aPHR®
and
aPHRi®
Associate in Human Resources Certification
Study Guide

aPHR® and aPHRi®

Associate in Human Resources Certification

Study Guide

2024 Exams

Sandra M. Reed, SPHR

James J. Galluzzo III, SPHR

SYBEX®

A Wiley Brand

Library of Congress Control Number: 2025902818
Paperback ISBN: 9781394295838
ePDF ISBN: 9781394295852
ePub ISBN: 9781394295845

Cover Image: Lighthouse in Maine. © Jeremy Woodhouse/Getty Images
Cover Design by Wiley

Set in Sabon LT Std 9.5/12pts by Lumina Datamatics

SKY10098495_021525

Dedicated to all HR practitioners, especially those just beginning—every one of us has stood where you are now. Your growth will shape the future of work!

Contents at a Glance

Contents

Acknowledgments

We want to express our heartfelt gratitude to everyone who made this book possible. To our families for their continued support and understanding when the deadlines came first, and to our colleagues who shared their experiences and insights with us. Your encouragement and wisdom helped create work that we are truly proud of.

To the team at Wiley: Kenyon Brown, Brad Jones, and our technical editor Thomas Mobley—thank you for your commitment to excellence and giving us the pushes needed to make this the best work possible. Working with professionals is an absolute gift!

Our hope is that those who read it are inspired to continue their journey into the world of HR with knowledge, passion, and purpose.

About the Authors

Sandra M. Reed, SPHR, has more than 25 years of experience in human resources, the last 20 of which have been spent in training and instruction. She holds her undergraduate degree in industrial-organizational psychology and her graduate degree in organizational leadership. Fun fact: it took her 30 years to complete her college degrees! She was certified before her first degree, and it is this that fuels her passion for helping others achieve HR certification, regardless of their educational level. Sandra is a master practitioner of the MBTI, Working Genius and the Profiles XT personality assessments. She is the author of *A Guide to the Human Resource Body of Knowledge (HRBoK™), The Big Book of HR Exam Questions,* and other certification study guides, all available through John Wiley & Sons. Sandra is the owner and founder of sandrareed.co, a consulting firm specializing in executive coaching and the unique needs of small to mid-size organizations. Find her on the web at https://sandrareed.co.

James J. Galluzzo III, SPHR, is a human resources strategic professional with nearly 30 years of experience. During his service in the United States Army, he found his professional calling in the human resources branch, the Adjutant General's Corps. He retired as chief of leadership development at the Adjutant General School, supporting the 40,000 Army HR professionals around the world. He has served as a director of HR in government and private sector organizations and is an HR subject matter and program manager helping to transform the Army's HR training and development as it fielded the most comprehensive human resources information system (HRIS) in its history. Additionally, James has been an adjunct instructor, author, and content creator for training HR professionals.

About the Technical Editor

Thomas Mobley, SHRM-SCP, SPHR, is an accomplished HR professional, consultant, and educator with more than 30 years of expertise in human resources. A professor and dedicated mentor, Thomas brings deep industry knowledge and practical insight to his clients and students. He holds a BS in business from Miami University and a MALER degree from the University of Cincinnati. This past January, Thomas joined the faculty at Miami University's Farmer School of Business in the Human Capital Management Leadership area. Previously, he served for over a decade as an assistant professor and educator in organizational leadership and HR at the University of Cincinnati. He has also taught in Dalian University of Technology's International Graduate Program in China. Thomas's approach to HR professional and student success blends mentorship, networking, and HR certification support, helping students apply theory through case studies and real-world examples. His HR consulting work includes designing leadership development programs for organizations as well as providing HR support to start-up organizations. His HR certification prep course students have achieved an impressive 90% exam pass rate. Learn more about his work on his website MobleyHR.com.

Introduction

Why should you learn about HR certification? It's a fast-growing field and an integral part of any business that values its people. Earning an HR certification, like the aPHR or aPHRi, can significantly boost your career, especially if you're just starting out. These certifications confirm that you have the foundational knowledge of HR principles, laws, and best practices, making you stand out in the job market. Whether you are thinking about transitioning to the HR career field or if you're already working in HR, earning an aPHR or aPHRi certification shows employers that you have a strong understanding of the field and are dedicated to professional growth.

The aPHR (Associate Professional in Human Resources) and aPHRi (international version) are great introductory certifications for people entering the HR field. These exams assess your knowledge of key HR operations, including recruiting, employee relations, and compliance. Understanding these topics will not only help you pass the exam but will also give you practical knowledge that can be applied directly to real-world HR tasks. Preparing for these exams will help you gain a solid understanding of the fundamentals, boost your confidence in your knowledge, and set you up for success as you advance in your HR career.

This guide is designed to help you study for and pass the aPHR or aPHRi exams by covering essential HR topics and providing practical tips for success.

What Is Human Resources?

Human resources (HR) refers to the department within an organization that is responsible for managing everything related to the people who work there. HR focuses on recruiting, hiring, training, and development of employees, ensuring that the company has the right talent at the right time to compete in their respective markets. HR professionals also work to maintain workplace safety, handle employee compensation and benefits, and resolve any issues or conflicts that arise. In short, HR helps both the organization and its employees succeed by balancing the needs of the business with the well-being of its workforce.

Why Become HR Certified?

HR Certification through the HR Certification Institute (HRCI) is an internationally recognized credential that validates the expertise and knowledge of HR professionals. HRCI offers several certifications, including the Associate Professional in Human Resources (aPHR) and Associate Professional in Human Resources, International (aPHRi). These exams are designed for entry level HR career professionals, or for non-HR individuals who are responsible for managing people.

There are several benefits to successfully certifying.

Career Advancement Opportunities   HR certification, such as those offered by HRCI, opens doors to higher-level positions and leadership roles. According to HRCI, certified professionals are often considered for promotions over noncertified colleagues because certification validates your expertise and commitment to the field.

Increased Earning Potential   Studies show that HR professionals with certifications typically earn more than those without them. HRCI reports that individuals with certifications often see higher salaries, making certification a solid investment in long-term financial growth.

Professional Credibility   Certification enhances your professional reputation, demonstrating your knowledge and commitment to staying current with HR practices and labor laws. It signals to employers and peers that you are a trusted and credible resource in the HR field.

Up-to-date Knowledge   HR certifications require continuing education, ensuring that certified professionals stay informed on the latest trends, regulations, and best practices in the rapidly evolving HR landscape. This helps professionals manage compliance and improve organizational performance.

How to Become HR Certified

To become certified, candidates must pass a comprehensive exam, demonstrating their skills and knowledge in the field.

There are no eligibility requirements for the aPHR and aPHRi exam. This means that these certifications are ideal for individuals just starting their careers in HR, students, or those looking to transition into the field. Both certifications focus on foundational HR knowledge and are open to anyone looking to build their HR expertise.

The exams are administered by Pearson VUE, a global leader in computer-based testing. To register for the exam, candidates need to visit the HRCI website at www. hrci.org. They can create an account, complete the application, and select a testing location and date. Once the application is approved and the exam fees are paid, the candidate will receive instructions to schedule the exam with Pearson VUE. For those outside of the United States, HRCI exams are available in many international locations, allowing candidates to sit for the exam at a Pearson VUE testing center near them. If you need assistance, HRCI's customer service can be reached at 1-866-898-4724 or info@hrci.org.

Who Should Buy This Book?

If you are preparing to take the aPHR or aPHRi exams, you can benefit from this study guide. If you're new to the HR field, this guide covers essential topics you'll need to understand from the very basics, leading up to the level of knowledge required to pass the certification exams. Even if you're just starting your HR career, this book will guide you through the material in a clear, structured way. If you already have some HR experience or are familiar with basic HR concepts, this guide can help you review key areas and fill any gaps in your knowledge. US military service members who perform HR functions as their military occupation can also use this guide to transition into civilian HR by demonstrating competency in key HR tasks.

This book assumes that you have a basic understanding of workplace environments and human resources, such as general knowledge of HR functions like recruitment, employee relations, and compliance. It's helpful if you've worked in HR or have some familiarity with it, but it's not a requirement. Whether you're just beginning your HR career or seeking to solidify your foundational knowledge, this book will help prepare you for the aPHR or aPHRi exams, ensuring you're ready to pass.

How This Book Is Organized

This book is broken down into three sections. Section 1 includes Chapter 1, which introduces you to both the aPHR and aPHRi exams. You should read this no matter which exam you plan to take. It outlines the fundamental exam content, the structure of the questions, and a few essential exam-day details to be aware of before test day.

If you are seeking to become aPHR certified, then Section 2 is for you. If you are focusing on the aPHRi certification, then you'll want to jump to Section 3.

Section 2 for aPHR contains chapters 2 through 6. Again, these cover the exam content for the aPHR exam.

Chapter 2   Functional Area 01 | Talent Acquisition

Talent acquisition involves sourcing, recruiting, and selecting the right candidates for a company. This function focuses on building a strong workforce by identifying job requirements, utilizing recruitment tools, and implementing strategies to attract diverse and qualified candidates. It includes everything from creating job descriptions to managing the interview process and ensuring an effective onboarding experience.

Chapter 3   Functional Area 02 | Learning & Development

Learning and development focuses on training and equipping employees with the skills and knowledge they need to succeed in their roles. This functional area involves creating and delivering training programs, providing ongoing education, and supporting career development. It also assesses training effectiveness to ensure employees can contribute to the organization's success.

Chapter 4   Functional Area 03 | Compensation & Benefits

Compensation and benefits management involves designing and administering pay structures, incentive programs, and employee benefits such as health care, retirement plans, and paid leave. The goal is to create a competitive package that attracts, retains, and motivates employees while ensuring internal and external equity.

Chapter 5   Functional Area 04 | Employee Relations

Employee relations is about managing the relationship between employers and employees to foster a positive work environment. It involves addressing employee concerns, mediating conflicts, and ensuring fair treatment. This area also covers handling grievances, conducting investigations, and maintaining open communication.

Chapter 6   Functional Area 05 | Compliance and Risk Management

Compliance and risk management is responsible for ensuring that the company follows all labor laws, regulations, and internal policies. This includes monitoring compliance with legal standards related to discrimination, workplace safety, and data protection. Risk management involves identifying potential risks, such as legal liabilities or operational hazards, and implementing measures to mitigate these risks.

Section 3 of the book focuses on the aPHRi exam. This section contains chapters 7 through 11, which are reviewed next.

Chapter 7   Functional Area 01 | HR Operations

In an international context, HR operations involve managing the global workforce's day-to-day administrative tasks. This includes navigating the complexities of international payroll, employee benefits across multiple countries, maintaining compliance with varied labor laws, and managing expatriate assignments.

Chapter 8   Functional Area 02 | Recruitment and Selection

Global recruitment and selection require understanding the diverse labor markets and legal frameworks across different countries. HR professionals in an international setting must adapt job descriptions, sourcing strategies, and selection processes to align with local employment laws and cultural differences. This could involve using international job boards, engaging in global talent sourcing, and navigating visa and work permit requirements.

Chapter 9   Functional Area 03 | Compensation and Benefits

Compensation and benefits in an international HR context must take into account the varying cost of living, tax regulations, and legal requirements in different countries. HR professionals are responsible for creating equitable pay structures that reflect local market standards while maintaining consistency with global corporate guidelines. This includes managing cross-border benefits packages, such as international health insurance, retirement plans, and tax considerations for expatriates.

Chapter 10   Functional Area 04 | Human Resource Development and Retention

Global HR development and retention strategies involve creating training and career development programs that are applicable across different cultural and regional contexts. HR professionals must consider language barriers, time zone differences, and the availability of training resources in multiple regions. Retention efforts focus on building leadership pipelines that prepare employees for international roles and adapting professional development opportunities to meet the unique career aspirations of employees in different countries.

Chapter 11   Functional Area 05 | Employee Relations, Health, and Safety

In an international environment, managing employee relations requires HR professionals to navigate different labor laws, cultural expectations, and conflict resolution strategies. Ensuring compliance with international health and safety standards, such as those set by the International Labour Organization (ILO), is critical to protecting employees. This includes creating policies that address workplace harassment, safety protocols, and employee well-being across multiple countries.

Chapter Features

Each chapter begins with a list of the aPHR and aPHRi objectives that are covered in that chapter. The book doesn't cover the objectives in order, but rather, connects key concepts to optimize learning. Thus, you shouldn't be alarmed at some of the odd ordering of the objectives within the book.

Within each chapter are key terms you should be familiar with to understand the concepts covered, along with an "HR Done Wrong" feature to highlight the exam content within a real-world context. At the end of each chapter, you'll find a couple of elements you can use to prepare for the exam:

Exam Essentials   This section summarizes important information that was covered in the chapter. You should be able to perform each of the tasks or convey the information requested.

Review Questions   Each chapter concludes with 20 review questions. If you can't answer at least 80% of these questions correctly, go back and review the chapter, or at least those sections that seem to be giving you difficulty. The answers to these review questions are covered in Appendix A.

WARNING   The review questions, assessment test, and other testing elements included in this book are *not* derived from the exam questions, so don't memorize the answers to these questions and assume that doing so will enable you to pass the exam. You should learn the underlying topic, as described in the text of the book. This will let you answer the questions provided with this book *and* pass the exam. Learning the underlying topic is also the approach that will serve you best in the workplace—the ultimate goal of a certification like the aPHR and aPHRi.

To get the most out of this book, you should read each chapter from start to finish and then check your memory and understanding with the chapter-end elements. Even if you're already familiar with a topic, you should skim the chapter; HR is complex enough that there are often multiple ways to accomplish a task, so you may learn something even if you're already competent in an area.

Interactive Online Learning Environment and Test Bank

This book is accompanied by an online learning environment that provides several additional elements. Items available among these companion files include the following:

Practice tests   All of the questions in this book appear in our proprietary digital test engine—including the 60-question assessment test at the end of this introduction and the 200+ questions that make up the review question sections at the end of each chapter. In addition, there are two 50-question bonus exams.

Electronic "flashcards"   The digital companion files include 150 questions—75 for the aPHR and 75 for the aPHRi—in flashcard format (a question followed by a single correct answer). You can use these to review your knowledge of the exam objectives.

Glossary   The key terms from this book, and their definitions, are available as a fully searchable PDF.

> **NOTE**   You can access all these resources at www.wiley.com/go/sybextestprep.

Conventions Used in This Book

This book uses certain typographic styles in order to help you quickly identify important information and to avoid confusion over the meaning of words such as on-screen prompts. In particular, look for the following styles:

- *Italicized text* indicates key terms that are described at length for the first time in a chapter. (Italics are also used for emphasis.)

- A `monospaced font` indicates an online url to provide additional online resources or references

In addition to these text conventions, which can apply to individual words or entire paragraphs, a few conventions highlight segments of text:

> **NOTE**
> A note indicates information that's useful or interesting but that's somewhat peripheral to the main text. A note might be relevant to a small number of networks, for instance, or it may refer to an outdated feature.

Sidebars

A sidebar is like a note but longer. The information in a sidebar is useful, but it doesn't fit into the main flow of the text.

Real World Scenario

A real world scenario is a type of sidebar that describes an example that's particularly grounded in the real world. This may be a situation we or somebody I know has encountered, or it may be advice on how to work around problems that are common in real, working human resources environments.

---

aPHR and aPHRi Exam Objectives

The *aPHR and aPHRi Exam Prep Study Guide* has been written to cover every exam objective at a level appropriate to its exam weighting. The following tables provides a breakdown of this book's exam coverage, showing you the weight of each section and the chapter where each objective is covered:

aPHR EXAM WEIGHTING

Subject area	% of Exam	Chapter
Talent Acquisition	19%	2
Learning and Development	15%	3

Subject area	% of Exam	Chapter
Compensation and Benefits	17%	4
Employee Relations	24%	5
Compliance and Risk Management	25%	6
Total	100%	

aPHRi EXAM WEIGHTING

Subject area	% of Exam	Chapter
HR Operations	33%	7
Recruitment and Selection	22%	8
Compensation and Benefits	15%	9
Human Resource Development and Retention	10%	10
Employee Relations, Health, and Safety	20%	11
Total	100%	

aPHR and aPHRi Assessment Exams

Use these practice questions to test your knowledge in the key functional areas of the exams. The following are two assessments. One is for the aPHR followed by one for the aPHRi.

aPHR Assessment Exam

1. What is the primary benefit of a matrix organizational structure?

    A. Simplifies decision-making

    B. Allows employees to report to multiple managers based on different projects

    C. Streamlines communication between departments

    D. Reduces employee supervision

2. What is a key feature of a flat organizational structure?

    A. Few levels of management and wider spans of control

    B. Many levels of management and narrow spans of control

    C. Employees reporting to multiple managers

    D. Teams divided by function

3. Which structure might work best for a small startup with limited staff?

    A. Bureaucratic structure

    B. Functional structure

    C. Geographic structure

    D. Flat organizational structure

4. What is the first step in handling an employee complaint?

    A. Notify the employee's supervisor

    B. Initiate an investigation

    C. Open a file to set up the record

    D. Listen and gather information

5. Which of the following is a common tool used to assess future staffing needs in an organization? (Choose all that apply.)

    A. Benchmarking

    B. AI

    C. Forecasting

    D. Regression analysis

6. What is the primary purpose of a job analysis in the hiring process?

    A. It analyzes for internal wage equity

    B. To differentiate jobs from each other

    C. To analyze external wage equity

    D. To identify the KSAOs for each position

7. Which recruiting strategy focuses on increasing the company's visibility and attractiveness to potential candidates?

    A. Employer branding

    B. Online job boards

    C. Job fairs

    D. Candidate pipelines

8. A company is experiencing high turnover and struggles to fill positions quickly when employees leave. The HR team wants to ensure they have a consistent pool of qualified candidates ready to fill these roles as they become available. Which of the following strategies would be most effective for addressing this issue?

    A. Increasing job postings on online job boards

    B. Holding quarterly job fairs to meet potential candidates

    C. Building a candidate pipeline to proactively engage qualified prospects

    D. Relying on internal promotions to fill vacant positions

9. A company is struggling to find qualified candidates for a technical role, despite using traditional job postings and social media ads. Which of the following strategies might be the most effective next step?

    A. Increase the job posting budget

    B. Focus on employer branding to better highlight the company's culture

    C. Partner with a recruitment firm specializing in technical roles

    D. Conduct more resume mining to find qualified applicants

10. A company is considering two internal candidates for a leadership role. Both have the necessary experience, but one has consistently scored higher on skills assessments, while the other received outstanding feedback from previous teams during reference checks. What should the company prioritize in making the final decision?

    A. The candidate with better skills assessment scores

    B. The candidate with better feedback from previous teams

    C. Biases should be removed, and the decision should be made based solely on qualifications

    D. The candidate who best fits the company's leadership style and culture

11. After completing an instructor-led training program, a company notices little improvement in employee performance. Which method would be most effective in identifying why the training did not have the desired impact?

    A. Reviewing the training content to ensure it aligns with company goals

    B. Conducting post-training evaluations to gather employee feedback on the training

    C. Switching to virtual training methods for the next session

    D. Reducing the training duration to increase engagement

12. A company is implementing a major technology upgrade and needs to ensure all employees are ready for the change. Which of the following should be a top priority in the change management process?

    A. Hiring external consultants to handle the training

    B. Conducting post-training evaluations after the change is complete

    C. Moving forward with the change to avoid delays

    D. Assessing employee readiness and creating a communication plan to address concerns

13. Which tool is commonly used to track employee development and measure the effectiveness of training programs?

  A. Job analysis

  B. Learning management systems (LMS)

  C. Employee performance reviews

  D. Post-training feedback from colleagues

14. In which of the following scenarios is the best choice to use an internal training provider?

  A. When the company is looking for cutting-edge, industry-wide insights on leadership

  B. When the training involves new technology that internal staff has not yet mastered

  C. When the goal is to provide employees with general skills applicable across industries

  D. When the training requires a deep understanding of the company's unique culture and long-term goals

15. What is the primary goal of a change management process in an organization?

  A. To make small, quick organizational changes

  B. To assess readiness, plan communication, and provide resources to support organizational change

  C. To restructure the company's workforce and strategies

  D. To respond to external competitive conditions

16. Which of the following is a suitable application of blended learning in employee training?

  A. When training is a combination of self-paced online modules and live instructor-led sessions

  B. When employees complete online synchronous training with instructor support

  C. When employees learn through hands-on, on-the-job training

  D. When training is conducted by external consultants with no internal resources

17. Which of the following is typically part of an organization's pay structure? (Choose all that apply.)

  A. Senior leader approval

  B. Market analysis to determine competitive pay rates

  C. Employee performance assessments

  D. Pay minimum and maximum

18. What is the main difference between a Health Savings Account (HSA) and a Flexible Spending Account (FSA)?

  A. Only an HSA allows you to carry over unused funds into the next year.

  B. Only an FSA allows you to invest funds for growth.

  C. An FSA is used only for dental expenses, while an HSA is for medical expenses.

  D. Only an HSA requires funds to be spent by the end of the year.

19. Which of the following is an example of a fringe benefit commonly offered by organizations?

    A. Health insurance coverage

    B. Employee assistance program

    C. Vacation pay

    D. Overtime pay

20. A company is experiencing a higher cost of living in its headquartered location. Which compensation strategy would best help employees manage this increase without completely overhauling the pay structure?

    A. Offering merit-based raises to high-performing employees

    B. Conducting a market analysis to determine pay adjustments

    C. Implementing a cost-of-living adjustment for all employees

    D. Increasing the number of performance evaluations

21. A company wants to improve employee wellness but has a limited budget. Which of the following supplemental wellness programs would provide the most benefit for all employees while remaining cost-effective for the organization?

    A. Offering free gym memberships to all employees

    B. Implementing an employee assistance program (EAP) for mental health support

    C. Offering remote work flexibility programs

    D. Increasing the number of milestone celebrations, such as birthdays and anniversaries

22. A company offers both short-term and long-term disability insurance to its employees. However, several employees have expressed confusion about the differences between the two. What is the most effective way for HR to address this issue and ensure employees fully understand their options?

    A. Send a detailed email to all employees explaining the differences

    B. Include a FAQ section in the benefits enrollment packet

    C. Add a brief summary of each program to the company handbook

    D. Conduct an in-person or virtual benefits information session with clear explanations of each program

23. Which law prohibits discrimination in the workplace based on race, color, religion, sex, or national origin?

    A. Title VII

    B. IRCA

    C. FLSA

    D. Title I

24. What is the primary purpose of Form I-9 in the hiring process?

    A. To record an employee's personnel file details

    B. To verify the employee's tax withholdings

    C. To verify an employee's work authorization and identity

    D. To document an employee's disability for accommodations

25. Which law requires employers to provide reasonable accommodations for qualified individuals with disabilities?

    A. OWBPA

    B. ERISA

    C. ADA

    D. ADEA

26. A manager has learned that an employee with a disability is struggling with a job task due to their condition. What is the manager's legal obligation under the Americans with Disabilities Act (ADA)?

    A. Dismiss the employee if they cannot complete the task

    B. Transfer the employee to a different department

    C. Work with the employee to provide reasonable accommodations based on a doctor's recommendations

    D. Ask the employee what kind of work they can do and make allowances based on that

27. An employer is reviewing hiring practices to ensure compliance with immigration laws. Which of the following actions would be most effective in verifying an applicant's work authorization without violating EEOC guidelines?

    A. Requesting that applicants provide their work authorization documents before the interview

    B. Completing the I-9 form and verifying work authorization only after a conditional job offer is made

    C. Asking about citizenship status during the interview

    D. Requiring all employees to provide their social security card during the post-hire process

28. A company's training program includes copyrighted materials sourced from external providers. Which law should the company follow to avoid legal issues when using these materials?

    A. IRCA

    B. Title VII

    C. Title 17

    D. HIPAA

29. Which law requires employers to provide a safe and healthy work environment for their employees? (Choose all that apply.)

    A. MSHA

    B. OSHA

    C. HIPAA

    D. FECA

30. What is the primary purpose of the WARN Act in the workplace?

    A. To ensure that employees are notified in advance of significant layoffs or plant closings

    B. To mandate drug testing for all employees

    C. To protect employee health records from unauthorized access

    D. To provide guidelines for sexual harassment policies

aPHRi Assessment Exam

1. What is a key challenge in global talent acquisition?

    A. Attracting qualified candidates from around the world.

    B. Adapting recruitment strategies to different cultures and legal requirements

    C. Using a single job description for global roles

    D. Limiting hiring to expatriates

2. What is the most important factor to consider when recruiting talent globally?

    A. The candidate's proximity to the company's headquarters

    B. Compliance with global labor laws and regulations

    C. Offering the same salary across all locations

    D. Compliance with local employment laws and visa requirements

3. How do companies benefit from a strong global talent acquisition strategy?

    A. They attract a more diverse and skilled workforce.

    B. They reduce the need for a local workforce.

    C. They increase options for hiring from multiple countries.

    D. They eliminate the need for the use of global recruitment agencies.

4. What role does technology play in global talent acquisition?

    A. It makes interviews unnecessary.

    B. It removes the need for job descriptions.

    C. It allows for efficient screening and communication with candidates.

    D. It narrows the candidate pool to local applicants.

5. What is a key focus of global risk management in organizations?

    A. Hiring risk management brokers that are familiar with the area and culture

    B. Identifying and mitigating potential risks across different countries

    C. Ensuring consistent risk management strategies worldwide

    D. Purchasing insurance to protect global workers

6. Which of the following is a common risk in global operations?

    A. Child labor

    B. Unregulated working hours

    C. Political instability

    D. Lack of infrastructure

7. Which of the following is a strategic approach to managing global risk? (Choose all that apply.)

    A. Educating global workers on relevant risks in their area

    B. Accepting the risk as a cost of doing business

    C. Purchasing gap insurance to hedge against losses

    D. Avoiding investments in high-risk regions

8. What is the primary goal of a learning and development program in organizations?

    A. To help employees gain skills and grow professionally

    B. To upskill older workers

    C. To reduce employee workload

    D. To better compete in the competitive market

9. Which of the following is a key benefit of employee training?

    A. Increased productivity from remote workers

    B. Improved quality and service

    C. Improved job performance

    D. Improved team collaboration

10. What is an effective way to deliver learning and development programs to a global workforce?

    A. Using online training platforms that can be accessed anywhere

    B. Invest in train-the-trainer programs for local facilitators

    C. Limiting training to individual contributors and not managers

    D. Providing training materials in the headquarters' primary language

11. What is a common challenge in global learning and development programs?

    A. Ensuring all employees have equal opportunities

    B. Keeping employees engaged with the content

    C. Tailoring content to meet different cultural and language needs

    D. Catering to the many different adult learning styles

12. What is a functional organizational structure?

    A. A structure where employees are grouped by geographic location

    B. A structure where employees report to multiple managers

    C. A structure where employees report directly to the CEO

    D. A structure where employees are grouped by their job departmental structure

13. Which organizational structure is best for a company with operations in multiple countries?

    A. Flat structure

    B. Matrix structure

    C. Divisional structure

    D. Informal structure

14. What is the main responsibility of HR operations?

    A. Aligning HR activities with company operations

    B. Executing business strategy

    C. Protecting the company from harmful risk

    D. Managing employee performance

15. Which tasks fall under the scope of HR operations? (Choose all that apply.)

    A. Creating HR programs that support the employee lifecycle

    B. Using data to drive decision-making

    C. Developing social media campaigns

    D. Conducting harassment prevention training

16. Which of the following best defines company culture?

    A. Company policies, procedures, and rules

    B. The shared values, beliefs, and behaviors that shape how employees interact and work together

    C. How employees are rewarded

    D. The organizational structure and reporting lines

17. Which of the following is a key HR operational function for an early career professional? (Choose all that apply).

    A. Setting HR goals

    B. Processing employee payroll

    C. Screening applicants

    D. Maintaining HR records

18. What is the term used to describe the practice of ensuring employees' values and behaviors align with the company's values and beliefs?

   A. Employee engagement

   B. Cultural fit

   C. Diversity and inclusion

   D. Role suitability

19. What is the primary goal of progressive discipline in the workplace?

   A. To provide employees with opportunities to correct behavior before severe action is taken

   B. To apply the same level of punishment for each type of violation

   C. To document errors for future reference

   D. To preserve the at-will relationship between the employer and employee

20. A company's HR department needs to analyze employee turnover rates, track attendance, and compile performance review data across multiple departments. Which of the following tools would be most effective for organizing and analyzing this information?

   A. Project management software

   B. An enterprise resource management (ERM) system

   C. Spreadsheets

   D. An AI program

21. What is the main difference between a histogram and a bar chart?

   A. A histogram displays categorical data, while a bar chart shows numerical data.

   B. A histogram groups data into ranges, while a bar chart represents distinct categories.

   C. A histogram uses vertical bars, while a bar chart uses horizontal bars.

   D. A histogram shows percentages, while a bar chart shows counts.

22. A company is experiencing a drop in employee morale and wants to understand the underlying reasons. They have already distributed anonymous surveys and conducted one-on-one interviews, but the feedback is still unclear and lacks depth. Which of the following would be the best approach to gain more detailed insights into the employees' concerns?

   A. Sending out another anonymous survey with different questions

   B. Holding a company-wide meeting to address all employees at once

   C. Setting up a focus group with a small, diverse group of employees to discuss their experiences

   D. Conducting one-on-one interviews with senior management only

23. When posting a job opening, which of the following is a legal consideration an HR professional must account for?

   A. Ensuring the job description is appealing to the candidates

   B. Avoiding language that could be perceived as discriminatory

   C. Including a list of ideal candidate personality traits

   D. Setting a high minimum experience requirement

24. Which of the following would be the best tool to manage and organize information about applicants for future job openings?

   A. Personnel files

   B. Applicant databases

   C. Chatbots

   D. Cross-indexing software

25. Which of the following is a potential disadvantage of using employee referrals as a recruitment source?

   A. It can lead to a lack of diversity in the workplace.

   B. It increases the chances of hiring unqualified candidates.

   C. It makes the recruitment process slower.

   D. It discourages internal promotions.

26. Which of the following best describes PTO?

   A. A type of leave where employees are paid for taking time off work

   B. Unpaid leave granted to employees for personal reasons

   C. Extra salary given for working overtime

   D. Time off granted only for illness or medical emergencies

27. What is the primary purpose of data collection for salary and benefits surveys?

   A. To compare company salary and benefits with industry standards

   B. To determine the number of employees eligible for retirement

   C. To calculate employee bonuses based on performance

   D. To decide how many vacation days employees receive

28. Which of the following is most likely required when filing a workers' compensation claim?

   A. Proof the injured was employed by the company

   B. Employee identification and work authorization

   C. Proof of an on-the-job injury

   D. A doctor's note

29. Which of the following is considered a behavioral interview question?

   A. "Tell me about a time when you worked through a difficult challenge."

   B. "What is your desired salary?"

   C. "How are you best motivated?"

   D. "How would your past supervisor describe you?"

30. Which of the following best describes succession planning in career development?

    A. A method for helping employees be successful in their current roles

    B. A plan to replace employees within the next 12 months

    C. A strategy for identifying and preparing employees to fill key roles in the future

    D. A performance improvement plan (PIP)

aPHR Assessment Exam Answers

1. B. The primary benefit of a matrix organizational structure is that it promotes flexibility and enables employees to work on various projects across different departments, enhancing collaboration. (A) The matrix structure can actually complicate decision-making with multiple reporting lines. (C) Streamlines communication between departments is not a direct benefit of a matrix structure, although it may improve project coordination.
(D) Reduces employee supervision is incorrect, as the matrix structure typically involves more oversight due to multiple managers.

2. A. A key feature of a flat organizational structure is that this structure allows for quicker decision-making and more direct communication between employees and leadership.
(B) Many levels of management and narrow spans of control describe a hierarchical structure, not a flat one. (C) Employees reporting to multiple managers refers to a matrix structure.
(D) Teams divided by function is typical in a functional structure, not a flat one.

3. D. A flat organizational structure would work best for a small startup with limited staff. This structure allows for quick decision-making, direct communication, and flexibility.
(A) Bureaucratic structure involves many layers of management, which is not ideal for a small, agile team. (B) Functional structure divides employees by specialized departments, which may not be necessary in a small startup. (C) Geographic structure is used by larger companies with operations in multiple locations and is not suitable for a small startup.

4. D. The first step in handling an employee complaint is to listen and gather information. It's important to fully understand the issue before taking any further action, as this helps ensure that the complaint is addressed appropriately. (A) Notifying the employee's supervisor is typically done later in the process if needed. (B) Initiating an investigation happens after understanding the details of the complaint. (C) Opening a file to set up the record is part of documentation but comes after gathering the necessary information.

5. B, C, D. Forecasting involves predicting future staffing requirements based on factors like company growth, industry trends, and historical data to ensure the organization has the necessary talent to meet its goals. Similarly, regression analysis is a statistical method used to find the relationship between variables, helping to predict outcomes based on past data. AI may be used to predict future staffing needs by analyzing large amounts of data, identifying patterns, and forecasting trends. (A) Benchmarking is used to compare performance against industry standards, but it's not specifically for staffing needs.

6. D. The primary purpose of a job analysis in the hiring process is to identify the knowledge, skills, abilities, and other characteristics (KSAOs) required for the position. This helps ensure that candidates meet the specific qualifications needed for the job. (B) Differentiating jobs from each other is a result of a job analysis but not its main purpose. (A), (C) Analyzing for internal and external wage equity are functions of job evaluation, not job analysis.

7. A. Employer branding highlights the company's culture, values, and reputation to appeal to potential candidates. (B) Online job boards and (C) job fairs are useful for posting jobs and connecting with candidates but don't directly enhance the company's overall image. (D) Candidate pipelines maintain a pool of potential candidates but do not focus on increasing company visibility or attractiveness.

8. C. Building a candidate pipeline is the most effective strategy in this situation because it ensures a steady stream of qualified candidates is ready when positions open, reducing time-to-hire. (A) Increasing job postings and (B) holding job fairs may help attract candidates but won't provide the consistency of a well-maintained candidate pipeline. (D) Relying on internal promotions alone may not always meet the company's staffing needs.

9. C. Since traditional methods are not yielding results, working with a specialized recruitment firm can help tap into a network of qualified candidates and provide targeted expertise in finding technical talent.

10. D. While both skills assessments and feedback are valuable, the most critical factor for a leadership role is how well the candidate's leadership style aligns with the company's culture and leadership needs, as this will impact team performance and organizational success. This approach also ensures that those with less traditional qualifications, such as education and experience, are equally considered, which increases diversity of leadership.

11. B. The most effective method for identifying why the training did not have the desired impact is to conduct post-training evaluations to gather employee feedback on the training. These evaluations allow the company to understand how employees perceived the training and whether it addressed their needs. (A) Reviewing the training content is important but won't directly reveal employee perspectives. (C) Switching to virtual training methods may not address the underlying issue. (D) Reducing the training duration without understanding the cause of the problem may not improve engagement or performance.

12. D. A top priority in the change management process when implementing a major technology upgrade should be assessing employee readiness and creating a communication plan to address concerns. This ensures that employees are prepared for the changes and helps reduce resistance by keeping them informed and engaged. (A) Hiring external consultants may help with training, but it does not address employee concerns or readiness. (B) Post-training evaluations are useful but should not be the first step. (C) Moving forward without ensuring readiness could lead to more issues and delays later.

13. B. The tool commonly used to track employee development and measure the effectiveness of training programs is a learning management system (LMS). An LMS allows an organization to manage, track, and assess the progress of employees through various training modules. (A) Job analysis is used to evaluate the requirements of a specific role, not track development.

(C) Employee performance reviews focus on evaluating job performance rather than measuring training effectiveness. (D) Post-training feedback from colleagues can provide insights but does not comprehensively track employee development like an LMS does.

14. D. Internal training providers are the best choice when the training needs to align closely with the company's specific culture and strategic objectives (D). External providers may be better suited for general skills or new technology that internal staff may not be familiar with, as mentioned in (A), (B), and (C).

15. B. The primary goal of a change management process in an organization is to assess readiness, plan communication, and provide resources to support organizational change. This ensures that employees are prepared for and engaged in the change, reducing resistance and improving the chances of success. (A) Making small, quick changes at the top level does not encompass the broader organizational support needed for effective change. (C) Restructuring the workforce can be part of a change, but it is not the primary goal of change management. (D) Responding to external conditions is important, but change management focuses more on internal preparation and communication.

16. A. A suitable application of blended learning in employee training is when training is a combination of self-paced online modules and live instructor-led sessions. This approach allows employees to learn at their own pace while still benefiting from direct instruction and interaction with trainers. (B) Synchronous training with instructor support is not fully blended, as it doesn't incorporate self-paced learning. (C) Hands-on, on-the-job training is a different method of learning, not blended. (D) Training conducted solely by external consultants without internal resources is not blended learning, as it lacks the combination of multiple learning formats.

17. A, B, D. An organization's pay structure typically includes senior leader approval (A), as leaders are often involved in finalizing pay decisions. It also involves market analysis to determine competitive pay rates (B), ensuring the company offers salaries that align with industry standards. Additionally, pay structures set pay minimums and maximums (D), which define the salary range for various positions. (C) Employee performance assessments are important for determining any performance-based payout but are not a standard component of the pay structure itself.

18. A. HSAs are designed to be long-term savings accounts for medical expenses, allowing unused funds to roll over. (B) FSAs do not allow fund investment; only HSAs may allow growth through investments. (C) FSAs are not limited to dental expenses and can be used for a wide range of medical costs, just like HSAs. (D) It's actually FSAs that typically require funds to be spent by the end of the year, not HSAs.

19. B. Employee assistance programs (EAPs) provide support services such as counseling and wellness resources that are designed to help employees with personal or work-related issues. (A) Health insurance coverage and (C) vacation pay are standard benefits, not considered fringe benefits. (D) Overtime pay is a compensation-related benefit rather than a fringe benefit, which typically includes nonwage perks like wellness programs or gym memberships.

20. C. A COLA adjusts salaries to reflect changes in the cost of living, ensuring employees maintain their purchasing power. (A) Offering merit-based raises only benefits high-performing employees and may not address the broader cost-of-living issue. (B) Conducting a market analysis could provide insights but doesn't immediately resolve the cost-of-living increase. (D) Increasing performance evaluations doesn't directly address compensation needs related to rising living costs.

21. B. EAPs offer valuable resources like counseling and mental health support at a relatively low cost to the organization. (A) Offering free gym memberships to all employees could be costly. (C) Remote work options may only benefit some employees, as not all jobs can be done from home. (D) Increasing the number of milestone celebrations may not provide as much value to employees and is not directly tied to wellness benefits.

22. D. Conducting an in-person or virtual benefits information session with clear explanations of each program allows employees to ask questions and get detailed, real-time answers. (A) Sending an email may not be as engaging or clear for all employees. (B) Including a FAQ section in the benefits packet is helpful but doesn't provide the depth of understanding needed. (C) Adding a brief summary to the handbook offers information but may not fully resolve confusion.

23. A. Title VII of the Civil Rights Act of 1964 is a key piece of federal legislation that ensures equal employment opportunities. (B) IRCA (Immigration Reform and Control Act) deals with work authorization and immigration status. (C) FLSA (Fair Labor Standards Act) focuses on minimum wage, overtime, and child labor laws. (D) Title I refers to the Americans with disabilities Act, which provides protections to qualified individuals with disabilities.

24. C. The primary purpose of Form I-9 in the hiring process is to verify an employee's work authorization and identity to ensure that employers are hiring individuals who are legally authorized to work in the United States. (A) Recording personnel file details is not the purpose of the I-9 form. (B) Verifying tax withholdings is done through other forms, like the W-4. (D) Documenting an employee's disability for accommodations is addressed under the ADA, not through the I-9 form.

25. C. The Americans with Disabilities Act (ADA) ensures that individuals with disabilities have equal opportunities in the workplace, including necessary accommodations. (A) OWBPA (Older Workers Benefit Protection Act) relates to protecting older workers in benefits and severance agreements. (B) ERISA (Employee Retirement Income Security Act) governs employee benefit plans. (D) ADEA (Age Discrimination in Employment Act) prohibits age discrimination against individuals aged 40 and older.

26. C. The ADA requires employers to make reasonable adjustments that enable employees with disabilities to perform their job duties, as long as it doesn't cause undue hardship for the employer. (A) Dismissing the employee without offering accommodations violates ADA protections. (B) Transferring the employee without first attempting accommodations is not required under the ADA. (D) Asking the employee about their abilities is important, but accommodations should be made based on professional medical advice to ensure the best support.

27. B. The most effective action in verifying an applicant's work authorization without violating EEOC guidelines is completing the I-9 form and verifying work authorization only after a conditional job offer is made. This ensures compliance with both immigration laws and anti-discrimination regulations. (A) Requesting work authorization documents before the interview could lead to potential discrimination. (C) Asking about citizenship status during the interview can violate EEOC guidelines by creating bias. (D) Requiring a Social Security card during the post-hire process is not required for all employees and may not be the most effective way to verify work authorization.

28. C. Title 17 of the US Code governs copyright law, which protects the use of copyrighted materials. A company must comply with copyright law to avoid legal issues when using materials from external providers. (A) IRCA relates to immigration and work authorization. (B) Title VII deals with workplace discrimination. (D) HIPAA protects personal health information, not copyrighted materials.

29. A, B, D. The Mine Safety and Health Act (MSHA) governs safety in the mining industry, the Occupational Safety and Health Act (OSHA) sets safety standards for most workplaces, and the Federal Employees' Compensation Act (FECA) indirectly promotes safe conditions for federal employees by compensating for work-related injuries. The Health Insurance Portability and Accountability Act (HIPAA) (C) is incorrect because it relates to the privacy and security of health information, not workplace safety.

30. A. The Worker Adjustment and Retraining Notification (WARN) Act requires employers to provide 60 days' notice before large-scale layoffs or facility shutdowns to allow employees time to prepare for job loss. (B) Mandating drug testing, (C) protecting employee health records, and (D) providing guidelines for sexual harassment policies are covered under other laws, not the WARN Act.

aPHRi Assessment Exam Answers

1. B. A key challenge in global talent acquisition is adapting recruitment strategies to different cultures and legal requirements. This is important because each country may have unique labor laws, recruitment norms, and cultural differences that need to be considered to attract and retain talent successfully. Attracting qualified candidates from around the world (A) is important, but it is not the main challenge compared to adapting to diverse legal and cultural contexts. Using a single job description for global roles (C) is incorrect because it doesn't account for regional differences in job expectations or qualifications. Limiting hiring to expatriates (D) is also incorrect as global talent acquisition seeks to attract a diverse pool of candidates, not just expatriates.

2. D. An important factor to consider when recruiting talent globally is compliance with local employment laws and visa requirements. This ensures that the company follows legal hiring practices specific to each country or region, including work permits and local labor regulations. (A) is incorrect because global talent acquisition focuses on hiring talent from different regions, not just near the headquarters. (B) is important but not as specific or practical as focusing on local employment laws and visas, which vary by location. (C) is incorrect because salary structures typically vary by country due to cost of living differences and market standards.

3. A. Companies benefit from a strong global talent acquisition strategy by attracting a more diverse and skilled workforce. This allows them to tap into a wide range of talent, bringing in varied skills and perspectives. (B) is incorrect because a global strategy doesn't reduce the need for a local workforce; it complements it. (C) is incorrect because while it increases hiring options, the main benefit is diversity and skill. (D) is wrong because global recruitment agencies may still be needed to navigate local hiring laws and practices.

4. C. Technology plays a key role in global talent acquisition by allowing for efficient screening and communication with candidate, streamlining the recruitment process, and making it easier to connect with and evaluate candidates from around the world. (A) is incorrect because interviews are still essential, even with technology. (B) is wrong since job descriptions are necessary for defining roles, regardless of technology. (D) is incorrect because technology expands, rather than narrows, the candidate pool beyond local applicants.

5. B. The key focus of global risk management is identifying and mitigating risks across different countries. This ensures that unique risks in each region are addressed effectively. (A) is incorrect because hiring brokers is helpful but not the primary focus. (C) is wrong as strategies often need to be tailored, and not always consistent. (D) is incorrect since insurance, similar to brokers, is just one part of managing risk, not the main focus.

6. C. A common risk in global operations is political instability, which can disrupt business activities, impact safety, and create economic uncertainty. (A) Child labor and (B) unregulated working hours are important concerns, but they are more specific labor-related risks rather than general risks that affect global operations. (D) Lack of infrastructure can be a challenge, but political instability is a broader and more frequent risk in international business.

7. A, B, C, D. In managing global risk, organizations can educate workers on relevant risks to mitigate potential issues, accept certain risks as a cost of doing business, purchase gap insurance to transfer financial liability, and avoid high-risk regions altogether. These strategies—mitigate, accept, transfer, and avoid—are common approaches to handling global risks effectively.

8. A. The primary goal of a learning and development program in organizations is to help employees gain skills and grow professionally. This focus on skill-building enables employees to advance in their careers and contribute more effectively to the organization. (B) Upskilling older workers is important but is just one aspect of development programs. (C) Reducing employee workload is not a direct goal of learning and development. (D) Competing in the market is a secondary benefit, achieved through employees' enhanced skills, but the primary focus remains on professional growth.

9. C. A key benefit of employee training is improved job performance. Examples of improved job performance include (A) increased productivity from remote workers, (B) improved quality and service, and (D) improved team collaboration. All of these outcomes contribute to better overall job performance, which is the primary goal of employee training.

10. A. An effective way to deliver learning and development programs to a global workforce is by using online training platforms that can be accessed anywhere. This allows employees across different regions to access training conveniently and consistently. (B) Investing in train-the-trainer programs for local facilitators can be useful, but online platforms provide more widespread access. (C) Limiting training to individual contributors and not managers would hinder overall development. (D) Providing materials only in the headquarters' primary language is not effective for a global workforce, as it limits accessibility.

11. C. A common challenge in global learning and development programs is tailoring content to meet different cultural and language needs. (C) ensures the material is relevant and accessible to employees from diverse backgrounds. (A) Ensuring equal opportunities is the function of diversity efforts. (D) Catering to different adult learning styles and (B) keeping employees engaged are challenges for all training programs, not specifically because of the global aspect.

12. D. A functional organizational structure is one where employees are grouped by their job functions, such as marketing, finance, or human resources. This allows employees to specialize in their areas of expertise within the organization. (A) Grouping by geographic location describes a divisional structure. (B) Reporting to multiple managers is characteristic of a matrix structure. (C) Reporting directly to the CEO is not specific to a functional structure but could occur in a flat structure with few management levels.

13. C. The best organizational structure for a company with operations in multiple countries is a divisional structure. This allows the company to organize its operations by region, product, or market, enabling each division to function semi-independently while still aligning with overall corporate goals. (A) A flat structure is less suited for large, multinational companies due to its minimal management levels. (B) A matrix structure focuses on dual reporting lines, which may complicate operations across multiple countries. (D) An informal structure lacks the organization needed for managing complex, global operations.

14. A. The main responsibility of HR operations is aligning HR activities with company operations. This ensures that HR processes such as payroll, benefits, and employee management support the overall goals and smooth functioning of the organization.
(B) Executing business strategy is a broader role usually handled by senior leadership.
(C) Protecting the company from harmful risk is a part of risk management, not the core focus of HR operations. (D) Managing employee performance falls under HR's performance management function, not specifically HR operations.

15. A, B, D. HR operations encompass a broad range of tasks, including creating HR programs that support the employee lifecycle (A), using data to drive decision-making (B), and conducting harassment prevention training (D). These activities demonstrate the value of HR programs and support organizational goals. (C) Developing social media campaigns typically falls under marketing or communications, not HR operations.

16. B. The best definition of company culture is the shared values, beliefs, and behaviors that shape how employees interact and work together. Company culture reflects how people in the organization collaborate and conduct themselves, which influences the work environment and employee satisfaction. (A) Company policies, procedures, and rules are important, but company culture is more about shared attitudes and beliefs. (C) How employees are

rewarded is a part of company operations but does not fully define culture. (D) The organizational structure and reporting lines describe how a company is organized, not its culture.

17. C, D. A key HR operational function for an early career professional includes screening applicants and maintaining HR records. These tasks involve clear operational procedures that require foundational knowledge and skills, supporting the recruitment process and ensuring employee information is accurately stored and managed. (A) Setting HR goals is typically a higher-level strategic function, not usually assigned to early career professionals. (B) Processing employee payroll is more commonly managed by specialized payroll reps or experienced HR staff rather than those in early career roles.

18. B. Cultural fit focuses on whether an employee's attitudes, work style, and values align with those of the organization, which can contribute to a positive work environment and higher job satisfaction. (A) Employee engagement refers to how motivated and committed employees are to their work but does not specifically address alignment with company culture. (C) Diversity and inclusion focus on ensuring a diverse and equitable workforce, which is about equal opportunity and belonging. (D) Role suitability relates to how well an employee's skills and role match their job responsibilities, not alignment with the company's culture.

19. A. The primary goal of progressive discipline in the workplace is to provide employees with opportunities to correct behavior before severe action is taken. (A) This system allows employees to address their mistakes through a series of escalating steps. (B) Applying the same level of punishment for each violation is incorrect because progressive discipline escalates consequences based on the situation. (C) Documenting errors is part of the process, but not the main feature of the practice of progressive discipline. (D) Progressive discipline can erode at-will employment by creating an expectation that employees will be given multiple chances to correct behavior before dismissal, potentially limiting the employer's ability to terminate employment without cause.

20. C. The most effective tool for organizing and analyzing employee turnover rates, tracking attendance, and compiling performance review data is spreadsheets. Spreadsheets allow HR to sort, filter, and analyze large amounts of data across multiple departments efficiently. (A) Project management software is useful for managing tasks and timelines but is not designed for detailed data analysis. (B) An ERM system helps integrate business processes but may not offer the same flexibility or simplicity for organizing and analyzing specific HR data. (D) An AI program can assist with insights but is not typically used for manual data compilation like spreadsheets.

21. B. The main difference between a histogram and a bar chart is that a histogram groups data into ranges, such as numerical intervals, making it ideal for showing the distribution of continuous data. A bar chart, on the other hand, represents distinct categories, making it better suited for comparing categorical data.

22. C. Focus groups allow for open discussion, providing detailed insights into employee concerns and creating a more interactive environment than surveys or interviews. This approach is especially useful when previous feedback methods, like surveys, have been too vague. (A) Sending out another anonymous survey is not ideal because the company has already tried this and found the feedback unclear. (B) Holding a company-wide meeting might not encourage the honest, in-depth feedback that smaller focus groups can provide. (D) Conducting more one-on-one interviews with senior management only misses the point of hearing from a broader and more diverse range of employees.

23. B. This choice highlights the need to ensure that job postings comply with employment laws, particularly anti-discrimination regulations. (A) Writing the job description that appeals to the candidate is useful but not a legal requirement. (C) Including a list of ideal candidate personality traits is not a legal one. (D) Setting a high minimum experience requirement isn't helpful.

24. B. Databases allow HR professionals to store and organize applicant details, making it easy to track, search, and retrieve information for future recruitment needs. (A) Personnel files are used for current employees, not applicants. (C) Chatbots assist with communication but don't manage or organize data. (D) Cross-indexing software is not typically used for applicant management; it's more focused on organizing data in general, not specifically for recruitment purposes.

25. A. One potential disadvantage of using employee referrals is that it can lead to a lack of diversity. Since employees often refer people from similar backgrounds or social circles, this method can limit the variety of perspectives in the workplace. (B) Hiring unqualified candidates is less likely since employees usually refer qualified individuals who understand the job requirements. (C) Employee referrals tend to speed up the recruitment process, not slow it down. (D) Internal promotions are not directly affected by employee referrals.

26. A. Paid time off (PTO) refers to the time employees are granted to take off from work while still receiving their regular pay. It covers various reasons such as vacations, personal time, and in some cases, sick leave.

27. A. Collecting data for salary and benefits surveys helps ensure the organization remains competitive in attracting and retaining employees. (B) Determining retirement eligibility and (C) calculating bonuses are not the primary purposes of salary surveys. (D) Vacation days are typically determined by company policy, not salary surveys.

28. C. Workers' compensation is designed to cover injuries or illnesses that occur in the course of employment, so it's essential to provide evidence that the injury happened while performing job-related duties. (A) Proof of employment and (B) employee identification are basic requirements for employment but are not the primary focus of a workers' compensation claim. (D) A doctor's note may be necessary later in the process, but the claim must first establish that the injury occurred on the job.

29. A. "Tell me about a time when you worked through a difficult challenge" is a behavioral interview question designed to assess how a candidate has handled specific situations in the past, which can indicate how they might behave in similar situations in the future. (B) "What is your desired salary?" is a compensation-related question, not behavioral. (C) "How are you best motivated?" focuses on personal preferences and work style but doesn't ask for past examples of behavior. (D) "How would your past supervisor describe you?" is more about perception than assessing past actions or behaviors in specific situations.

30. C. Succession planning is a proactive process used by organizations to ensure that there is a pipeline of capable employees ready to step into important roles when they become available. (A) A method for helping employees be successful in their current roles is incorrect because succession planning is focused on future leadership roles, not just improving current performance. (B) A plan to replace employees within the next 12 months is incorrect because succession planning is a long-term strategy that prepares employees for future leadership positions, not just immediate replacements. (D) A PIP is incorrect because PIP is designed to help underperforming employees improve in their current roles, whereas succession planning focuses on preparing high-potential employees for future leadership.

Human Resource Certification

Welcome to your guide for certifying as a human resource (HR) professional. Whether you are just starting your HR career or looking to advance, earning a certification can make a big difference. Certifications, like the aPHR (Associate Professional in Human Resources) and aPHRi (for international HR), show that you have the skills and knowledge needed to succeed in HR. They also make you stand out to employers who are looking for qualified professionals to join their teams.

HR plays an important role in supporting both employees and businesses. HR professionals manage everything from hiring and training to handling employee benefits and legal issues. By getting certified, you prove that you understand these responsibilities and are ready to take on the challenges that come with them.

This study guide will help you on your journey to becoming a certified HR professional. It covers the most important topics you need to know for certification exams, such as compliance, employee relations, recruitment, compensation, and much more. We'll also provide practice questions, study tips, and test-taking strategies to ensure you feel confident when exam day arrives.

Throughout the chapters, you'll find clear explanations of key concepts and terms, examples of real-world HR situations, and content mapped to the exam objectives.

HR Certification Institute and the Certification Exams

Exam content refers to the specific topics and areas of knowledge that are covered on the certification exams. Each exam is tailored to the level of certification, meaning the content will vary depending on whether you're taking an entry-level exam like the aPHR or an advanced exam like the Senior Professional in Human Resources (SPHR).

The HR Certification Institute (HRCI) follows a detailed process to create the content for its certification exams. The goal is to make

sure the exams are up-to-date and relevant to real-world HR work. There are several steps to how HRCI prepares the exam content, and these are covered next.

Job Analysis   HRCI begins by conducting a job analysis, which involves studying the roles and responsibilities of HR professionals at different levels. This helps identify the skills and knowledge HR professionals need to succeed in their jobs. Input from HR experts around the world is used to ensure the analysis reflects the current trends and practices in HR.

Developing the Exam Blueprint   Based on the job analysis, HRCI creates an exam blueprint. This blueprint outlines the key areas or topics that will be covered on the exam. It ensures that the exam focuses on what HR professionals need to know and do in their everyday work.

Subject Matter Experts   HRCI works with subject matter experts (SMEs) who are experienced HR professionals to write and review exam questions. These experts ensure the questions are accurate and align with the knowledge and skills identified in the exam blueprint.

Question Testing   Before a question becomes part of the exam, it goes through a testing phase to make sure it is clear and measures the intended knowledge. HRCI tests these questions to ensure accuracy and fairness. The aPHR exam, for example, consists of 125 total questions; 100 scored questions, and 25 field test questions that do not count toward the final score. The questions are indistinguishable from each other, but the field test questions are used to gather data on potential new exam items.

Ongoing Updates   HRCI updates the exam content approximately every five years to reflect changes in the HR field, including new laws, technology, and best practices. This ensures that HR professionals are tested on the most current and relevant information. The last updates to the aPHR and aPHRi were in 2023.

Associate Professional in Human Resources (aPHR) Content

The aPHR exam is considered an entry-level certification for individuals new to the HR career field or transitioning from another career and covers several fundamental functions of an operational HR department. The exam content includes the following:

- Functional Area 01 | Talent Acquisition (19%)
- Functional Area 02 | Learning & Development (15%)
- Functional Area 03 | Compensation & Benefits (17%)

- Functional Area 04 | Employee Relations (24%)
- Functional Area 05 | Compliance & Risk Management (25%)

As you can see, almost half of the aPHR exam content will be testing your knowledge in functional areas 4 and 5. This is important to understand when building a study plan as part of your preparation activities.

Associate Professional in Human Resources International (aPHRi) Content

The aPHRi exam is the international version for non-US-based test takers and also an entry level certification. It covers several fundamental functions of an operational HR department in an international setting. The exam content includes the following:

- Functional Area 01 | HR Operations (33%)
- Functional Area 02 | Recruitment and Selection (22%)
- Functional Area 03 | Compensation and Benefits (15%)
- Functional Area 04 | Human Resource Development and Retention (10%)
- Functional Area 05 | Employee Relations, Health, and Safety (20%)

The aPHRi exam not only tests knowledge but also includes tasks that are directly related to the practical application of that knowledge. These tasks reflect real-world HR responsibilities and are tied to the various topics covered in the exam.

Associated Tasks

Since the aPHRi is a knowledge-based exam, candidates are responsible for the five knowledge areas described previously. What follows is a list of tasks an individual certified with the aPHRi credential would likely be expected to perform early in an HR career.

aPHRi Tasks

01. Access, collect, and provide information and data to support HR-related decisions (for example: recruiting, employee relations, training, safety, budgeting, needs analysis, off-boarding, termination)

02. Comply with all applicable laws and regulations

03. Coordinate and communicate with external providers of HR services (for example: recruiters, employee recognition services)

04. Maintain employee data in HRIS or system of record

05. Maintain, file, and process HR forms (for example: notices, announcements, new hire forms, salary forms, performance, termination paperwork)

06. Prepare HR-related documents (for example: reports, presentations, organizational charts)

07. Provide internal customer service by answering or referring HR-related questions from employees as the first level of support

08. Communicate information about HR policies and procedures

09. Communicate the organization's core values, vision, mission, culture, and ethical behaviors

10. Identify risk in the workplace

11. Minimize risk by conducting audits (for example: workers' compensation, employee records)

12. Document and update essential job functions with the support of managers

13. Post job listings (for example: company website, social media, job boards)

14. Manage applicant databases (for example: enter data, access records, update records)

15. Screen applicants for managers to interview

16. Answer questions from job applicants

17. Coordinate interview logistics

18. Interview job candidates

19. Arrange for tests and assessments of applicants

20. Coordinate the employment offer (for example: start date, salary, benefits)

21. Administer post-offer employment activities (for example: execute employment agreements, work authorization, coordinate relocation, immigration)

22. Communicate compensation and benefits programs and systems

23. Coordinate activities to support employee benefits programs (for example: health and fitness, pension schemes)

24. Coordinate payroll-related information (for example: new hires, adjustments, paid time off, terminations)

25. Process claims from employees (for example: workers' compensation, insurance benefits)

26. Resolve routine employee compensation and benefits issues

27. Conduct orientation and onboarding for new hires, rehires, and transfers

28. Coordinate training sessions (for example: logistics, materials, tracking, registration, evaluation)

29. Conduct employee training programs (for example: safety regulations, emergency preparedness, basic presentation skills, time management skills)

30. Coordinate the logistics for employee relations programs (for example: recognition, special events, diversity programs)

31. Monitor completion of performance reviews and development plans

These tasks are designed to test how well candidates can apply their knowledge in practical situations they might encounter as HR professionals in an international setting and are covered in Chapters 7 through 11. The combination of knowledge and task-based questions ensures that aPHRi-certified individuals are prepared to take on real responsibilities in global HR roles.

When applying for the aPHRi exam, you will have an additional question related to your knowledge of local employment laws. The criteria may be met by holding another HR certification (such as the PHR or the GPHR), holding a bachelor's degree or global equivalent in an HR field, or having successfully completed a course in employment law. Refer to the *Certification Handbook* for a complete list of how you can confirm this step in your knowledge.

> **NOTE** HRCI's *Certification Policies and Procedures Handbook (aPHR, aPHRi, PHR, PHRca, SPHR, GPHR, PHRi, and SPHRi)* contains the most current listing of the HRCI exam requirements. Because the exams are built around these policies and procedures, we strongly urge those preparing for the test to review the handbook and familiarize themselves with the test specs for each functional area prior to reading the related chapter. The HRCI website (www.hrci.org) provides information on downloading or ordering this free publication.

Acronyms

For both exams, you should know your acronyms! See Table 1.1 for a list of the more common acronyms in HR. For aPHR candidates, you should also know your labor law acronyms. These are shown in Table 1.2.

TABLE 1.1   Human Resource Acronyms

Acronym	Term	Definition
ATS	Applicant Tracking System	A software used by HR departments to manage the recruitment process and track job applications
BFOQ	Bona Fide Occupational Qualification	A legal exception that allows employers to base hiring decisions on certain characteristics (like gender or religion) when they are essential for performing a specific job
DEI	Diversity, Equity and Inclusion	Initiatives that aim to create a more diverse, fair, and inclusive workplace environment

(Continued)

TABLE 1.1   Human Resource Acronyms (*Continued*)

Acronym	Term	Definition
EE	Employee	Refers to anyone who works for an employer under a contract of employment
EEO	Equal Employment Opportunity	Policies that ensure all employees are treated fairly and equally in the workplace, regardless of race, gender, or other characteristics
FTE	Full-Time Equivalent	A unit used to measure the number of full-time employees or the equivalent hours worked by part-time employees
HRCI	Human Resource Certification Institute	An organization that provides globally recognized certifications for HR professionals, validating their expertise and knowledge in various HR disciplines
HRIS	Human Resource Information System	A software system used to manage and track employee data, payroll, and other HR tasks
HRM	Human Resource Management	The practice of recruiting, hiring, training, and managing employees in an organization
JD	Job Description	A document that outlines the responsibilities, qualifications, and duties of a specific job role
KPIs	Key Performance Indicator	A measurable value that shows how effectively an employee, team, or organization is achieving specific goals or objectives
KSAOs	Knowledge, Skills, Abilities and Other	A framework used in HR to evaluate a candidate's qualifications for a job
ROI	Return on Investment	A metric used to evaluate the financial return or benefit gained from an investment compared to its cost

TABLE 1.2   aPHR Labor Law Terms

Acronym	Term	Definition
ADA	Americans with Disabilities Act	A law that prohibits discrimination against individuals with disabilities in all areas of public life, including employment
ADEA	Age Discrimination in Employment Act	A law that prohibits employment discrimination against individuals 40 years of age or older
COBRA	Consolidated Omnibus Budget Reconciliation Act	A law that allows employees to continue their health insurance coverage after leaving a job
EEOC	Equal Employment Opportunity Commission	A federal agency responsible for enforcing laws against workplace discrimination
EPA	Equal Pay Act	A law that mandates equal pay for equal work, regardless of gender
ERISA	Employee Retirement Income Security Act	A law that sets standards for pension and health plans to protect individuals in these plans
FLSA	Fair Labor Standards Act	A US law that sets minimum wage, overtime pay, and child labor standards
FMLA	Family Medical Leave Act	A law that allows eligible employees to take unpaid leave for family or medical reasons without losing their job protection
GINA	Genetic Information Nondiscrimination Act	A law that prohibits discrimination based on genetic information in health insurance and employment
HIPAA	Health Insurance Portability and Accountability Act	A law that protects the privacy and security of individuals' health information
IRCA	Immigration Reform and Control Act	A law that prohibits employers from hiring illegal immigrants and requires verification of employment eligibility
LMRDA	Labor-Management Reporting and Disclosure Act	A law that regulates labor unions' internal affairs and union officers' relationships with members, ensuring transparency, democracy, and financial accountability within unions

(*Continued*)

TABLE 1.2   aPHR Labor Law Terms (*Continued*)

Acronym	Term	Definition
NLRA	National Labor Relations Act	A law that protects the rights of employees to organize, form unions, engage in collective bargaining, and take part in strikes and other collective activities
NLRB	National Labor Relations Board	An independent federal agency that enforces the National Labor Relations Act, overseeing labor disputes, union elections, and investigating unfair labor practices
OSHA	Occupational Safety and Health Administration	A federal agency that sets and enforces standards to ensure safe and healthy working conditions
PDA	Pregnancy Discrimination Act	A law that prohibits discrimination based on pregnancy, childbirth, or related medical conditions
SCA	Service Contract Act	A law that sets wage and labor standards for employees working on contracts with the federal government
USERRA	Uniformed Services Employment and Reemployment Rights Act	A law that protects the employment rights of military service members upon their return from duty
VEVRRA	Vietnam Era Veterans' Readjustment Assistance Act	A law that requires federal contractors and subcontractors to provide equal employment opportunities to veterans, particularly those who served during the Vietnam era
WARN	Worker Adjustment and Retraining Notification Act	A law that requires employers to provide advance notice of significant layoffs or plant closings

Eligibility Requirements

The aPHR and aPHRi exams are strictly knowledge-based credentials, and thus, no previous HR work experience is required.

Recertification

To maintain the aPHR or aPHRi certification, you must recertify every three years. Here are the two primary ways to meet the recertification requirements:

1. **Earn 45 Recertification Credits**

    You need to earn 45 HR-related recertification credits during the three-year certification cycle. These credits can come from various professional development activities:

    - Continuing education (like attending HR workshops, webinars, or conferences)
    - On-the-job experience (practicing HR tasks in your workplace)
    - Research and publishing (writing HR-related articles or papers)
    - Community service (volunteering in HR roles or related fields)

    The activities must be related to HR and align with the competencies in the HRCI certification framework.

2. **Retake the Exam**

    If you prefer not to earn recertification credits, you can retake the aPHR or aPHRi exam before your three-year certification period ends. Passing the exam again will automatically renew your certification.

    Staying certified ensures that you remain knowledgeable about HR trends and best practices while demonstrating your ongoing commitment to professional development. Be sure to take a look at HRCI's Recertification Policies and Procedures Handbook for the most up-to-date recertification information. It can be found at `www.hrci.org/docs/default-source/document-control-2023/2023-hrci-recertificatin-handbook.pdf`.

The Exam

Many professionals who choose to sit for certification report having varying degrees of test-taking anxiety. Understanding as much as you can about how the test is administered and structured is one practical way to be as prepared as possible before test day. Figure 1.1 gives you a snapshot of both the aPHR and aPHRi exam basics.

The aPHR and aPHRi exams cover similar content areas, but the aPHRi focuses more on international HR. Here's a summary of the different types of questions you might find on these exams:

- **Knowledge-based Questions**

    These questions test your understanding of core HR concepts, laws, and processes. You will need to recall specific information about HR policies, laws, and procedures. For example, "What is the main purpose of the Family and Medical Leave Act (FMLA)?"

FIGURE 1.1   The aPHR and aPHRi exams at a glance

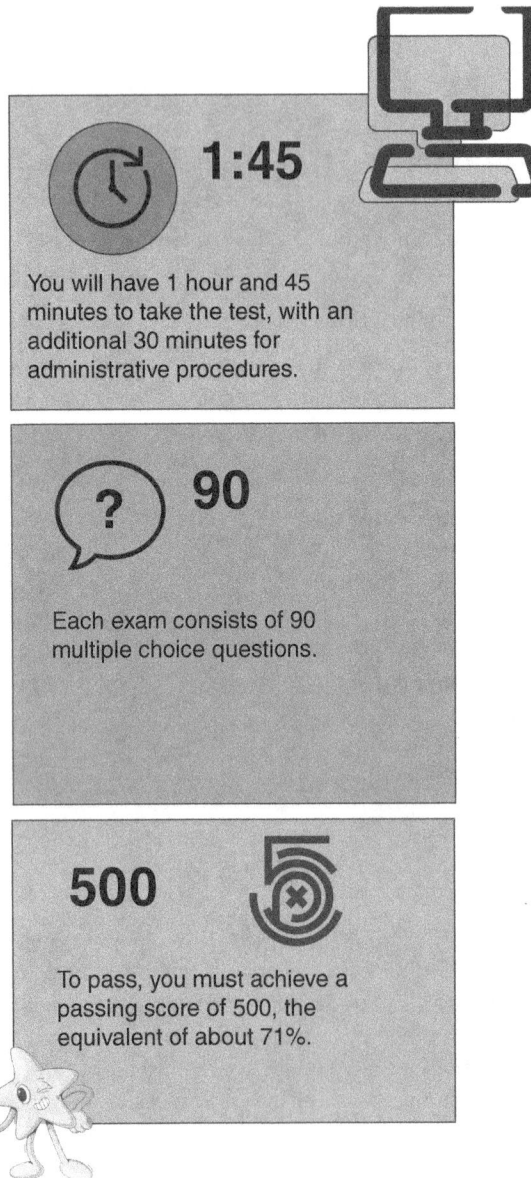

1:45

You will have 1 hour and 45 minutes to take the test, with an additional 30 minutes for administrative procedures.

90

Each exam consists of 90 multiple choice questions.

500

To pass, you must achieve a passing score of 500, the equivalent of about 71%.

- Application Questions

    These questions assess how well you can apply HR knowledge to practical situations. You will have to demonstrate an understanding of the steps to take in real-world HR situations. For example, "An employee requests leave under the FMLA. Which of the following actions should HR take first?"

- Scenario-based Questions

    Less common than the knowledge and application questions, a scenario involves a hypothetical situation, and you will need to decide the best course of action based on HR knowledge. These questions test problem-solving skills and your ability to handle workplace issues. For example, "A manager reports that an employee is frequently late. How should HR address this performance issue?"

- International HR Questions (for aPHRi)

    These focus on global HR practices, such as staffing international offices or understanding labor laws in different countries. This section will challenge your knowledge of international HR policies and practices. For example, "Which staffing approach hires host-country nationals to manage foreign operations?"

- Compliance and Legal Questions

    These questions test your knowledge of labor laws and regulations, such as those related to hiring, discrimination, and employee rights. You'll need to know US labor laws (aPHR) or international regulations (aPHRi). For example, "Which law prohibits discrimination based on race, color, religion, sex, or national origin?"

> Remember, there are plenty of opportunities within this book and online to practice for the exam. At the end of each chapter are 20 review questions, the introduction has a short assessment test, and the online resources have practice exams. You don't want to memorize the answers, but rather, get familiar with breaking down the exam question to understand what is being asked: knowledge, application or problem-solving scenarios.

Applying for the Exam

Before you can sit for the exams, you have to be approved to test. Applying for the aPHR and aPHRi exams is a simple process. Here's a step-by-step guide:

1. **Create an HRCI Account:** Go to the HRCI website and create an account.
2. **Complete the Application:** On the HRCI website, fill out the online application form with your personal details, exam type (aPHR or aPHRi), and payment information. Make sure all your information is correct.

3. **Submit the Required Documents:** You will need to upload an unexpired government-issued photo ID. Double-check that the name on your ID matches the name on your application exactly.

4. **Pay the Exam Fee:** There's an exam fee for both the aPHR and aPHRi, which you can pay during the application process. You'll also need to pay an additional application fee. As of 2024, the application fee is $100, and the exam fee is $300.

5. **Schedule Your Exam:** After your application is approved, you will receive an email with instructions to schedule your exam at a testing center or take it online. Pick a date and time that works for you, and also gives you plenty of time to prepare.

Once you receive your approval-to-test letter, it is time to get prepared!

Preparing for the Exam

Careful planning and preparation for the exams help you feel more confident and reduce stress on test day. By studying ahead of time and reviewing key topics, you'll increase your chances of passing and earning your certification. Here are some things you can do to be as ready as possible on exam day.

Understand the Exam Content   Start by reviewing the exam content outline. Understand which topics will be covered. For example, you might need to study areas like recruitment, employee relations, labor laws, or international HR practices. Focus on key areas by identifying which areas you are already comfortable with and which ones need more work. This can be done by taking a practice exam and noting where you scored highest and where you scored lowest.

Take Practice Tests   Take practice exams to get familiar with the types of questions you'll see on the real test. These will help you figure out which areas you need to improve. Use flashcards to memorize important terms, laws, and concepts. Both of these resources are offered online as part of your purchase of this study guide. Find them at www.wiley.com/go/sybextestprep.

Create a Study Schedule   Set daily goals and break your study time into small, manageable chunks each day. Instead of cramming, study a little each day leading up to the exam. Make sure to spend more time on topics that are difficult for you while also reviewing what you already know. Consider exam weights as well. For example, almost 50% of the aPHRi exam includes content from Compliance and Risk Management and Employee Relations, so plan to spend extra study time on these topics. Similarly, more than 50% of the aPHR exam comes from HR Operations and Recruitment and Selection, making these key areas for those preparing for that exam.

Join Study Groups   Joining a study group can be a good way to stay motivated. You can quiz each other and talk through difficult concepts. Don't be afraid to ask questions if you don't understand something. Another method is to research and take turns teaching the concepts to each other, which is a great way to both learn and share knowledge.

Practice Test-taking Strategies   Always read each question fully before answering. Don't rush. If you're not sure of the answer, try to eliminate obviously wrong choices. This increases your chances of picking the right one. Practice finishing practice exams within the time limit so that you don't run out of time during the actual test.

> Make sure to answer every question! Unanswered questions are marked as "incorrect," so if you get stuck, take your best guess instead of leaving it blank. Mark it for review at the end of the test if time remains.

On Test Day

The aPHR and aPHRi exams are administered as a computer-based test (CBT) by Pearson VUE. This approach provides candidates with greater flexibility in scheduling the test and has other benefits as well. Regardless of the exam you take, there are several best practices to consider for a successful exam day.

Arrive Early   Plan to get to the test center at least 30 minutes early. This gives you enough time to check in without feeling rushed. It's better to be super early and sit in your car for a bit rather than fight through the stress of unexpected road delays (or if you are like one of the authors, getting lost), so plan accordingly.

Bring Proper ID   Make sure to bring an unexpired government-issued photo ID, like your driver's license or passport, with a signature, and your test admission letter. The name on your ID must match your exam application exactly.

Expect to Be Searched   Exam centers are extremely vigilant to prevent unauthorized materials and electronic devices from entering the testing area. You will likely be asked to turn pockets inside out, lock up phones and digital watches, earbuds, or any other device. Hats and other clothing that could conceal training aids will be required to be stored in lockers. If you must leave the testing area to use the bathroom or during a break, you will be required to be searched again and identify yourself to the test proctor.

Dress in Layers   You will be sitting for an hour and 45 minutes to take the exam. To ensure a comfortable testing experience, it's advisable to dress comfortably in layers. This approach allows you to adjust your attire according to the testing room's temperature, which can vary. Keep in mind that while light jackets and sweaters are permitted, other outerwear such as heavy coats or hoodies with pockets may not be allowed.

Be Kind to Yourself   Get enough sleep, especially the night before the exam. Being well-rested helps you focus better. Eat a healthy meal before your test. Avoid too much sugar or caffeine, which can make you jittery. You will be able to use the restroom during your exam, but the clock does not stop while you are away from the computer.

Stay Positive   Stay positive, and remember that you've prepared for this! Take deep breaths and stay calm during the exam. If you don't know an answer, don't panic. Make your best guess, mark it to come back to later, and move on to the next question. Sometimes, the answer to a question you're unsure about might be found in another question, so stay calm and keep looking for clues.

Check the Rules Ahead of Time   Review the testing center's rules before you go so that you're aware of any specific guidelines for what is allowed. If you aren't sure, visit the testing centers website or give them a call. Figure 1.2 gives a snapshot of a few permitted and nonpermitted items.

In certain geographic locations, a live-proctored, virtual, online exam administration is also available, where you can schedule your test 24 hours a day, 7 days a week and 365 days a year.

FIGURE 1.2   Permitted and nonpermitted testing room items

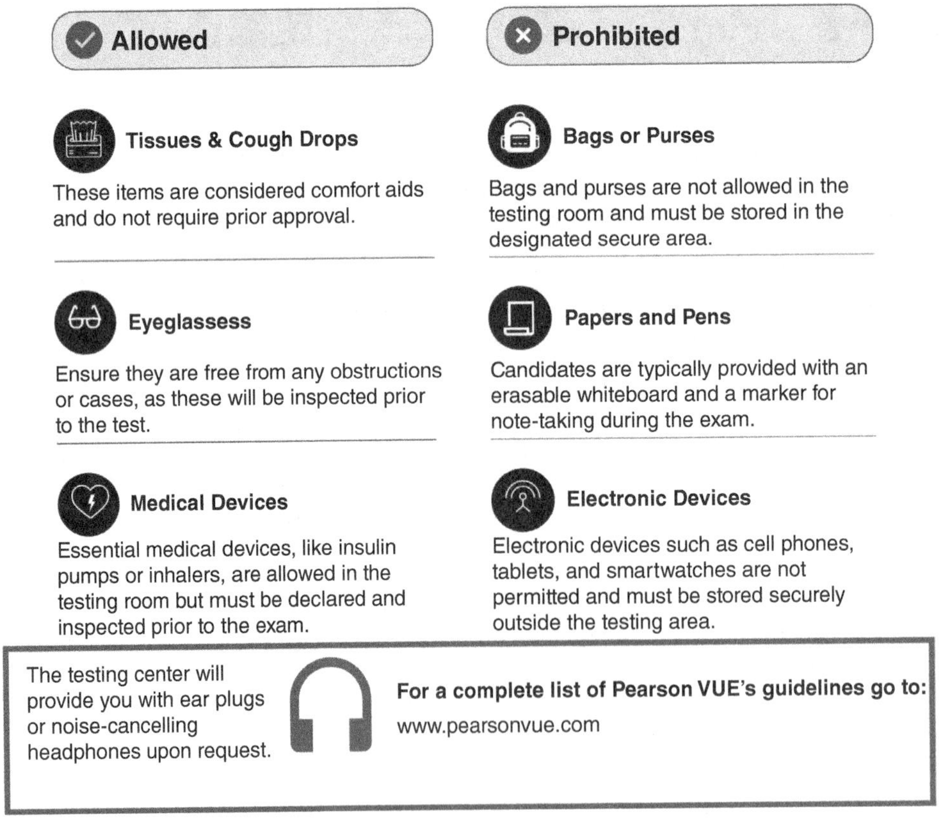

✓ Allowed	✗ Prohibited
Tissues & Cough Drops — These items are considered comfort aids and do not require prior approval.	**Bags or Purses** — Bags and purses are not allowed in the testing room and must be stored in the designated secure area.
Eyeglassess — Ensure they are free from any obstructions or cases, as these will be inspected prior to the test.	**Papers and Pens** — Candidates are typically provided with an erasable whiteboard and a marker for note-taking during the exam.
Medical Devices — Essential medical devices, like insulin pumps or inhalers, are allowed in the testing room but must be declared and inspected prior to the exam.	**Electronic Devices** — Electronic devices such as cell phones, tablets, and smartwatches are not permitted and must be stored securely outside the testing area.

The testing center will provide you with ear plugs or noise-cancelling headphones upon request.

For a complete list of Pearson VUE's guidelines go to: www.pearsonvue.com

The Aftermath

The great thing about CBTs is that you'll get a preliminary result before you leave the test site. If you're testing at a physical exam center, you'll see your results right away, and the official results will be available online within a few business days. If you're testing through an online proctor, you won't get your results immediately but will receive them by email within 24–48 hours. Here's a tip: you can usually log into your HRCI account (the one you used to register) and check your results within about an hour after finishing the test.

> **NOTE**   As of December 31, 2023, the aPHR exam had a pass rate of 71% and the aPHRi exam had a higher pass rate of 89%.

Both the aPHR and aPHRi exams are scored on a scale from 100 to 700, with a passing score set at 500. This means you need to achieve a scaled score of 500 or higher to pass either exam.

The scoring process involves converting your raw score—the total number of questions you answer correctly—to this scaled score. This conversion accounts for slight variations in difficulty across different exam forms, ensuring fairness for all candidates. To reach a scaled score of 500, you typically need to answer approximately 71% of the scored questions correctly.

> **NOTE**   In the aPHR and aPHRi exams, each comprising 90 multiple-choice questions, only 65 questions are scored while 25 serve as pretest questions. This design allows the exam administrators to evaluate the effectiveness and clarity of new questions for future exams without impacting your final score. These pretest questions are distributed randomly throughout the exam and are indistinguishable from the scored questions. By including them, the examiners can assess the performance of these questions across a diverse candidate pool, ensuring they meet the standards required for future assessments.

A Passing Score

Congratulations, you've passed! Many people feel a mix of excitement and relief now that the stress and sleepless nights are over. Now it's time to share your success! You can claim a digital badge that shows off your new certification. This badge can be used on social media and other platforms with digital signatures. HRCI will send you an email with instructions on how to claim it. You can also order a paper copy of your certificate from HRCI's online store.

A Non-passing Score

If you don't pass the exam, you'll get a report that highlights the areas where you didn't perform as well. This can help guide your study for the next attempt. It's a good idea to retake the test as soon as the 90-day waiting period is over so that the material is still fresh in your mind. If you were close to the passing score of 500, don't give up—get back in there and try again. Think about how far you came during the preparation period, and know that with a bit more preparation, you will be successful!

> **Second Chance Insurance**
>
> If you are really anxious about your ability to pass this exam on the first try, purchase the second chance insurance offered by HRCI. This insurance allows candidates to pre-purchase the ability to retake an exam if they are unsuccessful the first time. The $250 insurance must be purchased when you first apply to take the exam, and it is nonrefundable. HRCI often runs promos throughout each year offering free second chance insurance, and these are great times to sign up for your exam.

Summary

Choosing to take an HR certification exam like the aPHR or aPHRi is a strong step in committing to HR as a profession and demonstrating a commitment to life-long learning in this career field. The exam content is available from HRCI and so the information is available to understand what exactly the tests cover. It is important to remember that even though these are entry level exams, there are some minimum requirements and registration that is needed prior to sitting the exams. The first few chapters in the book are focused on the aPHR exam and content while the back half of the book covers the aPHRi. While the two exams are separate and distinct, there are concepts to HR that are universal and overlap and so candidates are encouraged to at least browse the other sections that do not pertain to the exam you are planning to take. In both cases, after successful completion of the exam, a new certificate holder will be required to recertify every three years through completion of continuing education units or retaking the exam.

Deciding to invest time in learning about HR and growing your career is a powerful commitment to yourself. The knowledge and skills you gain are invaluable, regardless of the outcome of the aPHR or aPHRi exam. The test may measure what you've learned, but it does not define your abilities or your potential. Every hour you spend learning and expanding your expertise is a step toward becoming the professional you aspire to be.

Testing can be stressful, but there are steps you can take to be prepared to sit in the testing room and complete the exam. The pointers and tips in the book help to be mentally prepared for a rigorous test. Using all of the available tools associated with this book, including practice tests and chapter questions, will help in the preparation. The good news is that the unofficial results of the test are shown to the test taker at the end of the test and do not require lengthy waits to learn the test outcome. In cases where an applicant does not pass, there are options for a follow-up test that can be obtained. Good luck in your testing journey, and we hope this book helps with that endeavor.

Exam Essentials

Know about the exam process, including registration, and what can be brought into the testing center.   While most of the exam essentials in this book talk about HR-related topics, for this chapter, it is more important to be knowledgeable about the process of taking the exam. Having a plan and understanding how the exam process works is helpful to new test takers.

Understand the tasks individuals should be expected to perform (aPHRi only).   The tasks listed in the chapter are all the expected duties of a new HR professional. You are likely to find these in any entry-level HR position description or job posting. Knowing how to do these tasks will set an applicant apart from other applicants and also provide context for many of the knowledge points in the exam content outline.

Associate Professional in Human Resources (aPHR)

PART

I

Chapter

2

aPHR Talent Acquisition

aPHR EXAM OBJECTIVES COVERED IN THIS CHAPTER REQUIRE KNOWLEDGE RELATED TO FUNCTIONAL AREA 01, TALENT ACQUISITION:

✓ **01–01** Methods to identify staffing needs and guide talent acquisition efforts (for example, forecasting, job analysis, the creation and structure of job descriptions, and alternative staffing approaches)

✓ **01–02** Talent sourcing tools and techniques to identify and engage prospective candidates (for example, employer branding, social media, candidate pipelines, resume mining, job postings, job fairs, and employee referrals)

✓ **01–03** Recruiting procedures and strategies for screening and selecting qualified applicants (for example, recruitment firms/staffing agencies, skills assessments, interview techniques and best practices, and biases)

✓ **01–04** The lifecycle of hiring and onboarding a selected applicant (for example, reference and background checks, offer letters and counteroffers, employment contracts, and the distribution and collection of company-mandated documents; such as employee handbook and policy acknowledgments, non- disclosure or other agreements, and benefits paperwork)

✓ **01–05** The use of technology for collecting, storing, reviewing and analyzing candidate/applicant information and recruiting data (for example, applicant tracking systems, human resource information systems [HRIS], return on investment [ROI], cost-per-hire, and time-to-fill)

Functional area 01, Talent Acquisition accounts for 19% of the aPHR exam. The HR Certification Institute (HRCI) summarizes this exam content as the "fundamental understanding of all aspects related to the talent acquisition process; including planning, sourcing, recruiting, screening, selection, hiring, and onboarding of a new hire." It involves various stages, from identifying job openings to sourcing candidates, screening resumes, conducting interviews, and then selecting the best fit for the role. This process is important because it ensures that companies have the right people at the right time and in the right positions to produce organizational results. HR professionals utilize a range of strategies, including job postings, networking, and leveraging technology platforms, to connect with potential candidates and build a pipeline of talent. By understanding the company's needs and culture, as well as the skills and attributes required for each position, talent acquisition specialists help companies successfully compete in their relevant markets.

HR Done Wrong

An article published in *Wired* magazine in March 2024 highlighted the personal stories of potential applicants competing for high tech jobs. Many of these individuals felt the hiring process had become "a nightmare" or "ridiculous." Lengthy interviews that demanded work samples often involved much more effort on the part of the applicant than was made known at the start of the process. Other examples of flawed talent acquisition such as poor job descriptions, a one-sided engagement method limiting questions and conversation, and a multi-round interview taking many months akin to trying to reach the boss level in a video game added to the frustration of recruits. Overall, a general lack of transparency followed by the employer ghosting the applicants not selected for hire created a sense that the process was more about obtaining free work or ideas than hiring qualified people.

HR professionals are responsible for finding and hiring the right people in the right positions at the right time in an organization. The process that is established often sets the tone for the initial impression of a company and can result in building brand loyalty when done well, but also creating frustration and negative emotions when executed poorly. It is important to remember that at the end of a hiring process are individual people who all have needs and desires that deserve respect for their time and compassion as they navigate the job search world. Do not trade off the human dimension of the hiring process in an attempt to be more efficient or thorough.

Source: Adapted from `https://www.wired.com/story/why-tech-job-interviews-became-such-a-nightmare/`

Talent Acquisition Defined

Talent acquisition in human resources (HR) is the process of finding and hiring the best people for a company. This process includes creating job ads, reviewing applications, conducting interviews, and selecting candidates who have the right skills and fit the company culture. It's about attracting and bringing in talented employees to help the company succeed.

The following is a list of key terms you should be familiar with for the aPHR exam in the area of Talent Acquisition:

- *Recruitment*: The process of finding and attracting qualified candidates for job openings. This can also be referred to as *Sourcing.*

- *Selection*: The method of choosing the most suitable candidates from those who applied for the job.

- *Staffing*: The overall strategy of hiring and managing employees to meet the company's needs.

- *Job requisition*: A formal request to fill a position within an organization.

- *Job posting*: The act of advertising a job opening on various platforms to attract candidates.

- *Employee referral program*: A program encouraging current employees to recommend candidates for open positions.

- *Candidate screening*: Reviewing applications and resumes to identify the best candidates for further evaluation.

- *Interviewing*: Conducting conversations with candidates to assess their suitability for the job.

- *Behavioral interviewing*: An interview technique that assesses a candidate's past behavior to predict future performances.

- *Applicant tracking system (ATS)*: Software that helps manage and streamline the hiring process by tracking candidates' applications.

- *Job offer*: A formal proposal to a candidate to join the company, including details about the position and compensation.

- *Talent pipeline*: A pool of potential candidates who are prequalified and ready to fill future job openings.

- *Employer brand*: The company's reputation as an employer and its appeal to current and potential employees.

- *Cultural fit*: The alignment between a candidate's values, beliefs, and behaviors and the organizational culture.

- *Candidate experience*: The overall impression and experience that candidates have during the hiring process.

- *Background check*: The process of verifying a candidate's history, including employment, education, and criminal records.

- *Skills assessment*: Test or evaluation used to determine a candidate's skills and abilities relative to the job.

- *Job description*: A detailed outline of the responsibilities, qualifications, and requirements of a specific job.

- *Job structure*: Also referred to as job architecture, it includes job levels, titles, grades, career paths, and criteria for career movement in a relative rank structure in terms of job values and complexity.

- *Realistic job preview (RJP)*: Providing candidates with a true picture of what the job will be like, including both positive and negative aspects.

- *Ghosting*: When a candidate or employer suddenly stops all communication without explanation during the hiring process.

- *Headhunting/Sourcing*: Actively seeking out and recruiting talented individuals, often for high-level positions.

Determining Staffing Needs

Forecasting in talent acquisition refers to the process of predicting future hiring needs based on factors such as business growth, turnover rates, and market trends to be able to proactively plan recruitment strategies and ensure a steady supply of qualified candidates. Forecasting is directly tied to the strategic planning process and takes into account company growth or downsizing plans.

Companies can grow in two main ways:

- *Business development*: growing a company by finding new customers, making new partnerships, or creating new products or services.

- *Mergers and acquisitions*: when companies join, or one company buys another, to become bigger or stronger. This is also a way that organizations can "buy" talent without necessarily going through a formal recruiting and selection process. Strategically, it also takes competitors out of the market.

Companies can downsize for two main reasons:

- *Business decline*: when a company starts to lose money or customers, usually because people aren't buying its products anymore or because other companies are doing better. A great example of this comes with technological advancements or changes to the business environment. Technological advancements impact workforces based on process changes that reduced human capital demand. Companies adapt by improving productivity to remain competitive in the market or lose business share.

- *Outsourcing/offshoring*: when a company hires another company to do some of its work, like customer service or making products, usually to save money or because the other company is better at it. Offshoring occurs when a company moves part or all of its operations to another country. While advancements in artificial intelligence (AI) is not considered outsourcing, as this technology advances, we do see a similar impact in replacing a workforce with a viable substitute.

Company growth or decline are factors that affect a company's talent acquisition strategy. For example, if a company is outsourcing part of its operations but is growing in another department, HR can help upskill or reskill employees to avoid layoffs. Upskilling is when employees learn new skills that make them better at the job they already have, like learning to use new software or getting better at talking to customers. Reskilling means learning new skills that are different from the ones the employees already have, usually because the job is changing or the employee is being transferred into a new department.

Building Job Structures

Building job structures using job analysis and job descriptions is important for companies to understand what each job involves and how it fits into the organization. *Job analysis* helps employers identify the tasks, duties, and responsibilities needed for a job, while an individual's job description is usually provided to the employee in a document to communicate these expectations. Having clear roles and responsibilities delineated in a job description helps managers make fair decisions about hiring, promotions, and salaries, and it helps employees know what's expected of them. It also makes it easier to plan for training and development because everyone knows what skills are needed for each job.

Several methods are used to analyze the tasks, duties, and responsibilities of a job:

- **Observation Method:** This method involves watching employees as they perform their jobs to understand the tasks they do, how they do them, and what skills are needed. The observer records detailed information about the job. An advantage to this method is that it provides firsthand information, which is especially useful for physically demanding jobs. However, to record the level of detail required for an accurate assessment can be time consuming and intrusive. Observing employees may also alter how they actually perform the work if they believe such observation may impact job security.

- **Interview Method:** With this method, managers or HR professionals talk to employees to gather information about their job duties, responsibilities, and the skills they use.

These interviews may be structured or unstructured conversations with the incumbents, supervisors, or other stakeholders, and the interviewer asks questions about the various aspects of the job, including duties performed, responsibilities, skills, and conditions of the job. This method provides in-depth and comprehensive information and is useful for capturing complex aspects of the job. Once again, this method takes time and also depends on the honesty of the individuals being interviewed to provide accurate responses.

- **Questionnaire Method:** In this method, employees fill out surveys or questionnaires about their job tasks, responsibilities, and the tools or equipment they use. The questionnaires typically include a series of questions about job tasks, responsibilities, required skills, and working conditions. This method has the advantage of being more efficient than the other two; however, it may lack detail or nuance. The method depends heavily on how well the questionnaire is designed and how the respondents interpret each question.

Table 2.1 shows the advantages and disadvantages of each job analysis method.

The output from the job analysis also helps to identify the knowledge, skills, abilities, and other (*KSAOs*) characteristics necessary to successfully perform the job.

Job descriptions are detailed documents that outline the responsibilities, qualifications, and expectations associated with a specific job within an organization. These descriptions serve as a roadmap for both employers and job seekers, providing clear guidelines on the duties and requirements of the position. Typically, they include information such as the title of the position, a summary of the role's purpose, essential job functions, required qualifications (such as education, experience, and skills), and any physical or environmental demands. Figure 2.1 shows the essential elements of a well-crafted job description.

TABLE 2.1   Job Analysis Methods Advantages and Disadvantages

Method	Advantages	Disadvantages
Observation	Provides real-time, accurate data by watching employees do their jobs.	Can disrupt work and may not capture all aspects of the job.
Interviews	Allows for in-depth answers and insights from employees about their tasks.	Time-consuming and may lead to biased answers depending on the person being interviewed.
Questionnaire	Can be given to many employees at once and is cost-effective.	May not gather detailed information if questions are not clear, and responses can be incomplete.

FIGURE 2.1   Essential parts of a job description

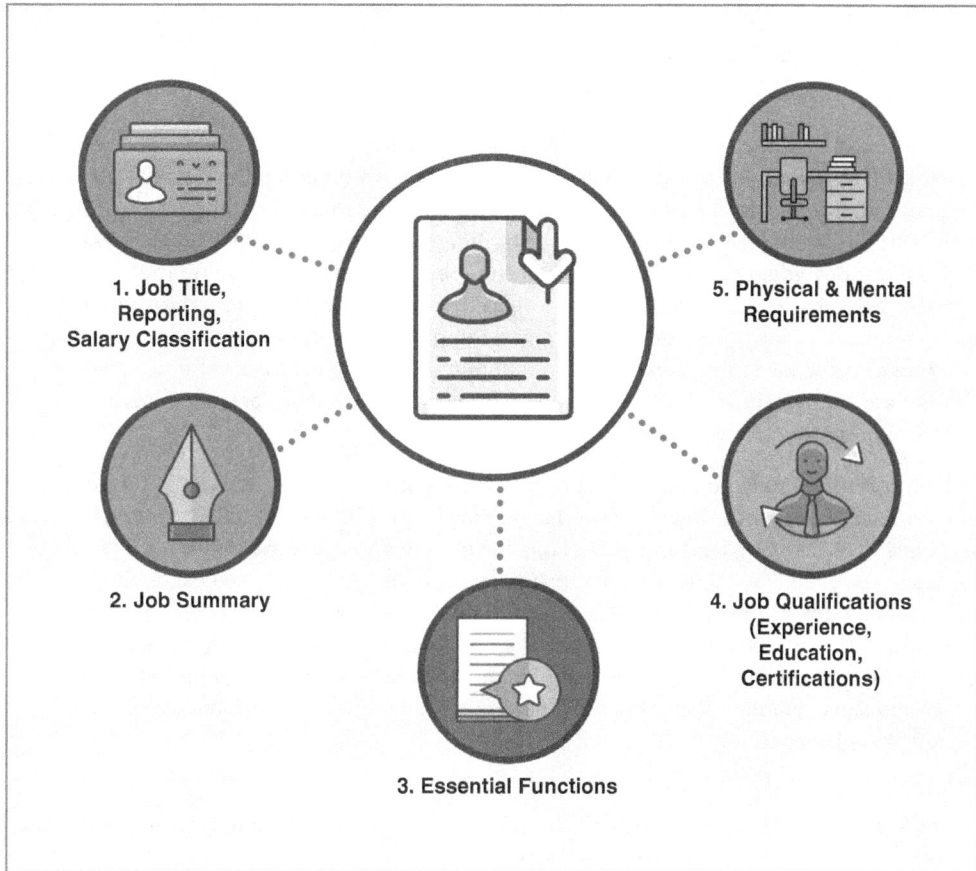

1. Job Title,
Reporting,
Salary Classification

2. Job Summary

3. Essential Functions

4. Job Qualifications
(Experience,
Education,
Certifications)

5. Physical & Mental
Requirements

A well-written job description not only helps job seekers understand what the role entails but also assists employers in evaluating candidates' suitability during the recruitment process. Job descriptions serve as a reference point for performance evaluations, career development discussions, modified duty assignments, and legal compliance, making them an important tool used throughout all of the stages of the employee lifecycle.

A realistic job preview (RJP) is another tool used to help candidates understand the day-to-day realities of an open role. An RJP is a concise overview provided to job candidates. It is different from a job description in that in addition to the tasks, duties, and responsibilities of a job, the RJP offers an honest portrayal of the challenges, demands, and aspects of the role and work environment.

Case Study

The Value of Realistic Job Previews

By Thomas Mobley

In a midsize tech company, rapid growth led to the hiring of several new software developers to meet increasing project demands. Eager to fill positions quickly, the HR department focused on the positive aspects of the job, such as the competitive salary, modern office environment, and potential for career advancement. However, they did not provide a realistic overview of the job's challenges, including the frequent overtime required to meet tight deadlines, the high-pressure environment, and the necessity for quick adaptation to changing project requirements. As a result, new hires, unprepared for these demands, began to experience burnout and dissatisfaction. Within six months, turnover rates spiked, causing project delays and increasing recruitment costs.

Had the company implemented RJPs during the hiring process, this turnover might have been avoided. RJPs would have provided candidates with a balanced view of both the positive and challenging aspects of the job, allowing them to make more informed decisions about their fit for the role. For instance, the company could have included testimonials from current employees discussing their experiences, highlighted the typical work schedule, and outlined the specific challenges associated with the role. Candidates who were not comfortable with these realities might have opted out of the process, while those who chose to join would have been better prepared and more resilient, resulting in higher job satisfaction and lower turnover.

Once an organization has forecasted its staffing needs and understands the job structure, the recruiting and selection process can begin.

Staffing

The purpose of the staffing process is to find, and attract, and select the right people to fill job openings within an organization. This involves searching for candidates who have the skills, experience, and qualities needed to succeed in specific roles. By identifying and engaging with potential candidates through various channels like job boards, social media, and networking, companies aim to build a pool of qualified candidates to choose from when hiring. The ultimate goal is to ensure that the organization has a talented and capable workforce to meet its current and future needs.

The job analysis process identifies the characteristics of jobs, and the staffing process identifies the characteristics of people. In this way, talent sourcing helps to predict "fit."

Fit during the talent sourcing process refers to the alignment between a candidate's qualifications, skills, values, and personality traits with the requirements and culture of the company or specific job role. There are two main types of fit:

- **Person-to-organization fit:** refers to how well an individual's values, beliefs, and work style align with the culture and goals of a specific company.
- **Person-to-job fit:** relates to the compatibility between an individual's KSAOs and preferences with the requirements and responsibilities of a particular job role.

The Employer Brand

Just as a product brand communicates what a customer might expect from a product or service, the *employer brand* is the overall reputation of the company as an employer. *Employment brand*, while often used interchangeably, actually refers to how a company communicates the values, culture, and overall experience that employees and potential candidates might expect from a company. A strong employer brand not only attracts top talent but also helps in retaining current employees. It communicates what makes the company unique and why it's a great place to work, influencing candidates' perceptions and decisions to apply for job openings. An *employer of choice* is the desirable status a company achieves when it is recognized as an exceptional place to work. Through employer branding initiatives such as employee testimonials, highlighting company culture, and promoting workplace perks and benefits, companies can effectively differentiate themselves in the competitive talent market and attract candidates who are the right fit for their organization. The employer brand may also help to attract *passive candidates*, those who are not actively looking for a job but might change their mind if they decide they want to come work for the company based on its employer brand.

One example of a negative employer brand is that of the company that laid off more than 900 workers via Zoom. This decision severely tarnished its employer brand because it received widespread negative attention, and the brand was further eroded when the company announced plans to lay off another 3,000 employees due to market disruptions. The mishandling of layoffs, including reports of some employees receiving severance pay before being notified, highlighted a lack of empathy and proper organizational management practices. It is also likely to make future candidates think twice before applying for open positions within the company due to perceptions of instability or lack of job security.

Recruiting

Recruiting is the process of finding and attracting individuals to fill job openings within an organization. It involves identifying the staffing needs and sourcing potential candidates through various channels such as job boards, social media, and networking events and assessing candidate qualifications and suitability for the roles available.

Recruiting can be the responsibility of a department manager, a staffing specialist, or an HR generalist. This is often a factor of company size, the turnover rate, and number of open positions at any given time. The process begins by working closely with the department manager to understand the requirements of the job and to make sure the job description is accurate and up-to-date. The wage range may need to be reviewed for competitiveness, and a target date for hiring established.

For hard-to-fill positions, HR may choose to engage in *continuous recruitment*, meaning that HR regularly advertises and screens for qualified individuals to build a *candidate pipeline* from which to choose as positions become available.

There are several methods for recruiting.

Social Media   Social media refers to online platforms and websites designed for social interaction and networking, which are increasingly used by organizations for recruiting purposes. Employers utilize social media channels such as LinkedIn, Facebook, X (formerly Twitter), and Instagram to promote job openings, engage with potential candidates, showcase company culture, and build their employer brand.

Candidate Pipelines   Candidate pipelines involve proactively sourcing and nurturing a pool of qualified candidates for current and future job openings. This strategic approach allows recruiters to maintain relationships with potential candidates, whether actively job searching or not, through networking, talent communities and talent relationship management systems. *Job bidding* is a method used internally that allows employees to express their interest in various roles for when they become open in the future.

Resume Mining   Resume mining is the process of using software tools or databases to search, extract, and analyze resumes and candidate profiles from various sources, such as job boards, social networks, and company websites. Recruiters use resume mining to identify potential candidates who match specific criteria, skill sets, and key words, helping streamline the candidate sourcing process and build talent pools. A *Boolean search* is a method used in information retrieval to find relevant information within a large set of data by using a specific set of operators. In recruitment and sourcing, Boolean search techniques are commonly used to refine searches when looking for candidates online. By combining keywords with Boolean operators such as "AND," "OR," and "NOT," recruiters can create more precise search queries to target candidates with the desired skills, experience, and other qualifications.

Job Fairs   Job fairs are events where employers, recruiters, and job seekers come together to network, discuss job opportunities, and explore career options. These events can be hosted by universities, professional organizations, or local communities and provide a platform for companies to showcase their employment opportunities while allowing job seekers to learn about different industries and connect directly with hiring managers.

Employee Referrals   Employee referrals are recommendations made by current employees of an organization for potential candidates to fill job vacancies. Companies often encourage employee referrals as a cost-effective and efficient way to source candidates, leveraging their employees' networks and relationships to identify qualified talent who may not be actively seeking job opportunities. One challenge of employee referrals is lack of diversity, as many individuals are likely to refer individuals who share their own demographic characteristics.

Recruitment Firms/Staffing Agencies   Recruitment firms, also known as staffing agencies or employment agencies, are companies that specialize in connecting employers with qualified candidates for temporary, contract, or permanent positions. These firms typically provide recruitment services, including candidate sourcing, screening, and placement, acting as intermediaries between employers and job seekers to facilitate the hiring process and find the best match for both parties.

Alternative Staffing Approaches

Alternative staffing approaches encompass nontraditional methods of sourcing and managing talent beyond traditional full-time employment. These approaches offer flexibility for both employers and workers, allowing organizations to adapt to changing business needs and access specialized skills on-demand. There are several alternatives to traditional staffing approaches.

Temporary Workers   Temporary workers, also known as contingent workers, are employed by organizations for a finite period to fulfill specific tasks or projects. This approach provides flexibility for employers to scale their workforce based on fluctuating demands without committing to long-term employment contracts. For workers, temporary roles offer opportunities to gain diverse experience, supplement income, or bridge employment gaps while retaining flexibility in their schedules and career paths.

Professional Employer Organization (PEO)   A professional employer organization (PEO) is a company that helps small and medium-sized businesses manage important tasks like payroll, benefits, human resources, and compliance with labor laws. When a business partners with a PEO, the PEO becomes a *co-employer*, meaning it shares some of the responsibilities of the employees, like handling taxes and providing health insurance, while the business still oversees daily operations and decision-making.

PEOs are different from staffing agencies because PEOs work with the employees a business already has, helping manage them long term, whereas staffing agencies focus on finding temporary workers or helping fill short-term job positions.

Independent Contractors   Independent contractors are self-employed individuals who provide services to businesses on a contract basis. Unlike traditional employees, independent contractors work autonomously and are responsible for managing their own taxes, insurance, and work arrangements. This staffing approach enables employers to access specialized skills and expertise without the overhead costs associated with hiring

TABLE 2.2 Differences Between an Employee and Independent Contractor

Employee	Independent Contractor
Is told when and where to do the work	Sets their own hours and works at a location necessary to perform the work
Gets feedback from a manager or supervisor	Does not have a formal feedback system beyond fulfillment of agreed upon deliverables
Has expenses reimbursed by the company	Often has unreimbursed expenses
Is guaranteed a regular wage for hours worked	Usually earns a flat or negotiated fee for services
Is usually offered employer-sponsored insurance plans	Generally provides their own insurance and pays their own taxes
Intent to keep the individual working as long as they are adequately performing	Understands that the work is project based
Services provided are a key aspect to the business	Services provided are often outside the scope of the business's core competencies

For more information on the behavioral, financial, and relationship guidelines visit. Adapted from https://www.irs.gov/businesses/small-businesses-self-employed/independent-contractor-self-employed-or-employee.

full-time employees. For contractors, it offers flexibility in choosing projects, setting rates, and managing their workload. See Table 2.2 for a description of the differences between an independent contractor and employee.

Independent Contractors

The guidelines for determining whether someone is an independent contractor or an employee come from a combination of IRS regulations, Department of Labor standards, state laws and regulations, court decisions, and other relevant agencies. It is essential for businesses to understand and apply these guidelines correctly to ensure compliance and avoid legal issues.

Freelancers/Project-based Workers   Freelancers are individuals who work independently on a project basis, offering their services to multiple clients simultaneously. This arrangement allows organizations to engage talent for short-term assignments or specific tasks without the constraints of traditional employment relationships. Freelancers enjoy autonomy in their work, the ability to work remotely, and the opportunity to build a diverse portfolio of clients and projects.

Gig Workers   Gig workers, often associated with the gig economy, perform short-term or freelance work on a flexible basis, typically through online platforms or apps. This staffing model allows individuals to earn income by completing tasks or providing services on-demand, such as driving for ride-sharing services, delivering groceries, or performing microtasks. For employers, gig workers provide a scalable workforce solution for time-sensitive projects or peak periods of activity, while gig workers appreciate the flexibility to choose when and how much they work.

Interview Techniques

Interview techniques include the method an employer chooses to engage applicants for hire and the qualitative elements of the interview itself. The urgency by which an open position in the company needs to be filled can impact the choice of the interview process as some ways are more expedient than others. Also, the interviewer(s) personalities, bias tendencies, and emotional intelligence are contributing factors to the quality of the interview and the overall results of a successful hire. There are several interview methods, which are reviewed next.

One on One   One-on-one interviews consist of a single applicant with a single representative of the company. The company representative may be a supervisor for the position, the hiring authority, or someone from HR. These interviews may be conducted in an office setting that is conducive to conversation and involves the applicant being asked a series of questions related to the job. Applicants should be afforded the opportunity to ask questions of the representative about conditions of employment, compensation, benefits, or other similar questions.

Panel   A panel interview is like a one-on-one interview with the exception that there is more than one interviewer from the company. This technique is helpful to have multiple perspectives and assessments provided by the interview team and shortens the hiring process by consolidating stakeholders who may have conducted separate one-on-one interviews otherwise. Panels usually divide the questions for the applicants, and when answering questions, can offer different viewpoints about the company. A panel that is representative of the diversity of an organization offers better insight into a candidate and improves the chances of a diverse candidate accepting an offer when they feel they are represented in the hiring process.

Distance   Remote work is becoming more available in organizations, and this is especially true following the global pandemic. Sometimes, it is not convenient for an applicant to be physically present with the interviewer(s). In such instances, video conferencing platforms such as Zoom or Teams that can be readily downloaded to the applicant's computer are used. The distance interview can be one-on-one or a panel with the same process used as described. Disadvantages to this technique include the limited ability to assess nonverbal communication (body language) and the potential for connectivity issues.

Behavioral   Behavioral interviews assess how an applicant might react or act in a possible workplace scenario. Often, the candidate is asked to comment on how they might handle an issue with a coworker or client or provide an example of something that occurred in their past work history and the actions they took. The purpose of this technique is to determine how a potential hire's behavioral tendencies align with the company's culture and values and if they would be a "good fit" with other members of the team.

The STAR method is one way to conduct a behavioral interview. The STAR method stands for Situation, Task, Action, Result. By describing a situation and a required task, the applicant can add the actions they took, along with the results of those actions. By providing this reference, an employer can have a clear picture of how an individual would act in a similar circumstance within the company.

Group   A group interview is when multiple candidates are assessed simultaneously. This may take the pressure off any one individual and instead focus on the interaction of the team and group dynamics. This interview technique is effective when hiring a team from scratch or when collaboration is an essential element of the job standards.

Working   A working interview may also be referred to as a technical interview. This is like an applicant and the employer taking each other for a test drive. When there is a strong technical requirement for the position, for example an automotive body repair technician, a working interview allows the employer to see exactly the outcome of the work product of the applicant. Technical skill and aptitude can be evaluated more closely without requiring the employer to commit to hiring the individual.

Informal   An informal interview is a conversational, in-person meeting with someone from the company who has a role in the hiring process to discuss aspects of a particular job and allow a potential applicant and prospective employer an opportunity to gauge mutual interest in exploring a working relationship. It might be an employer representative meeting an applicant over lunch or in a non-office setting. This technique may be used in initial interviews to get a sense of an applicant's interest in a company or position with an invitation to apply. It may also be used to introduce other members of the team such as a team lead or supervisor (if not involved in the initial interview) to assess compatibility or team cohesiveness. While informal interviews may offer additional insight into an applicant, they should not be used as the primary interview process.

Interviews take on many forms, but best practices have similar characteristics that should generally be followed when engaging potential future employees. Interviews can set the tone of how an employee perceives the organization as a first impression, so it is important to be mindful of the following interview standards:

▪   Courteousness: Treat others as you would expect to be treated in the company and reflect the company's values.

- Professional conduct: Strive to act in a professional manner even with informal interviews.

- Enthusiastic: Future employees judge the company on the level of commitment and enthusiasm of its current employees.

- Nonverbal: Be aware of how an individual's nonverbal communication is transmitted or received in an interview. Eye contact, posture, folded arms may send cues that can be misinterpreted.

- Conversational: Keep the engagement open, transparent, and a two-way discussion about the needs of the company with respect to this job opening and the qualifications of the applicant to fill the hire. An interview is not intended to be an interrogation.

Interviewers must be aware of any potential biases they might exhibit during the interview process. Biases are prejudices that could favor or inhibit an applicant's chances of successfully being hired. Biases are always present in interviews, but it is critical that they do not impact a hiring decision. In a working interview or in an assessment of performance, biases may also be present in a subjective evaluation. Bias and self-awareness are keys to ensuring a fair interview and hiring process. Common biases and prejudices are covered next.

Stereotyping   Stereotyping makes assumptions about an applicant by grouping the individual in with a larger population segment often based on an applicant's inherent characteristics. These biases could be based on ethnicity, gender, religion, or other similar attributes. You may note that these are also *protected classes*.

Inconsistency in Questions   When conducting a one-on-one or panel interview with multiple applicants, interviewers should be sure to ask the same questions of each applicant and assess the answers in a consistent approach. Asking different questions of applicants, especially based on the attributes of an applicant, can bias the outcome of the interview. For example, if one applicant was a woman, and the only applicant to be asked a question about intentions to start a family, that would be prejudicial based on gender.

First Impressions   Often an interviewer will have an initial impression of a candidate. That first impression may color future questions or cloud an unbiased judgment of follow on responses by the applicant. This can be both positive and negative to the applicant, depending on the first impression made. Interviewers must be sure that each question and response is evaluated on its own and not judged based on the initial thoughts of the interviewer.

Halo/Horn Effect   Similar to first impressions, the halo or horn effect are two extreme viewpoints of a candidate based on only one attribute that creates a very strong response. To illustrate, it could be discovered during an interview that a candidate shares liking a favorite sports team with the person conducting the interview. The interviewer may, in turn, have a more favorable view of the candidate giving that candidate a halo and ignoring other less favorable attributes. The horn effect is the opposite condition and would result in this situation if the candidate's favorite team was an opposing rival team.

Cultural Noise   Sometimes it is difficult to assess a candidate's truthful responses to questions. The applicant may be attempting to filter their answers in such a way as to guess what response the interviewer wants to hear. Applicants may be trying to fit culturally by limiting any potential answers that would be in conflict with the company's values to improve their chances for hire. As a result, hiring with this bias may result in someone that is unable to ultimately fit with a team dynamic and result in a mis-hire.

Similar to Me   Interviewers may have a bias to applicants who have attributes in common such as education or experience. Because they see themselves as a strong fit with the company, they may be biased in judging an applicant with a similar background history. A panel interview with multiple perspectives can reduce the impact of this bias.

Central Tendency   A central tendency bias results when an interviewer has similar ratings for all the applicants. This may come after many interviews for the same position and repeated questions with identical responses. If there is little differentiation, the interviewer may not be able to clearly choose a preference. Asking behavioral questions and using several interview techniques can help avoid this bias by offering multiple vantage points to assess candidates fully.

Contrast   If the first interviewed applicant generates a strong positive or negative response from the interviewer(s), the remaining candidates could be compared to that individual. This creates a contrast bias when an artificial metric or standard is put in place and all other comparisons are reduced to how a candidate measures up to the stand out applicant.

Nonverbal   Many inexperienced interviewers will rely too heavily on nonverbal responses of applicants. Some applicants may be nervous during an interview, which is a natural response to stressful situations, and not maintain eye contact or appear to shift and move while in the interview. This can create a nonverbal bias where an interviewer is focused more on what is not being said than what is actually being said during the interview.

Pre-offer Activities

In addition to the interview, several other activities can take place to help make a hiring decision. These activities can assess an applicant's KSAOs that demonstrate the potential to successfully fill the required position and how well aligned a candidate might be to the organizational values and culture. It is important to remember that all activities prior to an offer must fairly assess a candidate and be related to the job. Any activities must not create disparate treatment or cause disparate impact to any candidate on the basis of protected characteristics like race, religion, gender, national origin, or disability, for example.

Skills assessments are tools used by employers to evaluate the abilities, knowledge, and capabilities of candidates. These assessments can take various forms, including the following:

- **Technical skills assessments:** These assessments evaluate candidates' proficiency in specific technical areas relevant to the job, from simple skills such as typing speed to more advanced skills such as coding languages. They often include practical exercises or simulations to assess the candidate's ability to apply technical knowledge in real-world scenarios.

- **Cognitive ability tests:** Cognitive ability tests assess candidates' mental abilities, including problem-solving skills, critical thinking, numerical reasoning, and verbal comprehension. These tests help employers gauge candidates' potential to learn new tasks, adapt to changing environments, and effectively solve complex problems.

- **Personality and behavioral assessments:** Personality and behavioral assessments aim to evaluate candidates' personality traits, work styles, communication preferences, and interpersonal skills. These assessments provide insights into how candidates are likely to interact with colleagues, make decisions, handle conflict, and more. They help employers ensure a good cultural fit and predict candidates' job performance and potential for success within the organization.

Another pre-offer activity is conducting reference and background checks. These activities are done to verify the accuracy of information provided by job candidates, such as work history or educational credentials. Reference checks involve contacting previous employers or personal references to gather insights into the candidate's work ethic, performance, and character. Background checks typically involve reviewing an individual's criminal record, education, employment history, and other relevant background information to ensure they meet the employer's standards and requirements. Any additional information that is required in this process of background checks must comply with the Fair Credit Reporting and Disclosure Act.

The Offer

Once a qualified candidate has been identified, an offer is made. *Offer letters* are formal documents issued by employers to selected candidates, outlining the terms and conditions of employment, including job title, salary, benefits, start date, and any other pertinent details.

A candidate may come back with a counteroffer to the terms of employment. This negotiation process aims to reach mutually agreeable terms before finalizing the employment agreement.

In some cases, the company may choose to enter an *employment contract* with a potential hire. Often used for management and senior leaders, an employment contract is a legally binding agreement between an employer and an employee that outlines the terms and conditions of employment, including job responsibilities, compensation, benefits, and most importantly, the reasons the employment relationship may be terminated. An employment contract contrasts with *at-will employment*, which is a legal doctrine that allows either the employer or the employee to terminate the employment relationship at any time, with or without cause, and with or without advance notice. There are three main exceptions to the at-will doctrine:

- *Implied contract*: When an employer's actions or statements create an implied promise of job security, suggesting that termination will only occur for just cause.

- *Public policy*: When termination violates a well-established public policy, such as firing an employee for exercising legal rights or refusing to engage in illegal activities.

- *Implied covenant of good faith and fair dealing*: In some states, there's an implied covenant of good faith and fair dealing in every employment relationship, which prohibits employers from terminating employees in bad faith or with malicious intent.

Post-offer Activities

Post-offer activities refer to the tasks and processes that occur after a job offer has been extended and accepted by a candidate but before the individual officially begins employment. These activities typically include drug screenings, employment physicals, and completion of necessary paperwork.

Drug Screens and Physicals   Pre-employment drug screens and physicals are conducted by employers to assess a candidate's physical health and substance use prior to starting a new job. Drug screening typically involves urine or saliva tests to detect the presence of illegal substances or prescription medications that may impair job performance or pose a safety risk.

Physical examinations evaluate a candidate's overall health, including vital signs, mobility, and any pre-existing medical conditions that could impact their ability to perform job duties safely. These screenings and assessments help employers maintain a safe and productive work environment.

Just like employees, applicants are considered protected from unlawful discrimination. For this reason, drug screens and pre-employment physicals must be nondiscriminatory in both intent and outcome. The Americans with Disabilities Act (ADA) places certain restrictions on how pre-employment drug screens and physicals can be conducted to ensure they do not discriminate against individuals with disabilities. Under the ADA, employers are prohibited from conducting medical examinations, including drug tests and physicals, until after a conditional job offer has been made to the candidate. Any medical inquiries or examinations must be job-related and consistent with business necessity. This means that employers must have a legitimate reason to request a drug screen or physical exam, such as assessing an individual's ability to perform essential job functions safely. This is one reason why having accurate and up-to-date job descriptions that list the physical and mental requirements of the job are so important. Employers must provide reasonable accommodations to candidates with disabilities, such as alternative testing methods or adjustments to the examination process, unless doing so would impose undue hardship on the employer.

Form I–9 The Immigration Reform and Control Act (IRCA) of 1986 is a US federal law that focuses on controlling and regulating immigration, particularly with regard to employment. One of its key provisions is the requirement for employers to verify the identity and eligibility of their employees to work legally in the United States. This verification process is done through the completion of Form I-9, which documents the identity and employment authorization of each new employee. IRCA also established penalties for employers who knowingly hire unauthorized workers.

Verifying the identity and eligibility of new hires may also be completed through the Department of Labor's E-Verify system. E-Verify compares information provided by employees on Form I-9, such as Social Security numbers and immigration status, against data from the Department of Homeland Security and the Social Security Administration. Through E-Verify, employers can confirm the legal authorization of their employees to work in the United States, helping to maintain compliance with immigration laws and regulations. While participation in E-Verify is generally voluntary for most employers, some states have mandated its use for certain businesses or industries.

> **NOTE** Completing Form I-9 is complicated, and errors are costly. There is a 141-page Handbook for Employers (M-274) with instructions on how to accurately complete the two-page document. Find it at `https://www.uscis.gov/book/export/html/59502`.

New Hire Documents New hire document completion involves the process of filling out various forms and paperwork when an individual joins a company as an employee. This typically includes completing forms such as tax withholding forms (e.g., W-4 in the United States), direct deposit authorizations, emergency contact information, and company-specific policies and procedures acknowledgments. New hires often complete benefits paperwork to enroll in health insurance, retirement plans, and other employee benefits offered by the organization. These documents ensure that both the employer and employee are aligned on important administrative matters, legal obligations, and entitlements from the outset of employment.

Figure 2.2 shows a typical talent acquisition lifecycle.

FIGURE 2.2   The talent acquisition lifecycle

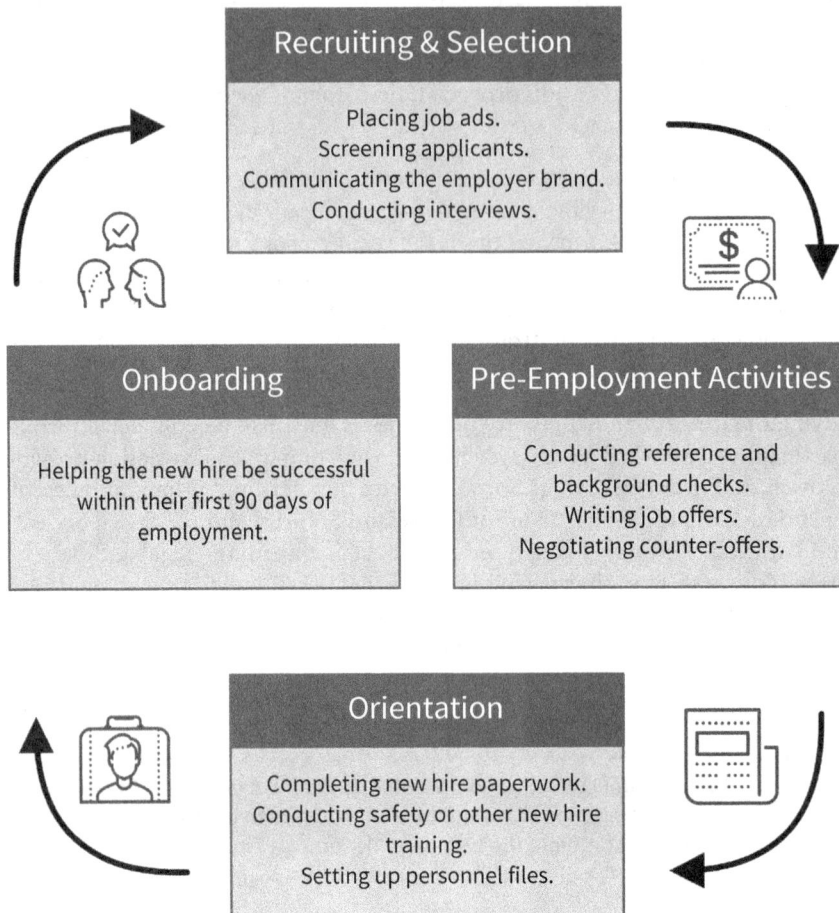

Talent Acquisition Technology

The use of technology during the talent acquisition process has streamlined how organizations attract, engage, and hire top talent. Advanced *applicant tracking systems* (ATS) streamline the recruitment process by automating job postings, resume screening, and candidate communication, enabling recruiters to efficiently manage large volumes of applicants. AI and machine learning algorithms help identify qualified candidates by analyzing resumes, predicting candidate fit, and even conducting initial interviews through chatbots or video platforms.

HRIS are software solutions aimed at integrating a wide range of HR processes, including payroll, benefits administration, time and attendance tracking, performance management, and *employee self-service* (allowing employees to access and manage their own personal information, such as payroll details, benefits enrollment, time-off requests, and performance evaluations). By centralizing employee information in a secure digital database, HRIS platforms enable HR professionals to access real-time data, automate routine tasks, and generate reports to support data-driven decision-making. HRIS systems often feature customizable dashboards and analytics tools that provide valuable insights into workforce trends, enabling HR leaders to identify areas for improvement, optimize resource allocation, and align HR strategies with organizational goals.

HRIS platforms also help employers comply with labor laws such as tax filings and regulatory reporting. With built-in security features and role-based access controls (tiers), HRIS systems ensure data integrity and confidentiality, safeguarding sensitive employee information from unauthorized access or breaches.

Another important aspect of technology is the ability to retain digital *personnel files.* Personnel files serve as a comprehensive record of employee information, documenting details throughout an individual's employment with the company. These files contain records related to recruitment, employment contracts (if relevant), performance evaluations, training and development, disciplinary actions, and any other relevant documentation. Retention periods vary depending on the type of document and applicable regulations, with some records needing to be retained for several years after an employee's departure. Implementing a structured retention policy ensures that personnel files are maintained securely, accessible when needed, and disposed of appropriately when no longer required. See Table 2.3 for a sample of federal document retention requirements.

TABLE 2.3   Federal Personnel Records Retention

Record	Retention Period	Relevant Laws
Selection, hiring, and employment records (job applications, resumes, interview notes; records relating to personnel actions, training, merit or seniority systems; copies of EEO-1 survey and self-identification forms)	One year after creation or one year from the date of termination Two years for qualified federal contractors with 150 employees or more or $150,000 in contracts otherwise one year	Age Discrimination in Employment Act Americans with Disabilities Act Civil Rights Act of 1964 (Title VII) Section 503 of the Rehabilitation Act Executive Order 11246 Vietnam Era Veterans Readjustment Assistance Act
Affirmative action plan records for federal contractors	Two years (all records of the current and preceding year)	Section 503 of the Rehabilitation Act Executive Order 11246

(*Continued*)

TABLE 2.3 Federal Personnel Records Retention (*Continued*)

Record	Retention Period	Relevant Laws
Payroll records, time sheets/cards (basic employee data and compensation records)	Three years	Age Discrimination in Employment Act Fair Labor Standards Act Service Contract Act Davis-Bacon Act Walsh-Healey Act (for federal contractors) Family Medical Leave Act
Form I-9	Three years from date of hire or one year after termination, whichever is later	Immigration Reform and Control Act Immigration and Nationality Act
Employment benefits (with certain exemptions from the Employee Retirement Income Security Act's report requirements) including summary plan descriptions, annual reports, notices of reportable events, and plan termination	Six years	Employee Retirement Income Security Act
Background checks (criminal reports, credit reports, driving records, consent and disclosure forms)	One year; however, recommendation of five years due to the statute of limitations in the Fair Credit Reporting Act	Civil Rights Act of 1964 (Title VII) Fair Credit Reporting Act (note: this law applies only to third-party investigations)
Tax records (employer identification number, wage and tip amounts, Social Security numbers, copies of W2s, absences, dates of employment, income withholding allowance certificates, copies of returns, records of fringe benefits provided)	Four years after filing the fourth quarter of the year	Federal Insurance Contribution Act Federal Unemployment Tax Act Internal Revenue Code

Record	Retention Period	Relevant Laws
Family Medical Leave Act leave records (employee data including dates of leave to include incremental hours or partial days, notices, substantiating documentation, premium payments, and any records of dispute between an employer and an eligible employee)	Three years	Family Medical Leave Act
Healthcare continuation (records of written notice to employees of their option to continue group healthcare coverage following qualifying events)	No retention requirements; however, recommendation of six years to be consistent with Employee Retirement Income Security Act	Consolidated Omnibus Budget Reconciliation Act
Polygraph test records (written statement of rights, written notice of employees being tested, copies of reports or such records)	Three years from the polygraph date (requested or performed)	Employee Polygraph Protection Act
Disability accommodations (any requests for reasonable accommodation from an employee and the employer response including any accommodations provided)	One year from date of action and retain for one year following an employee dismissal Two years for contractors and public employees	Americans with Disabilities Act as Amended Section 503 of the Rehabilitation Act Executive Order 11246 Vietnam Era Veterans Readjustment Assistance Act
Drug test records (a list of records is available at 49 C.F.R. #ss 382.401 for employees covered by the US Department of Transportation (DOT)	One year from test date Up to five years for DOT positions	DOT-covered safety-sensitive transportation positions in public transportation modes and pipelines
Military leave records (all records for absences for military duty and reemployment and other benefits bestowed upon return)	Indefinite (no statute of limitations under the Uniform Services Employment and Reemployment Rights Act	Uniform Services Employment and Reemployment Rights Act

Measuring Effectiveness

Measuring the effectiveness of all HR functions is important to ensure the company is attracting, hiring, and retaining talent in competitive markets. Companies use certain HR metrics to assess how sound their hiring process is relative to market benchmarks using key performance indicators (KPI). By assessing key metrics such as time-to-fill, cost-per-hire, quality of hires, and applicant satisfaction, HR can identify areas for improvement and optimize recruitment strategies to enhance efficiency and effectiveness. The following are some KPI metrics related to HR explained in further detail:

- **Return on investment (ROI):** measures the profitability or value gained from an investment relative to its cost, often used in talent acquisition to assess the effectiveness of recruitment strategies.

- **Cost-per-hire:** quantifies the total expenses incurred in recruiting and hiring new employees, typically calculated by dividing the total recruitment costs by the number of hires.

- **Quality of hire:** evaluates the caliber and suitability of new hires based on their performance, retention, and contributions to the organization.

- **Time to fill:** indicates the average duration it takes to fill open positions from the time they are posted until an offer is accepted, reflecting the efficiency of the recruitment process.

- **Applicant satisfaction:** gauges candidates' perceptions and experiences with the recruitment process, assessing factors such as communication, transparency, and overall satisfaction with the hiring process.

Summary

Talent acquisition is the functional area of human resource management that deals with finding, attracting, and hiring talented people. It starts by determining staffing needs to make sure the company has the right number of skilled workers for current and future output.

Building job structures is important and involves creating clear job descriptions and roles. Job analysis and job descriptions support the recruitment and selection process (also called staffing), which includes finding candidates and making hiring decisions to fill open roles.

Employers use several methods to recruit, and many employers use a combination of methods to ensure that there is a large enough qualified applicant pool to choose from.

Once a selection is made, HR engages in pre- and post-offer activities to ensure compliance with various labor laws and to help the new hire be successful from day one.

For all functions of HR, it is important to measure the effectiveness of HR activities. Metrics like time-to-fill, cost-per-hire, and employee retention rates help companies improve their hiring practices and get better results.

Exam Essentials

Be able to determine staffing needs of an organization.   Staffing needs are determined through forecasting and the creation of job structures. Companies experience growth and decline in a cyclical manner and are impacted by business development, mergers and acquisitions, offshoring, and loss of market share. Alternative staffing approaches are used in place of traditional full-time hires and may include temporary, freelance, gig workers, or independent contractors.

Be able to use job analysis and job descriptions to build job structures.   Job analysis determines the tasks, duties, and responsibilities needed for a job, while job descriptions explain these things to employees to help them understand what is expected. It enables employers to make fair decisions about hiring, promotions, and salaries. The output of a job analysis is the knowledge, skills, abilities, and other attributes needed for the position. Job descriptions are detailed documents that outline the responsibilities, qualifications, and expectations associated with a specific job role within an organization.

Be able to find and attract the right people to fill job openings within a company.   Talent sourcing helps to predict the alignment between a candidate's qualifications, skills, values, and personality traits with the requirements and culture of the company or a specific job role. Recruiting and recruiting methods such as social media, job fairs, and employee referrals help find potential candidates who align with the needs of the organization. Interview techniques can be in-person or over distance and may be one-on-one or involve multiple people. Interviews that can assess an applicant's behavioral actions in a known situation, with a given task, and analyze the results free of bias are preferred to hire the best qualified candidates.

Understand the impact of technology on the talent acquisition process.   Advanced ATSs streamline the recruitment process by automating job postings, resume screening, and candidate communication, enabling recruiters to efficiently manage large volumes of applicants. AI and machine learning algorithms help identify qualified candidates and perform various related tasks. HRIS software solutions integrate a wide range of HR functions and help employers comply with labor laws such as tax filings and regulatory reporting.

Be able to measure the effectiveness of HR functions in an organization.   Measuring the effectiveness of all HR functions ensures the company attracts, hires, and retains talent in competitive markets. HR uses key metrics such as time-to-fill, cost-per-hire, quality of hires, and applicant satisfaction to improve and optimize recruitment strategies to enhance efficiency and effectiveness.

Review Questions

You can find the answers in Appendix A.

1. Which of the following is a method to identify staffing needs in a company?

    A. Analyzing customer feedback

    B. Conducting a skills inventory

    C. Organizing team-building activities

    D. Monitoring social media trend

2. What is the primary purpose of a job analysis?

    A. To determine employee satisfaction

    B. To redesign jobs to improve productivity

    C. To understand the duties and responsibilities of a job

    D. To increase employee engagement

3. Why is forecasting important in human resources?

    A. It helps to predict future staffing needs.

    B. It helps determine the annual HR budget.

    C. It identifies employee training needs.

    D. It analyzes past seasonal staffing needs.

4. Which of the following is an example of employer branding?

    A. Offsetting commute costs for employees

    B. Creating a company blog to share employee success stories

    C. Reducing the number of meetings per week

    D. Increasing the company's team building budget

5. Which of the following best describes the practice of resume mining in recruitment? (Choose all that apply.)

    A. Manually reviewing each resume to find qualified candidates

    B. Using software to search and filter resumes based on specific keywords and criteria

    C. Hosting job fairs to meet potential candidates in person

    D. Conducting interviews to assess candidate suitability for a job

6. What is a candidate pipeline? (Choose all that apply.)

    A. A group of previous applicants for an open position

    B. A group of candidates who have been selected for an interview

    C. A list of current employees who have placed a job bid

    D. A group of employees identified to take on a future leadership role

7. Which of the following is considered a best practice for conducting interviews?

   A. Asking mostly yes or no questions to ensure consistency

   B. Letting the candidate lead the conversation to assess their communication skills

   C. Using a mix of behavioral and situational questions to gather comprehensive information

   D. Focusing primarily on the candidate's resume to avoid bias

8. During an interview, a hiring manager asks a candidate to describe a time when they had to handle a difficult customer situation. The candidate responds by explaining the context of the situation they encountered, the objective they needed to achieve, the steps they took to resolve the issue, and the outcome of their efforts. Which interview method is the candidate using?

   A. Structured interview method

   B. Case study interview method

   C. Unstructured interview method

   D. STAR method

9. Which of the following interview questions is the best example of a close-ended interview question? (Choose all that apply.)

   A. Have you ever worked in a customer service role?

   B. What are your strengths and weaknesses?

   C. Can you describe a challenging project you worked on?

   D. How do you handle conflicts with colleagues?

10. A document that outlines the duties, responsibilities, required qualifications, and reporting relationships of a specific job is called a _____.

    A. job analysis

    B. job posting

    C. job bid

    D. job description

11. Jenny is looking for resumes of candidates who have experience with both "marketing" and "social media." Which of the following search strings should she use in her Boolean search?

    A. marketing ALSO social media

    B. marketing AND social media

    C. marketing PLUS social media

    D. marketing WITH social media

12. What are the goals of the talent acquisition process? (Choose all that apply.)

    A. To improve employee engagement

    B. To attract and hire skilled employees

    C. To oversee the candidate experience

    D. To communicate the employer brand.

13. Which of the following is the first stage of the employee lifecycle?

    A. Performance management

    B. Onboarding

    C. Recruitment

    D. Retirement

14. What is the primary goal of the onboarding process?

    A. To evaluate employee performance

    B. To introduce new employees to company culture and procedures

    C. To plan future training sessions

    D. To conduct exit interviews

15. Which stage of the employee lifecycle focuses on skill improvement and career growth?

    A. Recruitment

    B. Onboarding

    C. Employee development

    D. Retirement

16. What is a counteroffer in the context of job offers?

    A. An offer made by an employer to a candidate after an interview

    B. A proposal made by a candidate to a company after receiving a job offer

    C. A job offer extended to multiple candidates simultaneously

    D. An offer made by an employer to fill a temporary position

17. What is the primary purpose of an employment contract?

    A. To outline the terms and conditions of employment between the employee and employer

    B. To create a commitment between the employer and a union

    C. To clarify the terms and conditions of employee dismissal

    D. To provide details on the company's policies, procedures, and rules

18. Why is the employee handbook considered a mandatory document for new employees?

    A. It provides detailed employment information about the company.

    B. It outlines the company's mission, vision, and values.

    C. It protects against employment at-will.

    D. It contains important policies, procedures, and expectations for employees.

19. Which of the following metrics is commonly used to measure ROI in the talent acquisition process?

    A. Employee satisfaction scores

    B. Cost per hire

    C. Number of job applications received

    D. Length of employee training programs

20. What is a key indicator of a successful ROI in the talent acquisition process?

    A. High turnover rates

    B. Low candidate response rates

    C. Short time-to-fill for job openings

    D. Increased number of training sessions

Chapter

3

aPHR Learning and Development

aPHR EXAM OBJECTIVES COVERED IN THIS CHAPTER REQUIRE KNOWLEDGE RELATED TO FUNCTIONAL AREA 02. LEARNING AND DEVELOPMENT:

✓ 02-01 The overall purpose and desired outcomes of employee orientation for new hires and/or internal hires (for example, setting expectations, building relationships, and acclimation)

✓ 02-02 The concept of instructional design and components of commonly used models and methods for developing an organizational learning strategy (for example, knowledge, skills, and abilities [KSAs], ADDIE model, needs analysis, goals/objectives, available training resources, and intended audience)

✓ 02-03 Elements and suitable applications for various training formats and delivery techniques (for example, blended, virtual, self-paced, instructor-led, on-the-job, role play, facilitation, and in-house vs. external training services)

✓ 02-04 The concept, purpose, and key/desired outcomes of a change management process (for example, assessing readiness, communication plans, identifying needs, providing resources, and training)

✓ 02-05 Methods and tools used to track employee development and measure the effectiveness of the training (for example, learning management systems [LMS], reporting, post training evaluation, and metrics)

Functional area 02, Learning and Development accounts for 15% of the aPHR exam. HRCI summarizes this exam content as "assessing the needs of the organization and understanding the techniques and methods for delivering training programs in order to provide employees with tools, skills, and knowledge to align with current and future organizational goals."

HR Done Wrong

In June 2022, the Society of Human Resource Management (SHRM) agreed to settle a lawsuit for $221,000 and make its professional development programs more accessible to those with disabilities, in compliance with the Americans with Disabilities Act (ADA). The suit alleged that SHRM did not comply with the provisions of the ADA regarding accommodations for disabled individuals specifically accessing their online learning. Training that is provided by an organization and made available must meet certain provisions, such as closed captioning for video content for individuals with hearing impairment.

This example is not isolated to SHRM as similar litigation has seen a dramatic increase over recent years. The Department of Justice has taken the position that accommodation and accessibility to comply with Title III of the ADA does not apply to just the employees but also the customers of a company. HR professionals must be aware of the requirements when building training for internal and external audiences. Additionally, Section 508 of the Rehabilitation Act amended in 1998 covers access to federally funded programs and services and includes electronic and information technology. Companies that may receive federal funding or are subject to these federal provisions must also adhere to the accessibility requirements. As more online learning has grown, especially following the recent pandemic, companies have rushed to implement needed training without ensuring it meets all the standards for accommodation.

For more information on the SHRM litigation, you can go to `Adapted from https://www.hrdive.com/news/shrm-will-pay-221k-improve-program-accessibility-to-settle-ada-suit/626213/`.

For more on Section 508 information, you can go to `https://www.access-board.gov/about/law/ra.html#section-508-federal-electronic-and-information-technology`.

Learning and Development

The learning and development (L&D) function of human resources (HR) helps employees grow their skills and knowledge. *Training* focuses on improving employees' current job performance through specific skills and knowledge and tends to have a short-term focus.

Development is long term and career oriented, aiming to prepare employees for future roles and overall personal growth through broader skill enhancement. The functional specialists of this key area of HR create training programs, workshops, and other activities to help employees improve in their jobs and advance in their careers. L&D ensures that employees stay updated with new techniques and information, which helps the company function as a *learning organization* and stay competitive in the marketplace. By supporting employees' growth, L&D helps make the workplace more productive and engaging.

L&D activities occur at many stages of the employee lifecycle, including at the time of hire, throughout their career development, and at the time of separation. Figure 3.1 shows typical L&D activities that occur at each stage.

Following are a few key terms that should be understood before test day:

- *Learning and development*: The process of improving employees' skills, knowledge, and abilities to help them grow and succeed in their jobs.

- *Orientation*: An introduction to a company's policies, procedures, and culture for new employees on their first days.

- *Onboarding*: A process that helps new employees adjust to their job and company through training and support.

- *Acclimation*: The period in which an employee gets used to their new workplace environment and responsibilities.

FIGURE 3.1 Learning and development in the employee lifecycle

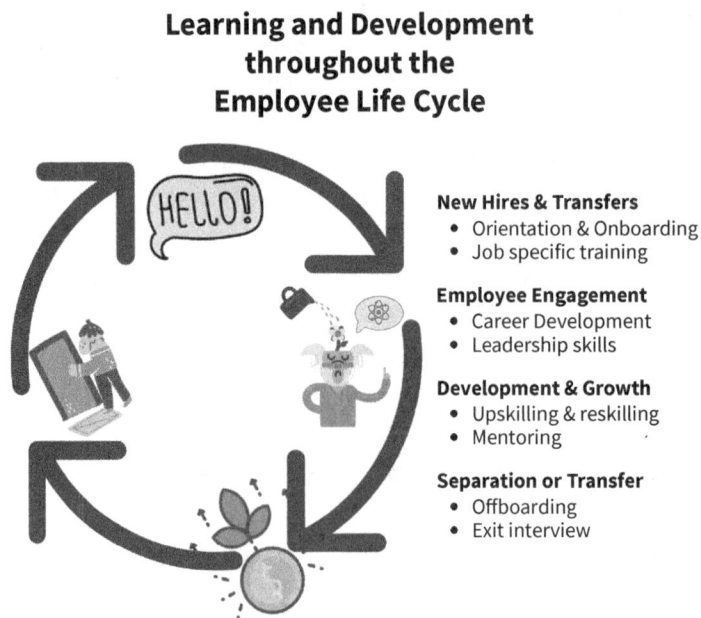

Learning and Development throughout the Employee Life Cycle

New Hires & Transfers
- Orientation & Onboarding
- Job specific training

Employee Engagement
- Career Development
- Leadership skills

Development & Growth
- Upskilling & reskilling
- Mentoring

Separation or Transfer
- Offboarding
- Exit interview

- *Instructional design*: The process of creating educational programs or materials that effectively teach new skills or knowledge.
- *Blended learning*: A method of education that combines online learning with traditional in-person instruction.
- *Change management*: Guiding employees through adjustments to new processes, systems, or organizational changes in the workplace.
- *Training evaluation*: The process of assessing how effective a training program is in teaching new skills or improving performance.
- *Learning management systems (LMS)*: Online platforms used to organize, deliver, and track employee training programs.

Developing New Hires

An important task of human resources is to support the hiring process. This involves understanding the *knowledge, skills, abilities, and other (KSAOs)* competencies employees need to be good at their jobs. The primary difference between a skill and an ability is that a skill is a learned competency that can be improved with practice, such as typing or coding, while an ability is a natural or innate talent, such as physical strength or hand-eye coordination. Knowledge speaks to a learned or general understanding of a concept or process. Other characteristics refer to personal traits, attitudes, and behaviors that contribute to job performance.

In some cases, it is necessary to support an existing employee who has moved into a new position within the company, called an *internal hire or transfer*. Hiring from within leverages the employee's familiarity with the company culture and operations while providing them with new growth opportunities.

A *realistic job preview (RJP)* is a tool used during the selection process when an employer gives a potential employee an honest look at what the job will be like, including both the good and the challenging aspects.

Once the individual starts their first day of work, HR facilitates the process of *employee orientation*, introducing new hires to their jobs, their department, and the company. Orientation is a short-term process, often lasting one or two days that reviews the company's basic policies, procedures, and culture. The orientation process includes completing paperwork, learning about company rules, completing safety training, and meeting immediate coworkers and supervisors.

Onboarding is a comprehensive and longer term process that can last several weeks to months. The term is often used interchangeably with orientation, but they are two distinct activities. Onboarding includes continuous training, mentoring, and support to help new employees fully integrate into their roles and the company, for example, through 30-, 60-, and 90-day onboarding success plans. These plans help equip new hires with the necessary skills, knowledge, and relationships to succeed in their positions and measure progress. Onboarding plans can also help objectively determine if the new hire is not a good fit for the role within the introductory period.

The main purpose of both orientation and onboarding is to make the new hire feel welcome and informed about the company and their role, set expectations, develop key relationships, and begin the process of acclimation.

Acclimation

Acclimation (also called socialization) refers to the process by which new hires or transferred employees adjust to their new roles and work environment. A successful acclimation process helps employees feel comfortable and confident in their new positions. Companies can facilitate acclimation through comprehensive onboarding programs, regular check-ins with managers, and providing resources and support for continuous learning. Proper acclimation can lead to higher job satisfaction, better performance, and reduced turnover. Many surveys have found that employees who do not experience a strong, positive, onboarding process feel far less attachment to the organization than employees who were welcomed with open arms and truly integrated into the organizational culture. This has a large impact on the retention of individuals as they do not share the same level of loyalty to their employer. Studies show that a new hire decides whether to stay or leave the company within the first six months of employment, so a positive, supportive early experience can make a difference.

Organizations should be careful that acclimation programs for new hires don't become barriers to diversity and inclusion. Encouraging new hires to engage with the company brand and identity is useful to build teams and help people feel included but should not be so rigid that it discourages individual preferences and identities. HR should ensure these programs value different perspectives, avoid stereotypes, and offer equal opportunities for everyone.

Establishing New Hire Expectations

Setting expectations involves clearly defining what is required from employees in their roles. This includes outlining job responsibilities, performance standards, and goals using tools such as job descriptions and onboarding plans. Effective communication of expectations helps employees understand what success looks like and aligns their efforts with the company's objectives. Managers play an important role in setting and reinforcing expectations through regular feedback, performance reviews, and goal-setting meetings. Some inexperienced managers will not conduct these initial meetings to communicate their intent, which can cause new hires to face challenges in trying to "guess" what the boss wants. They often have a difficult time knowing if what they are doing is the right thing or if they are meeting their performance objectives.

Building Relationships

Relationship building is an important HR competency because it helps create a positive work environment. Good relationships make it easier to resolve conflicts, support teamwork, and improve job satisfaction.

In geographically dispersed or remote teams, simply helping employees put a face to the names of people they are working with can help diffuse a sense of isolation that is a downside to virtual work. In some companies, these connections are built to support the entire employee lifecycle even when employees may desire to seek alternate employment and depart a company. HR that conducts *stay interviews* (conversations with employees about why they stay, what motivates them, and ways to increase job satisfaction) may alter the course of an employee's imminent departure to finding a better fit within the organization. Also, many employees become *boomerang* employees in that they leave an organization for what they perceive is a better opportunity only to return after a short-term realizing how good the job was. If HR maintains that close professional relationship, there is a stronger chance boomerang employees will return with a more positive outlook, especially if they are warmly received upon rejoining the company.

For HR teams, building relationships is an important competency to develop early on in their career. HR connects people with organizational results and thus need to be trusted and credible partners. Individuals new to HR can build relationships by doing the following:

- **Listening and communicating:** Actively listen to employees' concerns and communicate clearly. This shows respect and helps build trust.

- **Being approachable:** Make themselves available and approachable. Attend team meetings, introduce themselves, and engage in casual conversations.

- **Offering support:** Show genuine interest in helping employees with their needs and problems. Providing support and solutions makes HR a reliable and valued resource.

Employee Development

Employee development is the process of helping workers improve their skills and grow in their careers. It includes training, mentoring, and opportunities for learning new things. Companies invest in employee development to boost job performance, increase job satisfaction, and help employees reach their full potential. Employee development is especially desired by young professionals just starting to build their resumes. Effective employee development benefits both the company and its workers, leading to better productivity and higher morale. Techniques to develop employees involve mentoring, workshops, courses, and on-the-job training.

Other factors that must be considered are the unique development needs of multiple generations in the workplace. For example, as early career professionals, Generation Z wants more growth opportunities faster in the workplace. They measure their work status against their peers as to the level of progression they achieve and how quickly they rise in promotion. Contrast this to older workers nearing retirement, who may prefer to focus on upskilling to stay relevant. The older workers might value stability and the opportunities to mentor younger workers over rapid advancement.

Career Development

A *career path* is a series of jobs and experiences that lead employees toward their long-term career goals. HR supports employee career paths by providing resources and opportunities for growth, such as training programs, career counseling, and mentoring. HR helps employees identify their career goals, create development plans, and offer guidance on how to achieve these goals within the company. HR also works to ensure that there are clear advancement opportunities and pathways for employees to follow, aligning individual goals with organizational needs. A *dual-career path* is a career development strategy that allows employees to advance in their careers along two distinct tracks: a technical or professional path and a managerial path. This approach recognizes and rewards both technical expertise and managerial skills, providing opportunities for career growth without forcing employees into management roles if they prefer to continue specializing in their technical field. This alignment is important so that the investment a company makes in an individual benefits not only the person, but the company as well.

Coaching and mentoring are two related employee development techniques. *Coaching* typically involves a more experienced person helping an employee improve specific skills and achieve short-term goals through regular feedback and guidance. *Mentoring* focuses on long-term career development, providing broader advice, support, and opportunities for personal and professional growth. Both methods aim to enhance an employee's performance and help them reach their full potential. Mentoring has been found to be especially effective in building diverse teams, as underrepresented individuals have access to individuals who understand their unique needs. These mentors are often able to provide relevant and meaningful support and feedback. A great recent example of this concept has been in the US Army, which has formally trained some of its personnel as professional career coaches to help the organization better develop its mid-career leaders. Also, with the change in Department of Defense policy that enabled women to serve in direct combat occupations such as the infantry, opportunities for mentorship and the sharing of experiences greatly helped with the transition into these roles. While there are many ways to help employees achieve their desired career goals, it is ultimately the responsibility of employees to be their own best career managers. This is even to the point if they wish not to have any particular job path but choose job change on a frequent basis, choosing the work over the particular end-state in a job, career, or organization. Not every entry-level employee aspires to management, so development processes must cater to a variety of paths unique to every individual.

Appendix B includes case studies that highlight the evolving roles and challenges faced by women and LGBTQ individuals in the military. These case studies focus on key changes in policies and practices, such as the repeal of "Don't Ask, Don't Tell" and the integration of women into combat roles. The cases explore how these reforms have impacted military culture, inclusion efforts, and the career experiences of service members.

A *career development model* is a framework that guides individuals in planning and advancing their careers. It helps people identify their strengths, interests, and goals and provides structured steps for achieving professional growth and success. These models often include assessments, goal-setting strategies, and pathways for skill development. They can be used by individuals to make informed career choices and by organizations to support employee growth and align talent with business needs. Career development models aim to create clear, actionable plans for career progression and fulfillment.

The RIASEC career development model, developed by psychologist John Holland, categorizes careers and individuals based on six personality characteristics. Each type is associated with specific interests and skills, helping individuals find compatible career paths. The acronym is as follows:

- **Realistic:** Prefers hands-on, practical activities, often involving physical work and tools; enjoys solving concrete problems.

- **Investigative:** Enjoys working with ideas and thinking critically; prefers activities that involve research, analysis, and problem-solving.

- **Artistic:** Values creativity and self-expression; enjoys unstructured tasks and activities that allow for artistic creation and design.

- **Social:** Likes helping others and working in cooperative environments; prefers activities that involve teaching, counseling, or providing care.

- **Enterprising:** Enjoys leading and persuading others; prefers activities that involve management, sales, and starting new projects.

- **Conventional:** Prefers structured tasks and working with data; enjoys activities that involve organization, detail-oriented tasks, and following set procedures.

Let's look at the typical HR professional. In the RIASEC model, an HR professional mainly fits into the Social, Enterprising, and Conventional categories.

As a Social type, an HR professional enjoys working with people and helping them succeed. They spend a lot of time talking to employees, offering support and advice, and solving conflicts. They like being a trusted person that employees can turn to when they need help.

In the Enterprising category, an HR professional takes on leadership roles. They might lead a team of recruiters, plan new initiatives to improve the workplace, or organize company events. They enjoy making decisions, persuading others, and driving the company forward.

Under the Conventional category, an HR professional handles a lot of structured tasks. They keep detailed records of employee information, ensure the company follows labor laws, and manage the processes for hiring and training new staff. They are good at organizing and paying attention to details, making sure everything runs smoothly.

HR Career Paths

An HR professional can follow different career paths, and it's useful to start by understanding the difference between a job and a career.

A *job* is something a person does to earn money. It can be temporary or part time, like being an administrative assistant or doing data entry for HR records. These roles might not require a lot of special training or education.

A *career*, however, is a long-term professional journey within a specific field or domain, such as accounting or human resources. In HR, this often requires special training, education, or certification. People who choose a career in HR usually have an interest in helping others and improving workplaces, and they work to advance and achieve more in this field over time. One option of a career in HR is to be an HR generalist, handling tasks like hiring, training, and employee relations. Another path is recruitment and talent acquisition, where the focus is on finding and hiring the best candidates for jobs. Some HR professionals specialize in employee relations, helping resolve workplace issues and ensuring fair treatment. Others focus on training and development, creating programs to improve employees' skills. There is also compensation and benefits, which involves managing salaries and benefits packages. HR analytics specialists analyze data to help improve HR strategies. Those who become HR managers or directors lead HR departments and develop strategies for the company. Labor relations professionals work with labor unions and handle negotiations and disputes. Each path allows HR professionals to grow in their careers and help their organizations succeed.

HR professionals usually have a combination of education and work experience. Most HR managers and specialists hold a bachelor's degree in human resources, business, communications, or a related field. Some positions may require a master's degree.

HR managers generally need at least five years of related work experience and often start in roles such as HR specialists or labor relations specialists. HR specialists, on the other hand, usually enter the field with a bachelor's degree and do not require prior work experience, although internships or related job experiences can be beneficial.

Women make up a significant portion of HR professionals, particularly in leadership roles within HR departments. Employment in HR roles is expected to grow, with a 5% increase projected for HR managers and a 6% increase for HR specialists from 2022 to 2032.[1]

One challenge to HR teams is their lack of diversity. It's important that HR teams continue to seek diverse talent to ensure the employee populations being served have

---

[1] US Bureau of Labor Statistics. (2019). *Human resources managers: Occupational outlook handbook* (online). Available at: https://www.bls.gov/ooh/management/human-resources-managers.htm

adequate representation. This could be done, for example, by having HR representatives who speak the same language as a bilingual employee population, or that other protected groups are represented in HR to support employee programs that are inclusive. Another example of an underrepresented group in HR is veterans. While many companies seek to hire veterans, they often miss this opportunity to hire inside the HR department. This is because of the perception that military HR professionals don't have the same prerequisite skills needed for corporate HR. While some elements of this are true, many transitioning veterans often seek out credentials such as the aPHR, PHR, or even SPHR to demonstrate their competency and knowledge base.

Training Management

The aPHR exam summary of the functional area of L&D places heavy emphasis on the role of training. This is because training is at the heart of how an organization competes in its relevant market. For example, well-trained employees can adapt to new technologies, maintain high levels of productivity, and ensure the company remains compliant with industry standards and regulations. Effective training programs help employees develop the necessary skills and knowledge to perform their jobs efficiently, which in turn boosts the overall performance and competitiveness of the organization.

An HR professional new to L&D should have good communication skills, be organized, and understand how adults learn. They should also be good at problem-solving, able to use technology for training, and have a positive attitude to motivate and support employees in their growth and development. And because the aPHR is a knowledge-based exam, they should be familiar with several key principles of learning.

Adult Learning Principles

Adult learning principles focus on how adults learn best. Adults prefer learning that is practical and relevant to their life and work. They learn better when they can use their experiences, have control over their learning, and understand why what they are learning is important. The most common model of *andragogy* (adult learning principles) is Malcolm Knowles' model. It outlines that adults learn best when they understand why they need to learn something, have a say in their learning process, and can use their experiences. The learning should be practical and relevant to their personal or work life. Knowles' model includes the following:

- *Self-efficacy*: Adults want to take control of their own learning and feel confident in their abilities.
- *Experience*: Adults use their past experiences as a resource for learning.
- *Readiness to learn*: Adults are ready to learn things that help them in real-life situations.

- *Orientation to learning*: Adults prefer learning that is practical and helps them solve problems.
- *Motivation:* Adults are motivated to learn by internal factors, like personal growth and satisfaction.

Learning and Development throughout the Employee Lifecycle

There are several opportunities for employees to gain knowledge and develop skills throughout the employee life cycle. These are covered next.

Attraction

Description: The process of attracting potential candidates to the organization. This involves employer branding, recruitment marketing, and showcasing the company's culture and values.

Key Activities: Job postings, career fairs, social media campaigns, and company websites.

Recruitment

Description: The process of identifying, interviewing, and selecting candidates to fill open positions within the organization.

Key Activities: Screening resumes, conducting interviews, assessments, and extending job offers.

Onboarding

Description: The process of integrating new employees into the organization and equipping them with the tools, resources, and knowledge they need to become productive members of the team.

Key Activities: Orientation programs, training sessions, paperwork completion, and introduction to team members and company culture.

Development

Description: The continuous process of improving employees' skills, knowledge, and abilities to enhance their performance and support career growth.

Key Activities: Training programs, professional development courses, mentoring, and career development planning.

Retention

Description: The efforts made by the organization to keep talented employees engaged and motivated to reduce turnover.

Key Activities: Employee recognition programs, competitive compensation and benefits, work-life balance initiatives, and fostering a positive work environment.

Performance

Description: The ongoing process of evaluating and managing employees' work performance to ensure alignment with organizational goals.

Key Activities: Performance reviews, feedback sessions, goal setting, and performance improvement plans.

Offboarding

Description: The process of managing the departure of employees from the organization, whether through resignation, retirement, or dismissal.

FIGURE 3.2   Career stage key activities

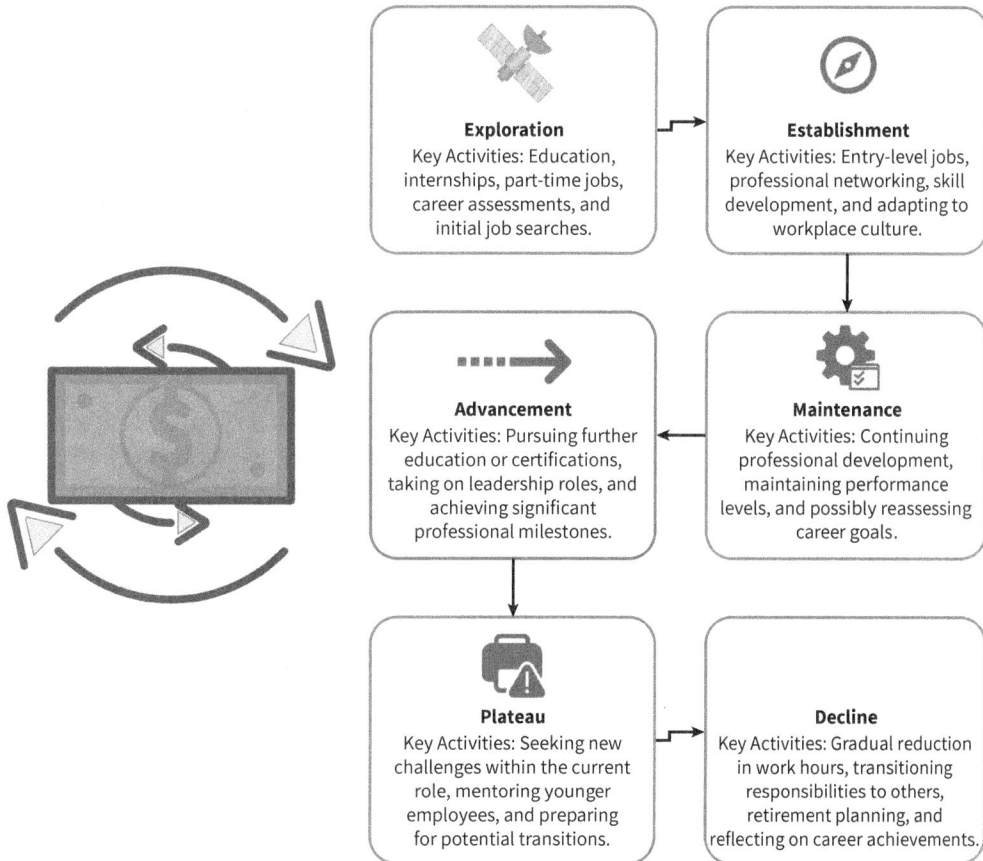

Exploration
Key Activities: Education, internships, part-time jobs, career assessments, and initial job searches.

Establishment
Key Activities: Entry-level jobs, professional networking, skill development, and adapting to workplace culture.

Advancement
Key Activities: Pursuing further education or certifications, taking on leadership roles, and achieving significant professional milestones.

Maintenance
Key Activities: Continuing professional development, maintaining performance levels, and possibly reassessing career goals.

Plateau
Key Activities: Seeking new challenges within the current role, mentoring younger employees, and preparing for potential transitions.

Decline
Key Activities: Gradual reduction in work hours, transitioning responsibilities to others, retirement planning, and reflecting on career achievements.

Key Activities: Exit interviews, knowledge transfer, final paperwork, and ensuring a smooth transition for both the departing employee and the organization.

Career development and coaching helps an employee follow a solid career path. An organization can track employee development through a performance appraisal process that has been established. Figure 3.2 shows key activities at each career stage.

Training Tools

Using technology in training has become more popular and beneficial. Technology makes learning more engaging and accessible for everyone. For example, asynchronous online learning allows employees to learn at their own pace and from any location. This flexibility helps people balance their training with other responsibilities. Hybrid learning, such as a class taught both in-person and via remote video conferencing where students can interact remotely with peers and the instructor in real time, allows for individuals to still get the classroom experience without the physical limitations of having to be at the location. This has grown in popularity following the recent pandemic as well.

Technology also enables better communication and collaboration. Discussion boards on a company intranet, instant messaging, and video conferencing allow trainees to interact with their instructors and peers, even if they are not in the same place. This interaction can lead to a deeper understanding of the material and help build a supportive learning community. *Gamification* in training at work makes learning more engaging and enjoyable by incorporating game-like elements, such as points, badges, and leaderboards, encouraging healthy competition and motivating employees through several small wins.

Case Study

Many companies are investing in the use of technology to enhance their training offerings. General Electric (GE) has integrated smart glasses to help workers assemble wind turbines, providing easy access to directions and training materials in their line of sight. This integration offers data layers and allows workers to view videos, receive voice commands, and interact with experts for real-time assistance, leading to a significant 34% improvement in productivity during initial use.

Another example is the University of Toledo, where the football team uses GoPro cameras to improve the performance of its quarterbacks. The GoPros provide footage that coaches can review to enhance players' techniques and strategies.

The use of current and emerging technologies helps team members and employees hone their skills to improve performance.

Training Formats

Training formats are important because they provide different ways to deliver information, making learning effective and suitable for everyone. Formats like virtual and self-paced learning offer flexibility, allowing employees to access materials when it fits their schedules. This is especially helpful for balancing work and personal life.

Accessibility is another key benefit; virtual and blended learning reach employees in various locations, ensuring equal training opportunities. Diverse formats keep employees engaged; interactive virtual sessions and hands-on on-the-job training make learning interesting and practical. Instructor-led and on-the-job training provide immediate feedback, helping employees apply new skills quickly. Self-paced and blended learning cater to individual speeds and preferences, offering a personalized experience. By using different training formats, organizations can effectively meet various learning needs, improve skills, and enhance job performance.

Each format has its own style and method of instruction:

- *Blended* training combines both online and in-person learning. It allows employees to benefit from the flexibility of online courses while still having face-to-face interactions with instructors or peers.

- *Virtual* training is done entirely online through video calls, webinars, or virtual classrooms. It allows employees to participate from any location, making it convenient and accessible.

- *Self-paced* training allows employees to complete courses at their own speed. They can access materials whenever they have time, making it flexible and personalized to their schedules.

- *Instructor-led* training is conducted in person by a trainer or instructor. This format is traditional and allows for direct interaction, questions, and immediate feedback.

- *On-the-job* training happens while employees are working. They learn by doing their tasks under the guidance of a supervisor or experienced coworker, which helps them gain practical skills directly related to their job.

Most adult learning occurs on the job. According to the 70–20–10 model, which is widely used in leadership development, about 70% of learning happens through challenging work experiences and assignments, 20% through developmental relationships, and only 10% through formal coursework and training. This model highlights the importance of real-world job experiences in developing skills and knowledge.

Delivery Techniques

Delivery techniques are methods used to present training and development programs to employees.

In-house training is conducted by the organization's own trainers. It is tailored to the company's specific needs and can be more cost-effective.

External training services are provided by outside organizations or consultants. They bring specialized expertise and new perspectives to the training program. In some cases, training can be purchased by an outside provider off the shelf or customized to suit the specific training needs.

HR professionals should be familiar with several delivery techniques:

- **Role play:** involves acting out scenarios to practice skills and problem-solving in a realistic setting. It helps learners understand different perspectives and improve their communication and decision-making abilities.

- **Facilitation:** when a trainer guides a group discussion or activity, helping participants learn from each other. It focuses on encouraging interaction and collaboration.

- **Simulation:** uses models or virtual environments to mimic real-world situations. It allows learners to practice skills and make decisions in a safe, controlled setting.

- **In-box:** involves giving learners a set of tasks and documents to prioritize and respond to, simulating a typical workday. It helps develop time management and decision-making skills.

- **Vestibule:** takes place in a separate area that mimics the actual work environment. It allows employees to practice their tasks using real equipment without impacting regular operations.

Legal Compliance

In learning and development, legal compliance means following all laws and rules that apply to training programs. Companies need to make sure their training methods and materials meet legal standards to avoid problems like lawsuits or fines. Many labor laws, such as the Occupational Safety and Health Act, the Fair Labor Standards Act, and the Equal Employment Opportunity laws, require that employees receive notification or training at the time of hire to ensure they are informed about their rights and responsibilities under these regulations. The following is a short review of how three acts affect L&D.

Americans with Disabilities Act, Reasonable Accommodation   The ADA requires employers to provide reasonable help for employees with disabilities so they can participate in training and development. This might involve changing training materials, using assistive technology, or making sure training locations are accessible. The aim is to ensure that employees with disabilities have the same training opportunities as others.

Rehabilitation Act (Color, Visual, Audio, Contrast, Images)   The Rehabilitation Act requires that federal agencies and contractors make their technology accessible to people with disabilities. This includes making sure training materials have good color contrast, captions for images, and audio descriptions for visual content. These adjustments help people with visual, hearing, and other disabilities fully engage with the training materials.

Copyright Act of 1976, Fair Use Doctrine The Copyright Act of 1976 and the Fair Use Doctrine allow for the limited use of copyrighted material without permission for specific purposes like teaching and research. In learning and development, this means that companies can use small parts of copyrighted materials in their training programs if they meet fair use guidelines. This includes considering how the material is used, the type of work, the amount used, and the impact on the market value of the original work. Following these rules helps companies use educational content legally.

Instructional Design

Instructional design is about creating effective training programs and materials. The goal is to make learning easier and more engaging, and directly relate to improved employee behaviors. Instructional designers (including HR professionals) plan and organize content, using methods that help people understand and remember information better. They use various tools and techniques to create training objectives, content, activities, and assessments that match the learning needs and goals of the company employees. These needs are identified by conducting a *skills gap analysis* or *training needs assessment*. These assessments are used to identify the difference between the skills employees currently have and the skills they need to effectively perform their jobs.

Many HR programs benefit from the systematic approach to instructional design. For example, HR might create onboarding programs for new hires, ensuring they understand company policies and procedures. They also design ongoing training for current employees to help them improve their skills and stay updated with the skills necessary to perform, including honing existing skills and developing new ones to help the company remain competitive. Three of the most common instructional design methods include the following:

- **ADDIE Model:** This is a five-phase process that stands for Analysis, Design, Development, Implementation, and Evaluation. It's a systematic approach used to create effective training programs and learning experiences by breaking down the process into manageable steps.

- **Successive Approximation Model (SAM):** This method emphasizes iterative (a process that is repeated and refined multiple times) design and development, allowing for continuous feedback and improvements.

- **Agile Learning Design (AGILE):** This approach applies agile project management principles to instructional design, promoting flexibility and collaboration. It involves iterative cycles, called sprints, consisting of planning, designing, developing, and reviewing, with a strong focus on learner feedback and quick adjustments to meet changing needs and objectives.

Learning Management Systems

A *learning management system (LMS)* is a software platform that delivers, manages, and tracks training programs at work. It provides a centralized place for accessing learning materials, conducting assessments, and maintaining records of learners' progress.

An LMS makes it easy for employees to access training materials online. With an LMS, all the lessons, videos, and resources are available in one place. This means that employees can learn anytime and anywhere, as long as they have an internet connection. It's important to note that training is considered compensable time under the Fair Labor Standards Act, so employees need to be paid for any mandatory training.

LMS platforms also help trainers create and give tests or quizzes to check what students have learned. These assessments can be multiple-choice questions, short answers, or even assignments that need to be submitted.

Keeping track of everyone's progress and results is another important feature of LMS. These systems record all the training activities, test scores, and completed assignments in one place. This makes it easy for trainers and administrators to see who has finished their training and who might need extra help.

Choosing an LMS involves a few important steps for HR professionals responsible for supporting the selection and integration. First, they should identify the specific needs of the organization, such as delivering lessons, tracking progress, or conducting tests. Next, they need to compare different LMS options by examining their features, ease of use, and cost. It's also beneficial for them to read reviews or seek recommendations from other organizations. Additionally, it is possible to arrange free trials or demos to evaluate which LMS platform best meets the company's requirements.

Integrating the LMS with other organizational software is important because it makes managing everything easier and more efficient. When an LMS works well with other tools, like an HRIS or communication platforms (think Slack or Teams), it helps keep all the data in one place.

Measuring Training Effectiveness

Measuring training effectiveness is important because it shows how well the training is working and if it's making a difference. It helps identify areas where training can be improved, ensures that learners are gaining the necessary skills, and proves that the investment in training is worthwhile.

One of the most common models of measuring training effectiveness comes from Donald Kirkpatrick. This model has four levels to evaluate training, with each level being more valuable than the last:

- **Level 1, Reaction:** This level measures how learners feel about the training. Did they like it? Was it useful and engaging?

- **Level 2, Learning:** This level checks what learners have actually learned. Did they gain the knowledge and skills that were intended?

- **Level 3, Behavior:** This level looks at whether learners are using what they learned in their jobs. Has their behavior changed as a result of the training?

- **Level 4, Results:** This level evaluates the overall impact of the training on the organization. Did it lead to better performance, increased productivity, or other positive outcomes?

Tracking Employee Development

Tracking employee development involves monitoring and recording the progress of employees' skills, knowledge, and career growth over time. This process helps HR identify training needs, plan professional development programs, and ensure that employees are advancing toward their career goals. By tracking development, HR can support continuous learning and align employee growth with organizational objectives. The LMS may have features that can customize training plans that have predetermined dates when training should be completed and can send reminders to both the employee and manager when they are on track or falling behind. Employees with demonstrated high potential can also be identified early and fast-tracked to have more exposure to learning in management settings if the intent is to create pathways for management opportunities from within the organization's available talent pool. Promoting talent from within is often preferable to hiring from outside the organization, as internal candidates are already acclimated to the organizational philosophy and values.

Performance Appraisals

Performance appraisals are systematic evaluations of employees' job performance and contributions to the organization. These appraisals provide valuable feedback to employees, identify areas for improvement, and set professional development goals for the next rating period. Several methods can be used; following is a review of the three most common:

360-degree Feedback   Also called multi-rating, this method involves collecting feedback from multiple sources, including peers, subordinates, supervisors, and sometimes even clients. This approach provides a well-rounded view of an employee's performance and behaviors from the perspective.

Behaviorally Anchored Rating Scales (BARS)   BARS combines elements of qualitative and quantitative data by rating employee performance against specific behavioral examples. These examples are linked to numerical ratings, providing clear standards for evaluating performance on specific tasks or competencies.

Management by Objectives (MBO)   MBO involves setting specific, measurable goals that an employee aims to achieve within a defined period. Performance is appraised based on the extent to which these goals are met, fostering alignment between individual objectives and organizational goals.

Rater bias is when someone's personal feelings or unrelated factors unfairly influence their judgment of an employee's performance. *Unconscious bias* is when people unknowingly have attitudes or stereotypes that affect their understanding, actions, and decisions about others. The following rater errors can occur when making any employment related decision, such as hiring, or when preparing performance feedback:

- *Halo Effect:* This bias occurs when an appraiser's overall impression of an employee, often based on one outstanding characteristic or achievement, unduly influences the appraiser's assessment of other unrelated areas of performance. This can lead to overly positive ratings.

- *Recency Bias:* This bias happens when appraisals are disproportionately influenced by the employee's most recent behavior or performance rather than considering their performance over the entire appraisal period. This can result in ratings that do not accurately reflect the employee's consistent performance.

- *Leniency, Severity, Central Tendency Bias:* Leniency bias involves appraisers giving consistently high ratings to all employees, while severity bias involves giving consistently low ratings. Central tendency occurs when the rater gives mid-zone scores to all applicants or employees, usually to avoid conflict or because they do not have enough awareness of the team members' performance. All three types of bias prevent a fair and accurate assessment of an employee's actual performance.

Rater bias can be avoided by using clear and consistent criteria to evaluate everyone the same way. It's also helpful to get multiple opinions and use anonymous feedback to reduce personal biases. HR supports the performance appraisal process by training raters on how to give unbiased performance feedback.

Learning and Development Reporting

Reporting in HR involves generating detailed and accurate reports on various HR metrics such as employee demographics, turnover rates, training effectiveness, and payroll data. These reports provide insights that help HR professionals and management make informed decisions about training, identify trends, and measure the impact of HR programs. This allows the corporate leadership to gain an understanding of the return of investment in the training that is developed. Effective reporting is essential for strategic planning from a resources perspective and maintaining compliance with legal and regulatory requirements. Here are a few examples of learning and development reporting:

- **Training completion rates:** This metric shows the percentage of employees who have finished their assigned training programs.

- **Employee satisfaction scores:** After training, employees can give feedback on how useful and engaging they found the sessions.
- **Skill improvement scores:** These scores measure how much employees' skills have improved after completing the training.
- **Time spent on training:** This tracks how many hours employees spend in training programs.
- **Assessment results:** These are the scores or grades employees get on tests or quizzes taken after training to measure what they've learned.

Change Management Process

Whenever an organization embarks on a new initiative, such as offering new products, obtaining a new customer, or responding to environmental conditions such as the economy or a global pandemic, change management will be necessary. This is because, as a rule, most employees tend to resist change, preferring the security of the status quo over the uncertainty of the unknown or new.

Change management is the process of planning, implementing, and monitoring changes in an organization to minimize disruptions and ensure smooth transitions. These processes provide a structured approach to preparing, supporting, and helping employees adapt to changes, reducing resistance, and increasing acceptance. By effectively managing change, organizations can achieve desired results such as successfully integrating new programs or technologies, changing processes, or establishing new employee expectations.

HR supports change management efforts by helping to assess a group's readiness for change. HR helps do this by evaluating their skills, attitudes, and adaptability through surveys, interviews, and other planned observations or intake. From here, HR can ensure the changes are properly communicated to make sure employees understand the new desired behaviors. HR also listens for and addresses employees, concerns about any changes, and advocates for the proper resources (people, training, tools, equipment, money) to embed the changes as the new normal.

Monitoring change involves regularly checking the progress of the change initiatives to address any issues promptly and ensure the desired outcomes are achieved.

Summary

L&D is a critical component of the HR function that touches every employee in the workplace. It reaches across the entire lifecycle of an employee from onboarding to separation and is essential to the proper development of an employee to be a productive member of the team. Starting with new hires, onboarding and acclimation sets the expectation of the individual employee and assists with building relationships that enable teams to grow, learn, and accomplish the company's mission.

As employees mature in the company, their career development can follow a variety of paths depending on the knowledge, skills, abilities, and other attributes they possess and what additional training they receive along the way. HR career paths are also a part of this and demonstrates that our functional area has many roles that are specializations with the HR career field, or an individual may choose to be a generalist that touches elements of many roles. This is also impacted by the size and nature of the organization.

To manage the training for all employees, HR learning and development specialists must be cognizant of adult learning principles and be versed in the variety of training tools, formats, and delivery techniques to effectively deliver training in a manner that the employee retains and uses what has been learned. Beyond basic instructional design, instructional developers must be aware of requirements of the laws and regulations that govern training accessibility to ensure legal compliance.

Training that is developed and delivered can be managed through an LMS. The LMS effectively tracks the employee's progress of mandatory and voluntary training that enhances their skills or abilities to further their capabilities to perform their job duties. This system also allows for reporting and analysis to determine the effectiveness of the training at multiple levels from how individuals received the training to the degree to which individuals modify their behaviors to better align with the job requirements.

Finally, companies that implement a new process, program, or policy must go through a change management process that plans, implements, and monitors the change to ensure a smooth transition and minimizes disruptions to the workflow in an organization. Overcoming obstacles and objections to change reduces stress to the employees while helping management successfully accomplish its goals and objectives that were the driving force behind the change.

Exam Essentials

Understand the concepts and components of employee development. HR professionals should understand the learning and development strategies at each stage of the employee lifecycle. This includes assessing the knowledge, skills, abilities, and other attributes of new hires as part of the onboarding and orientation process to set expectations and build a strong working relationship.

Understand the concept of instructional design and its use in developing an organizational learning strategy. The principles associated with training management include elements of design, such as the adult learning model and other training tools. Delivery techniques like facilitation conducted in various formats such as in-person or online learning help to solidify understanding of the training material presented. Organizations can measure the effectiveness of training at multiple levels, starting from initial impressions of the training to a resultant change or modification of behaviors that meet the needs of the company.

Understand the function of an LMS in employee learning and development.   The LMS allows for an integrated delivery and tracking of learning content provided by the organization. As employees complete content, reporting to managers and supervisors can be handled by the system in an automated manner. An LMS should easily integrate with other HR systems to prevent additional workload to the HR team, but also to assist the overall administration of the organizational learning and development strategy.

Review Questions

You can find the answers in Appendix A.

1. Which of the following is an example of knowledge in the workplace?

   A. Understanding how to operate specific software

   B. Typing at a speed of 60 words per minute

   C. Leading a team meeting

   D. Handling customer complaints

2. Resolving conflict between team members is the best example of which of the following?

   A. Knowledge

   B. Skills

   C. Abilities

   D. Other competencies

3. Which of the following is an example of abilities in the workplace? Choose all that apply.

   A. Memorizing company procedures

   B. Having 20/20 vision

   C. Lifting heavy objects

   D. Writing detailed reports

4. In which of the following circumstances would it be best to promote from within instead of hiring externally?

   A. When the company needs to fill a position quickly and efficiently

   B. When the position requires cutting-edge expertise not available in the current workforce

   C. When the company is undergoing significant changes and needs new approaches

   D. When the company is looking to diversify its talent pool

5. As part of the hiring process, your employer pays a potential candidate to job shadow a senior employee for a day. This is the best example of which of the following hiring tools?

   A. Structured interview

   B. Job bidding

   C. Paid internship

   D. Realistic job preview

6. Which of the following are examples of employee orientation activities? (Choose all that apply.)

   A. Introducing the new employee to their team

   B. Providing an overview of the company's mission, values, and culture

    C. Explaining company policies and procedures

    D. Assigning the new employee their first project

7. During onboarding, a new employee was not given proper training materials and the employee's workstation was not set up, causing confusion and frustration. What should the HR coordinator do next?

    A. Buy the new hire the proper equipment

    B. Apologize to the new hire and offer support

    C. Elevate the situation to the HR Manager

    D. Schedule additional training sessions

8. Which of the following is a challenge to employee acclimation programs?

    A. Struggles with clear communication of job expectations

    B. Lack of support from colleagues

    C. Focus on conformity rather than inclusivity

    D. Access to necessary resources

9. In which of the following ways can managers help set expectations for new hires? (Choose all that apply.)

    A. Providing a detailed job description and performance standards

    B. Offering regular feedback and check-ins

    C. Allowing peers to mentor them within their first 30 days

    D. Setting open goals to encourage creativity

10. What is the primary difference between coaching and mentoring?

    A. Coaching focuses on long-term career guidance, while mentoring focuses on short-term skill development.

    B. Coaching is typically done by a supervisor, while mentoring is usually done by a more experienced colleague.

    C. Coaching is informal and unstructured, while mentoring follows a specific plan.

    D. Coaching involves group sessions, while mentoring is always one on one.

11. Millie is interested in learning new skills to promote within the company. She meets with her manager to discuss her goals and the steps she needs to take to reach a higher position. What method is Millie's manager using to help her with her professional development?

    A. Performance feedback

    B. Coaching

    C. Mentoring

    D. Career pathing

12. How do HR teams help employees develop new skills?

    A. By conducting annual performance reviews

    B. By providing access to training courses and workshops

    C. By facilitating team meetings

    D. By offering flexible work hours

13. Which of the following is one of the six personality types in the RIASEC model?

    A. Analytical

    B. Realistic

    C. Charismatic

    D. Independent

14. Which of the following career paths would be most suitable for a person with SEC as their RIASEC code?

    A. Human resource professional

    B. Accountant

    C. Electrician

    D. Retail associate

15. In which of the following ways can HR utilize a career framework? (Choose all that apply.)

    A. To help determine employee pay increases based on performance

    B. To design employee development plans

    C. Helping individuals identify career paths

    D. To identify reskilling or upskilling needs

16. A job is characterized by _____, whereas a career is characterized by _____.

    A. short-term tasks; long-term growth and development

    B. personal fulfillment; financial rewards

    C. work-life balance; personal sacrifices

    D. individual achievements; teamwork

17. Why is it important for HR professionals to continually update their knowledge and skills?

    A. To maintain their current job position

    B. To reduce the workload of other employees

    C. To keep up with changing laws and best practices

    D. To ensure employee satisfaction

18. Which of the following is a principle of Knowles' model of adult learning?

   A. Adults learn best through rote memorization.

   B. Adults are motivated to learn by external rewards.

   C. Adults need to know why they need to learn something before engaging in the learning process.

   D. Adults prefer learning in a competitive environment.

19. According to Knowles' model of adult learning, how should learning activities be designed for adults?

   A. Learning activities should be lecture-based and passive.

   B. Learning activities should rely heavily on textbooks and exams.

   C. Learning activities should be unstructured and spontaneous.

   D. Learning activities should focus on real-life experiences and problem-solving.

20. What is the primary difference between asynchronous and synchronous learning?

   A. Asynchronous learning happens in real-time, while synchronous learning happens at the learner's own pace

   B. Asynchronous learning involves live interaction with instructors, while synchronous learning involves prerecorded materials

   C. Asynchronous learning happens at the learner's own pace, while synchronous learning happens in real-time with live interaction

   D. Asynchronous learning requires physical attendance, while synchronous learning can be done online

Chapter

4

aPHR Compensation and Benefits

aPHR EXAM OBJECTIVES COVERED IN THIS CHAPTER REQUIRE KNOWLEDGE RELATED TO FUNCTIONAL AREA 03, COMPENSATION AND BENEFITS:

✓ **03-01** The elements involved in developing and administering an organization's compensation strategy; such as pay structures, pay adjustments and incentive programs (for example, external service providers, market analysis, job evaluation/classifications, merit increases, pay scales/grades, cost of living adjustments, and service awards)

✓ **03-02** Health benefit and insurance programs including, eligibility requirements, enrollment periods and various designs (for example, high deductible plans, health savings accounts, flexible spending accounts, preferred provider organizations, and short- or long-term disability)

✓ **03-03** Supplemental wellness and fringe benefits programs commonly offered by organizations (for example, employee assistance program [EAPs], gym membership, online therapy, housing or relocation assistance, and travel/transportation stipends)

✓ **03-04** Employee eligibility for, and enrollment in retirement plans, and rules regarding contributions and withdrawals (for example, 401(k), 457(b), catch- up contributions, and hardship withdrawals)

✓ **03-05** Components of wage statements and payroll processing (for example, taxation, deductions, differentials, garnishments, leave reporting and final pay, and total reward statements)

Functional area 03, Compensation and Benefits accounts for 17% of the aPHR exam. HRCI summarizes this exam content as "understanding elements of the total rewards package including compensation, benefits programs, retirement planning, and how they support organizational competitiveness."

HR Done Wrong

According to the Economic Policy Institute,[1] "between 2017 and 2020, more than $3 billion in stolen wages was recovered on behalf of workers by the US Department of Labor… through class and collective action litigation." Wage theft is when employees do not receive wages to which they are entitled by law for their labor produced. Often it occurs in the lowest paid industries, like with service workers or similar minimum wage occupations. This also creates a disparate impact among some minority groups that tend to disproportionly work in these occupations.

Wage theft includes paying workers less than the minimum wage, failing to pay overtime, having employees work before or after shifts unpaid, illegal deductions, and misclassifying employees as independent contractors. Due to minimum wage violations, companies stole, on average, more than $3,000 per employee over the course of a year by failing to pay all the wages entitled. A lack of oversight and investigative resources compounds the problem in identifying and correcting violations.

HR professionals must understand the rules when it comes to paying wages and have the appropriate payroll recordkeeping systems in place that can maintain wage and hour information accurately. Properly classifying workers as employees and those who are exempt versus nonexempt from overtime pay eligibility are also critical tasks.

Compensation and Benefits Defined

Compensation and benefits refer to the total package of rewards that employees receive in exchange for their work. *Compensation* typically includes direct payments like wages or salaries, while *benefits* cover nonmonetary perks such as health insurance, retirement plans, and paid time off. Together, they form an essential part of what motivates employees and supports their well-being in the workplace. Key terms to be familiar with include the following:

---

[1] Mangundayao, I., McNicholas, C., Poydock, M., and Sait, A. (2021). More than $3 billion in stolen wages recovered for workers between 2017 and 2020. Economic Policy Institute. Available at: www.epi.org/publication/wage-theft-2021/

- *Incentives*: Incentives are rewards or bonuses given to employees to motivate higher performance or achieve specific goals.
- *Pay adjustments*: Pay adjustments involve changes in an employee's salary or hourly rate, often due to promotions, inflation, or performance reviews.
- *Wage surveys*: Wage surveys collect data on pay rates across different companies or industries to ensure competitive and fair compensation.
- *Wage statements*: Wage statements are documents provided to employees that outline their earnings, deductions, and net pay for a specific period.
- *Deductions*: Deductions are amounts taken out of an employee's paycheck for taxes, benefits, or other obligations like retirement contributions.
- *Garnishments*: Garnishments are legal orders that require a portion of an employee's wages to be withheld by their employer to pay off debts, such as unpaid taxes, child support, or loans.
- *Employee assistance programs (EAPs)*: EAPs are workplace programs that offer confidential support services, such as counseling, to help employees with personal or professional issues.
- *Eligibility*: Eligibility refers to the conditions an employee must meet to qualify for certain benefits, such as length of service or job status.
- *Fringe benefits*: Fringe benefits are noncash perks provided by employers, such as company cars, gym memberships, or tuition assistance.

Elements of Total Rewards

Total rewards programs in the workplace can help attract, motivate, and keep employees by offering fair pay, benefits, and recognition. They can improve job satisfaction, create a positive work environment, and support a healthy work-life balance. However, there are things total rewards alone cannot do, such as replace internal motivation and drive. Nor can they fix companywide problems, or performance that is due to lack of proper training. Total rewards also cannot guarantee that workers will stay at their organizations, but a properly structured compensation program can definitely aid in retention.

A single rewards plan might not meet everyone's needs, so it's important to regularly review and adjust the program to fit the workforce better. For this reason, total rewards is a holistic (whole system) approach to employee compensation and benefits that often include the following elements:

Competitiveness   In a competitive job market, companies work hard to offer total rewards packages that make them stand out from other employers. They compare their salaries, benefits, and perks with other companies to ensure they stay attractive to current and future employees. A strong total rewards plan helps companies differentiate (stand out in their labor market) and keeps their employer brand strong.

Compensation   Compensation refers to the direct financial rewards given to employees for their work. This includes monetary rewards and incentives such as the following:

- *Base salary*: The fixed amount paid regularly for the job. For example, hourly workers might be paid $15.00 for every hour worked in a day. If they miss work, they are not paid, unless it is covered under a benefit such as sick time or vacation time.

- *Bonuses*: Performance-based rewards given periodically for achieving specific goals. For instance, a customer service representative might receive a $500 bonus for achieving a customer satisfaction score above 90% over a quarter.

- *Incentives*: Other financial rewards tied to performance or project completion. One example of an incentive is profit sharing, where employees receive a portion of the company's profits based on its financial performance. For instance, if a company decides to share 5% of its annual profits with its employees, and it makes a profit of $2 million, the total amount shared among the staff would be $100,000. This amount is then distributed to employees based on criteria such as their role, tenure, or individual performance, encouraging them to contribute to the company's success.

- *Commissions*: Offered in sales roles as a percentage of revenue or profits generated. An example of commission pay is car sales where salespeople earn a percentage of the sale price for each car they sell. For instance, if a salesperson receives a 5% commission and sells a car for $20,000, they would earn $1,000 from that sale.

- *Piecework*: A payment method where workers are paid a fixed rate for each unit they produce or task they complete rather than receiving a regular salary or hourly wage. An example of piecework is a clothing factory where seamstresses are paid for each shirt they successfully sew. If a seamstress is paid $2 per shirt and she sews 50 shirts in a day, she earns $100 for that day's work. Employees must still be paid minimum wage, so if their piecework pay does not equate to the federal or state minimum wage, the employer must pay the difference.

Benefits Programs   Benefits programs provide indirect financial support and support employee well-being. Benefits programs often include the following:

- **Health insurance:** medical, dental, and vision coverage.

- **Life insurance:** financial protection for employees' families.

- **Disability insurance:** short-term and long-term income protection.

- **Paid time off (PTO):** vacation, sick leave, and personal days.

- **Work-life balance perks:** examples include flexible work arrangements, wellness programs, and childcare assistance.

Catch-up contributions are extra payments that people aged 50 or older can make to their retirement accounts to save more money as they approach retirement. These contributions allow older workers to increase their retirement savings beyond the usual annual limits.

Hardship withdrawals are special withdrawals from retirement accounts that employees can take out early, without penalty, in case of a financial emergency, such as medical expenses or avoiding eviction. However, these withdrawals often come with strict conditions and must be repaid or result in taxes.

With all of the options and regulations around retirement savings, it is helpful for employers to offer *retirement education*. This includes identifying resources and counseling to help employees make informed investment decisions.

Compensation Strategy

Having a compensation strategy is important for a company because it ensures that the salaries and benefits offered are fair, competitive, and align with the company's goals and labor budget. Labor costs are often the highest point on a company's financial statements, so a strategy helps attract and retain talented employees without overpaying for talent. A compensation strategy also helps to keep payments consistent across the company, preventing confusion, dissatisfaction, and perceptions of injustice among employees. A well-planned compensation strategy supports the company's financial health and strategic objectives.

Total rewards statements (also called hidden paychecks) give employees a clear view of their full compensation package, including salary, benefits, bonuses, and other perks. They help employees understand the total value of what they receive from their employer, boosting satisfaction and retention. These statements are a key part of effective compensation strategies. Figure 4.1 shows an example of a hidden paycheck.

Classifying Workers

As noted earlier, compensation refers to the monetary rewards employees receive in exchange for their work. The US Department of Labor (DOL) requires clear classification of workers to ensure proper compensation and legal protections. This classification helps determine which workers are entitled to overtime pay and minimum wage under the Fair Labor Standards Act (FLSA).

Hourly employees are those who are paid a flat rate calculated on an hourly basis; they are only paid for hours worked and must be paid time and a half their regular rate of pay for any hours worked over 40 in a workweek. The Federal minimum wage an employee must be paid under the FLSA in 2024 is $7.25 per hour; however, many states have minimum wage requirements that go beyond the federal minimum.

Salaried workers are those who are also paid a flat rate, but it is calculated on a weekly or biweekly basis; the minimum salary amount must be at least $684 per week. Salaried workers are exempt from overtime and as of 2024 meal and rest periods required under the FLSA. Salaried workers may be subject to an employer's attendance policy; however, they cannot be docked pay for tardiness or missed days of work.

FIGURE 4.1   Sample total rewards statement

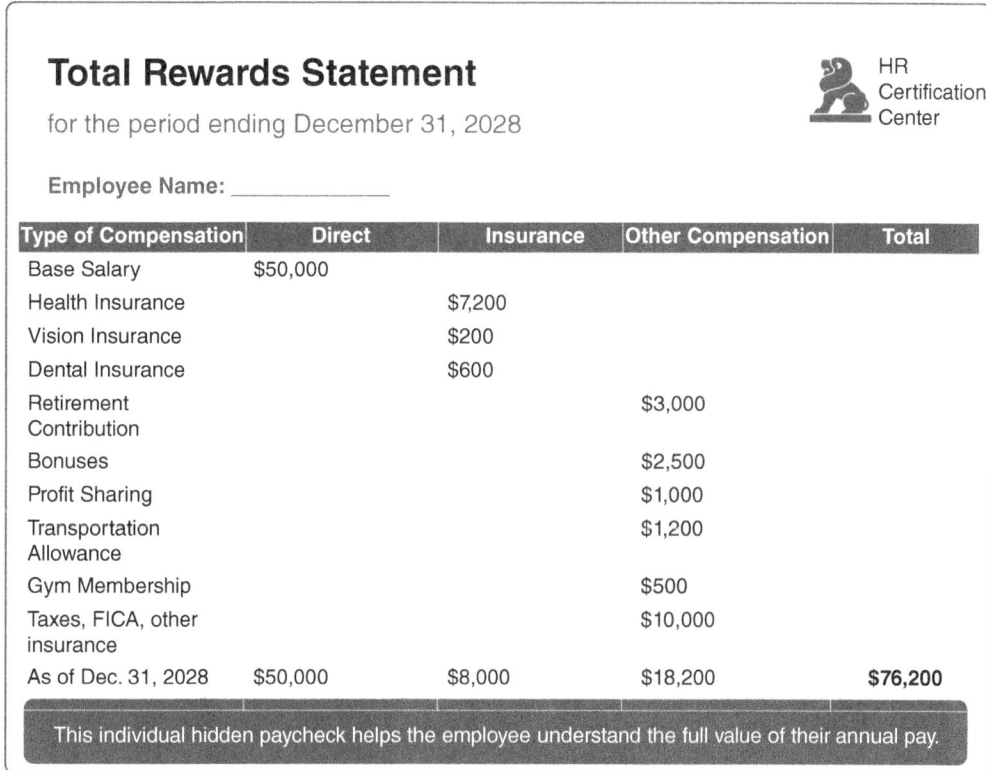

Total Rewards Statement

for the period ending December 31, 2028

HR
Certification
Center

Employee Name: _____

Type of Compensation	Direct	Insurance	Other Compensation	Total
Base Salary	$50,000			
Health Insurance		$7,200		
Vision Insurance		$200		
Dental Insurance		$600		
Retirement Contribution			$3,000	
Bonuses			$2,500	
Profit Sharing			$1,000	
Transportation Allowance			$1,200	
Gym Membership			$500	
Taxes, FICA, other insurance			$10,000	
As of Dec. 31, 2028	$50,000	$8,000	$18,200	**$76,200**

This individual hidden paycheck helps the employee understand the full value of their annual pay.

> **NOTE**
>
> The DOL final rule raising the salary threshold for exempt employees took effect on July 1, 2024. The weekly threshold increased from $684 to $844, or $35,568 to $43,888 annually. On January 1, 2025, the threshold will increase again to $1,128 per week, or $58,656 annually. However, on November 15, 2024, a federal district court in Texas vacated this DOL rule nationwide, determining that the DOL had exceeded its authority by emphasizing salary levels over job duties in defining exemptions. This continues to be worked out in the courts, so it is important to check for the most current requirement prior to sitting for your exam.

It is also important to understand the separate but related concepts of *exempt* versus *nonexempt* workers. Under the FLSA, workers are categorized as either exempt or non-exempt based on their job duties and how much they are paid.

Exempt workers are employees who are not required to be paid overtime for working more than 40 hours a week. They usually have jobs that are managerial, professional, or administrative and earn a salary rather than an hourly wage. Exempt workers typically have more flexibility in their schedules and job duties. Exempt workers can be paid a flat salary, or classified as "salaried, nonexempt."

Nonexempt workers must be paid overtime (1.5 times their hourly rate) if they work more than 40 hours in a week. This is calculated by hours worked, not counting vacation, sick, holiday pay, or other nonwork status. Nonexempt workers are often paid hourly and include various types of jobs that don't fall into the exempt categories, often classified as "individual contributors."

> **NOTE** States are allowed to write their own labor laws, such as minimum wage requirements, overtime rules, and mandated benefits. However, the state laws must always meet or exceed the federal requirements. As of July 2024, 30 states, 3 US territories, and the District of Columbia have minimum wage rates higher than the federal minimum wage of $7.25 per hour.

Internal Environmental Factors

A transparent compensation strategy can be easily understood through internal and external environmental standards. Internal methods for setting total rewards strategies involve assessing the organization's own job roles, employee performance, and business goals. This approach prioritizes aligning compensation and benefits with the company's objectives and the relative importance of each job internally.

Job evaluation is the process of determining the *relative worth* of different jobs in an organization to establish fair compensation. Relative worth is the value assigned to a job in comparison to other jobs within the company, based on factors like responsibilities, skills required, and complexity. The job evaluation process is a way for employers to make sure every job is given a fair salary based on what the job involves and how tough it is. Job evaluation is not to be confused with performance evaluations or how well employees perform their jobs, as previously discussed in Chapter 3. Several methods are used to conduct a job evaluation. The three most common are the following:

- *Ranking method*: Jobs are listed from the most important to the least important. The toughest or most important jobs are usually paid more.

- *Point method*: Jobs get points for different parts of the work, like skills needed or responsibilities. The more points a job gets, the higher the pay. An example of the point method would be assigning specific values for education level (a high school diploma may get 10 points where a doctorate or professional degree merits 50 points).

- *Factor comparison method*: This is a bit like mixing the ranking and point methods. Jobs are compared based on factors like skill levels, responsibilities, and working conditions. Each factor is given a score, and then those scores help decide the pay.

After using these methods, companies have a better idea of how to set salaries that are fair. The process also is the starting point for placing jobs into *pay ranges*, also called grades or scales. Pay ranges have a minimum and maximum for the range and an average that could be either a mean or median, depending on the methodology.

Establishing pay grades in the workplace involves grouping different jobs that have similar value and requirements into categories. First, the company completes the job evaluation process and then groups similar jobs into grades (categories). Each pay grade has a pay range with a minimum and maximum salary. The floor and ceiling of the range are determined using the market mid-point, data derived from conducting a market analysis, which is discussed in an upcoming section. Current employees are then mapped to their relative pay grade to determine where they are in the range. See Figure 4.2 for a look at how to handle employees who are paid out-of-range for their role.

External Environmental Factors

External methods for setting an employer's pay strategy focus on analyzing market data and industry standards. Companies compare their pay scales with similar roles in other organizations to ensure competitive salaries and benefits, aiming to attract and retain top talent in the industry.

FIGURE 4.2   Red circled and green circled employees

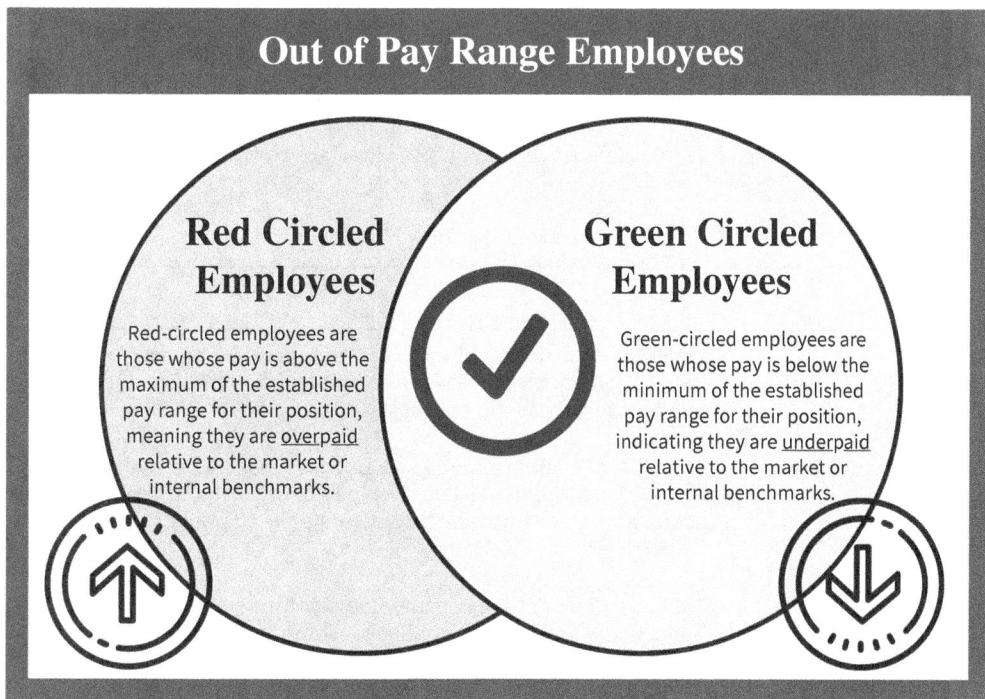

Out of Pay Range Employees

Red Circled Employees

Red-circled employees are those whose pay is above the maximum of the established pay range for their position, meaning they are overpaid relative to the market or internal benchmarks.

Green Circled Employees

Green-circled employees are those whose pay is below the minimum of the established pay range for their position, indicating they are underpaid relative to the market or internal benchmarks.

When a company wants to decide how much to pay its employees and what other benefits to offer, like health insurance or vacation time, it conducts a *market analysis*. In market analysis, companies look at what other similar businesses are paying their employees and what benefits they offer. They also look at factors such as how many employees those companies have and where they're located. By doing this, companies can decide if they're paying their employees enough compared to other companies (called competitiveness). They can also see if they need to add any new benefits to attract or keep good workers.

A *salary survey* is a tool used to collect and analyze data on wage rates for specific jobs within an industry. Employers conduct salary surveys by gathering pay information for different jobs from several companies in the same industry or area. They often use questionnaires or buy data from specialized compensation consulting firms, like Mercer or Aon Hewitt, that can provide customized reports. Surveys are also compiled by professional associations like SHRM or online platforms like PayScale that are more generic. Finally, employers may choose to create products for internal use. After collecting the data, employers analyze it to figure out the average salaries and benefits for similar jobs. This helps them set competitive pay rates and adjust their pay structures to attract and keep good workers, making sure their salaries are in line with what other companies are offering.

A *benchmark job* is a position within an organization that is commonly found across various industries and serves as a standard reference point for setting compensation levels. These jobs are typically well defined with stable duties, making them ideal for salary comparisons and market pay analysis. An example of a benchmark job is an administrative assistant. This position is common across many industries with well-defined responsibilities, such as managing office communications, scheduling meetings, and handling administrative tasks, making it a standard job used for salary comparison in compensation surveys.

Other external factors for establishing a compensation strategy include complying with wage and hour laws. The FLSA is the main law governing wages and hours in the United States. Several items are NOT required under the FLSA. These are covered in Table 4.1.

TABLE 4.1   What the Fair Labor Standards Act Does Not Require

Topic	Summary
Pay Raises	The FLSA does not require raises. Pay raises are typically negotiated between an employer and employee or through the collective bargaining process.
Extra Pay for Nights/ Weekends	The FLSA does not require extra pay for weekend or night work. However, it mandates overtime pay of at least 1.5 times the regular rate for nonexempt workers after 40 hours in a workweek.
Vacation, Sick, and Holiday Pay	The FLSA does not require payment for time not worked, like vacations, sick leave, or holidays. These benefits depend on employer-employee agreements.

Topic	Summary
Severance Pay	Severance pay is not required under the FLSA and depends on the employer-employee agreement.
Breaks and Meal Periods	Federal law does not require lunch or coffee breaks. However, when employers do offer short breaks (usually lasting about 5 to 20 minutes), federal law considers the breaks as compensable work hours. Most states have requirements for meal and rest periods, though some states have specific rules. All employers must provide unpaid break time and a private space for nursing mothers.
Performance Evaluations	The FLSA does not require performance evaluations, leaving it to employer-employee agreements.
Work Schedule Changes	Employers can change work hours without notice unless a prior agreement exists.
Notice of Separation	Neither the employer nor the employee is required to give notice of separation unless they are covered under a different law, such as WARN, or an employment contract/collective bargaining agreement that outlines specific notice requirements.
Double Time Pay	The FLSA does not require double time pay, which depends on employer-employee agreements.

Source: Adapted from US Department of Labor. (n.d.). Questions and answers about the Fair Labor Standards Act (FLSA). Adapted from The Department of Labor https://www.dol.gov/agencies/whd/flsa/faq

Pay Adjustments

Once salaries have been established, HR teams are also responsible for making pay adjustments. Pay adjustments are changes made to an employee's salary or hourly wage, often based on factors like performance, inflation, or changes in job responsibilities. Pay adjustments help maintain a competitive market position by ensuring employee salaries align with industry standards, attracting and retaining top talent, and preventing wage stagnation in a changing economic environment. When pay increases do not keep up with the market, *pay compression* can occur. Pay compression is when there is a small difference in pay between employees, despite differences in their experience, skills, or job responsibilities. It is usually the result of employers hiring new talent and paying them close to or the same as workers who have more *tenure* with the organization (time on the job).

Merit increases are pay raises given to employees based on their performance. Employees who do an excellent job may receive raises to recognize their hard work. These raises are usually agreed upon between the employer and the employee and can be calculated as a flat rate, such as $1.00 per hour increase, or as a percentage of salary, such as a 5% increase to their annual wages.

Employees may also receive a pay increase based on the cost of living. *Cost of living adjustments (COLAs)* are generally based on inflation, which reflects the rising costs of goods and services. These are sometimes referred to as market rate adjustments. Employers often use a measure like the Consumer Price Index (CPI) to determine how much prices have gone up over a certain period. The goal is to adjust wages so employees can maintain their purchasing power and standard of living as everyday expenses like housing, groceries, and transportation become more expensive.

Service awards recognize employees for their dedication and years of work at a company. Employees may receive gifts, certificates, or bonuses after reaching specific milestones, like 5 or 10 years of service.

Payroll Processing

Payroll processing is the overall task of managing employee pay, including calculating earnings, withholding taxes, and distributing paychecks. In some companies, processing payroll is a task that the accounting department handles; in others, it is up to human resources. There are several factors to be aware of when processing payroll.

Employer and Employee Taxes   Payroll processing involves calculating and withholding federal, state, and local taxes from employees' wages. Employers also pay taxes like Social Security, Medicare, and unemployment.

Deductions   Deductions are amounts taken out of an employee's paycheck for benefits like health insurance, retirement contributions, or charitable donations.

Differentials   Differentials are extra pay given to employees for special conditions, like night shifts or hazardous work. They ensure that employees receive fair compensation for working in less desirable situations.

Garnishments   Garnishments are court-ordered deductions from an employee's paycheck to pay off debts like child support, taxes, or loans.

Leave Reporting   Leave reporting tracks the paid and unpaid time off employees take, such as vacation, sick leave, and family leave, ensuring their pay is accurately adjusted.

Final Pay   Final pay is the last paycheck an employee receives when leaving a company. It includes their remaining earnings, unused vacation days, and any owed bonuses or deductions. Under the FLSA, there are no specific requirements that dictate when an employee's final paycheck must be paid upon dismissal. Instead, final pay requirements are typically governed by state laws. However, the FLSA mandates that employers must pay employees for all hours worked, including overtime, as required. It is also worth noting that employers cannot withhold an employee's final check. It must be paid in accordance with the laws and regulations relevant to the place of employment.

Workweek/Pay Period   Establishing the workweek for employee pay is required because it defines the period for calculating hours worked. An example of a workweek might be from Monday at 9:00 a.m. to the following Monday at 8:59 a.m. This setup defines the start and end of the period during which all hours worked are counted. If an employee works 42 hours within this period, they would be paid for two hours of overtime, assuming they are a nonexempt employee under the FLSA. The pay period is the time for which the employee pay is being calculated. For biweekly payroll, the pay period would be two workweeks.

Payroll Recordkeeping

Every employer covered by the FLSA must keep certain records for each nonexempt worker. The FLSA does not require a specific form for the records, but an employer must include certain information to be in compliance with the law. The following is a list of the basic records that an employer must maintain according to 29 CFR Part 516, which covers the recordkeeping requirements for the FLSA:

- Employee's full name and Social Security number
- Address, including zip code
- Birth date, if younger than 19
- Sex and occupation
- Time and day of week when employee's workweek begins
- Hours worked each day
- Total hours worked each workweek
- Basis on which employee's wages are paid (e.g., "$15 per hour," "$640 a week," "piecework")
- Regular hourly pay rate
- Total daily or weekly straight-time earnings
- Total overtime earnings for the workweek
- All additions to or deductions from the employee's wages
- Total wages paid each pay period
- Date of payment and the pay period covered by the payment

Pay Stubs

A *pay stub* (also called a wage statement) is a document provided to employees that details their earnings, deductions, and net pay for a specific pay period. The requirements for pay stubs are not directly specified by the FLSA, but the law does require that employers keep accurate records of employee wages and hours worked. Most states have their own requirements regarding the information that should be provided on employee pay stubs. The paystub is usually attached to the employees pay statement or physical check and usually includes some combination of the following:

Employee Information   This should include the employee's name and address and an employee ID number. This can be an internal number assigned to each worker, or a partial of the employee's social security number (protected against identity theft).

Earnings Information   A summary of all earnings for the pay period must be itemized, including an employee's gross wages, regular and overtime hours worked pay rate(s) (regular and overtime), and bonuses, commissions, or other earnings.

Deductions   Employers must itemize all deductions for the pay period including federal and state income taxes, Social Security and Medicare, health insurance deductibles, retirement contributions, garnishments, and any other voluntary or mandatory deductions. Under the FLSA, an employer may not legally make deductions from an employee's wages that would reduce their earnings below the minimum wage or cut into their overtime pay. Employers cannot deduct costs that are for the benefit or convenience of the employer. This includes things like uniforms, tools needed for the job, and damages or theft losses. In addition, certain types of deductions from an employee's paycheck require written authorization from the employee. This includes deductions that are not legally mandated (such as taxes or court-ordered garnishments) and are for other purposes, like contributions to retirement accounts, payment for company products or services, or other elective deductions. The written authorization helps ensure that employees are fully aware and agree to these deductions from their earnings. However, it's important to note that even with authorization, deductions cannot reduce an employee's earnings below the federal minimum wage or decrease their overtime compensation.

Net Pay   *Net pay* is the amount of money an employee takes home after all deductions are subtracted from their gross pay. For example, if an employee earns a gross salary of $1,000 per week, and $300 is deducted for taxes, health insurance, and retirement contributions, the net pay would be $700. This is the actual amount the employee receives in their paycheck.

Employers should ensure compliance with both federal and state requirements regarding the provision and content of pay stubs. Some states require employers to provide pay stubs either in physical or electronic form, while others simply require that the information is available upon request. A few states (like New York, California, and Texas) have stricter requirements and require specific information on pay stubs, such as accrued sick leave or paid time off balances.

Time Keeping

Employee time keeping involves recording the hours that employees work each day to ensure accurate payment and compliance with labor laws. This can include clocking in and out using timecards, digital systems, or apps, helping manage schedules, tracking overtime, and verifying that labor regulations are followed.

Retention Requirements

Payroll record retention involves keeping employee pay records for specific periods as required by law to ensure compliance and resolve any disputes about compensation. The FLSA notes that "each employer shall preserve for at least three years payroll records, collective bargaining agreements, sales and purchase records. Records on which wage computations are based should be retained for two years, i.e., timecards and piece work tickets, wage rate tables, work and time schedules, and records of additions to or deductions from wages." Written or digital records must be available upon request and can be stored in a central location.

> **NOTE**
>
> Using external service providers to process payroll can enhance efficiency, ensure compliance with tax laws, and reduce administrative burdens for businesses, especially in smaller organizations where HR is a department of one. Payroll is one of the most often outsourced function of human resources. Companies such as ADP or Paychex specialize in payroll and benefits processing solutions.

Health Benefits and Insurance Programs

Most employers now offer health and other types of insurance as a means to attract and keep workers. Health insurance helps employees cover medical expenses, like doctor visits and hospital stays. Other types of insurance include dental and vision plans and life insurance, which provides financial support to families if an employee passes away. These benefits improve employees' well-being and job satisfaction.

Voluntary benefits are extra perks that workers can choose to sign up for, like supplemental life insurance, dental and vision, flexible spending accounts (FSA), wellness programs, or critical illness insurance benefits. There are different benefit packages that can be designed based on the needs of the majority of the employees of an organization that provides the most benefit for the cost incurred.

Mandated benefits are those that employers are required by law to provide, such as Social Security and workers' compensation. Under the Affordable Care Act (ACA), employers with 50 or more full-time employees must offer health insurance, but other benefits, like dental and vision insurance, are voluntary. Employees can choose to enroll in these extra benefits if they want them, but they are not required to by law.

Eligibility requirements determine whether employees qualify for health benefits and other types of insurance provided at work. These requirements often vary based on several factors, including the following:

- **Employment status:** Full-time employees are often eligible for health benefits, while part-time workers might have limited options or none at all.

- **Employment classification:** Permanent employees usually qualify for benefits, but temporary or seasonal workers often don't.

- **Hours worked:** Many employers require employees to work a minimum number of hours per week (i.e., 30 hours) to qualify for benefits.

- **Length of service:** Some benefits require employees to work at the company for a certain amount of time, like 30 or 90 days, before becoming eligible.

- **Job classification:** Different classifications, such as managers or hourly workers, may have different eligibility rules.

- **Collective bargaining agreements (CBAs):** Union contracts may have specific eligibility requirements for employees covered by the agreement.

- **Dependent eligibility:** For family coverage, employees' dependents (spouse, children) may need to meet certain requirements, like age limits or marital status.

- **Special conditions:** Some benefits, like life or disability insurance, may require employees to complete a health screening or answer medical questions.

Employees must enroll during specific periods, such as annual open enrollment or within a window following a qualifying life event (like marriage or the birth of a child).

Health Plans

Health plans are benefits provided by employers to help cover the medical expenses of employees and their families. These plans can include coverage for doctor visits, hospital stays, prescriptions, and preventive care, ensuring employees have access to necessary health services while reducing out-of-pocket costs.

Employer-paid benefits are when the company partially or fully covers the cost of certain benefits for employees. For example, they might pay for the employee's full health insurance premium (the price of the insurance) without the employee having to contribute. Many employers choose to cost share, split the amount of the insurance premium between the employee and the employer. The total amount covered varies between the types of plans employees select for themselves or their dependent(s).

Pre-tax benefits are benefits that allow employees to pay for certain expenses before taxes are taken out of their paychecks. Examples include health insurance premiums, retirement contributions, or money saved in a Health Savings Account (HSA).

In a *fully funded plan*, an insurance company is in charge. Employers pay premiums to the insurance company, and the insurance company pays for employees' health expenses. In a *self-funded plan*, the employer handles the costs themselves. Instead of paying premiums to an insurance company, the employer directly pays for employees' health expenses.

Plan Designs

Insurance plan designs determine the specifics of coverage, including what services are covered, the cost to the insured through premiums, deductibles, and copays, and the network of providers available. There are several plan design choices to choose from.

Health Maintenance Organization (HMO)   An *HMO* is a type of health insurance plan. It provides health services through a network of doctors and hospitals. Employees must use these network providers for care. HMOs often require a primary care doctor and need referrals for specialist visits. They usually have lower costs.

Preferred Provider Organization (PPO)   A *PPO* is a type of health plan that lets employees see any doctor or specialist, but it costs less if they use the doctors in the plan's network. A PPO is usually more expensive than an HMO, but employees don't need a referral to see a specialist, which gives them more choices.

High Deductible Health Plan (HDHP)   An *HDHP* is a type of insurance where employees have to pay more out of pocket before the insurance starts to cover costs. The monthly premiums are usually lower, and it often pairs with an HSA to help save money.

Health Savings Account (HSA)   An *HSA* is a special savings account for people with an HDHP. Employees can put money in it tax-free and use it to pay for medical expenses like doctor visits or prescriptions.

Flexible Spending Account (FSA)   An *FSA* is a special account where employees can save money, tax-free, to pay for health-related expenses. Unlike an HSA, they don't need an HDHP to use an FSA, but the money often needs to be used within the year.

Dental Plan   A dental plan helps cover the costs of keeping teeth healthy. It usually pays all or a portion (such as 80%/20%) for regular check-ups, cleanings, and some treatments like fillings or braces.

Vision Plan   A vision plan helps cover the costs of taking care of eyes. It often includes paying for eye exams, glasses, or contact lenses, and sometimes offers discounts on laser eye surgery.

Supplemental Wellness and Fringe Benefits

Supplemental wellness and benefits programs aim to improve employees' overall health and well-being. They offer extra services like mental health support, nutrition advice, and stress management tools. These programs help employees stay healthy, reduce stress, and boost productivity, making the workplace a better and happier environment.

According to an executive report from Wellable, approximately 44% of companies plan to increase their investment in employee wellness benefits in 2024. Specifically, 91% are focusing more on mental health solutions, and 66% on stress management and resilience tools.[2] Additionally, 52% of companies are boosting investments in lifestyle spending accounts, which allow employees to tailor wellness benefits to their needs.[3] There are several choices HR can make when designing supplemental packages.

Paid Time Off (PTO)   *PTO* is time off work that employees still get paid for. It includes vacation days, personal days, and sometimes sick days. Employees can use PTO to relax, spend time with family, or take care of personal matters.

Sick Leave   *Sick leave* is time off that employees can use when they're feeling unwell or need to care for a sick family member. It lets them rest and recover without losing pay. Many states are beginning to mandate paid sick leave, so it is important to understand the state laws where the company has employees.

Accrual   *Accrual* is how employees earn time off over time. For example, an employee might earn one day of PTO every month they work. The longer they work, the more time off that is built up.

Other Leave (Military, Bereavement)   Many employers offer other types of leave. This type of leave is generally designed to be job-protected, but it is not necessarily paid by the employer. For example, employees may be granted *job-protected leave* to serve their duties in the military, but the employer is not obligated to pay for that time off. In other circumstances, such as bereavement leave, the employee may be granted a certain number of days off for the loss of an *immediate family member* (usually defined as a parent, spouse, child, sibling, or grandparent) and also be paid for that lost time. These rules are defined in an employee handbook.

Employee Assistance Program (EAP)   An *EAP* is a program that offers free, confidential help with personal or work problems. It includes counseling for stress, mental health, and financial or legal advice.

Online Therapy   Online therapy gives employees access to mental health support through video or chat. It's a convenient way to talk to a therapist from home and manage stress or other issues.

Housing/Relocation   Housing or relocation benefits help employees move to a new location for work. It can include finding a new home, paying moving costs, or providing temporary housing.

---

[2] Wellable. (2024). 2024 employee wellness industry trends report [online]. Available at: `https://www.wellable.co/resources/employee-wellness-industry-trends-reports/2024/`
[3] Kawamoto, D. (2023). 2024 benefits trends: Why healthcare plans are going retro [online]. HR Executive. Available at: `https://hrexecutive.com/2024-benefits-trends-why-healthcare-plans-are-going-retro-high-deductible-health-plans/`

Travel/Transportation   Travel and transportation benefits help employees with commuting costs. This could include free parking, bus or train passes, or discounts on ridesharing apps like Uber or Lyft.

Insurance Programs

There are several options for employers to offer insurance to employees as an added benefit to their total rewards package. It is not unusual for employers of all sizes to offer all or some combination of the following insurance programs.

Worker's Compensation   Worker's compensation is insurance that helps employees who get injured or sick because of their job. It covers medical bills, rehabilitation costs, and lost wages while they recover. In some cases, it may provide death benefits to the family if a worker dies from a job-related injury or illness. This insurance is required by law and varies based on state regulations.

Supplemental Life Insurance   Supplemental life insurance is extra coverage that employees can buy in addition to their employer-provided life insurance. It offers more financial protection for *dependents* in case of death and can help cover expenses like funeral costs or outstanding debts. Employees can often choose the amount of coverage they need.

Accidental Death and Dismemberment (AD&D)   AD&D insurance provides extra financial support if an employee dies or suffers severe injuries due to an accident. It covers specific situations like loss of limbs, vision, or hearing. This coverage pays a lump sum to the employee or their family to help with medical expenses, recovery costs, or funeral expenses.

Short-term and Long-term Disability Insurance   *Short-term disability* (STD) insurance provides a portion of an employee's salary if they can't work due to illness or injury for a short period, usually up to six months. *Long-term disability* (LTD) insurance offers financial support for extended periods of disability, often after STD benefits end. LTD coverage can last several years or until retirement.

Elder Care Insurance   Some employers offer elder care insurance as part of their employee benefits package. This type of insurance is considered an attractive benefit because it helps employees manage the potential future costs of long-term care for themselves or their family members. The availability of this benefit can vary widely depending on the employer's size, industry, and overall benefits strategy.

Pet Insurance   Pet insurance helps employees cover the cost of their pets' medical care. It typically includes coverage for accidents, illnesses, surgeries, and sometimes preventive care like vaccinations. By offering pet insurance as a benefit, employers help pet owners manage unexpected vet bills and provide peace of mind for their furry family members.

Deferred Compensation Plans

Deferred compensation plans are special savings accounts where employees can put part of their earnings to use later, such as after they retire. This money isn't taxed when it's first earned, which means employees can save more upfront. When they take the money out during retirement, they pay taxes on it. These plans are great for saving more money for the future because they grow over time without being taxed right away. Employers can offer several types of deferred compensation plans, each with unique features and tax implications. Following are the main types.

401(k) Plans   *401(k) plans* are the most common type of deferred compensation, where employees can elect to defer a portion of their salary into this plan. Taxes on these contributions are deferred until the money is withdrawn, typically at retirement.

403(b) Plans   *403(b) plans* are similar to 401(k) plans, but specifically for employees of public schools, nonprofit organizations, and certain churches.

529 Plans   *529 plans* are savings plans specifically for higher education expenses. Employers may offer matching contributions to employees saving a percentage of their salary that can be used by a beneficiary, including the employee themselves, to pay expenses related to their education for any college eligible for Title IV Federal Student Aid (includes flight schools, and vocational schools). Recent changes to this program also enable funds to be used for primary and secondary education as well.

457 Plans   *457 plans* are available for government and certain nongovernmental employers, allowing employees to defer compensation without paying taxes until it is withdrawn.

Nonqualified Deferred Compensation Plans (NQDC)   *Nonqualified deferred comp plans* allow executives and other highly compensated employees to defer larger amounts of their salary, bonuses, and other compensation beyond the limits typical of qualified plans like 401(k)s.

Profit-sharing Plans   *Profit-sharing plans* are where employers can make discretionary contributions to the employees' retirement savings based on the company's profits.

SEP IRA (Simplified Employee Pension Individual Retirement Accounts) and SIMPLE (Savings Incentive Match Plan for Employees) IRA   *SEP* and *SIMPLE IRAs* are retirement plans that allow employers (often smaller businesses) to make contributions to their employees' retirement savings.

Each of these plans has specific rules regarding eligibility, contributions, and withdrawals, and they offer different advantages depending on the employer's and employees' needs.

Qualified plans, like 401(k)s, follow strict guidelines set by the Internal Revenue Service (IRS). They offer tax benefits such as tax-deferred growth of earnings. Contributions are made from pre-tax income, and taxes are paid when the money is withdrawn.

Nonqualified plans are less regulated and more flexible than qualified plans. They are usually offered to executives or high earners. Taxes on these plans are deferred until the money is accessed, but they don't have the same tax advantages as qualified plans. See Table 4.2 for the differences in contributions, withdrawals, and loans. Understanding these rules can help employees make informed decisions about their retirement savings.

Vesting is the period an employee needs to work at the company to own 100% of what the company contributes to the retirement account. Some companies allow employees to be fully vested after a certain number of years, while others gradually increase the vested percentage each year. For example, an employee might be 20% vested after one year, 40% after two years, and so on, until they are fully vested.

Deferred retirement plans such as IRAs and 401(k) plans generally regulate when and how individuals may contribute and withdraw funds. *Catch-up contributions* are extra payments that people aged 50 or older can make to their retirement accounts, like 401(k)s or IRAs, to save more money as they approach retirement. These contributions allow older workers to increase their retirement savings beyond the usual annual limits. *Hardship withdrawals* are special withdrawals from retirement accounts that employees can take out

TABLE 4.2   Qualified and Nonqualified Plan Rules

Rules	Qualified Plans	Nonqualified Plans
Contributions	The IRS sets limits on maximum employee and employer contributions. Many advantages to employer and employee regarding taxes on contributions and complies with the Employee Retirement and Investment Savings Act (ERISA).	Use after-tax dollars to fund them and generally employers cannot claim their contributions as a tax deduction. Generally suited for highly compensated executives that would be ineligible to contribute to the qualified plan but still desires a retirement savings plan.
Withdrawals (Hardship, other)	Must meet certain eligibility criteria for qualified distributions (such as age or a certain number of years an account is active before making a withdrawal). May be subject to required minimum distribution based on age of owner. Taxes and penalty consequences set by the IRS to discourage the use of funds for reasons other than retirement savings.	These plans use IRAs to hold participants' retirement savings. Money can be withdrawn at any time. Taxes can be deferred until withdrawal.
Loans	Some plans are permitted but not required to offer loans at a reasonable interest rate. Restricted to the lesser of 50% of an account balance or $50,000.	Loans are generally not permitted from IRA-based plans. If a loan were taken, the value of the entire IRA would be included in the owner's income for tax purposes.

early, without penalty, in case of a financial emergency, such as medical expenses or avoiding eviction. However, these withdrawals often come with strict conditions and must be repaid or result in taxes.

Summary

Traditional compensation and benefits have focused on the monetary portion or salary of the employee and those mandatory health coverage programs where the employer paid at least a portion of the premium and enjoyed a tax benefit for its contributions. As talent has become scarce and businesses must compete for employees, total reward offerings have expanded to include many voluntary health and insurance programs, fringe benefits, and deferred compensation packages. Each of these elements can be attractive to different employee segments for different reasons. Ultimately, total rewards are in place to promote an employee's morale while retaining the best employees to meet the company's work-force demands.

Employers use a comprehensive compensation strategy to offer fair wages that respond to internal and external environmental factors. Internal factors determine the relative value of positions based on their job responsibility, skills required, or complexity. External factors include market influences, such as the available talent pool and the difficulty of recruitment. Employers must ensure that wages fall within a range that does not overly compensate individuals, increasing overall payroll costs unnecessarily, or undercompensating employees, which could result in retention issues as good employees are enticed to leave by more competitive wages. Payroll recordkeeping is an essential function of HR as well as compliance with timekeeping and retention of records that are pay–impacting, which allows companies to demonstrate compliance with laws and regulations at the federal, state, and local levels.

Health benefits and other insurance offerings by employers may be mandatory or voluntary. Benefits often have tax benefits to both the employee and the employer, and their availability can impact a company's ability to attract and retain talent in the marketplace greater than pay alone. The variety of supplemental wellness and fringe benefits has expanded in recent years as companies desire to be more competitive and differentiate themselves to attract the highest quality workers. Beyond life insurance, paid gym memberships, online or face-to-face therapy, accidental death and dismemberment, short- and long-term disability, housing assistance, and even pet insurance can be potential employee benefits offered by a company as part of the total rewards package.

Deferred compensation plans are special savings accounts that allow employees to defer some wages to grow through investments and be accessed later in life, such as at retirement. These plans are usually subject to IRS rules and offer some tax benefits to the participants. These types of plans are called qualified plans, in that in exchange for the tax benefits, there are eligibility requirements that must be met. Unqualified plans allow highly compensated executives and other employees who are not eligible for the traditional retirement savings program to still be able to save money for retirement but without the same tax benefits in most cases. Employers may offer more than one plan, such as 401(k) and 529 plans that have different savings goals to attract multiple employees with different financial goals and needs. The ERISA is the primary federal law that governs activities related to an employer's retirement programs and offerings.

Exam Essentials

Understand the elements of total rewards, including compensation and benefits.   Total rewards encompasses a variety of strategies designed to provide sufficient combination of compensation and benefits to meet the needs of a diverse workforce within an organization to attract and retain qualified people. Establishing a pay structure that is competitive in the market, fairly compensates employees for their work, and complies with current labor laws is a critical HR function for a company. Payroll records and practices keep track of changes of the total rewards for each employee over time and can be analyzed to facilitate decision-making by executives.

Understand the types of health benefits and insurance programs that are typically offered through an employer.   Employers provide a range of voluntary and mandatory health benefits to employees to improve their well-being and job satisfaction. Plan designs vary to provide different coverages and options that can meet the needs of the majority of employees. Plans for health, dental, and vision are the most common. Additionally, many companies have supplemental well-being and fringe benefits such as paid time off or voluntary insurance programs that enhance total reward packages beyond direct monetary compensation.

Understand the unique features and tax implications of certain deferred compensation plans.   Qualified plans governed by the ERISA allow employers and employees to defer some compensation through investment programs subject to IRS rules. These plan rules cover eligibility for contributions, withdrawals, and loans. Nonqualified plans often are reserved for highly compensated executives who are otherwise prohibited from contributing but still wish to have a retirement savings option. These IRS rules change often and can impact contribution limits or age restrictions and must be reviewed constantly to ensure plans remain compliant to avoid being disqualified and losing any tax benefits.

Review Questions

You can find the answers in Appendix A.

1. What does total compensation include? (Choose all that apply.)
   A. Health insurance premiums
   B. Bonuses
   C. Housing allowances
   D. Nonmonetary perks

2. Which of the following is considered an employee benefit?
   A. Monthly salary
   B. Bonuses
   C. Job satisfaction
   D. Alternative work schedules

3. What is the main difference between job analysis and job evaluation?
   A. Job analysis focuses on describing a job, while job evaluation assesses the job's value.
   B. Job analysis defines wage scales, whereas job evaluation prices jobs.
   C. Job analysis is used to define training needs, while job evaluation ranks jobs in order of importance.
   D. Job analysis data are used to create job descriptions, while job evaluation defines the characteristics of jobs.

4. What is the primary reason for a pay increase for an employee?
   A. To reward employees for daily above average performance
   B. To match the salary to market rates
   C. To increase employee retention
   D. To keep employees happy

5. Which of the following is a reason for determining the appropriate salary for a job based on its duties and market data? (Choose all that apply.)
   A. To create job descriptions
   B. To benchmark compensation points
   C. To price jobs
   D. To evaluate internal competitiveness of wages

6. Which of the following statements BEST describe a company's compensation philosophy?
   A. Total rewards include more than just salary; we also provide benefits like health insurance, retirement plans, and paid time off.

B. We strive to maintain transparency within our compensation systems and commit to paying our employees fairly and competitively to attract and retain top talent.

C. We offer nonmonetary perks as part of our total rewards, such as flexible work hours and remote-first options.

D. By offering a mix of financial and nonfinancial rewards, we aim to keep our employees motivated, satisfied, and well compensated.

7. Which of the following is a purpose of the Fair Labor Standards Act? (Choose all that apply.)

   A. To regulate child labor

   B. To establish a threshold for minimum wage

   C. To require employers with 50 or more employees to offer healthcare benefits

   D. To require all private employers to pay a minimum wage to nonexempt workers

8. What is the first step to creating a pay scale?

   A. Understanding the company's compensation philosophy

   B. Classifying workers as exempt or nonexempt

   C. Pricing jobs relative to market conditions

   D. Conducting a job analysis to determine the responsibilities and requirements of each position

9. Which of the following employees is most likely to be classified as an exempt worker under the Fair Labor Standards Act? (Choose all that apply.)

   A. A salaried manager who supervises a team of employees

   B. An hourly worker in a retail store

   C. A computer programmer who earns a high salary

   D. A part-time cashier at a grocery store

10. An hourly worker is paid $14.75 per hour. Based on the Fair Labor Standards Act, calculate the worker's overtime pay for the following total hours worked each day in a week. For the purposes of this example, the established workweek is Sunday to Saturday:

   Monday: 8.25 hours

   Tuesday: 8.5 hours

   Wednesday: 8 hours

   Thursday: 9 hours

   Friday: 6.5 hours, plus 2 hours of paid time off

   A. $5.53

   B. $14.75

   C. $83.00

   D. $94.00

11. Which of the following options best describes the feature of an HMO?

   A. Provides the flexibility to see any healthcare provider without a referral

   B. Requires members to use a network of doctors and get referrals for specialists

   C. Offers high-deductible health plans with health savings accounts

   D. Allows members to receive care from out-of-network providers at a higher cost

12. What is the primary reason employers choose to offer health insurance and other benefits?

   A. Most are required by regulations.

   B. It supports an employer brand.

   C. It increases employee job satisfaction.

   D. It helps the employer compete for talent.

13. Which of the following is not likely to qualify for health insurance benefits with an employer? (Choose all that apply.)

   A. Gig workers

   B. Full-time employees

   C. Grandparents as dependents

   D. Part-time employees

14. Why is it important for employers to comply with the information required on employee pay stubs?

   A. To ensure the employees' pay is accurate

   B. To comply with state and federal labor laws and avoid penalties

   C. To provide employees with written proof of payment

   D. To reduce the company's tax liability

15. Which of the following options is true about an employee's final paycheck? (Choose all that apply.)

   A. It can be withheld until the employee returns all company property.

   B. It must include payment for any unused vacation time, if state law requires it.

   C. It can include a lump-sum deduction for outstanding employee loans.

   D. It must comply with state laws.

16. In which of the following scenarios would outsourcing payroll be the most beneficial?

   A. For a small business without a dedicated HR department

   B. For a company with temporary or other contract workers

   C. For a company with more than 1,000 employees

   D. For a company with 200 employees and 1 HR person

17. Which of the following is the correct definition of pay compression?

    A. The process of adjusting employee salaries based on performance reviews

    B. The situation where there is a small difference in pay between employees regardless of their skills, experience, or seniority

    C. The strategy of increasing salaries to match market rates

    D. The practice of providing bonuses to employees during peak seasons

18. Which of the following is NOT required by wage and hour laws? (Choose all that apply.)

    A. Overtime pay

    B. Severance pay

    C. Two weeks' notice of separation

    D. Paid meal periods

19. Which of the following job evaluation methods is characterized by scoring jobs based on their level of skill and responsibility?

    A. Ranking

    B. Point method

    C. Point factor method

    D. Factor comparison

20. Which of the following is an internal method for setting a total rewards strategy?

    A. Job evaluation

    B. Benchmarking

    C. Salary surveys

    D. Market evaluations

Chapter

5

aPHR Employee Relations

aPHR EXAM OBJECTIVES COVERED IN THIS CHAPTER REQUIRE KNOWLEDGE RELATED TO THE FUNCTIONAL AREA 04, EMPLOYEE RELATIONS:

✓ 04-01 The purpose and difference between mission, vision, and values statements, and how they influence an organization's culture and employees

✓ 04-02 How HR supports organizational goals and objectives through HR policies, procedures, and operations (for example, function of human resource information systems [HRIS], organizational structures, preparing HR-related documents, basic communication flow & methods, SWOT analysis, and strategic planning)

✓ 04-03 Techniques used to engage employees, collect feedback, and improve employee satisfaction (for example, employee recognition programs, stay interviews, engagement surveys, work/life balance initiatives, and alternative work arrangements)

✓ 04-04 Workforce management throughout the employee life cycle, including performance management and employee behavior issues (for example, goal setting, benchmarking, performance appraisal methods & biases, ranking/rating scales, progressive discipline, termination/separation, off boarding, absenteeism, and turnover/retention)

✓ 04-05 Policies and procedures to handle employee complaints, facilitate investigations, and support conflict resolution (for example, confidentiality, escalation, retaliation, and documentation)

✓ 04-06 The elements of diversity and inclusion initiatives and the impact of organizational effectiveness in productivity (for example, social responsibility initiatives, cultural sensitivity and acceptance, unconscious bias and stereotypes)

Functional area 04, Employee Relations accounts for 24% of the aPHR exam. HRCI summarizes this exam content as "understanding the methods organizations used to monitor and address morale, performance, and retention by balancing the operational needs of the organization with the well-being of the individual employee."

HR Done Wrong

The corporate landscape is ever-changing and adapting as changes in technology, economics, and culture affect how companies engage their employees. The most recent revolution in business acumen has been the understanding that among some groups of employees, there have been historic barriers or obstacles that have created disparities within the workplace. These inequities have been perpetuated over time and have created in some ways social injustices that companies and corporate leaders have recognized and attempted to change. To counter the effects of these past practices, companies have embraced diversity, equity, and inclusion (DEI) programs to evaluate outcomes and ensure opportunities exist for all employees, but specifically focused on those groups of employees that may have been historically marginalized.

These programs are important and are discussed in this chapter. However, something of great value can be detrimental to an organization if executed or adopted poorly. Recent articles and surveys have highlighted the backlash DEI programs have faced. While a third of employees in a survey responded that there has been increased focus on DEI initiatives, nearly half also found that peers found those initiatives divisive.[1] The backlash comes when employees perceive DEI efforts to be a threat or disruption to their own social standing within the organizational community. HR leaders who do not effectively communicate the need for DEI initiatives and understand the possible resistance that can occur risk employees becoming disengaged and even leaving the organization.

Recognizing the sensitivity in implementing DEI practices, encouraging empathy amongst employees, and gaining buy-in from all stakeholders are required actions to ensure DEI objectives are achieved successfully.

---

[1] Rai, T. and Dutkiewicz, C. (2022). How to navigate pushback to diversity, equity and inclusion efforts [online]. Gartner. Available at: https://www.gartner.com/en/articles/how-to-navigate-pushback-to-diversity-equity-and-inclusion-efforts

Employee Relations Defined

Employee relations refers to the way a company manages the relationship with its employees. For HR, this requires the development of several competencies including business acumen, communication, problem-solving, and negotiation skills. These competencies support HR in an advocacy role, understanding and balancing the rights and responsibilities of the employees with the responsibilities and rights of the employer. Other relationships that fall into the category of employee relations include relationships between employees and their manager, coworker relationships, and when there is union representation, the relationship between the employer and the union.

Here is a list of a few key terms you should be familiar with in the context of employee relations:

- *At-will employment*: A doctrine in employment law that states either the employer or the employee can terminate employment at any time, with or without cause, and with or without notice, as long as it does not violate any laws or contractual agreements.

- *Collective bargaining:* The process of negotiation between employers and a group of employees (often represented by a union) to determine conditions of employment, such as wages, working hours, benefits, and other work-related conditions.

- *Grievance procedure*: A formal process through which employees can raise concerns, complaints, or disputes about workplace issues or violations of company policies or employment laws.

- *Employee engagement*: The level of an employee's commitment, involvement, and enthusiasm toward their work and the organization.

- *Progressive discipline*: A system of discipline that involves a graduated series of steps or actions taken by an employer to address employee misconduct or performance issues.

- *Employee rights and responsibilities*: The rules and protections for workers, like getting fair pay and working in a safe place (rights), along with the duties they need to do, like doing their job well and following company rules (responsibilities).

- *Competencies:* The skills and knowledge workers need to do their jobs well and help the company succeed.

- *Workplace conflict resolution*: Solving arguments or problems between workers or between workers and supervisors to keep respect in the workplace.

- *Collective bargaining*: When a group of workers agree to collectively be represented by a labor union and bargains with the company about work conditions, pay, and other job-related issues.

- *Labor laws*: The rules that govern how workers and employers should treat each other, including hiring, safety, and workers' rights.

- *Employee retention*: Methods to keep good workers in the company and reduce the number of people who leave.

- *Code of conduct*: A set of rules about how workers should behave at work, including things like honesty and respect.
- *Organizational Climate*: The overall feeling or atmosphere in the workplace, like whether it feels positive and supportive or negative and stressful.
- *Organizational Culture*: The shared values, beliefs, and behaviors in a company that shape how people work and interact with each other.

HR Strategic Support

Strategic planning is the set of actions or activities by which an organization establishes overarching goals with clearly defined objectives and determines the ends, ways, and means in achieving them. These goals and objectives must have the ability to impact the organization by achieving the mission or vision of the company. This process helps companies grow and succeed by making sure everyone is aligned to the same outcomes.

As HR business partners, it is important to have a "seat at the table." This means that HR functions are considered fundamental to the execution of business strategy, and HR acts as an advisor and partner to achieving strategic results. HR supports the strategic planning process by helping to align the workforce with the company's goals. They recruit and train employees, manage talent, and develop policies that support business objectives. The aPHR will test your knowledge on fundamental concepts related to business strategy, and how HR operations and workflows support the achievement of business goals.

Mission, Vision, and Values

Business strategy starts with understanding the company's mission, vision, and values. The mission, vision, and values work together to shape the company culture by providing a clear purpose, define future goals, and guiding principles that influence how employees interact and make decisions. These are important because they create a unified direction for the company and ensure consistent actions and decisions that align with the company's overall goals. Ultimately, the mission, vision, and values should guide employer behaviors and direction. When employees are aware of the mission, they understand what the organization aims to achieve; the vision helps them see the long-term objectives, and the values guide their behavior and decision-making processes. When employees do not understand these foundational elements, it can lead to a lack of engagement, misaligned priorities, reduced motivation, and inconsistent behavior, ultimately affecting overall productivity, employee morale, and the organization's ability to achieve its strategic goals.

A *mission statement* explains why a company exists. It describes the company's main goals and the kind of work it does. For example, a company's mission might be to provide high-quality products, deliver excellent customer service, or improve community well-being.

In employee relations, a clear mission helps employees understand their role in the company and motivates them to contribute to the company's success.

The *company vision* is a statement about what a company wants to achieve in the future. It is a big-picture idea of where the company sees itself going. This could be becoming a leader in the industry, expanding globally, or making a significant impact on society. For employees, a strong vision inspires them and gives them a sense of direction and purpose, helping them stay focused and committed to the company's long-term goals.

Values are the core beliefs and principles that guide a company's actions and decisions. These might include honesty, teamwork, innovation, and respect. Values influence how employees interact with each other, how they treat customers, and how they approach their work. When a company's values are clear and shared by its employees, it creates a positive work environment and builds trust within the team. Sometimes companies may ask for-hire candidates behavioral-based questions about values. This is done to determine if a candidate shares or is aligned to the values of the organization to judge if they are a best fit.

Case Study

Salesforce, founded in 1999, is a leading provider of customer relationship management (CRM) software that helps businesses manage their sales, customer service, and marketing efforts. As of January 2024, Salesforce employs approximately 72,682 people worldwide.[2] Here are the company's mission, vision, and values, and how they influence the company's business practices:

Mission   Salesforce's mission to empower companies to connect with their customers in a whole new way is evident in its comprehensive CRM solutions that drive customer engagement. For example, Salesforce's Customer 360 platform provides businesses with a complete view of their customers, allowing for personalized and efficient service across sales, service, marketing, and commerce.

Vision   Salesforce's vision to be the world's most trusted customer relationship management platform is reflected in its continuous innovation and commitment to security. Salesforce invests heavily in developing new technologies, such as artificial intelligence with Salesforce Einstein, to help businesses predict customer needs and automate tasks. This ensures that Salesforce stays ahead of the technology curve while maintaining high security and trust standards.

---

[2] Stock Analysis. (n.d.). Salesforce number of employees 2004–2024 [online]. Available at: https://stock analysis.com/stocks/crm/employees/

Values   Salesforce's values of trust, customer success, innovation, and equality guide its business practices:[3]

- Trust: Salesforce prioritizes data security and privacy, ensuring that customer data are protected and handled responsibly.

- Customer Success: Salesforce provides extensive support and resources to help customers achieve their goals, including training programs through Salesforce Trailhead and a vibrant user community known as the Trailblazer Community.

- Innovation: Salesforce constantly updates and expands its product offerings, integrating cutting-edge technologies like AI and machine learning to enhance its CRM solutions.

- Equality: Salesforce is committed to promoting diversity and inclusion within its workforce and beyond. The company actively supports various equality initiatives and has set ambitious goals to foster an inclusive environment for all employees.

These elements demonstrate how Salesforce integrates its mission, vision, and values into its everyday business practices to drive growth and create a positive impact both internally and externally.

The company mission, vision, and values are not expected to drastically change over time. Change certainly can and does happen, but when it does, it is often in response to a significant internal or external change. These may include an economic downturn, a merger, the acquisition of a new large customer, or the invention of new technology, just to name a few. A great example of this would be Tandy Leather (tandyleather.com). The original company was founded in 1919, first focusing on shoe sole leather and the needs of the Armed Services through the wartime period. However, in the post-war period, it shifted to focus on customers that saw leatherworking as a hobby, and then in 1963, it acquired Radio Shack. The Tandy Corporation would split into two companies by the mid-1970s and shift focus to retail electronics and include a line of computers bearing its name. Of course, as the technology changed, by the turn of the century, the electronics elements of Radio Shack disappeared and went bankrupt, but Tandy Leather still exists with more than 90 retail stores and focused on leatherworking.

Strategic planning attempts to get ahead of any changes such as those just described, and this is accomplished through the process of environmental scanning and forecasting.

---

[3] Salesforce. (2023). Our values guide every decision [online]. Salesforce. Available at: https://www.salesforce.com/company/our-values/

Environmental Scanning

Environmental scanning in strategic planning is when a company looks at internal and external factors that can affect its success. This includes studying trends, competition, laws, and the economy. By understanding these elements, companies can make better plans and adapt to changes. There are two primary scanning tools to be familiar with for the exams:

PESTLE Analysis   *PESTLE* is a scanning tool that helps employers understand the Political, Economic, Social, Technological, Legal, and Environmental forces affecting their ability to compete. It's a tool companies use to understand the external environment:

- **Political:** government policies, stability, and regulations.
- **Economic:** economic growth, inflation, and unemployment rates.
- **Social:** cultural trends, population demographics, and lifestyle changes.
- **Technological:** advances in technology, innovation, and automation.
- **Legal:** laws, regulations, and legal issues.
- **Environmental:** environmental protection, climate change, and sustainability.

SWOT Analysis   *SWOT* is a scanning tool that helps employers assess their Strengths, Weaknesses, Opportunities, and Threats. It helps companies evaluate their internal and external environment for areas to leverage, and risk:

- **Strengths:** An internal factor of what the company does well, its advantages. This could be products it creates that are in demand or processes that are an industry standard.
- **Weaknesses:** An internal factor of areas where the company needs improvement. The ability to respond to changes in the market or have large fluctuations in deliveries or quality might be examples of weaknesses.
- **Opportunities:** External factors the company can use to its advantage. This could be new innovation in the industry that the company can implement before peers or being able to branch out to new areas to expand operations.
- **Threats:** External factors that could harm the company. Changes in market demand, increased industry regulations, or a competitor's bid to corner the market are all external threats.

Both *PESTLE* and *SWOT* help companies make informed decisions and plan strategically.

Porter's Five Forces Analysis   This tool is used to analyze the competitive environment of an organization by examining five key forces: the threat of new entrants, the bargaining power of suppliers, the bargaining power of buyers, the threat of substitute products or services, and the intensity of competitive rivalry. Understanding these forces helps HR professionals and leaders assess the organization's position within its industry and develop strategies to enhance its competitive advantage:

- **Threat of new entrants:** Will the introduction of a new company or product alter the market to the disruption or disadvantage of a popular brand?

- **Bargaining power of suppliers:** Can suppliers strongly influence the end user through control of raw materials by cost or availability?

- **Bargaining power of buyers:** Do buyers in the market currently have brand preference or are they willing to obtain a substitute or forgo the product or service if the cost is too high?

- **Threat of substitute products or services:** Do substitute or alternative products or services exist in the market or is there a monopoly?

- **Intensity of competitive rivalry:** How close in market share is the next closest competitor, and how much influence does a competitor have in shaping the market?

Forecasting

Forecasting is another important part of strategic planning. It means predicting future needs and trends, such as how many employees will be needed and what skills they should have. This helps the company prepare for the future and stay competitive. Following are three common forecasting methods:

- *Trend analysis*: This method looks at past data to identify patterns or trends. By examining how things have changed over time, companies can predict future outcomes. For example, if sales have increased steadily over the past few years, trend analysis can help forecast future sales growth.

- *Delphi method*: The Delphi method involves getting opinions from a group of experts. These experts answer questions and provide their forecasts independently. Their responses are then summarized, and they can revise their answers based on the group's feedback. This process is repeated until a consensus is reached, providing a well-rounded forecast.

- *Scenario planning*: Scenario planning involves imagining different future situations and how they might impact the company. For instance, a business might consider scenarios like economic growth, recession, or technological changes. By planning for various possibilities, companies can be better prepared for whatever the future holds.

Regardless of the outcomes of scanning the external and internal environment, it is important that employers communicate the strategic plan with all stakeholders through meetings, emails, or newsletters to ensure everyone knows how they contribute to the overall strategy and its implementation. A great example would be communicating with bricklayers who are putting in a foundation. If they were simply told to lay the bricks, the employees would perhaps do the job competently and diligently but wouldn't understand how they fit into the overall project. However, if the architect first explained that these bricks being laid were the cornerstone of the project, which was actually a large cathedral, and the importance that each brick had to support the foundation of this massive structure, that would indeed focus and perhaps even motivate the bricklayers to do the absolute best job possible.

Organizational Structures

Organizational structures are ways that companies arrange their departments and reporting structures to make sure everyone knows their role and responsibilities. These structures influence business and HR strategies in several ways. For example, in a traditional *hierarchy*, decisions flow from top to bottom, which can slow down processes but ensure control. In a flat structure, there are fewer levels of management, promoting faster decision-making and more employee involvement. See Figure 5.1 for an example of a traditional hierarchical structure.

Another structure is when a company is divided into departments, like marketing, finance, and HR. This *functional* structure allows each department to focus on its specific goals and helps create specialized strategies that align with the company's overall objectives. See Figure 5.2 for an example of a functional structure.

Some organizations use a *matrix* structure, where employees report to multiple managers. This encourages collaboration and flexibility but can lead to confusion. Companies need to balance control with flexibility to support effective business and HR strategies. See Figure 5.3 for an example of a matrix structure.

A *divisional structure* organizes the organization into semiautonomous units or divisions, each responsible for a particular product line, market, or geographic area. Each division operates like a mini-company, with its own resources and objectives. This structure allows for greater flexibility and responsiveness to specific market needs but may lead to duplication of resources and efforts across divisions. See Figure 5.4 for an example of a divisional structure.

FIGURE 5.1   A hierarchical structure

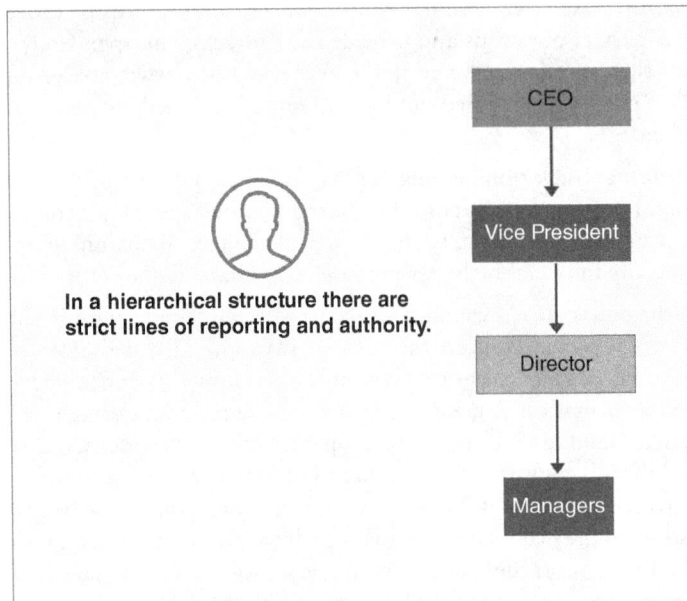

In a hierarchical structure there are strict lines of reporting and authority.

CEO

Vice President

Director

Managers

FIGURE 5.2   A functional structure

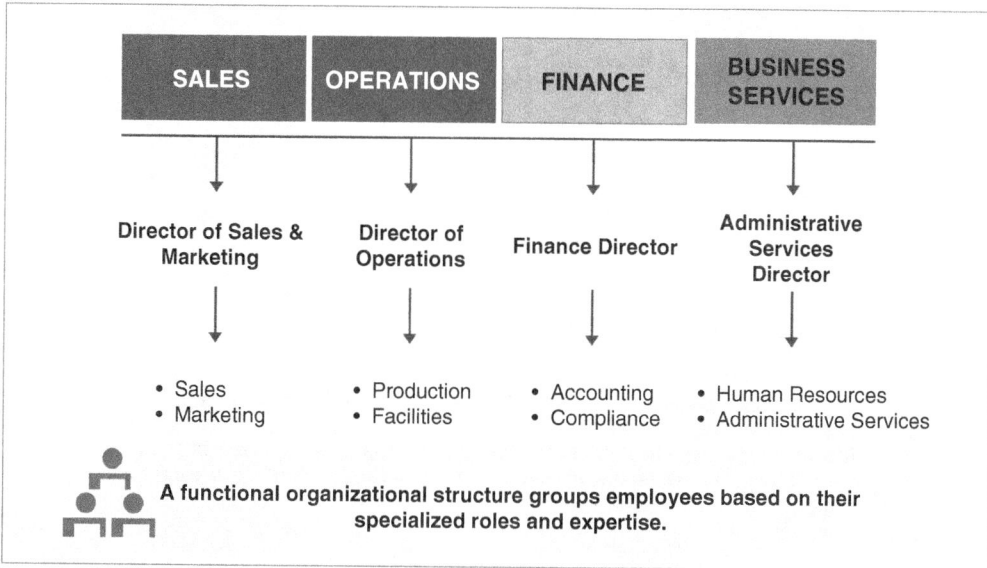

A functional organizational structure groups employees based on their specialized roles and expertise.

FIGURE 5.3   A matrix structure

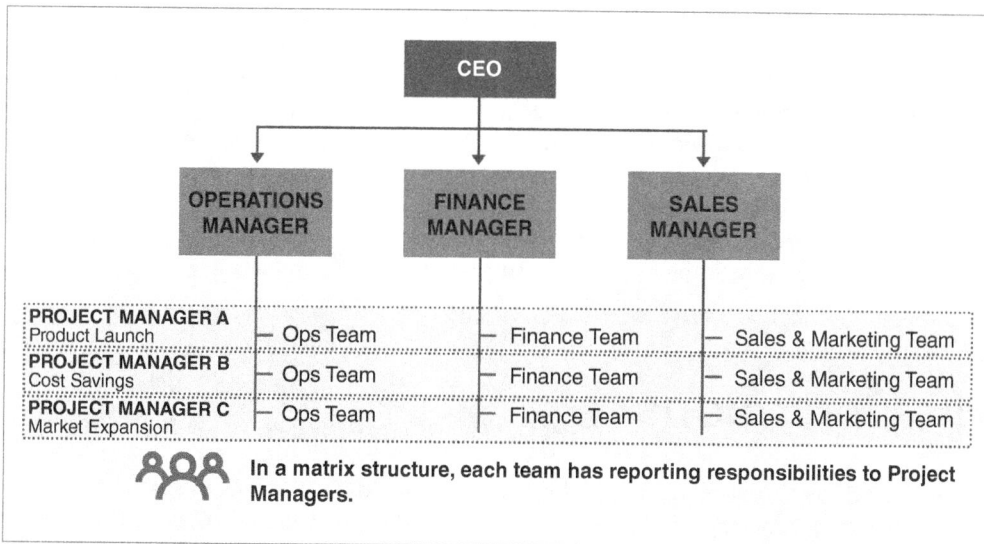

In a matrix structure, each team has reporting responsibilities to Project Managers.

FIGURE 5.4   A divisional structure

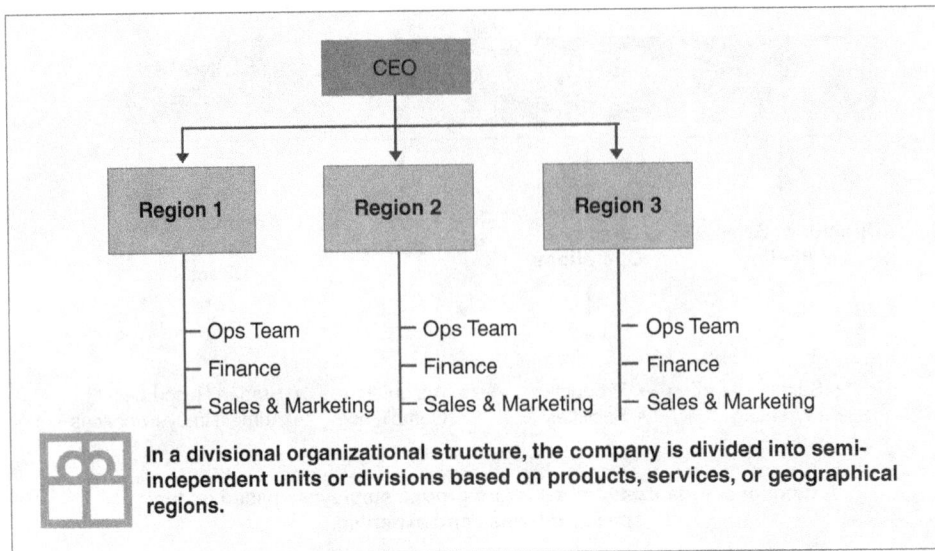

In a divisional organizational structure, the company is divided into semi-independent units or divisions based on products, services, or geographical regions.

The way a company is organized can greatly affect its HR policies and workflows. For example, in a large company with many departments, HR policies might need to be very detailed to handle the different needs of each department. This can make HR workflows more complex, as they have to keep track of many rules and procedures. On the other hand, in a smaller company with a simpler structure, HR policies might be more straightforward, allowing HR workflows to be quicker and easier to manage. The structure of the organization also determines how decisions are made and communicated, which can influence how quickly HR can respond to employee needs and changes within the company.

The organizational structure of a business is key to understanding how an HR department should be integrated into the organization. Proper alignment of HR inside the business architecture of the organization will ensure proper services and timely actions by the HR team working with the right supervisors and managers, and it will allow HR to be more effective overall as a business unit.

HR Operations

HR is often the go-between for the employer and the employee. This means that HR is responsible for helping align and influence employee behavior to ensure that employees' actions match the company's mission, vision, and values. This can be done through training, communication, and leadership. For example, if a company values teamwork, it might offer team-building activities and reward collaborative efforts. By aligning employee behavior with the company's goals and values, the company can achieve better results and create a more cohesive and motivated workforce. The most often used tools to achieve alignment are a company's policies, procedures, and rules:

- *Policies*: Policies are guidelines that outline the company's expectations for employees. It provides the "what" and "why" of a specific aspect of employment. For example, a company might have an attendance policy outlining the required steps or actions an employee must take if requesting time off due to illness. The policy can describe the standards of expected employee behavior.

- *Procedures*: Procedures are step-by-step instructions on how to perform specific tasks. For example, a procedure might detail how to assemble a product.

- *Rules*: Rules are specific regulations that employees must follow. For example, a rule might require employees to wear safety gear in certain areas of the workplace.

> A policy establishes the rule, while the procedure explains the specific steps needed to comply with the rule.

Technology plays an important role in providing operational support. An HRIS (Human Resource Information System) and other HR technology support employee relations by making communication and recordkeeping more efficient. These systems help manage employee records, track performance reviews, and store important documents, which in turn, help employers stay in compliance with the multiple recordkeeping requirements of various labor laws. Most employee-related documents must be both secure and accessible on demand.

HR technology helps to facilitate employee feedback through surveys and other mechanisms. This helps HR understand employee concerns and improve job satisfaction. By streamlining tasks like scheduling and benefits management, HRIS also reduces the administrative burdens, enabling HR to focus on the more important and strategic employee relations activities.

Employee self-service (ESS) is a feature of an HRIS that lets workers handle many of their own HR tasks online. Using a computer or smartphone, employees can update personal information, view paychecks, request time off, and check benefits. This saves time for both employees and HR staff, making processes more convenient and on-demand.

Workforce Management

Workforce management is about organizing and taking care of employees from the time they join a company until they leave. These stages are known as the *employee lifecycle*. The functions of an HR department are often organized around this lifecycle, such as recruiting, performance management, and separation. HR professionals support team members in ways that help employees achieve organizational results. Here is a brief overview of workforce management at each phase of the employee lifecycle:

- **Staffing:** During the staffing stage of the employee lifecycle, HR supports individuals by ensuring fair recruitment and selection, and properly communicates the status of applications to interested candidates.

> **NOTE**
>
> In recruitment, "ghosting" is when a company suddenly stops responding to a job candidate without any explanation, leaving the candidate unsure if they are still being considered for the job. It is true that employers may receive 1000s of applicants for an open position and, thus, cannot possibly personally respond to each one. However, especially for candidates who have gone through multiple rounds of interviews, it is important that HR balance the need for efficiency with respect for the candidate's time and effort. Never forget the "human" in human resources. Additionally, many company review platforms such as Glassdoor have the ability for candidates to offer feedback and rate the interview process. Negative ratings can reduce the potential applicant pool.

- **Onboarding:** During the onboarding phase of the employee lifecycle, HR supports new team members by helping them get comfortable with their new job, introducing them to coworkers, and helping coordinate any training the new hire needs to succeed.
- **Engagement:** During the engagement phase of the employee life cycle, HR supports team members by encouraging their involvement and commitment through regular feedback, team activities, and recognition of their hard work.
- **Performance management:** During the performance management stage of the employee lifecycle, the HR team supports employees by providing regular feedback, setting clear goals, and helping them improve their skills to succeed in their role.
- **Offboarding:** During the offboarding stage of the employee lifecycle, the HR team supports employees by ensuring all paperwork is completed and that the exit experience leaves employees feeling supported.

> **NOTE**
>
> A boomerang employee is someone who leaves a company and later returns to work there again. Post-pandemic, nearly 20% of global workers returned to their former employer.[4]

Figure 5.5 shows a few of the workforce trends HR will need to prepare for in the next several years.

---

[4] Nair, D. (2024). Are you a coffee-badging boomerang employee? Workplace trends for 2024. The National [online]. Available at: https://www.thenationalnews.com/business/money/2024/02/12/what-are-the-15-workplace-trends-set-to-dominate-2024/

FIGURE 5.5　Workplace trends

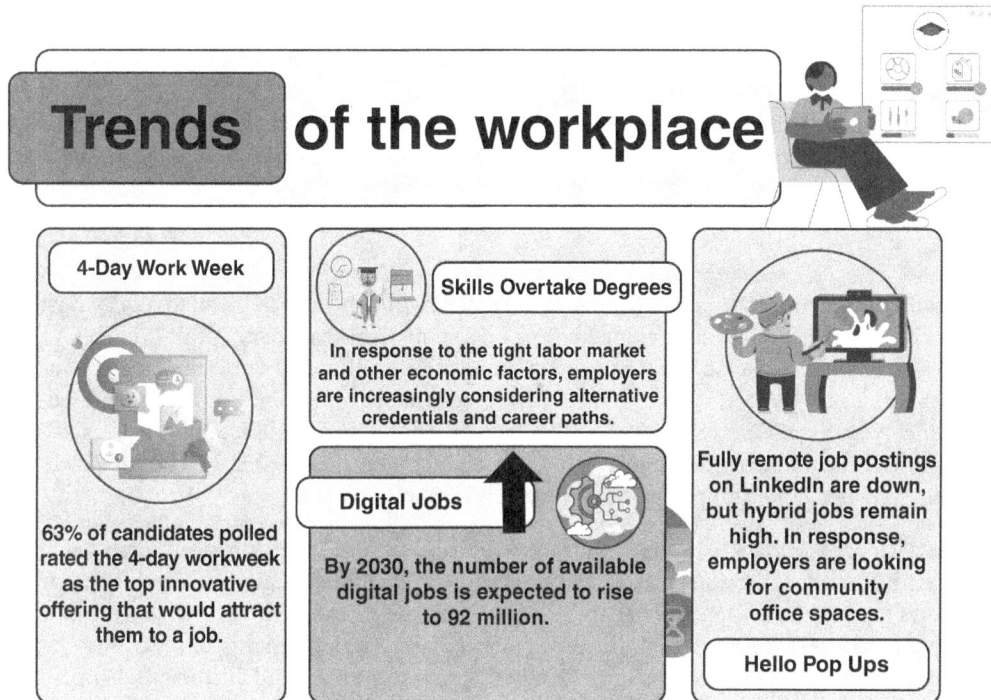

Trends of the workplace

4-Day Work Week

63% of candidates polled rated the 4-day workweek as the top innovative offering that would attract them to a job.

Skills Overtake Degrees

In response to the tight labor market and other economic factors, employers are increasingly considering alternative credentials and career paths.

Digital Jobs

By 2030, the number of available digital jobs is expected to rise to 92 million.

Fully remote job postings on LinkedIn are down, but hybrid jobs remain high. In response, employers are looking for community office spaces.

Hello Pop Ups

Source: The National News
https://www.thenationalnews.com/business/money/2024/02/12/what-are-the-15-workplace-trends-set-to-dominate-2024/

Performance Management

Part of the role of an HR business partner is to support the performance of the company and the employee. Supporting organizational performance comes through understanding the business strategy and designing the work of an HR department to support those outcomes. This was discussed at the beginning of the chapter.

HR plays a vital role in managing employee performance through the performance management process. The performance management process is a way to help employees do their best work and achieve their goals. It begins by employees and their managers setting realistic goals. Ideally, these goals should be specific, measurable, achievable, relevant, and time-bound (SMART). Setting *SMART goals* helps employees know what is expected of them and gives them something to work toward. It also helps the managers provide meaningful feedback at regular intervals to help team members be successful.

Benchmarking is another concept to understand in the context of employee performance management. Benchmarking involves comparing an employee's performance to a standard or to the performance of others in similar roles. This helps to understand how well someone is doing and identify areas where they can improve. For example, a sales team might compare their sales numbers to the industry average.

The most common understanding of the performance management process is the delivery of performance reviews, also called appraisals. *Performance appraisals* are regular reviews of how well employees are meeting their goals.

Several types of performance appraisal processes and techniques are commonly used in organizations:

Rating Scale Method   The rating scale method involves evaluating employees against a set of predefined criteria or competencies on a numerical scale (e.g., 1 to 5). These criteria may include job knowledge, communication skills, teamwork, punctuality, and other relevant factors. Each criterion is rated separately, and the ratings are then used to provide an overall performance score. This method is simple to use, allows for easy comparison, and provides quantitative data for decision-making but can be subjective and may not fully capture qualitative aspects of performance.

360-degree Feedback   In the 360-degree feedback method, performance is assessed based on feedback gathered from multiple sources, including supervisors, peers, subordinates, and even customers. This holistic approach provides a comprehensive view of an employee's performance from different perspectives, offering insights into various competencies, such as leadership, teamwork, communication, and customer service. While this method is thorough and encourages self-awareness and development, it can be time-consuming to administer and may result in conflicting feedback that needs careful interpretation.

Management by Objectives (MBO)   Management by objectives involves setting SMART goals collaboratively between employees and their managers. Each employee's performance is then evaluated based on the achievement of these agreed-upon objectives. This method promotes goal alignment between individual and organizational goals and encourages employee engagement and motivation by involving them in the goal-setting process. However, it can be less effective if objectives are not clearly defined, measurable, or if there is a lack of follow-up.

Behaviorally Anchored Rating Scales (BARS)   Behaviorally anchored rating scales (BARS) combine elements of the rating scale method with behavioral examples to evaluate performance. BARS provides specific behavioral examples for each level of performance (e.g., from "excellent" to "unsatisfactory") related to a particular job dimension. This method aims to reduce subjectivity by providing clear standards and examples of what constitutes different levels of performance. While BARS can increase accuracy and fairness in the appraisal process, it can be complex to develop and may require considerable time and resources.

Likert Scale   The Likert scale is a method where employees are rated on different aspects of their job performance using a scale, like 1 to 5, where 1 means "strongly disagree" and 5 means "strongly agree." For example, an employee might be rated a 4 on teamwork, indicating they mostly agree that they work well with others.

Forced Ranking   Ranking involves listing employees from best to worst based on their performance, comparing each employee directly to others. For example, in a sales team, the employee with the highest sales might be ranked first, while the one with the lowest sales is ranked last.

Self-evaluation   In self-evaluation, employees assess their own performance, reflecting on their strengths, weaknesses, and achievements. For example, an employee might note they have improved their customer service skills but need to work on meeting deadlines.

Peer Review   Peer review is when employees evaluate each other's performance, giving feedback based on their experiences working together. For example, a team member might praise a colleague for being very reliable but suggest they work on their communication skills.

There are several challenges to the performance appraisal process. Many supervisors and employees report dissatisfaction with the process, as the frequency of an appraisal—typically once a year—is not enough to have a significant impact on employee behaviors. This means they simply "go through the motions," checking the appraisal off a to-do list rather than using it to positively support employee performance. Employees often see reviews as a necessary evil to get through in order to get a pay increase. HR can help mitigate these challenges by increasing the frequency of an appraisal to quarterly or helping to design an informal feedback system that allows for more real-time feedback.

Biases are another challenge HR needs to address. *Biases* are unfair preferences or prejudices that can affect performance appraisals. The different types of performance appraisal bias are the same as the rater biases that can occur during the hiring process:

- **Recency bias:** focusing too much on recent events rather than the entire review period.
- **Halo effect:** letting one positive aspect of performance influence overall evaluation.
- **Horn effect:** letting one negative aspect of performance overshadow everything else.
- **Leniency (or severity) bias:** rater consistently gives higher (or lower) than deserved ratings to all employees
- **Similarity bias:** also referred to as "like-me," favors employees who are of similar background, personality, interest, or values of the rater.

HR can address these biases by training raters on the different types of biases, and building appraisals that are designed to accurately measure work behaviors.

Employee Discipline

Effective employee disciplinary processes are a critical component of effective human resource management. Employee disciplinary issues typically focus on three main areas: attendance, conduct, and performance. Attendance issues, such as frequent tardiness or unapproved absences, can disrupt workflow and productivity, negatively impacting team morale and overall organizational effectiveness. Conduct issues, including inappropriate behavior, harassment, or breaches of workplace policies, can create a hostile work environment and expose the organization to legal risks. Performance issues, such as failure to meet job expectations or consistently low productivity, can affect the quality of work and reduce the organization's ability to meet its goals. When employees are underperforming in any of these areas, it is often necessary to take disciplinary action. The good news is that there are two routes for discipline HR can support, and they are positive discipline and progressive discipline.

Positive discipline techniques are designed to support employees in improving their performance and behavior by focusing on constructive feedback and encouragement instead of punishment. Constructive feedback consists of three main components. First, it involves specificity, where the feedback clearly describes the behavior or issue with concrete examples. Second, it includes positivity by highlighting the employee's strengths and offering praise along with areas for improvement. Finally, constructive feedback provides actionable suggestions, giving practical advice on how to improve and supporting the employee in making those changes.

Supporting employees through positive discipline techniques often is done through coaching and mentoring. This involves guiding employees to recognize their strengths and areas for improvement in a way that leverages their strengths and either improves or mitigates their weaknesses. For example, a manager might work closely with an employee to set clear performance goals each week and provide regular feedback on their progress. Mentoring can also include sharing experiences and offering advice to help employees develop their skills and confidence. By focusing on growth and development rather than punishment, positive discipline helps create a supportive work environment where employees feel valued and motivated to improve.

Progressive discipline is a method of consequences used to address employee behavior and performance issues in a step-by-step manner. It usually starts with a verbal warning to let the employee know about the problem. If the behavior continues, a written warning follows, outlining the issue and the expected changes. For example, if an employee is consistently late, they might first get a verbal warning, and if the tardiness continues, they receive a written warning. If the problem still isn't fixed, more serious actions, like suspension or even dismissal, might be taken.

The concept of progressive discipline is important because it ensures that employees are aware of their behavior or performance issues and are given ample opportunity to improve. By documenting each step of the disciplinary process, organizations can protect themselves from potential legal claims of unfair treatment or discrimination. It also promotes a culture of accountability and responsibility, encouraging employees to take ownership of their behavior and performance.

At-will employment means that an employee can be fired at any time for any reason (except illegal ones), and the employee can also leave the job at any time, without notice. Progressive discipline can erode at-will employment because it creates a process that needs to be followed before an employee can be fired. For example, if a company has a progressive discipline policy, they might need to give several warnings before they can let an employee go. This process can make it harder for the company to fire someone immediately, even if at-will employment would normally allow it.

Both positive and progressive discipline techniques should ultimately be designed to support employee success and retention; however, in some cases, involuntary dismissal is the only or the best option.

Organizational Culture

Organizational culture shapes how employees interact and work together. A positive culture with strong values and open communication can make employees feel valued and more connected, while a negative culture can lead to misunderstandings and low morale.

The field of industrial-organizational (I-O) psychology exists to study the relationship between people and the workplace. One of the most studied phenomena is the relationship between company culture and job satisfaction. Researchers in the I-O field analyze how organizational culture influences employee attitudes, behaviors, and overall well-being. They explore factors such as leadership styles, communication patterns, and organizational policies to understand their impact on job satisfaction. By identifying these relationships, I-O psychologists can develop strategies that enhance positive outcomes for the employer and the employee. For example, a company with a strong culture of innovation might encourage employees to share new ideas and reward creative solutions, while a company that values customer service might focus on training employees to provide excellent support and care to customers.

A company's culture is defined by much more than the physical environment where the work is done. Culture is defined by the relationships and behaviors of both the employer and the employee.

Employer Behaviors

How an employer behaves is an important consideration in how employees feel about their work. Companies that are perceived to be unethical, for example, are likely to have more turnover than companies who act with transparency. Additionally, a company's culture is shaped significantly by the actions and attitudes of its leaders. For example, a leader who fails to provide meaningful feedback may contribute to a culture of disengagement and low morale. Several tools are available that can help guide employer behaviors.

Code of Ethics   A company code of ethics is a written guide to help govern human behavior in the workplace. This code shapes how decisions are made by setting rules for what is right and wrong. For example, if the code requires leaders to act with integrity, managers will be encouraged to be honest and transparent in their decisions and interactions.

Board of Directors   *Publicly traded companies* are those that are owned by stockholders. These stockholders obtain equity by purchasing shares of ownership, which can then be traded on the US stock market. For publicly traded companies, a *board of directors (BOD)* acts as oversight of the company's decision-making and represents the company's shareholders. The BOD set the company's direction and strategy, monitor financial health, and oversee audits. The board hires and evaluates the CEO and should enforce ethical behavior and compliance with laws. The board is responsible for protecting shareholders' interests and works to increase the company's value.

State and Federal Laws   US labor laws are rules set by the government to protect workers and ensure fair treatment in the workplace. These laws cover various aspects of employment, such as wages, working hours, and safety conditions.

Anti-discrimination laws exist to prohibit employers from treating employees unfairly based on race, gender, religion, or other protected characteristics. For example, it is unlawful to refuse to hire or promote someone based on their gender or ethnicity.

States have their own employment laws that employers must follow. HR should learn and follow the rules of the states where they have employees, including remote workers, adjusting company policies to meet the stricter standards when laws differ. One example of this is with minimum wage laws. The federal minimum wage is $7.25 per hour, but many states have set higher minimum wages. For instance, California's minimum wage is $15.00 per hour (2024), which employers in California must pay even though it's higher than the federal rate.

For the aPHR exam, you will be tested only on federal laws where applicable.

Employee Behaviors

Company culture is also influenced by how employees act and interact with each other every day. When employees are friendly, supportive, and work well together, it creates a positive workplace. If, however, employees are negative or disrespectful, it can lead to a toxic work environment. Several tools are available to help set employee behavior expectations.

Employee Handbook   The *employee handbook* is a guide that explains the rules, policies, and expectations of the company. It covers important topics like work hours, dress code, benefits, and workplace behavior. This handbook helps employees understand what is expected of them and what they can expect from the company.

Anti-discrimination Policies   *Anti-discrimination policies* ensure that everyone is treated fairly and equally at work. These policies prevent discrimination based on race, gender, age, religion, disability, or any other non-job-related characteristic. By following these policies, the company creates a respectful and inclusive environment where everyone feels valued.

Standard Operating Procedures   *Standard operating procedures (SOPs)* are detailed instructions on how to complete tasks and duties correctly. These procedures help ensure that everyone does their job in the same way, which makes work more efficient and consistent. Following SOPs helps prevent mistakes and keeps operations running smoothly.

Safety Code of Conduct   A *safety code of conduct* includes rules and guidelines to keep everyone safe at work. It explains how to use equipment properly, what to do in emergencies, and how to maintain a safe workspace. By following these safety rules, the company can prevent accidents and keep employees healthy and secure.

A simple way to understand how company culture is created is by looking at what behaviors an employer rewards and what behaviors get disciplined. For example, if a company consistently rewards teamwork and collaboration with bonuses and recognition, employees are likely to adopt these behaviors. Conversely, if an employer rewards alliances and politics, these behaviors are likely to increase.

Diversity, Equity, and Inclusion (DEI)

Laws prohibiting discriminatory treatment based on protected class characteristics such as age, race, and gender have been in effect since the 1960s. More recently, laws have been passed protecting the rights of the LGBTQ+ communities, attempting to afford this group the same protections offered to other underrepresented individuals in the workplace. However, as with many labor laws, regulations are not enough. Employers should engage in strategic initiatives to ensure that their workplaces are diverse and inclusive. The main purpose of DEI initiatives is to create within the organizational culture a sense of belonging and inclusion to a diverse group of employees.

Diversity means having a mix of people from different backgrounds, including race, gender, age, and abilities. *Equity* refers to fairness or justice in the way people are treated and especially freedom from bias or favoritism, while *inclusion* means creating an environment where all employees feel valued and respected. Together, DEI aims to build a workplace where everyone can thrive and contribute their best.

There are many benefits of DEI initiatives for the employer and the employee. DEI efforts can boost productivity and effectiveness by bringing in different ideas, improving employee happiness, and encouraging creativity. Companies that embrace DEI report employees that are more satisfied and, thus, stay with their companies longer.

Implementing DEI begins by building strategic (planned) diversity initiatives. For example, a company might implement a diversity hiring program to ensure a wide range of candidates from various backgrounds are considered for job openings or establish mentorship programs that support underrepresented groups, helping them to grow and succeed within the organization.

Managing DEI includes gathering feedback from affected groups to measure the effect of DEI efforts. When the feedback is negative, HR intervenes to help solve the issue(s). For example, HR can train employees on the concept of cultural sensitivity. *Cultural sensitivity* is understanding and respecting the differences between various cultures. It means being aware of how people's backgrounds, traditions, and values might be different from others. For example, a company could recognize and respect different religious holidays. If an employee needs time off to celebrate a holiday that isn't widely observed, the company allows them to take the day off. This shows respect for the employee's cultural and religious practices.

There are a few challenges to implementing and managing DEI initiatives in the workplace. One challenge is resistance to change, where some employees might be uncomfortable with new policies or feel threatened by a new practice such as using preferred gender pronouns. Another challenge is unconscious bias, where people might have hidden prejudices that unknowingly affect their decisions and interactions. *Stereotypes* are oversimplified and fixed ideas about a group of people that can lead to unfair assumptions and judgments and can also be a challenge in managing DEI goals. Lack of understanding and training can make it hard for employees to fully embrace DEI principles.

The *diversity tax* is a situation where, in addition to their regular responsibilities, diverse individuals are put in charge of diversity initiatives. This means, for example, that a woman of color is actually penalized because she is expected to take on more work to drive DEI outcomes. HR should be aware of these challenges and take active steps to advocate and problem-solve to ensure the success and reap the benefits of a diverse and equal place of work.

Corporate Social Responsibility (CSR)

Another aspect of a company's culture is the strategic initiative of corporate social responsibility (CSR), which is when companies act ethically and contribute to economic development while improving the quality of life for their employees, communities, and the environment. It continues to grow in importance as the market continues to encourage companies to take a view of the global community and enter a social compact to promote social justice and protect the environment.

The three Ps—people, profit, and planet—represent a balanced approach to business using CSR initiatives to have a positive effect:

- **People:** Focus on treating employees and communities well, ensuring fair labor practices, and supporting social causes.
- **Profit:** Achieve financial success and sustainability, ensuring the business can grow and thrive.
- **Planet:** Protect the environment through sustainable practices, reducing waste, and minimizing the company's ecological footprint.

Balancing these three aspects helps businesses operate responsibly and successfully.

Case Study

The following are real-world examples of CSR:

- **Starbucks:** Starbucks focuses on ethical sourcing of its coffee beans, ensuring fair trade practices, and investing in sustainable farming methods to support coffee farmers and the environment.

- **TOMS Shoes:** TOMS Shoes operates on a "one-for-one" model, donating a pair of shoes to a child in need for every pair sold. They also support clean water, eye care, and safe birth initiatives.

- **Patagonia:** Patagonia is known for its commitment to environmental sustainability, using recycled materials in its products and donating a portion of its profits to environmental causes.

- **Ben & Jerry's:** Ben & Jerry's actively supports social justice causes, fair trade practices, and environmental sustainability, ensuring its business practices align with its values.

These companies integrate CSR into their operations to make a positive impact on society and the environment.

Employee Engagement

Employee engagement is about how connected and committed employees feel toward their work and their organization. Engaged employees are enthusiastic, motivated, and more likely to go above and beyond in their roles.

Studies show that companies with high employee engagement are more profitable and productive. According to Gallup, highly engaged teams see a 21% increase in profitability and a 17% boost in productivity compared to less engaged teams. Organizations with engaged employees experience 41% lower absenteeism and 59% less turnover, which saves money on hiring and training new staff.

Here are some examples of how to increase employee engagement based on findings from I-O psychology:

- **Provide regular feedback:** Giving employees consistent and constructive feedback helps them understand their performance and how they can improve, which boosts their engagement and motivation.

- **Offer professional development:** Opportunities for training and career advancement make employees feel valued and invested in their work, increasing their commitment to the organization.

- **Survey employees:** Engagement surveys are tools used by organizations to measure how engaged and satisfied employees are with their work and the workplace. These surveys often include questions about job satisfaction, company culture, management practices, and overall morale. The results help companies identify areas for improvement and develop strategies to boost engagement.

- **Create a positive work environment:** Creating a supportive and inclusive workplace culture encourages employees to feel comfortable and engaged. This includes recognizing achievements and promoting teamwork.

- **Empower employees:** Allowing employees to have a say in decision-making and giving them more autonomy in their roles can increase their sense of ownership and engagement.

- **Ensure work-life balance:** Supporting employees in balancing their work and personal lives, such as through flexible working hours or remote work options, helps reduce stress and improve overall job satisfaction and engagement.

- **Offer alternative work arrangements:** Alternative work arrangements are different ways of working that are not the usual 9-to-5 office job. Examples include working from home, flexible hours, part-time work, job sharing, and compressed workweeks. These arrangements can help employees balance their work and personal lives better.

Job Satisfaction

Employee satisfaction refers to how content and happy employees are with their jobs. High employee satisfaction typically leads to increased engagement. HR can watch for several markers that suggest employees have low job satisfaction and engagement.

For example, *absenteeism* is when employees frequently stay away from work without valid reasons. High absenteeism can be a sign of underlying issues such as job dissatisfaction, health or other personal challenges, or poor work-life balance. It negatively impacts productivity and can increase the workload on other employees.

Quiet quitting is when employees do the minimum required work at their job without putting in extra effort or time. Quiet quitting often shows that employees are not happy with their job and no longer feel motivated to go above and beyond their basic duties.

Turnover refers to the rate at which employees leave a company and are replaced by new hires. High turnover can be costly and disruptive. *Retention*, on the other hand, focuses on keeping employees within the organization for longer periods. Effective retention strategies include providing competitive benefits, career development opportunities, and a positive work environment.

HR professionals can sometimes conduct *stay interviews* when engaging employees to determine whether they intend to seek employment elsewhere or to determine their current job satisfaction level. This type of interview asks what the employee likes about their job, the company, their supervisor, and what could be done better to improve their working conditions. The intent is to determine the reasons employees may be considering leaving an organization before they have made a decision to do so in an effort to reduce turnover. An *exit interview* is conducted when an employee has already been given their notice to leave the organization and are offered an opportunity to provide critical feedback about the working environment.

Employee recognition programs are initiatives designed to acknowledge and reward employees for their hard work and achievements. These programs can include formal awards, public recognition, bonuses, and other incentives. Recognizing employees helps boost morale, motivation, and loyalty, which in turn increases engagement and job satisfaction.

Alternative work arrangements

Alternative work arrangements are different ways of working that are not the usual 9-to-5 office job. Examples include the following:

- *Work from home (WFH):* Also known as remote work, employees do their job from their home instead of coming into the office, using technology to stay connected.

- *Flexible hours*: Employees have the freedom to choose their start and end times within certain limits, allowing them to work when they're most productive.

- *Part-time work*: Employees work fewer hours than a full-time schedule, often to balance other commitments like school or family.

- *Job sharing*: Two employees split the responsibilities and hours of one full-time job, each working part of the week.

- *Compressed workweeks*: Employees work their usual number of hours in fewer days, such as four 10-hour days instead of five 8-hour days, giving them an extra day off.

- *Hybrid work*: Employees split their time between working from the office and working from home, offering flexibility and a balance between remote and in-person work.

- *Hybrid at-will*: Employees have the option to choose when they work from home and when they come into the office, based on their personal and professional needs, without a fixed schedule.

These arrangements can help employees balance their work and personal lives better.

Disengaged Workers

Employees can become unhappy for several reasons. They might feel undervalued if their hard work is not recognized or rewarded. Poor communication or lack of support from managers can also lead to frustration. If the work environment is stressful or if there are conflicts with coworkers, it can make the job unpleasant. For the young professional, lack of professional development opportunities directly correlates (relates to) discouragement.

Employee complaints are when workers express concerns or issues they have at work. These can include problems with coworkers, managers, or working conditions. Addressing complaints quickly and fairly is important to maintain a positive work environment. One way to do this is to conduct formal or informal investigations.

Workplace Investigations

Formal investigations happen when a company looks into a serious complaint or issue to find out what really happened. This involves gathering facts, talking to witnesses, and reviewing evidence to ensure the situation is handled correctly and fairly. Informal investigations can occur for less serious complaints, although it is still important to focus on the facts and communicate as much as possible throughout the process. HR is responsible for maintaining neutrality during an investigation. This means they must be fair and unbiased, treating all parties equally and not taking sides.

Confidentiality within an investigation means keeping information private. When employees report issues or are part of an investigation, their information should be kept private to the greatest extent possible to ensure a fair process. It might not always be possible to keep information confidential during an employment investigation if the issue involves legal matters such as harassment or discrimination that require reporting to authorities. Additionally, sharing certain details might be necessary to gather all the facts and make sure all parties have the right to share their side of an issue.

Retaliation is when someone is punished for reporting a problem or participating in an investigation, and it is unlawful. Retaliation can include things like being demoted, fired, or treated unfairly. Retaliation does not need to come from management. Coworkers who create a hostile work environment that management had knowledge of or should have known as the result of an employee coming forward and participating in an investigation can also be classified as retaliation. An example would be if an employee raised a complaint against a popular boss, and in retaliation the employee's coworkers made the working conditions difficult or kept creating situations that impacted the employee's job performance in a negative manner. Companies must protect employees from retaliation to ensure they feel safe speaking up about issues. This is done by having a clearly stated policy prohibiting retaliation and training employees and managers on the policy.

Conflict Resolution

A common issue within employers of all sizes is when two or more workers don't get along. When this happens, it is important for HR to engage in conflict resolution. *Conflict resolution* is the process of solving disagreements or disputes between employees. This can involve mediation, open communication, and finding a compromise that everyone agrees on. Effective conflict resolution helps keep the workplace peaceful and productive.

In some cases, an issue cannot be resolved between the workers or between the team and their managers. When this happens, it is necessary to escalate the issue. *Escalation* is when a problem is moved up to higher levels of management because it can't be solved at the current level. This ensures that serious issues get the attention and resources needed to be resolved effectively.

Documentation

"If it isn't documented, it never happened." This HR saying underscores the critical importance of documentation in employee relations. *Documentation* is the process of recording important information about employee complaints, investigations, and resolutions. Keeping detailed records helps ensure transparency, fairness, and that procedures are followed correctly.

Employee documentation best practices involve keeping clear, accurate, and up-to-date records about employee performance, behavior, and any issues that arise. It's important to document both positive and negative aspects, using specific examples and dates. All records should be objective and factual, avoiding personal opinions.

Documentation should be kept confidential and stored securely, ensuring it's only accessible to authorized personnel. Regular updates and reviews of the documentation help keep it relevant and useful for performance evaluations and any necessary disciplinary actions.

Summary

Employee relations is an essential element of the HR function. The people in an organization are a company's most important and precious resource, and employee relations understands how employees, corporate leadership, stakeholders, and human resources interact and communicate. This interaction affects HR operations and organizational culture. Through effective employee relations, companies see positive employee engagement and more productive workers. Conversely, negative engagement leads to unhappy workers, which could increase attrition or behaviors that are inconsistent with the corporate values.

At the strategic level, companies use mission, vision, and values to communicate the company's purpose and desired end-state to their employees. Leadership will use techniques like environmental scanning and forecasting to gain an understanding about the operational environment in which the company conducts business. The political, economic, social, technological, legal, and environmental landscapes influence and impact a company's ability to operate. A company's strengths and weaknesses are the positive and negative internal capabilities, while opportunities and threats are external influences that all bear on a company's functionality.

HR conducts operations within the business structure to help manage the workforce. Using employee performance management, companies can report and track overall individual job performance over time. This tool can assist with development and productivity and provides the basis of justification for merit increases in salary and advancement through promotion. Employee discipline is used when an employee's actions or behaviors are not well aligned with the goals and efforts of the organization and should be administered so that the least amount of discipline needed to change and align proper behavior is used to affect the outcome.

Organizational culture is the norms and practices, ethical decision-making processes, and corporate and employee sentiments and attitudes toward management, between coworkers, and across the organization as a whole. How an employee behaves is an important indicator of how they feel about their work and the company. HR plays an important role in influencing how employees behave in the workplace through implementing policies and practices that promote and reward the behaviors that support the mission, vision, and values of the company. To ensure that all employees remain engaged, companies strive to maximize organizational diversity, equity, and inclusivity. To engage all stakeholders, including customers and the community, businesses must demonstrate corporate social responsibility.

Employee engagement shows how connected and committed employees feel toward their work and their organization. Engaged employees are enthusiastic, dedicated, and supportive of the company's objectives. They support the organization at a personal level and continue to demonstrate their overall commitment to the mission, vision, and values of the company. Unhappy workers conversely create conflict that must be resolved using a variety of techniques and also may generate more workplace investigations to determine the root cause of the problems. Documentation is a critical tool HR professionals use to maintain an understanding of each employee's engagement level and can show trends over time.

Exam Essentials

Understand the role strategic planning has in a company and how it relates to the mission, vision, and values the company professes.   For corporations to operate successfully in the modern market, they must set a vision and establish objectives with tasks that support the company's overall mission or reason of existence. As part of the planning process, organizational leaders will conduct environmental scans and forecasting to shape and understand the operational environment in which the strategic plans developed will be executed.

Understand how to conduct HR operations.   HR operations are the activities that HR professionals conduct that align and influence the behaviors of employees and management to successfully run the business and achieve its mission. Workforce management, performance management, and employee discipline are just some functions and tools that can be employed in the conduct of HR operations.

Understand how organizational culture is influenced by DEI and CSR initiatives.   An employee's behavior will be largely influenced by the corporate culture. How people are treated with respect and dignity will have a greater impact on operations than any other single point of influence. DEI programs show commitment by companies to a diverse workforce that feel they have a stake in the organizational outcomes and are included in the success of the company. CSR initiatives strive to the goal of maintaining a balance between profitability and environmental sustainability.

Know how to engage employees to determine their job satisfaction.   Employees cannot give to customers, coworkers, or a company what they do not already possess. HR professionals must know how to determine the sentiments and feelings of employees and how to organize information from surveys and interviews to relay to management the general feelings of employees. HR professionals must be able to understand the signs of a dissatisfied employee, such as absenteeism or quiet quitting that indicate they are unhappy at work.

Review Questions

You can find the answers in Appendix A.

1. Which HR competency is necessary to effectively manage relationships in the workplace? (Choose all that apply).

   A. Communication

   B. Conflict resolution skills

   C. Negotiation

   D. Data analysis

2. What is the primary difference between employee rights and employee responsibilities?

   A. Rights are what employees are obligated to do, while responsibilities are what they are entitled to.

   B. Rights are entitlements employees have, while responsibilities are duties they must perform.

   C. Rights are benefits provided by the employer, while responsibilities are optional tasks.

   D. Rights are guidelines for behavior, while responsibilities are legal requirements.

3. What is an effective strategy for managing conflict in the workplace?

   A. Ask the employees to try and work it out themselves first

   B. Train the supervisors to be effective conflict managers

   C. Facilitate open conversation to address the issue(s)

   D. Avoid discussions about the conflict to prevent escalation

4. Which of the following is the BEST example of a company mission statement?

   A. To provide the best customer service and improve lives through innovation.

   B. To become the global leader in our industry.

   C. Integrity, excellence, and teamwork.

   D. Our approach is centered on continuous learning and improvement.

5. Which of the following is an example of company values?

   A. Our goal is to expand to new markets and increase our customer base.

   B. Honesty, accountability, and respect for all individuals.

   C. To be the most trusted brand in our field.

   D. We believe in a work-life balance and employee well-being.

6. What is the primary purpose of employment laws in the workplace?

   A. For the government to collect payroll taxes

   B. To provide protections that collective bargaining agreements do not

    C. To increase employee retention through fair treatment

    D. To protect the rights of workers

7. Which of the following is an example of a political factor in a PESTLE audit?

    A. Electing a new president

    B. Advances in artificial intelligence

    C. An increase in the aging population

    D. A shift in consumer fashion trends

8. In a PESTLE audit, which factors would include the impact of climate change on a business? (Choose all that apply.)

    A. Social

    B. Economic

    C. Environmental

    D. Legal

9. Which of the following is an example of an opportunity in a SWOT audit?

    A. Employees gaining new skills

    B. Implementing new customer service management software

    C. A competitor being bought out

    D. An economic recession

10. The company you work for has begun to analyze market trends to determine how many employees you will need to hire to meet customer demand. This is the best example of which of the following strategic activities?

    A. Benchmarking

    B. Sensing

    C. Analyzing

    D. Forecasting

11. Which of the following decision-making methods involves getting opinions from a group of experts until consensus is reached?

    A. Scenario planning

    B. Trend analysis

    C. Delphi method

    D. Consensus building

12. What are the primary differences between a hierarchical and matrix organizational structure?

    A. Hierarchical structures have multiple leaders, while matrix structures have a single leader.

    B. Hierarchical structures focus on team collaboration, while matrix structures emphasize individual performance.

C. Hierarchical structures have a clear chain of command with one manager per employee, while matrix structures involve employees reporting to multiple managers.

D. Hierarchical structures are more flexible, while matrix structures are more rigid.

13. What is the primary difference among a policy, procedure, and rule?

A. A policy provides general guidelines, a procedure outlines specific steps, and a rule mandates strict requirements.

B. A policy mandates strict requirements, a procedure provides general guidelines, and a rule outlines specific steps.

C. A policy outlines specific steps, a procedure mandates strict requirements, and a rule provides general guidelines.

D. A policy and a rule are the same, while a procedure focuses on how work gets done.

14. Which of the following human resource activities are appropriate for employee self-service systems? (Choose all that apply.)

A. Updating personal contact information

B. Submitting a grievance

C. Conducting a self-appraisal

D. Viewing pay stubs and tax documents

15. What is the primary difference between positive and progressive discipline?

A. Positive discipline focuses on punishment, while progressive discipline focuses on immediate dismissal.

B. Positive discipline aims to correct behavior through encouragement, while progressive discipline involves escalating consequences.

C. Positive discipline is used for minor policy violations, while progressive discipline is used for major policy violations.

D. Positive discipline is not legally defensible, while progressive discipline is.

16. If a company wants to improve the effectiveness of its performance review process, which of the following should you recommend? (Choose all that apply.)

A. Increase the frequency of feedback

B. Avoid rater biases

C. Train supervisors and managers on how to deliver meaningful feedback

D. Replace the annual review with monthly feedback

17. Which of the following is a challenge to the performance appraisal process? (Choose all that apply.)

A. Lack of meaningful feedback

B. Unsatisfying pay increases

C. Frequency

D. Supervisor favoritism

18. What is rater bias in the context of performance appraisals?

   A. A method to improve employee skills

   B. A tendency to rate employees based on personal feelings rather than objective criteria

   C. A tool for measuring employee satisfaction

   D. A method for giving employee feedback

19. Which of the following techniques to improve company culture is within the scope of HR operations?

   A. Managing the performance review process

   B. Conducting wage surveys

   C. Reducing toxic workplace behaviors

   D. Integrating HR technology such as employee self-service

20. What is the primary difference between diversity and equity in the workplace?

   A. Diversity focuses on making sure everyone feels included, while equity focuses on equal opportunity.

   B. Diversity aims to reduce workplace harassment, while equity aims to increase opportunities for underrepresented groups.

   C. Diversity involves CRS, while equity involves compliance with nondiscrimination law.

   D. Diversity refers to having a variety of backgrounds and perspectives, while equity ensures fair treatment and opportunities for all employees.

aPHR Compliance and Risk Management

---

aPHR EXAM OBJECTIVES COVERED IN THIS CHAPTER REQUIRE KNOWLEDGE RELATED TO FUNCTIONAL AREA 05, COMPLIANCE AND RISK MANAGEMENT:

✓ 05-01 Applicable laws and regulations related to talent acquisition, training, and employee/employer rights and responsibilities; such as nondiscrimination, accommodation, and work authorization (for example: EEOC, DOL, I-9 form completion, employment-at-will, Title VI, ADA, Immigration Reform and Control Act, Title 17 [Copyright law])

✓ 05-02 Applicable laws, regulations, and legal processes affecting employment in union environments (for example, WARN Act, NLRA, collective bargaining, and alternative dispute resolution methods)

✓ 05-03 Applicable laws and regulations related to compensation and benefits, such as monetary and non-monetary entitlement, wage and hour (for example: ERISA, COBRA, FLSA, USERRA, PPACA, and tax treatment)

✓ 05-04 Applicable laws and regulations related to workplace health, safety, security, and privacy (for example: OSHA, Drug-Free Workplace Act, ADA, HIPAA, Sarbanes-Oxley Act, WARN act, and sexual harassment)

✓ 05-05 Risk assessment and mitigation techniques to promote a safe, secure, and compliant workplace (for example, emergency evacuation procedures, violence, business continuity plan, intellectual and employee data protection, and theft)

✓ 05-06 Organizational restructuring initiatives and their risks to business continuity (mergers, acquisitions, divestitures, integration, offshoring, downsizing and furloughs)

Functional area 05, Compliance and Risk Management, accounts for 25% of the aPHR exam. HRCI summarizes this exam content as "complying with laws, regulations and policies, and educating stakeholders in order to identify, mitigate, and respond to organizational risk. Awareness of records management, storage, and retention regulation and reporting requirements."

HR Done Wrong

The Boeing Aircraft Company is one of the oldest and most familiar airline manufacturers in the world. It has existed since before World War I, well over 100 years ago. It boasts military and civilian commercial aircraft that are readily identifiable to the average person. Today its production facilities manufacture, among other items, large commercial passenger aircraft including one of its bestselling models, the 737 Max 8.

However, two crashes in 2018 and 2019 resulted in the deaths of nearly 350 people in just a few months' time. The highly publicized crashes resulted in discoveries of systemic failures in compliance and safety procedures, which led to an agreement with the US Department of Justice to avoid lengthy and costly legal battles. Among the conditions, in addition to the $2.5 billion penalty, was an agreement to include more software and training improvements and to add individuals on the corporate board with experience in aircraft operations and especially aircraft safety. Shareholders in 2021 also settled for $237.5 million dollars for the loss of share price and damage to the company's reputation that resulted in losses exceeding $20 billion.

In 2024, the Justice Department claimed that Boeing was in violation of the agreement and in its communications with the federal court stated, that Boeing had failed to "design, implement and enforce" a compliance and ethics program to prevent and detect violations of US fraud laws in the company's operations." This decision came after a door "plug" was blown out during flight of an Alaska Airlines aircraft in January and a subsequent follow up. This time, there is also the added possibility of criminal penalties for board members in addition to all the civil litigation. Victims' families of all the accidents are seeking punitive damages to the maximum of $24 billion calling it the "deadliest corporate crime in US history."

As HR professionals, training, ethics, compliance, and risk management are all areas of profound importance to keep companies and corporate leadership from legal jeopardy. Having a resolute attitude toward the requirement of a strong compliance and risk management program is the foundation of ethical business practices and the safety and well-being of employees and consumers.[1]

---

[1] Valinsky, J. (2024). Boeing committed 'the deadliest corporate crime in US history' and should be fined $24 billion, victims' families say. *CNN Business*. Available at: `https://www.cnn.com/2024/06/19/business/boeing-families-lawsuit/index.html`

Compliance and Risk Management Defined

Compliance and risk management in entry-level HR involve ensuring that the company follows all the laws and regulations related to employees and their work. This means paying close attention to various aspects of the workplace to create a safe, fair, and lawful environment.

Compliance is first about adhering to the rules that govern the workplace. This includes following labor laws to ensure fair wages, safe working conditions, and proper working hours. It also means avoiding discrimination by making sure no one is treated unfairly because of their race, gender, religion, or other protected characteristics. Proper documentation is crucial, so HR must keep accurate records during the entire employee lifecycle from I-9s during hiring, benefits, performance documentation and post-termination COBRA paperwork in the United States. Additionally, compliance involves educating employees about company policies and procedures, ensuring everyone knows and follows the rules.

Risk management is about identifying and addressing potential problems that could harm the company or its employees. The roles for HR include identifying, assessing, and mitigating risks that could impact employee well-being, organizational compliance, and overall business operations. HR professionals play a key role in developing policies to manage the risks associated with workplace safety, employee relations, legal compliance, and organizational culture. This involves preventing workplace issues by creating a safe and respectful work environment to avoid accidents and conflicts. Handling employee complaints efficiently is essential, as listening to and resolving concerns quickly can prevent bigger problems from arising. Legal compliance plays a significant role in risk management, requiring HR to stay up to date with laws and regulations to avoid fines or lawsuits. Protecting company information is also critical, ensuring that confidential employee data are secure and not misused.

For someone in an entry-level HR position, compliance and risk management mean paying close attention to details, being aware of the laws, and helping to make the workplace safe and fair for everyone. This role requires diligence and a commitment to maintaining a lawful and positive work environment. It's worth mentioning here that sometimes being the voice of compliance also means having to speak truth to power. Some areas of compliance are complex and tedious to rigorously follow. For some managers, the urge to find shortcuts can drive decisions that have limited short-term outcomes that have really serious negative long-term consequences. It is always important to present facts and information about associated risks so leaders can make informed decisions.

Following is a list of a few key terms to be familiar with regarding this functional area of human resources:

- *Organizational restructuring*: Organizational restructuring is the process of changing a company's structure, which can include mergers, downsizing, or shifting departments to improve efficiency or reduce costs.

- *Alternative dispute resolution*: Alternative dispute resolution is a method of solving conflicts outside of court through processes like mediation or arbitration.

- *Immigration*: Immigration refers to the movement of individuals into a country to live or work, which requires legal authorization for employment.

- *Employer rights and responsibilities*: Employer rights and responsibilities include the authority to hire, fire, and manage employees while ensuring compliance with labor laws, providing a safe workplace, and treating employees fairly.

- *Employee rights and responsibilities*: Employee rights and responsibilities include the right to fair treatment, safety, and pay while being responsible for performing job duties and following company policies.

- *Form I-9:* A document that employers must complete to verify an employee's identity and eligibility to work in the United States.

- *Employment-at-will*: A legal doctrine allowing employers or employees to terminate employment at any time, for any reason, unless there's a contract or law stating otherwise.

- *Collective bargaining*: The process by which employees, through their unions, negotiate with employers for better wages, benefits, and working conditions.

- *Risk assessment*: The process of identifying potential hazards in the workplace and implementing strategies to reduce or eliminate them.

- *Business continuity plan*: A strategy that ensures essential business functions can continue during or after a disaster or major disruption.

- *Mergers and acquisitions*: The combining or purchasing of companies, which can lead to changes in operations and workforce structure, posing risks to business continuity.

- *Incident reporting*: A formalized process for documenting accidents, injuries, or unsafe conditions in the workplace.

- *Risk mitigation*: The strategies and actions taken by HR to reduce or eliminate potential risks within the workplace. This could involve updating policies, conducting employee training, or implementing safety protocols to prevent legal or operational issues.

- *Compliance audit*: A risk mitigation technique that is a systematic review of an organization's adherence to regulatory guidelines, internal policies, and labor laws.

Laws and Regulations

American labor laws have evolved significantly since the late 19th century. The early labor movement, driven by poor working conditions and low wages, including the hazardous risks to children exploited for labor, led to the formation of unions and strikes. Key milestones include the Fair Labor Standards Act of 1938, which established minimum wage, regulated child labor and overtime pay, and the National Labor Relations Act of 1935, which protected workers' rights to unionize. The Civil Rights Act of 1964 addressed workplace discrimination. Over time, additional laws have been enacted to improve workplace safety, protect employee benefits, and ensure fair treatment. These include the Family and Medical Leave Act (FMLA) of 1993, which provides unpaid, job-protected leave for certain family and medical reasons, and the Affordable Care Act (ACA) of 2010, which expanded healthcare coverage and required employers to provide health insurance. These laws continue to evolve, reflecting changes in the workforce and economy. States play an important role in labor laws by setting additional regulations that can be more stringent than federal laws. They can establish their own minimum wage rates, workplace safety standards, and labor protections to address specific needs and conditions within the state. State laws must be equal to or better than their federal law equivalent. When there is a conflict between state and federal law, it is a best practice to err on the side of the employee.

Many labor laws are triggered once an employer reaches a certain size. Table 6.1 shows the employer size requirements for the major US federal labor laws, along with a brief description of the labor laws you should understand for exam success.

TABLE 6.1   Employer Size Requirements

Act	Employer Size	Description
Americans with Disabilities Act	15 or more employees	Prohibits discrimination against individuals with disabilities in employment and requires employers to provide reasonable accommodations
Family Medical Leave Act	50 or more employees within a 75 mile radius	Provides eligible employees with up to 12 weeks of unpaid, job-protected leave for family or medical reasons
Title VII of the Civil Rights Act	15 or more employees	Prohibits employment discrimination based on race, color, religion, sex, or national origin
Age Discrimination in Employment Act	20 or more employees	Protects individuals 40 years of age or older from employment discrimination based on age
Equal Pay Act	Employers of any size	Requires employers to provide equal pay to men and women performing the same job in the same workplace

(Continued)

TABLE 6.1 Employer Size Requirements (*Continued*)

Act	Employer Size	Description
Genetic Information Nondiscrimination Act	15 or more employees	Prohibits discrimination in employment based on genetic information
National Labor Relations Act	Applies to most private-sector employers, regardless of size, but excludes federal, state, and local government employees	Protects employees' rights to organize, form unions, and engage in collective bargaining
Occupational Safety and Health Act	Applies to most employers, regardless of size, with few exceptions (such as certain family-run businesses)	Ensures safe and healthy working conditions by setting and enforcing workplace safety standards
Fair Labor Standards Act	Applies to most employers, regardless of size, covering minimum wage, overtime, recordkeeping, and child labor standards	Establishes minimum wage, overtime pay, and child labor standards
Consolidated Omnibus Budget Reconciliation Act	20 or more employees	Allows employees to continue their health insurance coverage after leaving their job, under certain conditions
Pregnancy Discrimination Act	15 or more employees	Prohibits discrimination based on pregnancy, childbirth, or related medical conditions
Uniformed Services Employment Reemployment Rights Act	Applies to all employers, regardless of size, including government and private employers	Protects the employment rights of military service members upon their return from duty
Immigration Reform and Control Act	Applies to all employers, regardless of size, requiring verification of employment eligibility for all employees	Requires employers to verify the legal work eligibility of employees in the United States and prohibits hiring illegal immigrants

Act	Employer Size	Description
Employee Retirement Income Security Act	Applies to most private-sector employers, regardless of size, that offer pension and health benefit plans to their employees	Sets minimum standards for retirement and health benefit plans in private industry to protect individuals in these plans
Worker Adjustment and Retraining Notification Act	100 or more employees	Requires employers to provide advance notice to employees before large layoffs or plant closures

You can find a complete list of major American labor laws in Appendix C.

Enforcement

A federal agency is an organization established by the US government to carry out specific functions and enforce laws at the national level. These agencies operate under the authority of the executive branch of the federal government and are responsible for implementing and administering federal laws and regulations in various areas, such as healthcare, finance, environment, and, of course, labor law.

Many of these agencies are created by specific laws that define their roles and duties. For example, the Equal Employment Opportunity Commission (EEOC) was formed by the Civil Rights Act of 1964 to fight workplace discrimination. The Occupational Safety and Health Administration (OSHA), created by the Occupational Safety and Health Act of 1970, ensures safe working conditions. The Environmental Protection Agency (EPA), established by the National Environmental Policy Act of 1970, protects the environment and human health. Additionally, the Americans with Disabilities Act (ADA) gave the Department of Justice the job of enforcing laws against disability discrimination. These agencies make sure the laws they were created by are followed.

Agencies and courts serve different roles in the legal system. Agencies like the EEOC or OSHA operate with their own procedures and focus on their specific areas, such as workplace safety or discrimination. On the other hand, courts handle a wide range of legal disputes through a formal process. Criminal courts deal with cases where people are accused of crimes, and these courts can impose punishments like jail time or fines. Civil courts resolve disagreements between people or organizations, often involving money or other forms of compensation. While agencies have a limited focus, courts have the authority to hear many types of cases, including those that agencies investigate.

A workplace situation can be filed in civil court if it involves disputes over issues like discrimination, wrongful termination, or unpaid wages. The process usually involves obtaining a determination letter from the EEOC after an investigation that may or may not substantiate allegations or claims. The agency issues a "Right to Sue" letter in cases where the EEOC declines to intervene or does not have sufficient evidence to warrant federal action. Most federal regulations require that the federal agency with jurisdiction on a claim first investigate and substantiate the claim's validity. The agency may enter into a consent agreement whereby a company agrees to certain conditions. These conditions can range from fines or stipulations to a change in policies and practices, such as including mandatory training provided at the company's expense. Companies will enter into such agreements to avoid lengthy court actions and the possibility of substantial judgments. If an agency is unable to substantiate a claim or determines that no action is warranted by the agency, then they will issue the "Right to Sue" letter, giving a green light for further action in court should the plaintiff wish to pursue it. In almost all federal cases, arbitration is required prior to the start of a court case and both parties have a chance to resolve differences without further legal proceedings. The vast majority of employment cases are settled this way, well prior to any courtroom. A claim could be filed in criminal court if it involves criminal activities such as fraud, embezzlement, or workplace violence, where the accused could face criminal charges and penalties like imprisonment.

A large part of an HR team's responsibilities lies with compliance with state and federal labor laws and responding to charges filed with one of the above agencies. The aPHR exam will focus primarily on knowledge of US labor law.

Wage and Hour Laws

Fun fact! The first federal minimum wage was set at just 25 cents per hour in 1938, when the Fair Labor Standards Act (FLSA) was passed. This was a significant step in protecting workers and ensuring fair pay during the Great Depression. Wage and hour laws have evolved to provide much more worker protection than setting the minimum wage floor. These laws are designed to protect workers and ensure fair treatment in the workplace in the area of pay and benefits. Wage and hour law violations are some of the most common complaints filed with the Department of Labor. Figure 6.1 shows a few current trends in the area of wages and benefits.

Fair Labor Standards Act (FLSA)

The FLSA was passed in 1938. It was created during the Great Depression to fix problems like child labor, low wages, and long working hours. The FLSA set rules for minimum wages, overtime pay, and child labor to protect workers from being taken advantage

FIGURE 6.1 Top five wage and hour trends

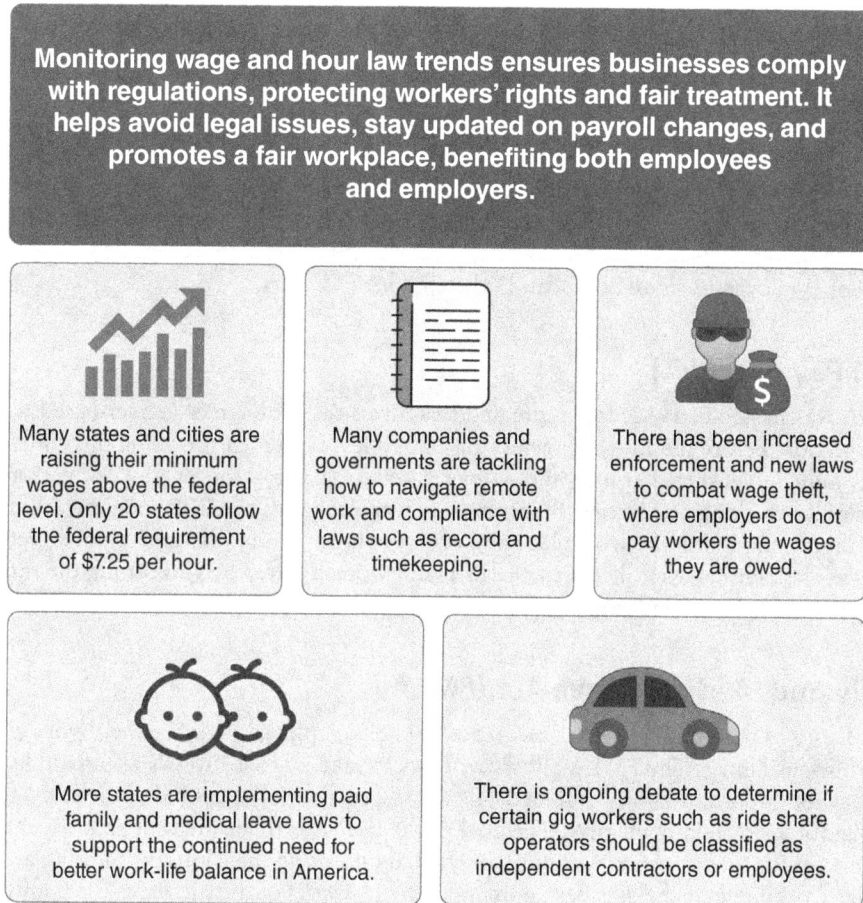

Monitoring wage and hour law trends ensures businesses comply with regulations, protecting workers' rights and fair treatment. It helps avoid legal issues, stay updated on payroll changes, and promotes a fair workplace, benefiting both employees and employers.

Many states and cities are raising their minimum wages above the federal level. Only 20 states follow the federal requirement of $7.25 per hour.

Many companies and governments are tackling how to navigate remote work and compliance with laws such as record and timekeeping.

There has been increased enforcement and new laws to combat wage theft, where employers do not pay workers the wages they are owed.

More states are implementing paid family and medical leave laws to support the continued need for better work-life balance in America.

There is ongoing debate to determine if certain gig workers such as ride share operators should be classified as independent contractors or employees.

of. It aimed to make sure workers got fair pay and had better working conditions. By doing this, the FLSA also hoped to help the economy by giving people more money to spend and reducing unemployment. This law also set the standard 40-hour work week in the United States as the baseline before overtime. During the Depression, individuals attempted to work as many hours as possible, which had a negative social impact as well. In many cases, employers were able to take advantage of the economy as there was no disincentive to regulate working hours. This led to fatigue, lower levels of productivity, and safety concerns. By setting 40 hours as the standard workweek, and by mandating overtime be 1.5 times the earned wage, a company could hire two individuals for 80 regular hours for the same cost as one individual working 60 hours, 20 of which was overtime. This put two people to work when there was an abundance of labor and fewer jobs, by encouraging employers to hire more people for the same cost. This created more productivity and allowed employees to spend more time with their families, which had positive societal impacts.

The FLSA sets the federal minimum wage at $7.25 per hour, though as of July 2024, 34 states, territories, and districts have minimum wage laws that exceed the federal mandate of $7.25 per hour. The FLSA also requires employers to pay overtime at 1.5 times the regular rate for hours worked over 40 in a week. The FLSA also has rules about child labor, limiting the hours minors can work and the types of jobs they can do. Employers must keep detailed records of employees' wages, hours, and other work conditions.

Equal Pay Act (EPA)

The EPA was passed in 1963. It was created to address the problem of gender-based wage discrimination. Before the EPA, women often earned less than men for doing the same work. The law aimed to ensure that men and women receive equal pay for equal work performed under similar working conditions. By promoting wage equality, the EPA sought to eliminate gender discrimination in the workplace and promote fairness and justice in employment practices. The EPA makes it illegal to pay men and women differently for doing the same job under similar working conditions.

Family and Medical Leave Act (FMLA)

The FMLA was passed in 1993. It was created to help employees balance their work and family responsibilities. The FMLA allows workers to take up to 12 weeks of unpaid leave each year for important family and medical reasons, such as having a baby, adopting a child, or caring for a sick family member. The goal of the FMLA is to ensure that employees can take time off for these reasons without worrying about losing their jobs, promoting a healthier work-life balance. Besides allowing up to 12 weeks of unpaid leave for family and medical reasons, the FMLA has a few other important requirements:

- **Job Protection:** When employees return from FMLA leave, they must be given their original job back or a similar job with the same pay and benefits.

- **Eligibility:** To qualify for FMLA leave, employees must have worked for their employer for at least 12 months and have worked at least 1,250 hours in the past year. The employer must also have at least 50 employees within 75 miles of the workplace.

- **Health Benefits:** During FMLA leave, employers must continue to provide health insurance coverage as if the employee were still working.

- **Notice:** Employees should give 30 days' notice if the leave is foreseeable, like for a planned surgery. If the leave is unexpected, they should inform their employer as soon as possible.

Davis-Bacon Act

The Davis-Bacon Act was passed in 1931. It was created to make sure that workers on federal construction projects are paid fairly. Before this law, some contractors would hire workers at very low wages to win government contracts by offering the lowest bid. The Davis-Bacon Act requires that workers on these projects be paid at least the local prevailing wages and benefits, which are the standard pay rates in the area for similar work. This law helps to ensure that workers are paid fairly and that local wage standards are not undercut by low bids on government projects. The Davis-Bacon Act requires that workers on federally funded construction projects be paid at least the local prevailing wages and benefits for similar work in the area. An example of this act is how it applies to federal grants issued to states that administer low incoming housing programs to developers. The land developers that are building housing communities often will apply for grants or loans at favorable rates to reduce the overall expenses in exchange for a portion of their community being set aside for low-income residents. As part of the proposals, the developers must agree to abide by the Davis-Bacon Act throughout the construction of the housing.

Walsh-Healey Public Contracts Act

The Walsh-Healey Public Contracts Act was passed in 1936 to make sure workers on US government contracts were treated fairly. Before this law, some companies paid very low wages and didn't provide good working conditions just to get government contracts by offering the cheapest prices. The Walsh-Healey Act requires that workers on these contracts be paid at least the minimum wage and receive overtime pay for hours worked over 40 in a week. It also sets standards for safe and healthy working conditions. This law helps protect workers from being exploited and ensures they get fair pay and good working conditions. This act applies to US government contracts over $10,000 for manufacturing or supplying goods. It mandates that workers be paid at least the minimum wage and receive overtime pay for hours worked over 40 in a week.

Service Contract Act (SCA)

The SCA was passed in 1965 to protect workers on federal service contracts. Before this law, some companies paid very low wages and didn't provide good benefits to win government contracts with the lowest bids. The SCA requires that workers on these contracts be paid wages and benefits that are common for similar jobs in the area. This law helps ensure that workers are paid fairly and receive good benefits, preventing companies from winning contracts by underpaying their employees. These benefits may be paid as direct compensation if an employee subject to the SCA already has those benefits. For example, a military spouse that receives TRICARE insurance through the military would not need an employer to pay for healthcare benefits, but the SCA still mandates that the benefit be given to the employee in some form.

Portal-to-portal Act

The Portal-to-portal Act was passed in 1947. Its purpose was to clarify what counts as work time under the FLSA. Before this law, there was confusion about whether activities like traveling to work or getting ready for work should be paid. The Portal-to-portal Act says that employers don't have to pay for time spent on activities before or after the main work tasks, like commuting to work or changing clothes. This law helps employers and employees understand what time is considered paid work time. This act clarifies what counts as work time under the FLSA, such as travel time and activities that happen before or after the main work tasks. See Table 6.2 for a review of the main requirements of the Portal-to-portal Act.

TABLE 6.2 Top Requirements of the Portal-to-portal Act

Requirement	Description
Commute Time	Employers are not required to pay for time spent traveling to and from the workplace.
Postliminary Activities	Time spent on activities before the main work begins, like changing clothes or washing up, is generally not compensable.
Principal Activities	Employers must pay for time spent on the main work tasks and activities that are integral and indispensable to those tasks.
Worksite-to-Worksite Travel	Travel time between different worksites during the workday is compensable.
On-call Time	On-call time is compensable if the employee is required to remain on the employer's premises or so close that they cannot use the time effectively.
Training Time	Time spent in training, meetings, and lectures is compensable if it is related to the employee's job and is required by the employer.
Waiting Time	Time spent waiting while on duty is compensable if the employee is unable to use the time effectively for their own purposes.
Rest and Meal Periods	Short rest breaks (usually 20 minutes or less) are compensable, but bona fide meal periods (typically 30 minutes or more) are not.
Preparatory and Concluding Activities	Employers are required to pay for time spent on activities that are necessary for the job, such as setting up equipment, even if performed before or after the main work.

Source: Department of Labor www.dol.gov

Employee Retirement Income Security Act (ERISA)

ERISA is a federal law that sets standards for most retirement and health plans in private industry. It aims to protect individuals in these plans by ensuring that plan funds are handled responsibly. ERISA requires plans to provide participants with important information about plan features and funding, sets minimum standards for participation and funding, and gives participants the right to sue for benefits and breaches of fiduciary duty. ERISA guarantees payment of certain benefits if a defined plan is terminated through a federally chartered corporation called the Pension Benefit Guaranty Corporation (PBGC). ERISA was passed in 1974.

Case Study

ERISA was partly inspired by the collapse of the Studebaker Corporation's pension plan in the early 1960s. When Studebaker, a major automobile manufacturer, went out of business in 1963, its pension plan was so underfunded that thousands of employees lost much or all of their promised retirement benefits. This incident highlighted the need for federal regulation to protect workers' pensions, leading to the creation and eventual passage of ERISA in 1974.

However, ERISA's limitations were exposed during the Enron scandal in the early 2000s. Many employees lost their retirement savings when Enron collapsed because the law did not adequately protect their investments in the company's stock within their 401(k) plans. The Enron scandal led to the bankruptcy of the Enron Corporation and significant financial losses for its employees and shareholders. As a result, many top executives were convicted of fraud and other crimes. The scandal also prompted the creation of the Sarbanes-Oxley Act in 2002, which aimed to increase corporate accountability and prevent future fraud.

Sarbanes Oxley Act (SOX)

SOX, passed in 2002, was created to prevent corporate fraud and protect investors. It set new rules for public companies, including stricter financial reporting and increased accountability for company executives. The main requirements of SOX in the workplace include the following:

- **Accurate financial reporting:** Companies must provide accurate and truthful financial statements.
- **Internal controls:** Companies need to have strong internal controls to prevent and detect fraud.
- **CEO/CFO certification:** Top executives must personally certify the accuracy of financial reports.

- **Whistleblower protection:** Employees who report fraud are protected from retaliation.

- **Audit independence:** External auditors must be independent and cannot provide certain consulting services to the companies they audit.

Consolidated Omnibus Budget Reconciliation Act (COBRA)

COBRA was passed in 1985. Its purpose is to allow employees to keep their health insurance coverage for a limited time after leaving their job, whether they quit or are laid off. This helps workers and their families avoid losing their health insurance suddenly. However, most employees do not realize the amount a company is paying as a portion of the healthcare costs compared to what the employee contributes. Generally, if the employee wishes to remain in coverage, they must pay both portions, which can be prohibitively expensive. Following are the main features of COBRA:

- **Continuation of coverage:** Allows employees and their families to keep their health insurance after leaving a job.

- **Eligibility:** Applies to employees who quit, are laid off, or have a reduction in work hours.

- **Coverage period:** Coverage can continue for up to 18 months, sometimes longer under special circumstances.

- **Cost:** Employees may have to pay the full premium, including the part previously paid by the employer, plus a small administrative fee.

- **Notification:** Employers must inform employees of their COBRA rights when they leave the job.

Health Insurance Portability and Accountability Act (HIPAA)

HIPAA was passed in 1996. Its purpose is to protect the privacy of patients' medical information and ensure that this information is kept confidential. HIPAA also helps people keep their health insurance when they change or lose their jobs and sets standards for how healthcare providers and insurance companies handle and share medical data. Employers comply with HIPAA by ensuring that any employee health information they handle is kept private and secure, following strict guidelines for confidentiality and data protection.

Uniformed Services Employment and Reemployment Rights Act (USERRA)

USERRA was passed in 1994. Its purpose is to protect the job rights of individuals who voluntarily or involuntarily leave their jobs to serve in the military. USERRA ensures that these employees can return to their civilian jobs with the same status, pay, and benefits they would have had if they had not been called to service. For example, if a worker at a manufacturing plant chose to enlist in the armed forces with a four-year contract and at the end of that time chose to return to the company, the company would be compelled to offer an equivalent position to the one the person had previously occupied. They would have four years added to their seniority in the company (which may impact the number of earned vacation days, longevity pay increases, and promotions for which they would have been competitive). The Employer Support for Guard and Reserve (ESGR) is an organization that advocates for military service members called to duty and forced to leave their employer. They often work directly with HR departments when a service member transitions from active duty to help reestablish employment. They also often recognize strong employers that support their employees through programs that benefit the company from a public relations standpoint.

Patient Protection and Affordable Care Act (PPACA)

The PPACA, also known as the Affordable Care Act, ACA, and Obamacare, was passed in 2010. Its purpose is to make health insurance more affordable and accessible for Americans. The law requires most people to have health insurance, provides financial help for those who need it, and sets rules for insurance companies to ensure they cover essential health benefits and don't deny coverage for pre-existing conditions. The PPACA also expands Medicaid and creates health insurance marketplaces where people can compare and buy insurance plans. The main criteria of the PPACA in the workplace include the following:

- **Employer mandate:** Companies with 50 or more full-time employees must provide health insurance to their employees or face penalties.

- **Coverage requirements:** The health insurance provided must cover essential health benefits like emergency services, maternity care, and prescription drugs.

- **Affordability:** The insurance offered must be affordable, meaning it should not cost more than a certain percentage of an employee's household income.

- **No pre-existing condition exclusions:** Insurance plans cannot deny coverage to employees based on pre-existing health conditions.

- **Reporting:** Employers must report information about the health coverage they provide to the IRS and to their employees.

The PPACA has bronze, silver, gold, and platinum medical plan categories. These categories, known as the "metal tiers," were introduced to help consumers compare the value of different health insurance plans. Each category represents a different level of coverage and cost-sharing between the insurer and the insured. See Figure 6.2 for a review of the tiers.

Tax Treatment

Exam Objective 05-03 refers to how different types of compensation and benefits are taxed under applicable laws and regulations. It includes understanding how wages, salaries, bonuses, and various employee benefits (such as health insurance, retirement contributions, and fringe benefits) are treated for tax purposes. This ensures that both employers and employees comply with tax laws regarding reporting, withholding, and paying taxes on different forms of compensation. For example, employer contributions to employee health insurance premiums are usually tax-free for employees. This means employees do not have

FIGURE 6.2 PPACA metal tiers

Platinum — Highest premiums, lowest out-of-pocket costs. ★★★★

Gold — Higher premiums, lower out-of-pocket costs. ★★★

Silver — Moderate premiums, moderate out-of-pocket costs. ★★

Bronze — Lower premiums, higher out-of-pocket costs. ★

to pay income tax on the value of these contributions, making it a tax-advantaged benefit. Contributions to employer-sponsored retirement plans, such as a 401(k), are often made with pre-tax dollars. Employees do not pay income tax on these contributions until they withdraw the funds, typically in retirement, deferring the tax liability to a later date.

When employers establish benefits plans, they can deduct certain expenses from corporate tax liability. The Internal Revenue Service places many rules on exactly how those tax benefits work. For example, employers often contribute a percentage portion of healthcare premiums for their employees that qualify for the company healthcare plans in conjunction with the Affordable Care Act (ACA). As a tax benefit, the employee portion of the healthcare premiums are deducted before taxes, lowering their overall taxable wage, and the employer gets the cost of the plan shielded as a business expense. For a plan to qualify, the premium cost for a single individual employee cannot exceed an established percentage of the employee's wage. In 2024, that percentage was 8.39 percent. This is so the healthcare plans remain affordable as defined by the law.

There are also provisions for certain health savings plans that can be attached to the benefits package of a company. Some plans may have a flexible spending account (FSA), which is a savings account attached to an employer-based health insurance plan. Funds are contributed before taxes are taken from the paycheck. There are annual contribution limits, and the funds do not roll over, which means the funds must be used during the year or they are lost. A health savings account (HSA) must be used in conjunction with a company's high deductible health plan, defined as a minimum deductible of $1,500 for an individual or $3,000 for a family plan. The HSA can be rolled over year to year and can also be tied to an investment account, so it grows over time. You can use the funds in your FSA or HSA to pay for qualified healthcare services and items such as medical devices or prescription drugs.

The term *safe harbor* is used to describe plans that have been established to be compliant with the rules established by the IRS. Another safe harbor provision is deferred compensation plans such as a 401(k) plan. The rules establish minimum contributions, automatic enrollment of employees when eligible, and other provisions. However, some plans allow employees' contributions to be withheld prior to taxes being withheld (pre-tax or traditional 401(k)) or paying the tax on the contributions at the time of investment (called a Roth 401(k)) but receiving a distribution of those contributions and their earnings may possibly be tax-free. Determining the various permutations often depends on individual financial circumstances and HR professionals must maintain awareness of the changes and adjustments to benefits plans and their tax consequences year over year and its impact to the company. HR professionals often work closely with benefits and financial advisor specialists who are experts in these areas to provide employees with the knowledge to make informed decisions.

Some companies also offer supplemental insurance benefits, the premiums of which could be pre-tax or after-tax deductions from payroll. However, if the premium is pre-tax, then the benefit is subject to tax while after-tax premiums have the benefit of being tax-free. This is important when calculating short-term and long-term disability payments for employees who are injured and unable to work for a period but are still able to have some income and how the income is treated for tax purposes.

Understanding tax treatment is important for HR professionals because it helps manage payroll and benefits correctly. They need to know which benefits are tax-free and which are taxable to follow the law and avoid penalties. This knowledge helps in designing attractive compensation packages and explaining their tax advantages to employees. It also ensures accurate payroll processing and the correct tax withholding. HR professionals can also guide employees on how their benefits affect their taxes, helping them make informed choices.

Enforcement and Compliance

The Department of Labor's Wage and Hour Division enforces federal wage and hour laws, while states have their own agencies for state laws. Employers who violate these laws can face penalties, be required to pay back wages, and provide other remedies to affected employees.

When the DOL's Wage and Hour Division processes a wage and hour claim, it starts by receiving a complaint from an employee. It then investigates the claim by reviewing the employer's records and interviewing employees. If it finds that the employer violated wage and hour laws, it works to resolve the issue by making the employer pay any back wages owed. If necessary, the division can take legal action to ensure the employer complies with the law. Throughout the process, it keeps the complainant informed about the status of their claim.

Anti-discrimination Laws

Anti-discrimination laws in the workplace are rules that protect employees from unfair treatment based on characteristics like race, gender, age, religion, disability, or national origin. These laws ensure that everyone has an equal chance at getting hired, promoted, and treated fairly at work. They aim to create a work environment where all employees feel respected and valued, regardless of their background.

Title VII of the Civil Rights Act of 1964

Title VII of the Civil Rights Act of 1964 prohibits discrimination based on race, color, religion, sex, or national origin. It applies to employers with 15 or more employees and covers a wide range of employment practices, including hiring, promotion, and dismissal.

Age Discrimination in Employment Act (ADEA)

The ADEA protects employees who are 40 years old or older from discrimination based on age. It prevents employers from using age as a factor in decisions about hiring, firing, promotions, and compensation.

Americans with Disabilities Act (ADA)

The ADA prohibits discrimination against individuals with disabilities and requires reasonable accommodations for them. This law applies to all areas of public life, including jobs, schools, transportation, and public and private places open to the general public.

Equal Pay Act (EPA) of 1963

The EPA requires that men and women be given equal pay for equal work. This act covers all forms of pay, including salary, overtime pay, bonuses, stock options, profit sharing, and benefits.

Genetic Information Nondiscrimination Act (GINA)

This act prohibits discrimination based on genetic information about an employee or their family members. This law also restricts employers from requesting, requiring, or purchasing genetic information about an employee.

Pregnancy Discrimination Act (PDA)

The PDA prohibits discrimination on the basis of pregnancy, childbirth, or related medical conditions. It requires that pregnant employees be treated the same as other employees who are similar in their ability or inability to work.

Rehabilitation Act of 1973

This act prohibits discrimination on the basis of disability in federal employment and by federal contractors. This act also mandates that federal agencies provide reasonable accommodations and ensure accessibility in their programs and activities.

Enforcement and Compliance

The Equal Employment Opportunity Enforcement Agency (EEOC) investigates discrimination complaints, provides guidance on compliance, and litigates cases. In fiscal year 2020, the EEOC received 67,448 discrimination charges, with retaliation being the most common type of charge. In fact, retaliation claims have been the most frequently filed type of discrimination charge since 2009.

Employee Safety

The purpose of workplace safety laws is to protect workers from getting hurt or sick on the job. These laws set rules that employers must follow to keep the workplace safe, like providing proper equipment, training, and making sure the work environment is free from hazards.

A *workplace injury* is a physical harm that happens suddenly due to an accident or incident at work, like a fall or a cut. A *workplace disease*, on the other hand, develops over time due to exposure to harmful conditions or substances at work, like lung disease from breathing in dust or chemicals.

Table 6.3 shows the top five most prevalent types of workplace injuries.

Occupational Safety and Health Act (OSHA)

OSHA is a law that helps keep workers safe on the job. An *OSHA standard* is a set of rules to prevent workplace injuries and illnesses. The law requires employers to provide a safe work environment and follow safety standards. If workers have concerns about their safety, they can report them, and the law ensures that these concerns are investigated and addressed.

TABLE 6.3   OSHA's Top Five Workplace Injuries

Injury	Description
1. Slips, Trips, and Falls	When workers slip on wet floors, trip over objects, or fall from heights
2. Overexertion	Injuries from lifting, pushing, pulling, or carrying heavy objects
3. Repetitive Strain Injuries (RSIs)	Injuries from repeating the same motion over and over, like typing or using tools
4. Struck by Objects	When workers are hit by falling tools, equipment, or other objects
5. Cuts and Lacerations	Injuries from sharp objects like knives, machinery, or broken glass

Source: www.osha.gov

The Act also provides training and resources to help everyone understand and follow the safety rules. Examples of OSHA compliance standards include the following:

- **Providing proper safety equipment:** Ensuring workers have and use appropriate protective gear like helmets, gloves, and goggles

- **Training employees:** Offering regular safety training on how to handle equipment and hazardous materials safely

- **Maintaining clean workspaces:** Keeping work areas clean and free of clutter to prevent slips, trips, and falls

- **Regular inspections:** Conducting routine checks of equipment and facilities to ensure everything is in safe working order

- **Emergency preparedness:** Having clear emergency plans and conducting regular drills for situations like fires or chemical spills

Under OSHA, the *general duty clause* requires employers to identify and correct any known hazards that could cause death or serious injury, even if there isn't a specific OSHA standard addressing those hazards. This means employers must proactively ensure a safe work environment for their employees.

OSHA follows a set of inspection priorities to focus its resources on the most hazardous situations. Here are the five main priorities for OSHA inspections, ranked from highest to lowest:

1. **Imminent Danger:** This is the top priority for OSHA inspections. Imminent danger refers to any situation where there is a reasonable certainty that an immediate hazard could cause death or serious physical harm to employees. OSHA inspectors will act quickly to resolve these situations.

2. **Fatalities and Catastrophes:** OSHA gives priority to workplaces where a fatality has occurred or where three or more employees have been hospitalized due to a workplace incident. Employers are required to report such events to OSHA within specific time frames, and inspections are initiated to determine the cause and prevent future occurrences.

3. **Complaints and Referrals:** Inspections are also initiated based on employee complaints or referrals from other agencies or sources. When a worker submits a formal complaint about unsafe or unhealthy working conditions, OSHA may conduct an inspection to address the concerns, especially if the situation poses a significant risk.

4. **Programmed Inspections:** These are planned inspections of high-hazard industries or workplaces that have statistically higher injury and illness rates. OSHA schedules these inspections to address industries known to have more safety and health risks, focusing on specific hazards or processes.

5. **Follow-up Inspections:** OSHA may conduct follow-up inspections to ensure that employers have corrected violations from previous inspections. This is essential to verify that hazards have been eliminated and that compliance with safety standards is maintained.

These priorities help OSHA effectively allocate resources and address the most critical safety and health risks in the workplace.

Mine Safety and Health Act (MSHA)

MSHA is a law that protects miners by setting safety and health standards for mines. It requires mine operators to follow rules to keep mines safe and prevent accidents. MSHA also involves regular inspections of mines to make sure they are following these safety standards. If a mine is found to be unsafe, MSHA can issue fines and require changes to improve safety. The goal of MSHA is to protect miners and ensure they have a safe working environment. As of recent data, approximately 300,000 miners in the United States are protected by MSHA (www.msha.gov/data-and-reports).

Federal Employees' Compensation Act (FECA)

FECA provides workers' compensation benefits to federal employees who are injured or become ill due to their job. It covers medical expenses, wage replacement, and rehabilitation for affected workers. The act also provides benefits to the families of employees who die from work-related injuries or illnesses. This helps ensure that federal workers and their families are supported during times of injury or illness. FECA is enforced by the Office of Workers' Compensation Programs (OWCP), which is part of the US Department of Labor.

Workers' Compensation Laws

Workers' compensation laws are designed to protect employees who get injured or become ill due to their job. These laws ensure that workers receive medical treatment and financial benefits without having to prove the employer was at fault. Benefits can include payment for medical expenses, replacement of lost wages, and compensation for permanent injuries. Each state has its own workers' compensation system, but all aim to support employees while they recover and to protect employers from lawsuits.

Enforcement and Compliance

Workplace safety laws are primarily enforced by OSHA. When a complaint is made with OSHA, it starts by reviewing the information provided. It may then inspect the workplace to see if any safety rules are being broken. If violations are found, OSHA will require the employer to fix them and may issue fines. OSHA does take anonymous reports, so workers can report problems without revealing their identity.

Whistleblowing is when an employee reports illegal or unsafe activities happening at their workplace. This can include violations of laws, regulations, or company policies. Whistleblowers help bring attention to problems that might harm workers, the public, or the environment. They can report these issues to their employer, government agencies like OSHA, or other authorities. OSHA handles whistleblowing by protecting employees who report safety violations from retaliation. If a worker is punished for reporting a safety issue, OSHA can investigate and take action against the employer. This can include requiring the employer to reinstate the employee, pay back wages, and stop any further retaliation. Whistleblowers can file complaints confidentially to protect their identity.

> **Case Study**
>
> A well-known example of whistleblowing in the workplace is the case of Dr. Jeffrey Wigand, who was an executive at the tobacco company Brown & Williamson. In the mid-1990s, he revealed that the company knew about the harmful effects of smoking and was deliberately increasing nicotine levels to make cigarettes more addictive. Dr. Wigand's testimony and the documents he provided became critical evidence in lawsuits against the tobacco industry. His actions led to significant legal and regulatory changes and greatly increased public awareness about the dangers of smoking. His story was later depicted in the movie *The Insider.*

Immigration

The primary purpose of US immigration laws related to employment is to regulate the hiring of foreign nationals, protect the domestic workforce, and ensure fair labor practices. These laws require employers to verify employees' legal work status, prevent the hiring of undocumented workers, and address labor shortages through regulated work visas.

Immigration Reform and Control Act (IRCA)

The IRCA, passed in 1986, made it illegal for employers to knowingly hire undocumented immigrants. The purpose was to curb illegal immigration by ensuring that only individuals with proper work authorization are employed.

It also required employers to verify the legal status of their employees using Form I-9, which is used to document an employee's identity and authorization to work in the United States. Employers must use Form I-9 to verify the identity and employment authorization of all employees, regardless of citizenship or immigration status. This form must be completed within three days of an employee's start date. Employers are required to review and record the documents presented by the employee to establish their identity and work authorization.

In addition to the I-9 form, some employers use the E-Verify system, an internet-based program that compares information from an employee's I-9 form to government records. E-Verify helps confirm the eligibility of employees to work in the United States. While E-Verify is voluntary for many employers, it is mandatory for federal contractors and employers in certain states.

The fines for Form I-9 errors can vary depending on the nature and severity of the violations. As of recent guidelines, fines can range from the following:

- **Paperwork Violations:** These occur when an employer fails to properly complete, retain, or make the Form I-9 available for inspection. Fines for paperwork violations can range from $272 to $2,701 per form, depending on the percentage of violations and whether the employer has committed previous offenses.

- **Unlawful Employment of Unauthorized Workers:** If an employer knowingly hires or continues to employ unauthorized workers, fines can range from $676 to $27,018 per violation, depending on the employer's history of violations and the number of unauthorized workers involved.

These fines are subject to adjustment for inflation and may increase if the employer has committed multiple violations. Employers must ensure accurate and timely completion of Form I-9 to avoid these penalties.

Work Visas

The United States has a variety of work visas available for foreign nationals, including H-1B visas for skilled workers, L-1 visas for intracompany transferees, and O-1 visas for individuals with extraordinary abilities. These visas allow employers to hire foreign workers for specific roles, often when there are shortages of qualified US workers. There is a cap set on how many of these work visas may be issued every year, with additional visas granted for those with advanced degrees. Generally speaking, most of the work visas require that the employer seeking foreign workers demonstrate that the skill or talent pool is not readily available from US citizens or is insufficient to meet the needs of the company. This burden of proof is often a high bar to overcome.

Enforcement and Compliance

The US Department of Homeland Security (DHS) is primarily responsible for the enforcement and compliance of immigration laws. Within DHS, the US Citizenship and Immigration Services (USCIS) handles the administration of immigration benefits, such as visa applications, naturalization, and asylum requests. It also oversees the E-Verify system used for employment verification.

Labor Relations

Labor relations refers to the relationship between employers and employees, particularly concerning the negotiation and enforcement of work conditions, wages, and benefits. It often involves communication between the company management and labor unions, which represent the workers. Labor relations focus on resolving issues like disputes, grievances, and contract negotiations to maintain a fair and productive work environment.

The Worker Adjustment and Retraining Notification (WARN) Act

The WARN Act requires large employers to give a 60-day notice before closing a plant or conducting mass layoffs. This law is designed to give employees time to prepare for the loss of employment and seek new jobs. Also included in this Act is notice to the local community, for example, a large factory that shuts down could have considerable impact on a small community that depends on this business for the majority of its residents' livelihood. If such an anchor business were to close, it could affect smaller secondary businesses such as restaurants, retail stores, schools, and other infrastructure.

Union Relations

The main purpose of unions is to protect workers' rights, improve working conditions, and negotiate fair wages and benefits. Unions provide a collective voice for employees to advocate for their interests. The first unions were formed in the late 18th and early 19th centuries during the Industrial Revolution when workers sought to address poor working conditions and low pay. The three main laws related to unions and employers in the United States are:

National Labor Relations Act (NLRA)   Also known as the Wagner Act, this law protects the rights of employees to form, join, or assist labor unions and to engage in collective bargaining. It also prohibits employers from interfering with these rights and outlines unfair labor practices.

Taft-Hartley Act   This law, also known as the Labor Management Relations Act, amended the NLRA to balance the power between unions and employers. It prohibits certain union practices, such as secondary boycotts and jurisdictional strikes, and allows states to pass "right-to-work" laws that prevent mandatory union membership as a condition of employment.

Landrum-Griffin Act   Also known as the Labor-management Reporting and Disclosure Act, this law regulates the internal affairs of labor unions. It ensures union members' rights, promotes transparency, and requires unions to file financial reports and disclose certain activities to protect members from corruption and abuses of power.

Both unions and employers run the risk of committing an *unfair labor practice* (ULP). A ULP is an action by employers or unions that violates the rights of employees or the rules established by labor laws, such as interfering with the formation or administration of a union. See Table 6.4 for examples of ULPs.

TABLE 6.4   Unfair Labor Practices

Employer ULPs	Union ULPs
Interfering with, restraining, or coercing employees in the exercise of their rights to form, join, or assist a union	Restraining or coercing employees in the exercise of their rights to refrain from union activities
Dominating or interfering with the formation or administration of any labor organization or contributing financial or other support to it	Causing or attempting to cause an employer to discriminate against an employee for not being a union member
Discriminating against employees for union activities or sympathies	Refusing to bargain in good faith with the employer

Employer ULPs	Union ULPs
Retaliating against employees for filing charges or giving testimony under the NLRA	Engaging in jurisdictional disputes with another union
Refusing to bargain collectively with the duly chosen representatives of the employees	Charging excessive or discriminatory fees to join the union

Collective bargaining is the process by which employees, through their unions, negotiate with employers to establish wages, hours, benefits, and other working conditions. This process allows workers to have a voice in their workplace and reach agreements that benefit both parties.

Alternative Dispute Resolution (ADR)

ADR refers to methods for resolving conflicts without going to court. Common types of ADR include mediation and arbitration. *Mediation* is a process where a neutral third party, called a mediator, helps people in a dispute communicate and reach a mutually acceptable agreement. The mediator doesn't make decisions but helps the parties find common ground. *Arbitration* is a process where a neutral third party, called an arbitrator, listens to both sides of a dispute and then makes a decision that is usually binding. It's like a less formal version of a court trial. ADR methods are often quicker, less formal, and less expensive than traditional legal proceedings.

An *arbitration agreement* is a written contract in which two parties agree to resolve their disputes through arbitration instead of going to court. Best practices for arbitration agreements include asking employees to sign them at the time-of-hire, ensuring that the terms are clear and fair, and making sure the employee understands their rights.

Drug-free Workplace Act

The Drug-free Workplace Act requires federal contractors and grantees to maintain a drug-free environment. Employers must develop a written policy explaining the rules against drug use, inform employees about the dangers of drugs, and provide a copy of the policy to all workers. They must also act if an employee violates the policy, such as providing assistance programs or taking disciplinary measures. The goal is to ensure a safe and productive work environment.

Employers can require drug tests before hiring, randomly, after accidents, or if they suspect drug use. However, they must follow specific guidelines to protect employees' rights, such as keeping test results confidential and providing clear policies.

> **NOTE**   Candidates will be tested on the laws that are in effect on their testing date, so it's important to stay as up-to-date as possible. In addition, while some states have passed laws that differ from or conflict with federal laws, for the purposes of the test, you must be familiar with federal law requirements.

Americans with Disabilities Act (ADA)

The ADA prohibits discrimination against individuals with disabilities in employment, public services, public accommodations, and telecommunications. Employers must provide reasonable accommodations to qualified employees with disabilities, unless it causes undue hardship. There are several key terms to be aware of in order to comply with the ADA:

- **Disability:** A physical or mental impairment that substantially limits one or more major life activities

- **Reasonable accommodation:** Changes or adjustments to a job or work environment that enable a person with a disability to have equal employment opportunities

- **Qualified individual:** A person with a disability who meets the skill, experience, education, and other job-related requirements of a position and can perform the essential functions of the job, with or without reasonable accommodation

- **Essential functions:** The fundamental job duties of a position that an employee must be able to perform, with or without reasonable accommodation

- **Undue hardship:** Significant difficulty or expense for the employer in providing reasonable accommodation, considering factors like the nature and cost of the accommodation, the overall financial resources of the business, and the impact on the operation

Harassment

Harassment in the workplace is any unwelcome behavior or conduct that creates a hostile, intimidating, or offensive work environment. It can include actions, words, or physical contact that target an individual's race, color, religion, sex, national origin, age, disability, or other protected characteristics. It is prohibited by law and employers are responsible for preventing and addressing it.

There are two main kinds of harassment in the workplace:

- **Quid pro quo:** This occurs when a person in authority, like a supervisor, demands sexual favors in exchange for job benefits, such as promotions, raises, or continued employment. It involves a power imbalance where the victim feels pressured to comply to avoid negative consequences.

- **Hostile work environment:** This type of harassment involves unwelcome conduct that is severe or pervasive enough to create an intimidating, hostile, or offensive work environment. It can include offensive jokes, slurs, threats, physical assaults, or other behavior that makes it difficult for someone to work. This harassment can come from supervisors, coworkers, or even customers.

An *affirmative defense* is a legal argument that allows an employer to avoid liability for harassment claims, even if harassment occurred, by proving certain conditions. Employers can create an affirmative defense by showing they took reasonable steps to prevent and correct harassment. This includes having a clear anti-harassment policy, providing regular training, and having a process for reporting complaints. Additionally, the employer must show that the employee unreasonably failed to take advantage of these preventive measures, like not reporting the harassment. This defense can help employers if they can prove they did everything possible to stop the harassment and the employee didn't use the resources provided.

Risk Assessment and Mitigation

Risk assessment and mitigation involve identifying potential hazards in the workplace and taking steps to reduce or eliminate them. This process helps prevent accidents, injuries, and other issues that could harm employees or the business. It includes several best practices that help to keep employees and company assets safe. Part of risk management is establishing controls that are systems or practices that employees follow to minimize hazards that exist. To properly assess a hazard and the risk level it poses, first determine the likelihood of occurrence of a particular hazard—how often it happens. Next determine the severity of the hazard such as minimal or catastrophic.

Emergency Plans and Procedures

Emergency procedures are plans for how to respond to unexpected situations like fires, natural disasters, or medical emergencies. These procedures outline steps to keep everyone safe, such as evacuating the building, calling for help, and providing first aid. Employees should be trained on these procedures to be prepared. OSHA requires employers to have *Emergency Action Plans* (EAPs) to ensure the safety of employees during various emergency situations. These are covered next.

Safety and Health Management Plan   A Safety and Health Management Plan outlines a company's strategies for maintaining a safe and healthy workplace. It includes policies and procedures for identifying, preventing, and managing workplace hazards. The plan covers aspects like employee training, emergency response, accident investigation, and compliance with safety regulations. The purpose is to reduce risks and ensure that all employees work in a safe environment.

Emergency Response Plan   An Emergency Response Plan (ERP) is a set of procedures and guidelines designed to help an organization respond effectively to various emergencies, such as fires, natural disasters, medical crises, or hazardous material incidents. The plan outlines specific actions to protect the safety of employees, visitors, and the public, including evacuation routes, communication protocols, and designated roles for emergency response teams. The goal of an ERP is to minimize harm and ensure a coordinated and efficient response during emergencies.

Business Continuity Plan   A Business Continuity Plan (BCP) is a strategy that outlines how a business will continue to operate during and after a major disruption, such as a natural disaster, cyberattack, or other emergencies. The plan includes procedures for maintaining essential functions, protecting data and assets, and recovering quickly. It often covers backup systems, alternative work sites, communication plans, and critical supply chain management. The purpose of a BCP is to minimize downtime and financial losses, ensuring that the business can quickly return to normal operations.

Fire and Evacuation Plans   Fire and Evacuation Plans are procedures for reporting fires, evacuating the building, and accounting for all employees after evacuation. This includes designated escape routes and assembly points.

Data Protection

Data protection involves safeguarding personal and sensitive information from unauthorized access, theft, or damage. This includes using passwords, encryption, and other security measures to protect data, whether it's stored electronically or on paper.

Most data security breaches are from within the organization resulting from poor practices and lack of cyber awareness training for employees. *Social engineering* describes the intentional psychological manipulation of an individual to gain access to information they are not entitled to possess. Cyber attackers will get pieces of information from company websites, social media posts, or other publicly available sources and craft messages that can be sent to employees, often with some urgent demands or time–sensitive window, pretending to be someone in corporate leadership, an important client, or the government. Unaware employees, wanting to be compliant and good customer service representatives, will provide information or click on attachments embedded in emails that trigger malicious software called malware that can then open the company's data storage or proprietary information to exploitation or theft. For example, an employee received a company email from the "executive director" instructing the employee to complete some mandatory training. The link embedded in the email looked to be a training site, but upon clicking the link, a malicious code infected the employee's computer and locked the hard drive and all data stored on the computer. It demanded a payment to release the data or the data would be completely destroyed and wiped clean. It took the company IT department several days to restore and clean the individual's computer, three days of productivity were lost as well as the previous day's work back to the point of the previous company data backup.

Employee data that must be protected includes personal information such as their names, addresses, Social Security numbers, and employment history. Protecting this data is important to maintain employees' privacy and prevent identity theft.

In the United States, there isn't a single federal law that applies broadly to all types of personal data across all sectors. However, there is a comprehensive federal privacy bill under discussion called the American Data Privacy Protection Act (ADPPA). This proposed legislation aims to establish a national standard for data privacy, providing more consistent protection for personal data across the country.

The ADPPA, like the GDPR in the European Union, seeks to give individuals more control over their personal information, requiring organizations to implement data protection measures, obtain consent for data collection, and allow individuals to access, correct, and delete their data. While it is still in the legislative process, the ADPPA reflects growing recognition of the need for comprehensive federal data protection regulations in the United States.

Note that there are elements of data protection laws such as the Fair Credit Reporting Act and the Health Insurance Portability and Accountability Act that currently does provides some data protection for employees.

Intellectual Property (IP)

IP refers to creations of the mind, like inventions, designs, brand names, and artistic works. Protecting IP means ensuring that these creations cannot be used without permission, which helps businesses maintain their competitive edge and ensures creators get credit for their work. Companies that create content such as internal training might want to use certain commercial media found on the internet. However, use might be restricted because of the laws that protect IP and permission might be needed or proper attribution given before inserting any protected content into the training materials. In the United States, most intellectual property is covered by the following legislation:

Patent Act   Provides protection for new and useful inventions, granting the inventor exclusive rights to make, use, and sell the invention for a limited time, typically 20 years from the filing date. The US has three types of patents:

- **Utility patents:** These are granted for new and useful inventions or discoveries, such as machines, processes, compositions of matter, or improvements to existing inventions. Utility patents provide protection for how an invention works and can last up to 20 years from the filing date.

- **Design patents:** These protect new, original, and ornamental designs for an article of manufacture. Design patents cover the appearance or aesthetic aspects of a product, rather than its function. They last for 15 years from the date of grant.

- **Plant patents:** These are granted for the invention or discovery and asexual reproduction of a distinct and new variety of plant. Plant patents protect new plant varieties that have been reproduced asexually, meaning not through seeds. They last for 20 years from the filing date.

Copyright Act   Protects original works of authorship, such as books, music, films, and software, by granting the creator exclusive rights to reproduce, distribute, perform, display, and create derivative works. Copyright generally lasts for the life of the author plus 70 years.

Trademark Act (Lanham Act)   Protects brand names, logos, slogans, and other symbols used to identify goods and services, preventing others from using similar marks that could confuse consumers. Trademarks can be renewed indefinitely as long as they are in use.

Trade Secret Protection   Although not governed by a specific federal statute, trade secrets are protected under state laws and the federal Defend Trade Secrets Act (DTSA). This protection covers confidential business information, such as formulas, practices, processes, and designs, that provide a competitive advantage.

Workplace Violence

Workplace violence refers to any act of physical violence, threats, harassment, or intimidation that occurs at work. It can come from coworkers, customers, or other people. Businesses need to have policies and training in place to prevent and respond to workplace violence, ensuring a safe environment for everyone. To protect employees from workplace violence, companies can implement several best practices:

- **Establish a zero-tolerance policy:** Develop and communicate a clear policy that prohibits any form of violence, threats, or harassment. Make sure all employees understand that such behavior will not be tolerated and outline the consequences for violations.

- **Conduct regular training:** Provide training for employees and management on how to recognize, prevent, and respond to workplace violence. This includes understanding warning signs, de-escalation techniques, and emergency procedures.

- **Implement security measures:** Enhance workplace security by installing surveillance cameras, controlled access points, and proper lighting. Ensure that areas like parking lots and entrances are secure and well-monitored.

- **Develop a reporting system:** Create a safe and confidential system for employees to report incidents of violence or threats. Encourage reporting and ensure that all complaints are taken seriously and investigated promptly.

- **Support employee well-being:** Offer resources such as EAPs that provide counseling and support services. Encourage employees to seek help if they feel stressed, threatened, or uncomfortable.

- **Screen job applicants:** Conduct thorough background checks on potential employees to identify any history of violent behavior. This can help prevent hiring individuals who may pose a risk to others. *Negligent hiring* is the legal concept that holds an employer liable for harm caused by an employee if the employer failed to reasonably investigate the employee's background and qualifications before hiring them, particularly if the employee has a history of behavior that suggests they may pose a risk to others.

One of the most important aspects of any workplace violence is being proactive to see the symptoms and signs of potential violence in order to de-escalate a dangerous situation. After an incident has occurred, HR must be prepared to respond to the aftermath. Notification of other workers, contacting law enforcement, assisting with investigations, helping family members of potential victims of workplace violence, and executing insurance policies, workers' compensation, and other benefits such as crisis response from an EAP are all possible actions that fall within an HR professional's area of responsibility. Many schools, small businesses, and large corporations conduct "active shooter" drills to plan actions and responses to potential violence in their space. HR will have a role to play in these scenario-based training sessions.

Counterproductive Work Behaviors (CWB)

CWB refers to actions by employees that harm an organization or its members. These behaviors can include theft, sabotage, workplace aggression, absenteeism, dishonesty, and violation of company policies. CWBs negatively affect productivity, employee morale, and overall organizational performance.

Organizational Restructuring

Organizational restructuring initiatives, such as mergers, acquisitions, divestitures, integration, offshoring, downsizing, and furloughs involve significant changes to a company's structure and operations. A description of each follows.

Mergers and Acquisitions   Mergers and acquisitions involve the combining of two or more companies. A *merger* is the joining of two companies to form a new entity, while an *acquisition* occurs when one company buys another. These transactions can enhance market share, diversify products or services, and increase competitiveness, but they may also lead to cultural clashes, integration challenges, and potential layoffs.

Integration efforts refer to the process of combining systems, processes, cultures, and operations following a merger or acquisition. This includes aligning business practices, consolidating systems, and unifying company cultures. Effective integration is critical for achieving the desired synergies, but it can be complex and time-consuming, with risks of operational disruptions and employee dissatisfaction.

Divestitures   *Divestitures* involve a company selling off a portion of its business, such as a subsidiary, division, or product line. This strategy can help a company focus on its core operations, raise capital, or eliminate underperforming assets. However, it can also lead to job losses, disruptions in service, and potential loss of expertise and customer relationships.

Downsizing   Downsizing, also known as layoffs or workforce reduction, involves cutting the number of employees to reduce costs and improve efficiency. This is often a response to economic downturns, technological changes, or organizational restructuring. While downsizing can help a company remain financially viable, it can also harm employee morale, reduce productivity, and result in the loss of valuable skills and knowledge.

Furloughs   Furloughs are temporary, unpaid leaves of absence for employees, often used as a cost-saving measure during economic downturns or financial challenges. Unlike layoffs, furloughed employees typically retain their jobs and benefits and are expected to return to work when conditions improve. Furloughs can help companies avoid permanent layoffs, but they can also lead to employee financial hardship and decreased morale.

Offshoring   Offshoring involves relocating business processes or services to another country, often to reduce costs. Commonly offshored functions include manufacturing, customer service, and IT support. While offshoring can lead to significant cost savings, it may also result in job losses in the home country, communication challenges, and potential quality control issues.

While these strategic initiatives can offer benefits like cost savings, increased efficiency, and expanded market reach, they also pose risks to business continuity. Potential risks include disruptions to daily operations, loss of key talent, cultural clashes, reduced employee morale, and integration challenges. Additionally, restructuring can lead to uncertainties among employees and customers, impacting productivity and brand reputation. Proper planning, clear communication, and a focus on maintaining core business functions are ways that HR teams help to mitigate these risks and support a smooth transition.

Summary

Compliance can be summarized as doing the right thing and following the rules, even when it may be unpopular, inconvenient, or expensive. What is important to realize is that by not being compliant with regulations or the law, a company can become even less popular, be significantly inconvenienced with litigation and additional oversight, and pay hefty fines that can have long-term consequences to the financial well-being of the organization. HR professionals must be acutely aware of how laws and regulations are enforced, and how they apply to the specific circumstances of their organization.

Wage and hour laws refer to a series of various federal laws that set standards, define employment terms, rolls, and responsibilities of the employee and employer, and create a series of protections for the administration of pay and benefits in a fair and legitimate manner. This serves both the employee and employer by creating a set of rules that all can abide by. Many of these laws are the bedrock of HR compliance and create processes and procedures that can be followed and later audited by outside parties to assure investors, shareholders, corporate executives, and government regulators that the company is acting as it should with respect to its employees' well-being.

Inherent in these laws is the fundamental rule that all employees are treated equally and that any disputes or grievances are addressed in a fair and reasonable manner. Protected classes are defined in Title VII of the Civil Rights Act of 1964 and prohibit employers from discriminating against an employee on the basis of one or more of the protected characteristics. Other laws add additional provisions and protections for other characteristics including disability, genetic disorders, and pregnancy. Employers and HR must be aware of the various components of these laws to ensure compliance.

In addition to establishing a fair working environment, employers are also required to provide a safe working environment. HR practitioners must understand how to assess risk to operations, equipment, or people by identifying hazards that are present in the workplace. Hazards that are identified can then be mitigated by putting controls in place to remove or reduce risk levels. Physical risks may include workplace accidents, illnesses, or injuries, including incidents occurring after or resulting from workplace violence. In addition to physical risks, there are also risks to data and information, including intellectual property that is proprietary to the company. HR is involved in protecting these various assets from hiring qualified individuals, to training on proper procedures, to recordkeeping and documentation to show compliance.

Finally, companies in a corporate lifecycle may go through the process of organizational restructuring. This can happen as a result of market influences, changes in product technology, or through internal decisions of corporate leadership. In all these circumstances, HR will have the responsibility of due diligence to provide records and information on the status of the company workforce, to communicate with employees of expected changes and any impact to jobs, and to assist with assimilating the changes that do come after the restructuring happens.

Exam Essentials

Understand the compliance requirements associated with various laws and regulations. Federal agencies are established by various laws to provide regulatory oversight and enforcement for companies and their workforce. The United States has laws such as the FLSA, FMLA, ERISA, COBRA, SOX, HIPAA, USERRA, and PPACA that provide compliance standards for companies with respect to their employees' conditions of employment. HR professionals should be keenly aware of periodic changes to any of the provisions related to the workforce, tax treatment, and other aspects of enforcement and compliance.

Know how OSHA has oversight of workplace safety and the demands placed on HR for safety compliance. Companies are responsible for providing a safe working environment by identifying hazards, determining the level of risk to employees or business operations, identifying and implementing controls to mitigate the hazards and any residual risk. Be familiar with OSHA and other employee safety laws such as MSHA, FECA, the Clean Air Act, and Workers' Compensation Laws at the federal level.

Understand the I-9 and E-Verify as they relate to employee eligibility. The primary means to validate an employee's eligibility to work in the United States is documented on Form I-9 from Customs and Immigration Services. E-Verify is a web-based system that confirms the employment credentials of a worker based on documentation provided by the employee. While the form and system have user guides that are hundreds of pages, the basic requirement is to understand how these are used to confirm a hired employee is eligible to work in the United States prior to starting work in the company.

Understand the elements of labor relations.   Labor relations as it relates to compliance with the law, covers certain responsibilities to inform and notify employees of major layoffs or plant closures as defined in the WARN Act. HR professionals must be aware of how unions impact business and HR and how ADR is often the preferred method of handling employee legal actions. Additionally, be familiar with laws that affect workplace behaviors including the Drug-Free Workplace Act, the Americans with Disabilities Act and Amendments, and laws protecting employees from harassment in the workplace.

Know mitigation procedures and responses to common workplace hazards.   HR professionals must understand how to establish and execute emergency plans and procedures to protect company infrastructure, resources, and people from hazards. They must recognize the signs and actions of counterproductive work behaviors, including those that could lead to workplace violence. They must acknowledge that some workplace violence begins outside the workplace but can be introduced into the environment through customers, vendors, employees, and people associated with employees, such as family members. In addition to protecting employees, HR must also be vigilant to protect corporate digital information from unauthorized access and secure intellectual property from corporate theft or espionage.

Understand elements of organizational restructuring.   As companies experience organizational restructuring, HR must understand the role it has with the due diligence process during merger and acquisition, divestitures, downsizing, furloughs, and offshoring. Each of these business decisions has significant impact to the workforce, and care and prudence must be taken to ensure a successful restructuring occurs. Understand the differences between these types of restructuring and what actions HR might take in each circumstance.

Review Questions

You can find the answers in Appendix A.

1. Which law establishes the minimum wage and overtime pay requirements in the United States?
    A. NLRA
    B. ERISA
    C. FLSA
    D. COBRA

2. Under which law are employees allowed to continue their health insurance coverage after leaving a job?
    A. ADA
    B. COBRA
    C. FLSA
    D. OSHA

3. Which of the following is an example of an unfair labor practice under the NLRA? (Choose all that apply.)
    A. An employer firing an employee for joining a union
    B. A union threatening employees who refuse to join
    C. An employer offering higher wages to employees who oppose unionization
    D. An employer holding regular staff meetings

4. Which of the following is a key provision of the Family and Medical Leave Act (FMLA)?
    A. Provides up to 12 weeks of unpaid leave for qualified family or medical reasons
    B. Provides up to 12 weeks of paid leave for qualified family or medical reasons
    C. Is administered on a state level, so whether it is paid or unpaid is left up to the states to decide
    D. Requires employees to first use any PTO or other available leave

5. Which law ensures that employees receive retirement and health benefit protections?
    A. FLSA
    B. WARN Act
    C. ERISA
    D. NLRA

6. What law requires employers to ensure a safe and healthy work environment?
    A. OSHA
    B. ADA
    C. FMLA
    D. COBRA

7. Maria works in an office where a male coworker frequently makes jokes about her appearance that make her uncomfortable. She has asked him to stop, but the comments continue. Maria is hesitant to report it because she is a DACA (deferred action for childhood arrivals) worker and does not believe anti-discrimination laws apply to her. Which of the following statements is true?

- **A.** Anti-discrimination laws do not protect DACA workers, so Maria cannot report the behavior.
- **B.** Maria should get an attorney to make sure her rights are protected.
- **C.** Anti-discrimination laws protect all workers, including DACA recipients, so Maria can report the harassment.
- **D.** Maria can report the behavior, but she is not guaranteed protection unless she has a permanent residency card.

8. John overhears a group of coworkers making inappropriate comments about another employee's race. He feels uncomfortable about what he heard. What is the best way for John to handle the situation?

- **A.** Tell the employee being talked about what was said
- **B.** Tell the group to stop
- **C.** Report the comments to HR or a manager
- **D.** Stay out of it because it doesn't involve him directly

9. Which of the following are examples of organizational restructuring? (Choose all that apply.)

- **A.** Mergers and acquisitions
- **B.** Hiring
- **C.** Downsizing or layoffs
- **D.** Outsourcing

10. What should an HR department do if harassment complaints continue after being reported?

- **A.** Escalate the issues to senior leadership
- **B.** Dismiss the harasser
- **C.** Tell the employee there is nothing more HR can do
- **D.** Enforce disciplinary actions if necessary, and protect the victim from retaliation

11. Which of the following are acceptable documents for verifying identity and employment eligibility for Form I-9? (Choose all that apply.)

- **A.** US passport
- **B.** Driver's license and Social Security card
- **C.** Birth certificate
- **D.** Arrival/departure record

12. What are some possible penalties for I-9 violations? (Choose all that apply.)

    A. Fines ranging from $200 to over $2,000 per form for first offenses

    B. Employee dismissal

    C. Criminal charges for knowingly hiring unauthorized workers

    D. Reassignment of employees to different roles

13. Which of the following is an example of workplace retaliation? (Choose all that apply.)

    A. Moving an employee to a different department after they file a complaint

    B. Offering training opportunities to an employee who raised a safety concern

    C. Firing or demoting an employee for reporting harassment

    D. Providing feedback to an employee who participated in an investigation

14. Which agency is responsible for enforcing anti-discrimination laws in the workplace?

    A. Equal Employment Opportunity Commission (EEOC)

    B. Department of Labor (DOL)

    C. Occupational Safety and Health Administration (OSHA)

    D. Internal Revenue Service (IRS)

15. Which of the following is a key requirement of the PPACA for large employers?

    A. Offering health insurance to all employees, regardless of status

    B. Offering health insurance to full-time employees and their dependents

    C. Providing free health insurance to all employees

    D. Offering health insurance only to part-time employees

16. Which of the following are considered compensable time under the Portal-to-portal Act? EQ: (Choose all that apply.)

    A. Time spent traveling between work sites during the workday

    B. Time spent working through a lunch break

    C. Time spent on mandatory training required by the employer

    D. Time spent performing essential job duties before or after the official workday starts or ends

17. Which of the following is a key way companies can ensure compliance with ERISA?

    A. Securing employment practices liability insurance

    B. Filing regular reports with the Department of Labor

    C. Allowing employees to manage their own retirement funds without interference

    D. Matching employee contributions equally

18. What is the primary difference between the Davis-Bacon Act and the Walsh-Healy Public Contracts Act?

    A. The Davis-Bacon Act applies to government contracts over $10,000, while the Walsh-Healy Act applies to contracts over $2,000.

    B. The Walsh-Healy Act covers workers on federal construction projects, while the Davis-Bacon Act covers workers on manufacturing and supply contracts.

    C. The Davis-Bacon Act requires prevailing wages on federal construction projects, while the Walsh-Healy Act sets standards for wages, hours, and safety for manufacturing and supply contracts.

    D. The Walsh-Healy Act focuses on minimum wage standards, while the Davis-Bacon Act focuses on health and safety regulations.

19. How does OSHA enforce workplace safety? (Choose all that apply.)

    A. By creating safety standards and conducting inspections

    B. By offering tax incentives to safe companies

    C. By issuing citations and fines for violations

    D. By hiring private companies to inspect workplaces

20. Which of the following are effective ways companies can prevent repeated harassment issues? (Choose all that apply.)

    A. Ignoring minor complaints to avoid conflict

    B. Providing regular harassment prevention training

    C. Establishing clear anti-harassment policies and reporting systems

    D. Delaying investigations until multiple complaints are made

Associate Professional in Human Resources, International (aPHRi)

Chapter

7

aPHRi HR Operations

---

aPHRi EXAM OBJECTIVES COVERED IN THIS CHAPTER REQUIRE KNOWLEDGE RELATED TO FUNCTIONAL AREA 01, HR OPERATIONS:

✓ 01-01 Organizational strategy and its connection to mission, vision, values, business goals, and objectives

✓ 01-02 Organizational culture (for example: traditions, unwritten procedures)

✓ 01-03 Legal and regulatory environment

✓ 01-04 Confidentiality and privacy rules that apply to employee records, company data, individual data

✓ 01-05 Business functions (for example: accounting, finance, operations, sales, marketing)

✓ 01-06 HR administration, policies and procedures (for example: personnel management, progressive discipline)

✓ 01-07 HR metrics (for example: cost per hire, time to recruit, turnover rate)

✓ 01-08 Tools to compile data (for example: spreadsheets, statistical software)

✓ 01-09 Methods to collect data (for example: surveys, interviews, observation)

✓ 01-10 Reporting and presentation techniques (for example: histogram, bar chart)

✓ 01-11 Impact of technology on HR (for example: social media, monitoring software, biometrics)

✓ 01-12 Employee records management (for example: electronic/paper, retention, disposal)

✓ **01-13 Reporting requirements about the workforce (for example: new hires, involuntary/voluntary termination)**

✓ **01-14 Purpose and function of human resources information systems (HRIS)**

✓ **01-15 Job classifications (for example: hourly, salary, full-time, part-time, contractor)**

✓ **01-16 Job descriptions**

✓ **01-17 Reporting structure (for example: flat organizational charts)**

✓ **01-18 Types of external providers of HR services (for example: recruitment firms, benefit brokers, staffing agencies, consultants)**

✓ **01-19 Communication techniques (for example: written, oral, email, intercultural awareness)**

Functional area 01, HR Operations, accounts for 33% of the aPHRi exam, which is the most content of all the functional areas. HRCI summarizes this exam content as "understanding the tactical and operational tasks related to workforce management and the HR function and complying with the regulations and policies that affect the organization."

Following is a list of key terms you should be familiar with to understand the functional area of HR operations:

- *Organizational goals*: How a company's mission, vision, and values connect with its goals and plans for the future.

- *Workplace culture*: The traditions, unwritten rules, and habits that shape how people behave at work.

- *Laws and regulations*: The rules companies must follow to stay legal, such as labor laws and workplace safety.

- *Data privacy*: Protecting personal and company information from being shared without permission.

- *Business departments*: Key areas of a business like accounting, marketing, and sales that work with HR.

- *HR policies*: The rules a company uses to manage employees, like discipline and handling problems.

- *HR metrics*: Numbers that show how well HR is doing, like how long it takes to hire someone or how many employees leave.

- *Recruiting*: The process of finding and hiring new employees for the company.

- *Records management*: Organizing and storing employee information, either on paper or electronically.

HR Done Wrong

"Company Announces Plans to Track Workers," read headlines in September 2024 when the UK branch of the international company PricewaterhouseCoopers (PWC) told employees that they would be subject to increased monitoring of their location in an effort to return people to in-person working. The company goal is to increase face-to-face time with the clients or being in the office 60% of the time. This action follows similar return to site efforts of companies that are concerned with lower productivity and/or accountability of a remote work force and the discomfort of management challenges that are associated with such working conditions.

Ironically, PwC is primarily an audit and assurance consulting organization whose tag line is "building trust for today and tomorrow" (https://www.pwc.com). With more than 360,000 employees worldwide, it seems remote working is problematic when there is a need from a business connection sense to build personal client relationships that are most effective when done in person. This decision to move to a teleworking model was out of necessity from the global pandemic, and there is much discussion in the business community about the pros and cons of remaining in such a configuration now that the risks have been reduced. However, too many in the current workforce have found freedom and comfort in the previous arrangement and are less motivated to return.

Part of the issue in this specific case is how and why the decision to return to in-person work was communicated and its apparent conflict with the company's corporate values of independence and trust. The tracking and monitoring of employees during their workday, even if it's just their physical location, can have potential negative unintended consequences. The policy may have challenges being successfully implemented if there is a strong backlash from the employees. HR professionals must understand how strong policy changes can affect the operations of an organization, the impact to corporate culture, and how HR operations are conducted to meet the intent and goals of the corporate leaders. HR professionals can leverage technology, establish metrics, and find alternative solutions when ones initiated by management may have poor results.

The Operational Environment

HR operates in a complex environment that is influenced by many different factors, which can be understood using the PESTLE framework. *PESTLE* stands for political, economic, social, technological, legal, and environmental factors. Each of these areas affects how HR functions in a company.

Political factors include government policies, regulations, and labor laws that HR must follow to keep the company compliant and avoid legal issues. Economic factors, like changes in the job market or inflation, can affect hiring, salaries, and employee benefits. Social factors, such as shifting workforce demographics and changing employee expectations, influence how companies recruit and retain workers. US-based companies that have international divisions must understand the cultural norms and differences that impact an international workforce. Many corporate leaders may have a home bias and expect workers and operations to run exactly as they do in the host nation of the corporate headquarters. They must look at each international operation as independent elements with a similar mission but a different composition. It is similar to driving across a country along two different routes. The end state may be the same, but the path and all that occurs along the way is decidedly different.

Technological advances also shape HR, as new tools like HR software and social media change the way companies manage employee records, recruitment and communication. Legal factors require HR to stay up to date on laws related to employee rights, discrimination, and data privacy. Lastly, environmental factors, such as a company's approach to sustainability, can impact HR policies related to corporate social responsibility and workplace practices.

In this environment, HR must be flexible, informed, and prepared to adapt to changes while keeping the company's workforce engaged and compliant with all relevant laws and trends.

Legal and Regulatory Environment

The legal and regulatory environment in which businesses must operate is made up of rules and laws that companies need to follow to stay in business and avoid getting into legal trouble. These laws come from the government and cover many areas of a business, from how they treat their employees to how they handle their money.

For example, there are employment laws that protect workers by setting rules for things like minimum wage, overtime pay, working conditions, and safety standards. Companies must also follow anti-discrimination laws, which ensure that employees are treated fairly no matter their race, gender, age, or disability. These laws help create equal opportunities for everyone in the workplace.

Additionally, businesses must follow environmental laws that regulate how they use natural resources and manage waste, which can impact the environment. Financial regulations ensure that businesses keep accurate records of their money and pay taxes. There are also privacy laws, like the General Data Protection Regulation (GDPR) in Europe, that protect personal information and prevent companies from misusing people's data.

Confidentiality and privacy rules that apply to employee records, company data, and individual data are designed to protect sensitive information and ensure it is only shared with authorized people. For employee records, this includes personal information like government identification numbers, health records, and performance reviews. HR must keep these records secure and prevent unauthorized access. Companies often have an affirmative duty to protect and safeguard personally identifiable information or other information of a sensitive nature and must be able to demonstrate that due diligence has been done to reduce the risk of data compromise.

Company data, such as financial reports or business strategies, are also protected to prevent leaks or misuse that could harm the company. For individual data, especially in today's digital age, privacy rules ensure that personal information is handled responsibly, following legal standards like data protection laws. These rules create trust between employees and the company and help avoid legal problems related to data breaches or misuse. In today's world of cybercriminals, hackers, and corporate espionage, proprietary information is at risk, and companies may face legal repercussions for failing to take appropriate measures in securing corporate information of clients and customers. Negligence, lack of training, or insider threats are all areas where a company should have known or anticipated vulnerabilities and may have failed to take action risking legal exposure.

Legal Compliance in a Transnational Organization

Legal compliance in a transnational organization means that the company must follow the laws and regulations of every country in which it operates. This can be complicated because each country may have different rules about things like employment, taxes, trade, and data protection. Examples include the following:

- **Labor Laws and Employment Contracts:** Different countries have varying rules on employee rights, such as minimum wage, working hours, overtime pay, and job security. For example, some countries have strict regulations on employee dismissal, while others have more flexible rules.

- **Benefits and Compensation:** Employee benefits, such as health insurance, paid leave, and retirement plans, differ widely across countries. In some places, companies are required by law to provide specific benefits, while in others, it's left up to the employer.

- **Paid Time Off and Holidays:** The amount of paid vacation days and public holidays varies significantly. Some countries, like France, have mandatory long vacations, while others offer fewer days off by law.

Transnational companies must comply with international trade regulations, environmental laws, and privacy rules like the GDPR in Europe. Failure to follow these laws can result in fines, legal action, or damage to the company's reputation. To stay compliant, transnational organizations often have legal teams or experts in each country to ensure they are following the local and international laws. This is especially important when some of these laws conflict with each other across international boundaries. Companies must take precautions to avoid operating practices that are valid in one country being used in another country that could be against the law. This is sometimes found in certain countries where there are religious, legal, or societal restrictions to performing certain work based on gender.

Employee Records Management

Employee records management involves keeping accurate and secure records of employee information, such as job applications, performance reviews, and payroll data. These records must be organized and easily accessible while ensuring privacy and protection from unauthorized access. HR is responsible for managing both digital and paper records to meet legal and company standards.

Here's a short list of the different types of records HR must keep:

- **Employee personal information:** Basic details like name, address, contact information, and emergency contacts
- **Job application and resume:** Records of the employee's application materials and work history
- **Employment contracts:** Agreements between the employee and employer about job terms, salary, and benefits
- **Performance reviews:** Records of employee evaluations, feedback, and goals
- **Payroll records:** Information on salaries, bonuses, taxes, and deductions
- **Attendance and leave records:** Tracking sick days, vacation days, and absences
- **Personnel reports:** A summary of an employee's overall work performance, achievements, and any disciplinary actions taken
- **Training records:** Details of any professional development, training, or certifications an employee has completed

HR creates records when employees are hired, promoted, or evaluated, and these records are kept for a specific period, depending on company policy and legal requirements. Retention periods often vary based on the nature of the information or for operational need, but payroll records that impact tax collection or withholding often have a much longer retention period. Generally, once records are no longer needed for current operations, they must be disposed of properly, often through shredding or secure deletion, to protect sensitive information and comply with privacy laws.

Many countries have their own compliance requirements when it comes to data management. For example, the General Data Protection Regulations (GDPR) is the primary law that must be followed by companies that collect or manage data of individuals residing in the European Union (EU). However, several EU countries also have specific labor laws that supplement GDPR for employee data and recordkeeping. One example is Germany, where under the Federal Data Protection Act (Bundesdatenschutzgesetz, BDSG), stricter requirements exist for employee data processing, and employee works councils often have a say in how data are handled. For HR, this means that several best practices should be maintained, including the following:

- Clear documentation and data retention policies for employee data, specifying what data are stored and for how long.
- Employee consent where necessary, particularly for sensitive data.

- Transparency in data processing and clear privacy notices to employees about how their data will be used.

- Robust data security measures to prevent unauthorized access, breaches, or misuse of employee information.

Workforce Reporting Requirements

Companies are often required to report certain workforce data to government agencies:

- **New hires:** Companies must report information about new employees, including their start date and personal details, to government agencies for tax, employment verification, or benefits purposes.

- **Voluntary and involuntary dismissal:** When an employee leaves a company, whether they quit (voluntary) or are fired/laid off (involuntary), HR must report the dismissal, often for unemployment insurance and workforce data tracking. This helps the company and government agencies manage records and benefits for departing employees.

Workforce reporting requirements can vary significantly by region, as different countries and local governments have their own rules and regulations for what data must be reported and when. Following are some examples of how this might differ:

- **United States:** Companies must report new hires to state agencies within a specific number of days for tax purposes and to assist with child support enforcement. Additionally, organizations must report involuntary terminations for unemployment insurance purposes. Companies also report data on diversity, such as the Equal Employment Opportunity (EEO) reports, to ensure compliance with anti-discrimination laws.

- **European Union:** In the EU, companies have strict data protection rules under the GDPR and must report any data breaches affecting employees. Additionally, companies are required to provide detailed records on working hours, overtime, and employee contracts to ensure compliance with labor laws, which can vary from country to country within the EU.

- **Canada:** Employers must report new hires and terminations to provincial agencies for tax, social insurance, and pension purposes. The rules for reporting employee information can vary by province, especially regarding paid leave, health insurance, and pension contributions.

- **Middle East (Gulf States):** In some Gulf states, workforce reporting includes data on the ratio of local nationals to expatriates, as many countries have specific quotas (such as "Saudization" in Saudi Arabia) to ensure that local citizens are employed.

Basically, what this means is that factors such as tax regulations, labor laws, and government policies all influence workforce reporting requirements. One example in the United States was the reporting of a new hire that may have been receiving unemployment benefits or had some barrier to employment. When reporting this hire, the company may have been eligible for certain tax benefits for a qualified hire. The tracking and reporting served as a verification on someone returning to the workforce and simultaneously providing the justification and evidence for the company to meet the tax rebate requirements.

Organizational Strategy

Organizational strategy is the plan a company creates to reach its long-term goals and succeed in its business. This strategy guides how the company operates and makes decisions to stay competitive and grow.

The mission, vision, and values help to shape a company's identity and help employees understand what they are working toward. The *mission* is its main purpose or reason for existing. The *vision* is what the company wants to achieve in the future. *Values* are the core beliefs that guide how the company operates, such as honesty or teamwork.

Business goals are the big things a company wants to accomplish, like increasing profits or expanding to new markets. *Objectives* are the specific steps or actions needed to reach those goals. Setting clear goals and objectives helps keep the company on track to achieve their strategy.

Company Culture

Organizational culture refers to the shared beliefs, values, and behaviors that shape how people work together in a company. Traditions are the practices that employees follow, which can include everything from how meetings are run to how people celebrate milestones. A strong culture can create a positive work environment.

Culture has a strong influence on business strategy because it shapes the way employees think, act, and make decisions. A company's culture reflects its values, beliefs, and traditions, which can impact how strategies are developed and carried out.

For example, a company with a culture that values innovation and creativity might focus its business strategy on developing new products and entering new markets. A company with a more traditional, risk-averse culture may adopt a strategy that focuses on maintaining stability and improving existing products.

Culture also affects how employees respond to strategic changes. In a positive, supportive culture, employees are more likely to embrace new goals and work together to achieve them. In a less open culture, resistance to change might make it harder to implement new strategies.

Overall, when a company's culture aligns with its strategy, employees are more motivated, communication is clearer, and the organization is better positioned to achieve its business goals.

Companies can communicate their organizational strategy by sharing clear and simple messages that explain their goals and plans. This can be done through meetings, emails, presentations, and company-wide updates. Leaders should explain how the strategy connects to the company's mission, vision, and values, so employees understand why it matters. Each employee's tasks or performance objectives can be nested and tied directly to a line of effort or large goal that supports or drives the company toward achieving a desired end state. Visual tools like charts or videos can help make the strategy easier to understand. It's also important for leaders to encourage feedback and answer questions so that everyone feels involved and knows how they contribute to achieving the company's goals.

Leaders should also be aware of the intercultural differences of their teams. In global companies, employees come from diverse backgrounds, so it's important to be aware of cultural differences in communication styles, customs, and values to work well together. This includes awareness of the unwritten practices and procedures, which are the informal rules and ways of doing things that are understood by employees. For example, everyone may know that certain meetings are always held at a specific time, even if it's not in the official schedule. These practices help the company run smoothly.

Unwritten rules and expectations can cause problems on international teams when team members from different cultures don't understand or follow these informal practices. Since these rules aren't written down, people from other countries may not know they exist. For example, some cultures may have specific expectations about how meetings are run, how people communicate, or how decisions are made. Without clear communication, international team members might unknowingly break these unwritten rules, leading to misunderstandings or frustration. This can be something as simple as the shape of the meeting table. In some configurations a table with a head position may create a perception of a hierarchy and where an individual sits directly correlates to the individual's level of importance (even if this is not the case, it may be an unintended result). Whereas a circular table for a team may convey or infer a different intention or meaning.

Different cultures also have different ways of showing respect or handling conflict. If unwritten rules clash with these cultural differences, it can create confusion or tension. To avoid problems, it's important for international teams to openly discuss expectations and clarify any informal practices so everyone understands how to work together smoothly. A great example is certain cultures in the Middle East. Be cognizant when asking for or requiring a deadline for delivery of goods or services that an individual may have cultural difficulty in telling you they cannot meet that timeline. They may wish to avoid conflict or not look incapable or inhospitable by stating the request cannot be met. Instead of agreeing outright that something will be ready at a certain agreed-upon time, they will obfuscate and say something to the effect that they certainly wish it so. Hence they give agreement without commitment or confirmation.

Business Operations

Business operations are the daily activities and processes a company uses to produce goods or provide services. This includes managing resources, employees, and systems to ensure the business runs smoothly and meets its goals. *Business functions* are specific areas within a company that handle different tasks, such as accounting, finance, HR, marketing, and sales. Each function plays a key role in supporting the overall success of the business. Business functions are often sorted into individual departments:

- Human Resources manage employee-related tasks, including hiring, training, benefits, and workplace policies.

- Accounting handles a company's financial records, tracking income, expenses, and taxes to ensure proper financial management.

- Production is the process of creating goods or services that the company sells to customers.

- Sales and Marketing work together to promote products and services, attract customers, and close deals to generate revenue for the company.

- Research and Development (R&D) involves creating new products or improving existing ones to stay competitive and meet customer needs.

- Customer Service provides support to customers by answering questions, solving problems, and ensuring satisfaction with products or services.

The *reporting structure* is how employees are organized and who reports to whom in a company. There are a few different structures to be familiar with for the aPHRi exam:

- *Hierarchical*: A hierarchical organizational structure is like a pyramid, where employees report to one boss, and that boss reports to someone higher up. Each level has more authority than the one below it, with the top leader at the very top.

- *Functional*: A functional organizational structure groups employees based on the type of work they do. Each department has its own manager, and everyone works on tasks related to their job specialty.

- *Matrix*: A matrix structure has employees reporting to more than one manager, typically a functional manager and a project manager, allowing for flexibility across departments.

- *Divisional*: A divisional structure divides the company into separate divisions based on products, markets, or geography, with each division operating semi-independently but reporting to the overall company leadership.

Organizational charts visually show the hierarchy of a company, detailing who reports to whom and how different departments are structured.

HR Operations

HR operations is the part of human resources that handles the daily tasks related to managing employees. This includes things like keeping employee records, handling payroll, organizing benefits, and making sure company policies are followed. HR operations also helps with hiring new employees, onboarding them, and managing any issues that come up, like performance problems or conflicts. Overall, it ensures that the company runs smoothly, and employees are supported in their roles. One of the critical tasks to conducting successful HR operations is a firm understanding of the supported business operations. Many HR professionals are proud of their understanding of HR practices, employment law, policies, and human relations, which are all important pillars to our field. However, among the chief criticisms of HR is a perceived lack of business savvy or expertise. HR professionals must strive to understand the business to be more involved from a strategic and operational perspective.

Aside from people management, HR operations and administration also handle tasks like payroll management, making sure employees are paid correctly and on time, and benefits administration, which includes organizing health insurance, retirement plans, and other employee benefits. HR also manages compliance with labor laws and company policies, ensuring the organization follows legal requirements. Additionally, HR takes care of employee records management, organizing and securing important documents, and HR metrics, where data are used to measure things like recruitment success, turnover rates, and employee performance. They also handle training and development, helping employees grow in their roles through workshops and courses.

To better align with the organizational goals and business, HR professionals must be able to evaluate how well they are conducting HR operations. All of the HR functions discussed require some measures of performance. *Measures of performance* examine how well a task is performed while *measures of effectiveness* determine if the tasks are the right ones to do. More simply, is HR doing the tasks correctly (performance) versus is HR doing the correct tasks (effectiveness).

HR Performance Measures

Measures of HR performance are a key part of HR operations that focus on evaluating how well HR is supporting the organization. One important aspect of this is providing internal customer service, where HR answers or directs employee questions about policies, benefits, or procedures as the first level of support. Clear communication about HR policies and procedures is essential to ensure employees understand expectations, benefits, and company rules. HR performance is assessed using metrics and data collection to track important areas such as employee satisfaction, turnover rates, recruitment efficiency, and time to hire. By analyzing these measures, HR can make informed decisions to improve processes, enhance the work environment, and better support both employees and the organization.

Today's digital platforms that collect and store HR data and information have made performing transactional tasks such as entering personnel information much more efficient. This provides for higher data accuracy and facilitates the ability to analyze and interpret the data that have been obtained. New technology and business intelligence software provides tools to visualize data to see patterns and predict future trends. This higher level of performance measures gives a competitive advantage to companies and enables corporate leaders to make better, more informed decisions.

Policies, Procedures, and Rules

Human resources often seek to manage people through the use of policies, procedures, and rules. This gives supervisors and other organizational leaders a guidebook to help establish expectations to support employee success. *Policies* are the official guidelines that define how things should be done in the organization, covering areas like attendance, behavior, and safety. *Procedures* are the specific steps or processes employees must follow to meet these policies, ensuring consistency in how tasks are performed. *Rules* are the specific do's and don'ts that help maintain order and set clear boundaries for acceptable behavior in the workplace. Following is a brief example of an HR policy, procedure, and rule, all focused on attendance:

Attendance Policy The company expects employees to be present and on time for all scheduled work hours. Excessive absenteeism or frequent tardiness without a valid reason may result in disciplinary action, up to and including dismissal.

Attendance Reporting Procedure

1. Employees who will be late or absent must notify their supervisor as soon as possible, preferably no later than one hour before their shift starts.
2. Submit an absence report via the HR system or call the HR department.
3. HR will track the absence and notify payroll of any adjustments needed.

Attendance Rule Employees are required to clock in within 5 minutes of their scheduled start time. Failure to clock in on time more than three times in a 30-day period without prior notice may result in a written warning.

These examples demonstrate how an attendance policy sets expectations, procedures outline the steps employees must follow, and rules set specific guidelines for punctuality and absences.

Employee discipline is an important part of ensuring that policies, procedures, and rules are followed in the workplace. When employees don't meet expectations or break the rules, discipline helps correct the behavior and maintain a fair and productive environment. Some companies use a system called *progressive discipline*, where issues are addressed step by step, starting with a warning and escalating if the problem continues. HR metrics play a role in this process by tracking patterns in behavior, such as repeated lateness or poor performance, to identify when discipline may be needed. By using metrics alongside clear rules and procedures, HR can make sure that discipline is applied fairly and consistently, helping employees improve while keeping the organization running smoothly.

HR Metrics

Companies use policies, procedures, and rules to guide how employees should behave and perform at work, but they also need a way to measure how well these guidelines are working. This is where HR metrics come in. HR measures key aspects of employee performance and company operations to ensure the workplace runs smoothly and efficiently. By tracking certain metrics, HR can spot issues like high employee turnover, long hiring processes, or low job satisfaction. These measures help HR understand where improvements are needed and make better decisions to support both employees and the company. The top five HR performance measures often include the following:

- *Employee turnover rate*: This measures how often employees leave the company and can indicate issues with retention or job satisfaction.

- *Time to hire*: This tracks how long it takes to fill a job vacancy, showing the efficiency of the recruitment process.

- *Cost per hire*: This metric calculates the total cost involved in hiring a new employee, including advertising, recruiter fees, and onboarding.

- *Employee engagement/satisfaction*: This measures how happy and engaged employees are in their roles, often through surveys, and can impact overall productivity and retention.

- *Absenteeism rate*: This tracks how often employees are absent from work and can indicate issues with job satisfaction, health, or workplace morale.

Because many of these metrics are analyzed over time, companies may not realize how much money is being spent on flawed processes. Corporate executives focus on net profits or productivity and have difficulty visualizing costs associated with turnover because it is much harder to track the total cost invested in training a new employee that suddenly quits, the sunk costs of recruiting and marketing for open positions, and the lost productivity being short staffed because of vacancies that go unfilled for long periods. Poor HR practices can result in thousands of dollars in lost revenue. Take an example of a small business that spends roughly $13,000 to recruit, hire, onboard, and train every new hire. However, the company invests very little in improving workplace culture or aligning people with the right fit job. As a result, in one year, the company hires and replaces 100 people. That is $1.3 million spent with very little return on investment. In today's work environment, people job hop every two to three years. Imagine the amount of savings a company can achieve by setting conditions such that employees remain engaged with the organization to a five-year point.

HR Data Collection

HR data collection is the process of gathering information to help measure and improve how a company manages its employees. There are different methods HR can use to collect this data. One simple way is through spreadsheets, where information like employee attendance, performance, and salaries can be tracked and organized. For more complex data, companies might use business intelligence software, which helps analyze larger sets of information and gives insights into trends, such as employee turnover rates or hiring patterns. Statistical software is another tool HR can use to analyze data more deeply, helping to find patterns and make predictions, like forecasting future hiring needs. All these methods help HR make informed decisions to support both the company and its employees.

> **Providing data analysis to support HR-related decisions**
>
> As the availability of business intelligence software grows in the market, the demand for HR professionals to be proficient in building queries, automated reports, and data visualization products increases. HR professionals must embrace data literacy and assist managers to be good data consumers to make timely decisions based on relevant data.

HR can collect data using several methods to better understand employee performance and workplace trends. *Surveys* are one of the most common methods, where employees answer questions about their job satisfaction, work environment, or other issues. *Interviews* allow HR to get more detailed feedback by asking specific questions in a one-on-one setting, giving deeper insight into employee concerns. *Observation* involves watching employees at work to understand how they perform their tasks and interact with others.

Once data are collected, *data analytics* can be used to analyze it. Analytics ranges from *descriptive analytics*, which simply explains what has happened (like tracking how many people were hired last year), to *prescriptive analytics*, which uses data to recommend actions (like suggesting strategies to improve future hiring).

To share the insights from data collection, *data visualization techniques* are used. This involves creating charts and graphs that make it easier to understand the data. For example, a *histogram* can show the distribution of data, like how a comparison of managers salaries by department, while a *bar chart* compares different groups. See Figure 7.1 for an example of a histogram, and the same data reflected in a bar chart in Figure 7.2.

FIGURE 7.1   Sample histogram

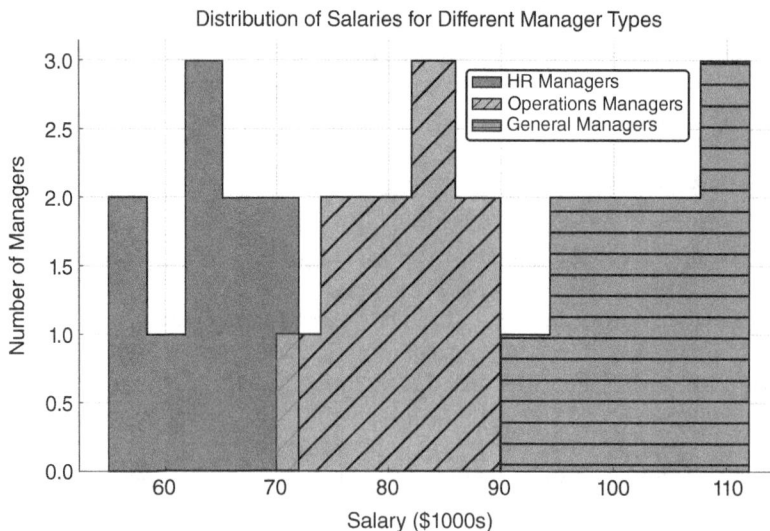

Distribution of Salaries for Different Manager Types

FIGURE 7.2   Sample bar chart

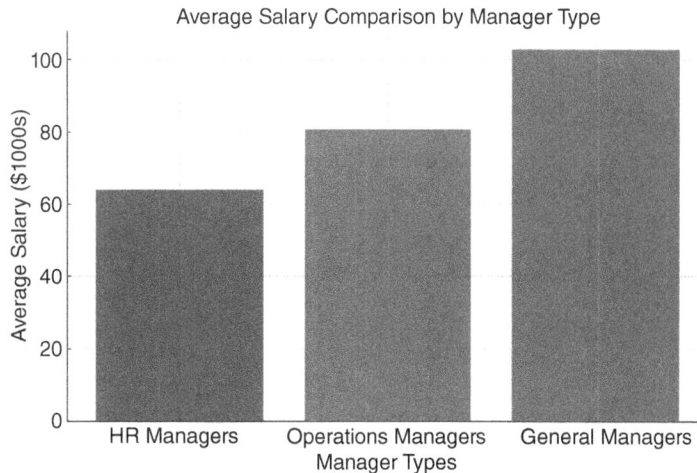

The key difference between a histogram and a bar chart is that histograms are used to show the distribution of data within different ranges or intervals, whereas bar charts are used to compare distinct categories or groups, showing the relationship between these categories and a particular measure.

Building Job Structures

Building job structures means organizing jobs within a company by grouping similar roles and responsibilities together. In HR operations, job structures help create consistent pay scales, promotion paths, and job classifications, ensuring that employees have a clear understanding of how each role fits into the organization. In the employee lifecycle, job structures impact every stage, from recruitment to retirement. During recruitment, clear job structures help HR create accurate job descriptions, making it easier to find the right candidates. Once hired, employees understand their role and potential career paths within the company. As employees develop, job structures provide guidelines for performance evaluations, promotions, and potential job transitions. Finally, these structures play a role in succession planning, helping companies identify replacements prior to a position becoming open.

There are two key areas to understand when it comes to building job structures:

- *Job classification*: Job classification categorizes jobs based on how employees are paid, the nature of their work, and their relationship with the employer. See Table 7.1 for examples of the different types of job classifications that you will be tested on.

- *Job descriptions*: A job description is a written document that outlines the main tasks, responsibilities, and qualifications for a specific job. It helps employees understand what is expected of them and assists HR in hiring the right candidates for the role, developing salary bands, and managing employee performance.

TABLE 7.1   Job Classifications

Job Classification	Definition
Hourly	Hourly workers are paid based on the number of hours they work, typically at a set rate per hour.
Salary	Salaried employees earn a fixed amount of money for their work, regardless of the number of hours they work.
Full Time	Full-time employees work a set number of hours per week, usually 35 to 40, and may receive benefits like health insurance.
Part Time	Part-time workers work fewer hours than full time, often under 30 hours per week, and may or may not get benefits.
Contractor	Contractors are hired for a specific project or period and are usually not considered an employee of the company.

NOTE

Essential functions are the key duties or tasks that an employee must be able to do in a specific job. These are the most important parts of a job and are necessary for the position to exist. For example, if you're a delivery driver, an essential function would be driving and delivering packages. In many cases, essential functions are listed in the job description so employers are transparent about a job's rigor and potential for accommodation. The Americans with Disabilities Act (ADA) classifies essential functions based on several factors:

▪ **Importance:** Essential functions are the core tasks that are fundamental to the job. The job exists to perform these duties, and without them, the role wouldn't be necessary.

▪ **Frequency:** How often the task is performed helps determine if it's essential. If a task is done regularly or takes up a significant part of the employee's time, it's likely considered essential.

▪ **Specialized Skills:** If the job requires specific skills or expertise that only the employee is hired to perform, those duties are considered essential.

▪ **Consequences of Not Performing the Function:** If not completing the task would affect the operation of the business or create significant problems, it's an essential function.

Employers focus on these tasks when hiring, training, or evaluating employees to make sure the most important parts of the job are done well.

In order for a job description to be effective, it should include several key components:

- **Job title:** The official title of the position that clearly reflects the nature of the role.

- **Job summary/overview:** A brief statement summarizing the main purpose and responsibilities of the position. It provides a high-level view of the role within the organization.

- **Duties and responsibilities:** A detailed list of the tasks and responsibilities the employee will be expected to perform. This section outlines specific functions and expectations for the position.

- **Qualifications/requirements:** The skills, experience, education, certifications, and other qualifications required or preferred for the job. This section may also include soft skills, such as communication abilities or teamwork.

- **Working conditions:** Information about the work environment, such as whether the job involves office work, fieldwork, travel, physical demands, or irregular hours. It may also outline any potential hazards or special conditions related to the job.

- **Reporting structure:** Specifies the position's place in the organizational hierarchy, including who the employee will report to and, if applicable, any direct reports.

- **Job location:** The location where the job will be performed, whether it's at a specific office, remote, or requires travel.

Outsourcing HR Functions

Outsourcing HR functions involves hiring external companies or specialists to handle tasks like payroll, benefits administration, recruiting, or employee training. The purpose of outsourcing is to allow businesses to focus on their core operations while experts manage HR tasks, often leading to cost savings and increased efficiency. Key considerations when outsourcing include ensuring that the service provider understands the company's culture and legal obligations, maintaining data security and privacy, and regularly monitoring the quality of services to ensure that they meet the company's needs and standards.

Recruitment firms are companies that help businesses find and hire the right employees. Similarly *staffing agencies* provide temporary or long-term workers for companies. Businesses that need to fill positions quickly or for short periods can outsource to staffing agencies, which supply qualified workers without the need for a long hiring process.

When a business outsources recruiting and hiring to these companies, it saves time by allowing experts to search for candidates, screen them, and recommend the best ones for the job. Another commonly outsourced HR function are employee benefits. *Benefit brokers* help companies choose and manage employee benefits, like health insurance and retirement plans. Outsourcing to benefit brokers helps businesses get the best deals and packages for their employees without having to handle the complex details themselves.

HR consultants are experts that give advice on specific HR issues, such as improving company policies or handling employee relations. Companies may outsource to consultants when they need specialized guidance or a fresh perspective on how to manage their workforce more effectively.

> **Choosing Employer of Record or Legal Entity**
>
> An employer of record (EOR) is a third-party organization that handles the legal responsibilities of employing workers on behalf of a company. This includes managing payroll, taxes, benefits, and ensuring compliance with local labor laws. The company using the EOR still manages the employees' day-to-day tasks. An EOR is particularly helpful when a company wants to hire workers in different locations or countries without establishing its own legal entity in those areas. Setting up a legal entity can be time-consuming and expensive, requiring knowledge of local regulations, tax systems, and employment laws. By choosing an EOR, companies can hire employees quickly while ensuring compliance with local laws, without the need to go through the complex process of creating a legal entity in each location.

When outsourcing HR functions, companies can face several challenges. One major issue is co-employment, which happens when both the company and the outsourcing provider share control over employees. This can lead to confusion about who is responsible for managing the employee, handling legal issues, or providing benefits, especially if workers are temporary or contracted through staffing agencies.

Another challenge is communication. Since the outsourced provider may not be fully integrated into the company, misunderstandings can arise regarding company culture, goals, or expectations. This can lead to inconsistencies in how HR functions are handled.

Data security is also a concern, as sensitive employee information, like payroll and personal details, are shared with a third-party provider. Ensuring the outsourced company follows strict data protection rules is critical to avoid breaches or leaks.

Lastly, quality control can be difficult to manage. Companies may find that outsourced services don't always meet their standards or that the external provider doesn't fully understand the unique needs of their business, which can impact employee satisfaction and HR effectiveness.

Managing these challenges requires clear contracts, regular communication, and careful selection of outsourcing partners.

HR Technology

HR technology refers to the tools and software used to help manage employees and HR tasks. This includes things like tracking attendance, handling payroll, managing benefits, and storing employee records. Technology has transformed how HR departments operate by making tasks faster, more accurate, and more efficient. By using technology, HR departments can work more efficiently and make better decisions with the help of data.

Human Resource Information Systems (HRIS)

A *human resource information system (HRIS)* is a type of software that helps companies organize and manage important HR tasks. The purpose of HRIS is to store employee data, track things like job performance and training, handle payroll, and make sure the company follows labor laws. It helps HR departments save time by automating many processes, and it provides useful data to help with decision-making and planning.

Entry-level HR professionals often use HRI systems to help manage the many administrative tasks of a busy HR department. This software makes it easier for them to organize employee data, create reports, and ensure everything is up-to-date. By using an HRIS, HR workers can save time on administrative tasks and focus on other areas, like helping with recruitment or answering employee questions.

Employee self-service (ESS) is a feature in many HR systems that allows employees to manage their own information. Through ESS, employees can update their personal details, view their pay stubs, request time off, and check their benefits without needing to contact HR. This saves time for both employees and HR staff, and it helps make sure that records are accurate and up-to-date.

NOTE

Maintaining employee data in a system of record

One of the challenges in handling HR data is ensuring its accuracy. People are constantly changing. Addresses, beneficiaries, marital status, even name changes are typical life events that impact employee data inside a HRIS. Companies must establish processes to audit and verify employee data periodically and encourage employees to validate critical data fields.

Social Media

Social media has become a key tool in HR for recruiting and employer branding. Companies use platforms like LinkedIn, Facebook, and X (previously known as Twitter) to post job openings, connect with potential candidates, and promote their company culture to attract top talent.

In multinational companies, social media is a powerful tool for communication and connecting employees across different countries. It helps teams share ideas, collaborate on projects, and stay updated on company news. It's important for employees to follow company guidelines when using social media to make sure they respect cultural differences and maintain a professional image.

All enterprises should have social media policies that provide clear guidelines for employees across different countries. These policies should include the following:

- **Professional conduct:** Employees should represent the company in a positive and respectful way, keeping language and content professional.

- **Respect for cultural differences:** Since employees in different countries may have varying customs and norms, the policy should encourage cultural awareness and sensitivity when posting on social media.

- **Confidentiality:** Employees must be reminded not to share sensitive company information, trade secrets, or personal data of clients and coworkers on social media.

- **Personal vs. professional use:** The policy should clarify the difference between personal and professional accounts and guide employees on how to responsibly mention or link to the company.

- **Legal Compliance:** Employees should be informed about the importance of following local laws and regulations regarding social media use, including rules about advertising or privacy.

In some countries, strict internet restrictions control what people can see or do online. Governments may block certain websites, social media platforms, or news sources. These restrictions can affect how employees in multinational companies communicate and access information. For example, in countries with heavy internet censorship, employees might not be able to use common tools like Facebook, X (also referred to as Twitter), or Google. Companies need to be aware of these restrictions and find alternative ways to help their employees stay connected and get the information they need.

Some of the most restricted countries for internet usage include the following:

- China has one of the most heavily censored internet systems in the world, known as the "Great Firewall." Many popular sites like Google, Facebook, and YouTube are blocked, and the government closely monitors online activity.

- In North Korea, internet access is extremely limited. Only a small, elite group has access to the global internet, while most citizens can only use a government-controlled intranet with restricted content.

- Iran heavily restricts internet usage, blocking social media platforms like X (formerly Twitter), Facebook, and YouTube. The government monitors online activity and frequently shuts down internet access during protests.

In these countries, the government controls and monitors online access, limiting what people can view, share, or discuss online.

Monitoring Software

Monitoring software helps companies track employee activity, such as computer usage or time spent on tasks. This can improve productivity and ensure that employees are following company policies, but it can also raise concerns about privacy. Many companies use this software to ensure that remote workers are staying on task.

Companies use various types of monitoring software to track employee activity, manage productivity, and ensure compliance with company policies. Some common types include the following:

- **Time tracking software:** This monitors how much time employees spend on tasks, projects, or specific applications, helping manage productivity and workflow.

- **Keystroke logging:** Keystroke loggers record all keyboard activity on a computer, allowing companies to track what employees are typing, often used for security purposes.

- **Screen monitoring software:** This software captures screenshots or live video feeds of employees' computer screens to ensure they are working on assigned tasks.

- **Email and communication monitoring:** This software tracks emails, instant messages, and other communications to ensure that company policies are followed and to detect potential data leaks or inappropriate behavior.

- **Website and app monitoring:** This software tracks which websites and applications employees use during work hours, helping to ensure they aren't spending excessive time on non-work-related activities.

- **GPS tracking:** Often used for remote or mobile employees, GPS tracking software monitors the location of workers to ensure they are where they need to be for work-related tasks.

Each type of monitoring software has a different purpose, and companies must balance using these tools while respecting employees' privacy. Many companies have an acceptable use policy (AUP) or other agreement employees must acknowledge or consent to in order to access confidential information or proprietary systems. Some organizations will even put a banner on the log-in screen to highlight a user's consent to monitoring. Use of these systems implies consent and surrenders any expectation of privacy. Employees must be aware of what rights they may be waiving when using a company-provided computer.

Biometrics

Biometrics refers to using physical characteristics, like fingerprints or facial recognition, for security or attendance tracking. Companies are starting to use facial recognition systems to verify employees' identities as they enter the workplace or log into systems, replacing traditional keycards or passwords. This technology ensures that only authorized people access certain areas or systems and prevents time fraud by ensuring accurate attendance records. Biometrics combined with geo-locating software can pinpoint where an individual is located for the purposes of tracking remote workers or people who must be on a worksite that is geographically separated from a headquarters.

Communication Techniques for an Entry-level HR Professional

As an entry-level HR professional, strong communication skills are used every day to connect with employees, managers, vendors, and job applicants. On the exam, several key components should be understood, including the following:

- **Written communication:** Writing clearly and professionally in emails, reports, or company policies is important. Avoid slang, check for grammar mistakes, and be concise so your message is easy to understand.

- **Oral communication:** When speaking in person or on the phone, listen carefully and speak confidently. Use a friendly but professional tone to make others feel comfortable while ensuring your message is clear.

- **Email communication:** Emails should always be polite, clear, and to the point. Include a proper greeting, organize your thoughts in short paragraphs, and close with a professional signature.

- **Intercultural awareness:** No matter which mode of communication you choose, be respectful of cultural differences when communicating. Learn about other cultures to avoid misunderstandings, and use inclusive language to make everyone feel valued.

Summary

Human resources operations play an important role in helping companies achieve their goals while managing their employees effectively. HR ensures that the company's mission, vision, and values are reflected in how it hires, manages, and supports its workforce. By shaping a positive workplace culture and providing clear job descriptions, HR helps employees understand their roles and responsibilities. This goes beyond what many people think HR is about, such as event planning or employment terminations.

Another important aspect of HR is making sure the company follows laws and regulations to avoid legal issues. HR also protects the privacy of employee information and manages their records securely. Recruiting is a key HR function, as finding the right employees is essential for the company's success. HR sets policies and procedures to guide how employees are treated, from handling disciplinary issues to managing day-to-day personnel tasks.

HR uses data and metrics to measure how well it's performing in areas like hiring and employee retention. Overall, HR operations tie together the company's people, processes, goals, and technology to ensure a strong, well-managed workforce that helps the organization thrive.

Exam Essentials

Understand how HR operations are impacted by the operational environment.   HR professionals must understand aspects of the business' operating environment to include legal and regulatory considerations, organizational strategy, and company culture to successfully integrate HR operations and navigate the corporate landscape that is unique to the organization. HR must understand how basic functions like employee records management or workforce reporting requirements impact operational decisions by providing accurate information about the available workforce.

Understand how key HR performance indicators are measured and the importance of data literacy in HR.   Measures of performance tell a story of a company's health in the marketplace. HR professionals must be able to collect, analyze, and interpret relevant data to help managers make informed decisions in a timely manner. Understanding how HR collects data and uses the information helps HR develop the right policies, procedures, and rules to govern personnel actions and activities in the workplace.

Be able to identify key elements of an HRIS and how it supports HR operations.   An HRIS is an essential resource for a modern company HR department that enables the organization to comply with laws and regulations, monitor HR activities, generate reports, and provide information for business intelligence software to create visualizations for managers. HR technology also includes monitoring software designed to track employee activity related to the company. HR professionals must understand the impact of privacy concerns of employees related to data that are collected and to communicate the need or purpose of a company acquiring such information.

Review Questions

You can find the answers in Appendix A.

1. What does PESTLE help businesses analyze?

   A. Internal finances

   B. External factors

   C. Customer complaints

   D. Employee productivity

2. Which of the following are examples of social factors that can influence how businesses operate? (Choose all that apply.)

   A. Changes in cultural trends

   B. Population growth

   C. Shifts in consumer preferences

   D. New government regulations

3. Which of the following is a major international organization that helps protect workers' rights worldwide?

   A. World Trade Organization (WTO)

   B. International Labour Organization (ILO)

   C. United Nations Security Council (UNSC)

   D. World Health Organization (WHO)

4. What is the main goal of the General Data Protection Regulation (GDPR)?

   A. To protect companies from data breaches

   B. To control how individuals use the internet

   C. To safeguard personal data and privacy rights

   D. To promote free trade within the European Union

5. Which of the following documents are protected by privacy laws? (Choose all that apply.)

   A. Employee personal data

   B. Employee records

   C. Business records

   D. Performance reviews

6. What should be the priority for employee records management?

   A. Maximizing the amount of data collected

   B. Minimizing the amount of data collected

C. Keeping records for only as long as necessary

D. Ensuring data privacy and security

7. What is the primary purpose of an organization's strategy?

   A. To define the company's vision and values

   B. To plan for short-term decisions

   C. To guide the company in reaching its long-term goals

   D. To focus solely on increasing profits

8. Which of the following best describes the difference between goals and objectives?

   A. Goals are about employee performance, and objectives are about customer satisfaction.

   B. Goals are short-term, and objectives are long-term.

   C. Goals are related to values, while objectives relate to mission.

   D. Goals are the overall purpose, while objectives are specific actions to achieve them.

9. How does organizational culture influence business strategy?

   A. By setting the company's financial goals

   B. By shaping how employees think, act, and make decisions

   C. By limiting the company's access to new markets

   D. By focusing on employee performance

10. What is one effective way companies can communicate their organizational strategy to employees?

    A. By sharing strategy with top management

    B. By implementing the strategy and asking questions as it evolves

    C. By focusing on unwritten practices and informal rules

    D. Through meetings, emails, and presentations

11. Which of the following best describes business operations?

    A. The specific departments within a company

    B. The hiring and training of employees

    C. The financial management of a company's income and expenses

    D. The daily activities and processes a company uses to produce goods or provide services

12. In which reporting structure do employees typically report to more than one manager?

    A. Flat

    B. Product

    C. Matrix

    D. Divisional

13. Which reporting structure has few or no levels of management, allowing for quick decision-making?

    A. Flat

    B. Product

    C. Matrix

    D. Divisional

14. What is a key characteristic of a matrix reporting structure?

    A. Employees report to both functional and project managers.

    B. The company is organized around specific products or product lines.

    C. The company is divided by geographic regions.

    D. There are few or no management levels.

15. What is one of the key challenges HR professionals must overcome to improve HR operations?

    A. Being distracted by underperforming employees

    B. Overcoming the vast amount of documentation requirements

    C. Developing a stronger understanding of business operations

    D. Being limited to administrative tasks

16. What is the purpose of having policies, procedures, and rules in human resources management? (Choose all that apply.)

    A. To ensure employees are treated fairly

    B. To provide supervisors and leaders with guidelines for managing employees

    C. To make sure employees understand what is required of them

    D. To ensure compliance with labor laws

17. A policy provides general guidelines for how things should be done in an organization, while a rule _____.

    A. is a broad suggestion for behavior

    B. outlines specific do's and don'ts for acceptable behavior

    C. is a strict interpretation of the policy

    D. is what is required by a labor law

18. Which metric is most likely to predict employee turnover?

    A. Retention rate

    B. Turnover in the first six months

    C. Time to hire

    D. Employee engagement

19. What is the key difference between HR performance measures and measures of effectiveness?

    A. HR performance measures track how well HR systems are supporting overall company goals, while measures of effectiveness focus on individual employee performance.

    B. HR performance measures assess the efficiency of HR activities, while measures of effectiveness evaluate the impact of those activities on the company's success.

    C. HR performance measures focus on employee satisfaction, while measures of effectiveness track employee engagement.

    D. HR performance measures focus on company profits, while measures of effectiveness track workplace safety.

20. A company has been struggling with processing payroll accurately and efficiently. Which part of HR operations would help resolve this issue?

    A. Developing more training programs for employees

    B. Conducting more employee satisfaction surveys

    C. Improving recruitment strategies

    D. Implementing better employee record management systems

Chapter

8

aPHRi Recruitment and Selection

aPHRI EXAM OBJECTIVES COVERED IN THIS CHAPTER REQUIRE KNOWLEDGE RELATED TO FUNCTIONAL AREA 02, RECRUITMENT AND SELECTION:

✓ **02-01 Applicable laws and regulations related to recruitment and selection (for example: work authorization, job requisition, job posting)**

✓ **02-02 Applicant databases**

✓ **02-03 Recruitment sources (for example: employee referral, social networking/social media, company website)**

✓ **02-04 Recruitment methods (for example: advertising, job fairs, university)**

✓ **02-05 Alternative staffing practices (for example: recruitment process outsourcing, job sharing, remote workers)**

✓ **02-06 Interviewing techniques (for example: structured, non-structured, behavioral, situational, panel)**

✓ **02-07 Pre- and post-offer activities (for example: background checks, medical exams)**

✓ **02-08 Orientation and onboarding (for example: logistics, introducing culture, facilitating/training)**

Functional area 02, Recruitment and Selection, accounts for 22% of the aPHR exam. HRCI summarizes this exam content as "understanding the hiring process including regulatory requirements, sourcing of applicants, formal interview and selection process, and onboarding of a new hire."

HR Done Wrong

In April 2021, the University of Toronto was censured by the Canadian Association of University Teachers following a recruiting and hiring controversy of the director of the school's International Human Rights Program. A search committee comprising several key stakeholders at the university conducted interviews and performed the necessary due diligence to select its recommended candidate. While some contract negotiations still remained, it was clear that this was the choice best qualified and agreed upon unanimously by the hiring panel.

One month later, the applicant was informed that the school would not be hiring her and had made a change in their decision. While it was stated that the justification for the change was the result of visa problems and the relocation of the individual, further investigation and reporting yielded the fact that a high level donor to the institution had contacted the university's administration and strongly urged reconsideration of this hiring recommendation because the individual disagreed with the applicant's views and previous published works on the Palestinian/Israel conflict in the Middle East and related human rights issues.

Much concern was raised about an outside wealthy influencer having so much influence on the school's hiring process as to disrupt the fair and unbiased panel hiring process. As a result, several internal employees resigned from posts or committees to which they were appointed, and several organizations chose to terminate partnerships, negatively impacting the prestige of a top university in the country. An additional independent inquiry was conducted to examine the interference, which did not seem to quash the concerns that the rejection of the applicant was more politically motivated than due to lack of qualifications.

In the recruitment and selection of candidates, especially for highly visible positions that can impact public relations and are viewed as tied to the organizational values of business, HR must be aware of the potential for outside influence and stakeholders' attempts to "tip the scale" in favor of against preferred applicants. Processes and procedures must be established and followed to create a fair selection that can stand up to scrutiny. It is especially egregious when processes are in place that are then subverted and biases are permitted to change the outcome of a hiring action. Damage to reputation, employee backlash, and other negative consequences, including potential litigation are likely outcomes when this is allowed to happen.

Adapted from https://www.newyorker.com/news/our-columnists/did-a-university-of-toronto-donor-block-the-hiring-of-a-scholar-for-her-writing-on-palestine

Recruitment and Selection Defined

Recruitment is the process of finding and attracting qualified candidates for job openings in an organization. *Selection* involves evaluating these candidates to choose the most suitable one for the position. Together, recruitment and selection help ensure that companies hire the right people with the skills and qualifications needed to succeed in the role.

Global recruitment and selection involve identifying and hiring candidates from different countries to fill job positions within multinational companies. This process requires navigating diverse cultural, legal, and logistical challenges, such as differences in labor laws, work visas, and local recruitment practices. Companies use global recruitment to access a broader talent pool and fill specialized roles that may not be available locally. Regardless of the region for finding qualified talent, you should be familiar with several key terms on exam day, including the following:

- *Job posting*: A public announcement by a company about an open position, listing qualifications and responsibilities
- *Applicant tracking system*: A software used by employers to manage and screen job applications
- *Outsourcing*: Hiring external companies or individuals to perform tasks or services traditionally done in-house
- *Multinational enterprise (MNE)*: A company that operates in multiple countries across the globe
- *Interviews*: A formal meeting where candidates are evaluated for a job
- *Orientation*: An introductory session to familiarize new employees with the company
- *Onboarding*: The process of integrating new employees into an organization
- *Work authorization*: Legal permission for an individual to work in a specific country

Recruitment

Recruiting is the process of identifying and attracting qualified candidates for a specific job within an organization. It involves various marketing activities designed to gain interest from qualified individuals both inside and outside of the organization. In 2023, the Secretary of the US Army announced that the Army needed to fundamentally change how it recruited its soldiers. As a result, the Army created a new position series called talent acquisition specialists. This change recognized a reality that has existed in the civilian corporate world for many years—that recruiting and the recruiter are a very specific subset of HR skills that require focus, attention, training, and resources to be done properly. This section looks at some of these concepts and the structure around successfully finding and choosing the right people for a company.

As with all functions of human resources, complying with labor laws and aligning with business strategy are two specific aims of the recruiting process.

Legal Compliance

The laws related to recruitment can vary depending on the country and region. However, several key principles and laws commonly govern recruitment practices to ensure fairness, nondiscrimination, and legal compliance.

In 2017 the European Union Agency for Fundamental Rights (FRA) was commissioned to study business-related human rights abuses, including how business is related to human rights. Many of the findings related to employment conditions and violations related to environmental protection, fair and just working conditions, nondiscrimination, prevention of forced labor or slavery, protections from unjustified dismissal, collective bargaining, and even the freedom to choose an occupation as some of the causes.[1] The laws and legal concepts discussed in this chapter, in many ways, offer some assurance and prevention of these abuses of employees from their employers to exploit their labor.

Anti-discrimination Laws

Anti-discrimination laws are regulations that protect individuals from unfair treatment based on characteristics like race, gender, age, religion, or disability. Recruiting practices such as job requisitions and job postings must comply with anti-discrimination laws by making sure the position description is unbiased and provides equal opportunity for protected class groups to apply.

In the EU, anti-discrimination laws are comprehensive and apply to areas like employment, education, and access to goods and services. The EU's legal framework includes directives that prohibit discrimination and promote equality, ensuring that everyone is treated fairly regardless of their background.

Outside the European Union, other countries also have anti-discrimination laws. For example, Canada has the Canadian Human Rights Act, which protects people from discrimination in federally regulated activities and promotes equal opportunity. In the United Kingdom, the Equality Act 2010 consolidates previous anti-discrimination laws and also includes protections against discrimination based on characteristics such as race, gender, age, disability, and sexual orientation.

In Australia, the Racial Discrimination Act and the Sex Discrimination Act are key laws that prevent discrimination based on race and gender, among other factors. In contrast, some countries may have less robust anti-discrimination protections or may not enforce them as strongly.

---

[1] European Union Agency for Fundamental Rights. (2019). *Business-related human rights abuse reported in the EU and available remedies.* Available at: https://fra.europa.eu/sites/default/files/fra_uploads/fra-2019-business-and-human-rights-focus_en.pdf

In the United States, the Civil Rights Act of 1964, specifically Title VII, prohibits employment discrimination in recruitment and hiring based on race, color, religion, sex, or national origin. The Age Discrimination in Employment Act (ADEA) protects individuals aged 40 and over. The Americans with Disabilities Act (ADA) prohibits discrimination against individuals with disabilities.

Immigration and Work Authorization

Immigration laws vary greatly across countries, including in the European Union and other regions. In the European Union, member countries generally allow free movement for EU citizens, meaning they can live and work in any EU country without special permits. However, non-EU citizens face stricter rules, including visa requirements, work permits, and often long application processes for residency. Some multinational companies will employ *third-country nationals* (TCNs) who work in a host nation but are not local or citizens of the company's international headquarters. HR must be aware of not only the work requirements for those from the company's country of origin but also any other company.

In the United States, work authorization is often granted through work visas, like the H-1B for specialized jobs or the L-1 for internal company transfers. These visas usually require an employer to sponsor the applicant. In the European Union, citizens from member countries generally don't need special work permits to work in other EU countries. However, non-EU citizens usually need a work visa or permit. In Germany for example, a US citizen could work for up to 90 days in a 180-day period under a Schengen visa to gain some experience. Beyond this time, both a resident permit and work permit are needed. Form I-9 must be completed for all workers in the United States. This document verifies the person's identity and authorization to work in the United States.

Outside the European Union, different countries have their own rules. For example, Canada is known for its points-based system, where applicants earn points based on factors like age, education, and work experience. Australia also uses a points-based system, focusing on skilled workers. In contrast, Japan has stricter immigration policies, with limited pathways for permanent residency.

The cruise line industry is a great example of having multinational employees working for a company that may be based in the United States but have ships of registry in other countries while sailing internationally. For example, if a US-based cruise ship was registered in Australia, having any Australian citizen aboard that ship might trigger certain employment laws for that one employee related to their home country. In those circumstances, it is likely the Australian employee might still work for the company but on a different ship with registry in another country, like the Bahamas.

Employment Contracts and Offer Letters

Employment contracts are agreements between employers and employees that outline the terms and conditions of employment. In the European Union, employment contracts are governed by both national laws and EU regulations. These contracts typically cover aspects such as job duties, salaries, working hours, benefits, and termination conditions. The European Union also has directives that protect workers' rights, such as ensuring fair treatment and preventing unfair dismissal.

Outside the European Union, employment contracts can vary significantly depending on the country's labor laws. In Canada, employment contracts are subject to both federal and provincial laws, which may include provisions for minimum wage, overtime pay, and notice periods for termination. In Australia, the Fair Work Act governs employment contracts, ensuring that employees receive basic rights like paid leave and fair pay. In Japan, employment contracts often emphasize loyalty and job security, but recent trends show a shift toward more flexible and varied contract types.

Offer letters generally have several components that should be addressed in this important initial communication with a prospective employee: the job title and position, compensation details, start date, work schedule, and employment status (full-time or part-time). Additional items might include information on benefits, but this could also be in separate correspondence. There may be confidentiality or noncompete clauses, but that is region or nation-specific, as some countries may have significant restrictions on this kind of language and would not include it as part of the offer but as a separate contract. This also holds true for employment "at-will." This concept is common in the United States, but internationally, there are vast differences, and employees cannot be dismissed for no cause in some cases. Finally, this document should have a place for the employee to sign and accept to formalize the agreement.

Targeting the right audience is also important, so HR professionals must carefully select the platforms where their target candidates are likely to see the job ad. This can include online job boards, social media platforms, niche job sites, newspapers, or university career services. The placement of ads in these channels should be strategic, focusing on reaching the right demographics and skill sets.

Recruitment Advertising

Many multinational companies and international organizations promote best practices in recruitment advertising. These practices include focusing on job-related qualifications, promoting diversity and inclusion, and ensuring transparency in job requirements and application processes. The International Labour Organization (ILO) also provides guidelines and recommendations for fair recruitment practices, encouraging countries and employers to adopt nondiscriminatory and ethical practices.

There aren't specific global rules governing recruitment advertising across all countries, but many countries have national laws and guidelines that regulate how job advertisements can be written and what can be included. These laws generally aim to prevent discrimination, ensure transparency, and promote fairness in the hiring process.

In the United States, employers must avoid misleading or discriminatory job advertisements. In many areas, false advertising can lead to legal penalties. It is also worth mentioning that there are a great many hiring scams, especially in the service industry in Europe, that lure unsuspecting applicants from poorer countries to the European Union or even the

United States and into a situation where they become trafficked persons. The applicants may believe that they are going to work in hotels or as domestic support workers only to have their documentation withheld and charged exorbitant fees to be released, or be placed into a forced labor or prostitution situation.

For the aPHRi exam, HR professionals must understand the key aspects of recruitment advertising to effectively attract qualified candidates. A well-crafted job advertisement should accurately reflect the essential duties, qualifications, and expectations of the position. Misrepresentation can lead to higher turnover and dissatisfaction, so clarity is critical. Additionally, recruitment ads serve as a platform for showcasing employer branding, allowing companies to communicate their values, mission, and unique benefits. This helps differentiate the organization from competitors and appeals to potential candidates who align with the company culture.

Background Checks

Global background check practices also vary widely, depending on the country and the specific purpose of the check. In general, a background check is a process used to verify a person's identity, employment history, criminal record, and other relevant details. In some countries, like the United States and Canada, background checks are common for employment. These checks often include verifying past employment, checking criminal records, and sometimes reviewing credit history.

In Europe, data protection laws like the General Data Protection Regulations (GDPR) place strict limits on what information can be gathered and how it can be used. This means that companies must be careful about how they conduct background checks and must often get the individual's consent. The GDPR applies to any organization, regardless of location, that processes the personal data of individuals within the EU.

In some countries, background checks are more limited or less common. For example, in Japan, it's not typical to conduct extensive checks for most jobs. However, for specific roles, like those in finance or government, more thorough checks may be conducted.

In the United States, laws vary regarding what employers can check and consider in hiring decisions. For instance, some regions have "Ban the Box" laws that limit when employers can inquire about criminal history.

Job Openings

When a job position opens up, it means that a company is looking for someone to fill a role that's available. From an HR perspective, the process starts with identifying the need for a new employee. This could be because someone left the company, there's a new position, or the company is growing and needs more staff.

Many employers use a *job requisition*, which is a formal request to hire a new employee. It outlines the need for the position, including the job title, department, and a brief description of the role. Managers use job requisitions to get approval from higher-ups before starting the hiring process.

Once the requisition has been approved, HR works with the hiring manager to create a job description (if one is not already available). This description includes the tasks the new employee will do, the skills needed, and any qualifications required. HR then starts the recruitment process.

Recruitment Methods

There are several methods for recruiting new employees. *Recruitment methods* can be sorted into internal and external approaches. Internal and external recruiting each offer distinct advantages and challenges. *Internal recruiting*, which involves filling roles with current employees, promotes employee morale, increases retention, and reduces onboarding time since internal candidates are already familiar with the company's culture and processes. It also tends to be less costly. However, it can lead to limited fresh perspectives and may cause resentment among employees who are passed over for promotions. *External recruiting* brings new talent and ideas into the organization, potentially sparking innovation and diversifying the workforce. But it is often more expensive, time-consuming, and carries a higher risk since external hires may take longer to adjust or might not fully fit the company's culture. Balancing these approaches depends on organizational needs and goals.

Job bidding is a process where current employees apply for open positions within their organization. Employees can bid for positions based on their qualifications, experience, and career interests. This process encourages internal mobility and allows employees to advance their careers within the company.

External methods include the use of online job boards like Indeed or LinkedIn, where companies post job openings to attract candidates from outside. Campus recruiting targets upcoming and recent graduates by visiting colleges, while recruitment agencies help find and screen external candidates. Social media platforms are used to reach a wider audience, and job fairs provide opportunities to meet potential hires in person.

Employee referrals can also be seen as a mix of internal and external, as current employees recommend potential candidates, who may or may not already be connected to the company. Employee referrals are often one of the most effective recruiting methods because generally in a strong positive company, employees want to work with colleagues that they can generally get along with. Hiring people they know and trust builds teamwork and cohesion among the workers. Some companies will pay referral bonuses, which gives incentives to the current workers to enhance their teams but also is less expensive than hiring marketing firms or professional recruiting agencies, which, if they find a candidate, often take a percentage of that new hire's first year salary.

Applicant Databases

Applicant databases are collections of information about people who have applied for jobs at a company. These databases store résumés, contact details, and other relevant information about applicants. Companies use applicant databases to keep track of potential candidates for current and future job openings. This helps them quickly find and review qualified individuals when a position becomes available. These databases are often part of an applicant tracking system (ATS) that helps streamline the hiring process.

From an entry-level perspective, HR is responsible for entering and updating data so that it is accurate. While ATS programs are useful, they are only one small part of a recruiting process. HR must be aware that some potential for bias exists in the programming of filters or questions and should make every effort to reduce or eliminate the influence of these biases from the selection process. For example, some duty descriptions, or word choices from applicants in work history, could all influence how the artificial intelligence (AI) readers interpret or rate a candidacy. Human eyes should always be the last quality control measure to ensure some viable candidate wasn't erroneously screened out.

To manage the database, HR regularly updates applicant profiles with new information, such as interview notes or changes in availability. They also use the database to search for candidates with specific skills or experience when new job openings arise. HR maintains the database's security by protecting sensitive applicant information and ensuring that only authorized personnel have access.

AI is transforming recruitment by automating tasks such as resume screening, candidate matching, and initial communications with applicants. It helps HR teams process large volumes of data more efficiently, reducing hiring time and bias. AI tools also improve candidate sourcing by identifying potential hires through predictive analytics and social media platforms.

Alternative Staffing Practices

Alternative staffing practices are different ways companies hire workers besides the traditional full-time employee model. Companies use alternative methods to be more flexible and quickly adapt to changing business needs. For example, they might hire temporary workers during busy seasons or use gig workers for specific projects. These alternative staffing options allow companies to save on costs and access a broader range of skills without committing to long-term employment.

Types of Workers

The distinction between an employee and other types of workers, like independent contractors, matters for many reasons. An *employee* is simply a person who works for a company or organization in exchange for a salary or wages. They typically have a specific job role and responsibilities, and they work under the direction of a manager or supervisor. Employees usually work for a single employer at a time, often establishing a long-term relationship. They may receive benefits like health insurance and paid time off as part of their compensation. Distinctions between employees and other types of workers are covered in Table 8.1.

Many employers use a combination of employment structures to address the variable needs of a business. These needs include seasonality, budgets, and availability of qualified workers in the labor pool. A *labor pool*, or applicant pool, refers to the group of individuals available and qualified to apply for job openings within a specific industry or company.

TABLE 8.1 Distinction Between Types of Workers

Distinction	Traditional Workers	Alternative Workers
Employment Relationship	Have a long-term relationship with a single employer. They usually work under the employer's direction and follow company policies.	Typically work on a project-by-project basis or for a limited time. They often work with multiple clients and have more control over how and when they complete their tasks.
Benefits	Often receive benefits like health insurance, retirement plans, paid time off, and other perks provided by the employer.	Generally do not receive traditional employee benefits and are responsible for securing their own insurance and retirement savings.
Taxes	Employers withhold taxes from their paychecks and contribute to Social Security and Medicare.	Must manage their own tax payments, including self-employment taxes, as they do not have taxes automatically withheld.
Job Security	Typically have more job security and may be entitled to severance or unemployment benefits if they are laid off.	Often have less job security, as their work is usually based on short-term contracts or gigs.
Work Flexibility	Usually have a set schedule and may work in a specific location, like an office.	Often have more flexibility in choosing their work hours and location, allowing for a better work-life balance.
Control over Work	Generally have less control over the work they do and how it's done, as they follow the employer's guidelines.	Typically have more control over the tasks they take on and how they complete them, as they are seen as independent business entities.

Gig Workers

Gig workers are people who work on short-term projects or tasks instead of having a full-time job with one company. This alternative staffing practice allows businesses to hire workers for specific needs, like a single project or busy season, without committing to long-term employment. Gig workers offer flexibility for both companies and workers, as they can quickly adapt to changing workloads and work on multiple projects for different clients. This setup is common in fields like freelance writing, graphic design, and ride-sharing services.

Remote Workers

Remote workers are considered an alternative staffing practice because they work from locations outside the traditional office setting. Instead of coming to a physical office every day, remote workers can do their jobs from home, a coworking space, or any place with internet access. This practice offers companies flexibility in hiring, as they can find talented people from anywhere in the world, not just from the local area.

By hiring remote workers, companies can also save money on things like office space and utilities. Remote work also allows businesses to quickly adjust to changes in workload. For example, during busy times, companies can hire temporary remote workers to handle the extra work without needing more office space.

Expatriates

Expatriates, often referred to as "expats," are people who live outside their native country, typically for work, study, or personal reasons. The experience of being an expat can vary widely depending on the destination country, the individual's background, and the reason for living abroad.

For work, expats usually move abroad due to a job assignment, either by their employer or by seeking opportunities on their own. Companies often send employees to other countries for roles that require specific expertise or to oversee operations. These international assignments are often seen as a fast track to promotions and other career opportunities. These expats might receive special support, such as relocation packages, housing allowances, and help with navigating the new culture. There are three main types of expatriates you should be familiar with for the exams:

▪ **Parent-country Nationals (PCNs):** These are employees who are citizens of the country where the organization's headquarters is located and are sent to work in a foreign subsidiary. They bring knowledge of the company's core values and practices to the foreign location.

▪ **Host-country Nationals (HCNs):** These expatriates are citizens of the country where the foreign subsidiary is located. They are typically hired locally but can be considered expatriates when they transfer between branches within the same country or company region.

▪ **Third-country Nationals (TCNs):** These are employees who are citizens of a country different from both the parent company's home country and the host country where the subsidiary operates. TCNs often bring international experience and specialized skills.

Living as an expat involves adapting to a new country and culture. This can include learning a new language, understanding local customs, and adjusting to different lifestyles. Many countries have expatriate communities that provide support and help newcomers connect with others who are also living away from their home country.

Expats need to consider legal aspects, such as visas and residency permits, which vary depending on the country. They may also need to handle taxes in both their home and host countries, which can be complex.

The fail rate for expatriate assignments, often defined as the percentage of expats who return home early or do not meet the objectives of their assignment, varies but is generally estimated to be between 20% and 40%. Reasons for failure can include the following:

- **Cultural adjustment:** One of the biggest challenges for expatriates is adapting to a new culture. This includes understanding different social norms, communication styles, and workplace practices. Culture shock can impact both personal life and job performance.

- **Family adjustment:** If expats move with their families, ensuring that everyone adjusts well can be challenging. This includes finding suitable schools for children, adapting to a new lifestyle, and dealing with the emotional stress of being far from home.

- **Language barriers:** Not being fluent in the local language can make everyday tasks difficult and lead to misunderstandings in both personal and professional settings. It can also hinder social integration and limit access to resources.

- **Legal and administrative issues:** Navigating visa requirements, work permits, and tax regulations can be complex and time-consuming. Expats must also understand local laws and healthcare systems, which may be very different from those in their home country.

Effective training, ongoing support, and clear communication can help reduce these failure rates.

Outsourcing

In some cases, the decision is made to outsource the recruitment. *Outsourcing* is when a company hires an external firm to manage its hiring process. This can include sourcing candidates, conducting interviews, and even onboarding new employees. It helps companies save time and focus on their core business activities.

Staffing agencies help companies find employees by matching job seekers with open positions. They make the hiring process easier by screening candidates and handling paperwork, which saves time and effort for the company.

Job Sharing

Job sharing is a work arrangement where two people share the responsibilities of one full-time job. Each person works part-time, allowing them to balance work with other commitments. It offers flexibility and helps employers retain skilled employees who prefer a part-time schedule.

Selection

Selection refers to the process of evaluating and choosing candidates for a job. It involves assessing applicants' qualifications, skills, and cultural fit through interviews, tests, and background checks to identify the most suitable candidate for the position. Suitability must consider many factors, not just one skill or qualification. A highly organized company with detailed procedures may not be the right fit for an applicant that enjoys more flexibility, spontaneity, or unstructured working conditions. They may be able to do the job well, but will they enjoy working day by day into the future? Wrong fit candidates who are hired purely for skill without considering the organizational culture or environment often leave a company within six months. Now the company incurs not only the cost of recruiting a replacement, but loses the sunk cost of the training time invested in the person that quit.

There are many logistical considerations during the selection process. These include all of the practical arrangements and details involved in organizing and conducting interviews. Examples are scheduling interview times, booking appropriate locations or virtual meeting platforms, coordinating with interviewers and candidates, and ensuring all necessary equipment and materials are available. Other things to consider include accessibility, time zone differences, and providing clear instructions to all participants, from telling the applicant what to bring to the interview to sharing location and dress code details. Many applicants form an early impression of the company at this stage, and so being as organized and professional as possible increases the likelihood that a qualified candidate will be interested in hearing an offer of employment.

Interviewing

An employment *interview* is a meeting between a job applicant and a company representative, like a manager or someone from HR. The purpose of the interview is to learn more about the applicant's skills, experience, and personality to see if they are a good fit for the job and the company. During the interview, the interviewer asks questions about the applicant's past work, education, and how they handle different situations. The applicant can also ask questions about the job and the company. It's a chance for both sides to decide if they want to work together.

Interviewing techniques are methods used to assess a candidate's suitability for a role during the interview process. There are several different types of interviews, including the following:

▪ *Structured interview*: A structured interview is a type of interview where the interviewer asks a set list of questions in a specific order. The same questions are asked of every candidate to ensure fairness and consistency.

  ▪ **Example Question:** "Can you describe a time when you worked on a team project and what role you played?"

▪ *Unstructured interview*: An unstructured interview is more casual and open-ended, with the interviewer asking different questions based on the conversation. There is no specific set of questions, allowing for more natural discussion.

  ▪ **Example Question:** "Tell me about yourself and what led you to apply for this position."

▪ *Behavioral interview*: A behavioral interview focuses on how a candidate has handled past situations to predict future behavior. The questions usually start with "Tell me about a time when..."

- **Example Question:** "Tell me about a time when you had to deal with a difficult customer and how you resolved the situation."

- *Situational interview*: A situational interview is an interview technique where the interviewer presents hypothetical scenarios related to the job and asks the candidate how they would handle them.

  - **Example Question:** "Imagine you're serving a table, and one of the guests complains that their meal is not cooked properly. The rest of the table is satisfied with their food and ready to eat. How would you handle the situation to ensure all guests have a positive dining experience?"

- *Panel interview*: A panel interview involves multiple interviewers asking questions to one candidate. The panel usually includes people from different parts of the company, like HR, the department head, and a team member. Panel interviewers can use any of the previously listed types of interview questions.

Interview logistics refer to the organizational details involved in setting up and conducting an interview. This includes scheduling the interview time and date, selecting the interview location or platform (in-person, phone, or virtual), ensuring the right technology is available (like video conferencing software), and organizing interview materials (such as resumes or assessment forms). It also involves communicating the interview details to both the interviewer and candidate, confirming participation, and making sure the environment is prepared for a smooth interview process.

A realistic job preview is a recruitment tool used to provide potential employees with a clear, honest, and balanced view of what a job will actually be like. It presents both the positive and challenging aspects of the role, giving candidates a realistic understanding of the work environment, responsibilities, and expectations. The goal is to allow candidates to make an informed decision about whether they are a good fit for the job, which can reduce turnover and improve job satisfaction.

Rater Bias

Rater bias refers to the tendency of interviewers or evaluators to let their personal opinions or feelings affect how they rate or judge a candidate. Following are a few different types of rater bias:

- *Halo effect*: This occurs when an interviewer lets one positive trait or experience overshadow all other aspects of a candidate, leading to an overall positive rating.

- *Horns effect*: The opposite of the halo effect, this happens when one negative trait or experience influences the interviewer to have an overall negative impression of the candidate.

- *Similarity bias*: This bias occurs when interviewers favor candidates who are similar to them in terms of background, interests, or personality, even if those factors aren't relevant to the job.

- *First impression bias*: This happens when the interviewer makes a quick judgment about a candidate based on the first few minutes of the interview, and this impression influences the rest of the evaluation.

- *Leniency or strictness bias*: Some interviewers are naturally more lenient or strict in their ratings. Leniency bias means they give higher ratings than deserved, while strictness bias means they give lower ratings.

- *Recency bias*: This occurs when an interviewer remembers only the most recent interactions or answers from a candidate and bases their evaluation on those rather than considering the entire interview.

To avoid rater bias, interviewers can use a structured interview format with standardized questions for all candidates. While this is not always possible, it does reduce the chances of unintentional discrimination. Training interviewers to recognize and manage their own biases can help make the evaluation process more objective and balanced.

Job Offers

Once a candidate has been selected for an open position, a *job offer* is made. These offers can be verbal or written and typically include details about the job role, salary, benefits, start date, and any other important terms and conditions of employment.

After receiving a job offer, candidates may have the opportunity to negotiate the salary. During this process, they can discuss their desired compensation based on their experience, skills, and market rates. It's important for both the candidate and the employer to communicate openly and find a mutually agreeable salary that reflects the value the candidate brings to the role.

There are global and cultural considerations as well. In some countries, it's common to receive a written job offer detailing all terms before any negotiation, while in others, verbal offers and informal discussions may precede the formal offer. Cultural norms also play a significant role; for instance, in some cultures, negotiating salaries is expected and encouraged, while in others, it might be seen as impolite or uncommon. Additionally, benefits and perks included in job offers can vary widely, depending on local labor laws and common practices.

Pre- and Post-offer Activities

Before making a job offer, companies typically go through several steps to find the right candidate. This includes reviewing resumes, conducting interviews, and possibly checking references or doing background checks. The purpose of pre-offer activities is to thoroughly evaluate candidates and ensure that the company selects the best person for the job. These activities help in assessing the candidates' qualifications, skills, and fit with the company's culture. They also help in verifying information provided by the candidates, such as their work history and references, to make an informed hiring decision.

Employment tests are assessments designed to predict a candidate's performance on the job. There are several types of employment tests that help employers assess a candidate's qualifications:

- **Cognitive ability tests:** Measure reasoning, problem-solving, and intellectual abilities

- **Skills tests:** Evaluate specific job-related abilities, like typing or software proficiency

- **Personality tests:** Assess traits like teamwork, leadership, and work ethic
- **Physical ability tests:** Determine physical fitness for jobs requiring strength or endurance
- **Aptitude tests:** Predict how well candidates can learn new skills or adapt to the job

When using employment tests, it's important that they are both valid and reliable. *Validity* means the test accurately measures what it claims to measure, ensuring it is relevant to the job. For example, a typing test for an administrative position should assess typing speed and accuracy. *Reliability* means the test produces consistent results over time. If a candidate took the test multiple times, their score should be similar each time.

Background screens, or *background checks*, typically involve verifying a candidate's history and qualifications to ensure they are suitable for a job. Common elements of a background check include the following:

- **Criminal record check:** Verifying if the candidate has any criminal history, such as arrests, convictions, or pending charges
- **Employment verification:** Confirming the candidate's past employment history, including job titles, dates of employment, and reasons for leaving
- **Education verification:** Checking the candidate's educational background, such as degrees earned and institutions attended
- **Reference check:** Contacting previous employers or professional references to gather information about the candidate's work performance and character
- **Credit check:** Reviewing the candidate's credit history, often done for positions that involve financial responsibilities
- **Identity verification:** Ensuring the candidate's identity by checking government-issued IDs, such as a driver's license or passport

A *medical exam* for employment is a health assessment conducted to ensure that a candidate is physically and mentally fit to perform the duties of a job. These exams may check for physical abilities, drug use, or specific health conditions relevant to the job. In some cases, they are required by law, especially for roles involving safety or heavy physical labor. Medical exams are typically considered *post-offer, pre-hire activities*. This is because an employer cannot consider the findings of the medical exam in making the job offer but can use the exam to evaluate if the potential new hire is physically qualified to do the job.

Another post-offer, pre-hire activity are work authorizations. After a job offer is made, an employer must verify that the candidate is legally authorized to work. In the United States, for example, new hires complete Form I-9 to confirm their work eligibility, and they may need to provide documents like a visa, Employment Authorization Document (EAD), or Green Card.

Employment agreements or contracts are also typically post-offer, pre-hire activities. After a job offer is accepted, the employer and employee may sign an employment agreement that outlines the terms and conditions of the job, such as salary, job responsibilities, benefits, and termination policies. This agreement serves as a legal contract that defines the working relationship between the two parties. It is completed before the employee starts work to ensure that both sides agree on the expectations and conditions of employment.

Orientation and Onboarding

Once a candidate has accepted an offer of employment and passed any initial background screenings, the processes of orientation and onboarding begin.

Orientation is the introductory phase for new employees, providing them with basic information about the company, its culture, policies, and procedures. It helps new hires understand their roles, meet colleagues, and get acquainted with the organizational structure. This is also when a new team member completes new hire paperwork and any required training, such as safety.

Onboarding is an extended process that integrates new employees into the company. It includes providing the necessary tools and resources, setting job expectations, and building relationships within the organization. The goal is to help new hires transition smoothly and become productive members of the team. Following are a few best practices for successful onboarding:

- **Clear communication:** Provide clear information about job expectations, responsibilities, and goals. This includes explaining the company's policies and procedures, as well as any specific tools or systems new employees will use.

- **Training and resources:** Offer thorough training and access to resources that new employees need to do their jobs effectively. This might include technical training, access to company software, and information on where to find help if needed.

- **Mentorship and support:** Assign a mentor or buddy to guide the new hire through the first few weeks. This person can answer questions, provide support, and help the new employee settle into their role.

- **Regular check-ins:** Schedule regular check-ins to see how new employees are adjusting and to address any concerns. This helps ensure they feel supported and can provide feedback on their onboarding experience.

An important part of a new hire's experience is paying attention to the simple details, for example arranging the workspace. Ensuring equipment is available and working and granting access to necessary systems and facilities helps new employees have everything they need to perform their job functions effectively from day one. A disorganized orientation and onboarding process does not instill confidence in a new hire and can cause early turnover.

Cultural acclimation involves helping new hires adapt to the company's culture, values, and social norms, and generally takes more than a week or so to occur. Employees need time to adapt to their new work environment and culture, and HR plays a key role in helping the new team member during this process. This includes understanding the company's work environment, communication style, unwritten rules, and fostering a sense of belonging and alignment with the organization's norms.

Personnel Files

It is often the responsibility of HR assistants to create and maintain employee *personnel files*. This includes organizing and securely storing documents such as employment contracts, tax forms, performance reviews, benefits information, and records of disciplinary actions. They also ensure that these files are up-to-date and comply with legal and company policies, providing a comprehensive record of each employee's history with the organization.

The personnel file is established at the time of hire and can be created and maintained digitally, such as through an employer's human resource information system (HRIS).

Certain parts of the personnel file must be kept confidential or stored separately to protect employees' privacy and comply with legal requirements:

- **Medical records:** Information related to an employee's health, including medical evaluations, health insurance information, and any disability accommodations, should be stored separately from the main personnel file to comply with privacy laws like the Health Insurance Portability and Accountability Act (HIPAA) in the United States.

- **Background check information:** Criminal history reports, credit checks, and other sensitive background information should be kept confidential and stored separately from other employment records.

- **Form I-9:** Employment eligibility verification forms (I-9) should be stored separately to protect sensitive information, such as Social Security numbers, and to facilitate inspection by government officials if required.

- **Legal and investigation documents:** Records related to internal investigations, legal actions, or complaints (such as harassment or discrimination claims) should be stored securely and separately to maintain confidentiality.

- **Payroll and tax information:** Details about an employee's pay, deductions, and tax information should be kept confidential to protect financial privacy.

By maintaining these records separately and securely, HR ensures that sensitive information is protected and only accessible to authorized personnel.

Summary

Recruiting and selecting employees who align with a company's mission, vision, and values involves both technical skills and understanding people. Entry-level HR professionals need a solid grasp of recruitment basics, starting with legal compliance. This includes anti-discrimination laws, which ensure hiring based on qualifications rather than race, gender, age, religion, or disability, as well as laws that protect fair and safe working conditions.

Employment contracts and offer letters set expectations for new hires, while recruitment rules cover everything from advertising positions to conducting background checks and verifying work eligibility. Applicant tracking systems (ATS) help manage applicant data through the hiring process, but they must be securely maintained to protect sensitive information.

Companies sometimes use alternative staffing for flexibility, such as hiring gig workers for short-term projects or remote workers to expand the talent pool. Expatriates bring valuable cultural insights in global roles, and outsourcing allows companies to transfer recruiting tasks to third parties.

The selection process often involves interviews and assessments to choose the best candidate, with an emphasis on avoiding bias. After a job offer is accepted, onboarding integrates new hires into the company culture and provides the resources they need for successful performance on the job.

Exam Essentials

Understand how laws and regulations affect the recruitment of qualified employees. Legal compliance is at the heart of good recruiting practices. HR should conduct recruiting activities free from discrimination to hire authorized workers who operate in a fair and safe working environment. HR should handle all the administrative actions related to the recruitment process, including advertising, background checks, and determining employment eligibility (such as immigration status).

Understand the uses and limitations of an ATS. ATSs are automated databases that collect, store, and process information regarding the applications of candidates seeking employment for a company. Candidates can communicate through this system to provide critical hiring information such as resumes and authorize processes that validate a candidate's eligibility for a position. An ATS can be used to screen candidates based on input from the company; however, HR must ensure these screens do not create an impermissible barrier or disadvantage viable candidates causing a disparate impact against employees based on protected characteristics. Timely responses and actions taken when applicants apply should be done as part of both efficiency and create positive recruiting experiences even for nonselected applicants.

Know the types of workers who are part of alternative staffing practices. Alternative staffing practices are a way to provide a workforce where full-time regular employees may not be the right fit or where it is difficult to find those workers. Companies can hire gig workers that only work project to project and do not become fully immersed in the company or its culture. Remote workers can be used to expand an applicant pool when it is not necessary to have the individual at a specified location and can reduce the overhead of needing a large corporate gathering location. Expatriates have knowledge of the country of origin for the company as well as the host nation where the work will be performed. They are able to blend cultural awareness and technical knowledge to accomplish the job in the most effective manner. In addition to types of workers, companies can outsource recruiting to a third party that is designed specifically for recruiting such as a staffing agency. Finally, when full-time workers are not available, job sharing may be a means to permit two individuals to cover all the regular work of a full-time worker but part time. This has the added benefit to the company of potentially saving the cost on certain benefits that part-time workers are not eligible for.

Be aware of how rater bias can affect the interview process.   Various biases can exist in individuals who are tasked with the selection process, which can be seen when conducting interviews. HR must know when an interviewer lets one trait or experience, whether positive or negative, overshadow all other aspects of a candidate. Interviewers may favor candidates who are like them in terms of background, interests, or personality, or make a quick judgment about a candidate based on the first few minutes of the interview. Some interviewers are naturally more lenient or strict in their ratings, and others remember only the most recent interactions or answers from a candidate and base their evaluation on those rather than considering the entire interview.

Be familiar with the pre- and post-offer activities related to a new hire.   HR should understand the activities that are conducted prior to an offer going forward to an applicant. This includes the interviews, testing, and other actions to conduct due diligence in making sure the hire is the right fit for the company. This process may include reference checks to former employers or validating education such as degrees and transcripts. Other background checks may include criminal checks, credit checks, and drug testing, which should only be done if there is a true nexus to a *bona fide* job requirement. Once an offer has been accepted, the focus of activities is to create a smooth transition to employment in the company, which may include orientation, gathering information to place into company personnel databases, and possibly the election of benefits that begin on day one of employment.

Review Questions

You can find the answers in Appendix A.

1. What is the primary purpose of the GDPR?
   A. To protect companies from data breaches
   B. To enforce employee work hours
   C. To protect personal data and privacy of individuals in the European Union
   D. To regulate international trade

2. Under the GDPR, what must companies do in the event of a data breach?
   A. Report it to the authorities within 72 hours
   B. Notify employees immediately, regardless of the severity
   C. Wait until the breach is fully resolved before taking action
   D. Ignore the breach if it involves fewer than 100 people

3. How does the GDPR affect non-EU companies?
   A. It only applies to companies that physically operate within the European Union.
   B. Non-EU companies are exempt from GDPR regulations.
   C. It applies to any company, regardless of location, if they handle the personal data of individuals in the European Union.
   D. It only applies to companies that do business with EU governments.

4. What is the primary difference in results between social media recruiting and university recruitment programs?
   A. Social media recruiting typically leads to hiring for entry-level positions, while university recruitment attracts mid-career professionals.
   B. Social media recruiting primarily targets active job seekers, while university recruitment is aimed at passive candidates.
   C. University recruitment programs are less effective for building long-term talent pipelines compared to social media recruiting.
   D. Social media recruiting can reach candidates with a wide range of experience levels, while university recruitment focuses on entry-level talent.

5. How is artificial intelligence (AI) most commonly used in recruitment?
   A. Conducting online interviews
   B. Automating resume screening and candidate matching
   C. Training new employees
   D. Negotiating salaries with potential hires

6. What is a common concern about bias in applicant tracking systems (ATS)?

   A. ATS only screens candidates using technical terms.

   B. ATS can unintentionally filter out qualified candidates based on word choices in resumes.

   C. ATS favors candidates from specific geographic locations.

   D. ATS does not allow manual resume screening.

7. What documents can be required for foreign nationals to work legally in the United States? (Choose all that apply.)

   A. An employment visa

   B. A Green Card or Employment Authorization Document (EAD)

   C. A Social Security card

   D. A US passport

8. Which of the following is typically required for a US citizen to work abroad in another country? (Choose all that apply.)

   A. A work permit or visa from the home country

   B. A work permit or visa from the host country

   C. A US driver's license

   D. A letter of recommendation from a US employer

9. What is the primary difference between an employment contract and an offer letter?

   A. An offer letter is legally binding, while an employment contract is not.

   B. An employment contract is legally binding, while an offer letter is typically not.

   C. An offer letter specifies job title only, while an employment contract covers salary.

   D. An employment contract is only for senior employees or executives.

10. Which of the following is a common mistake in a job offer letter?

   A. Omitting details about benefits

   B. Stating job title and start date

   C. Failing to include information about compensation

   D. Using unclear or ambiguous language

11. Which of the following is an example of an alternative global staffing method?

   A. Hiring employees exclusively from the company's home country

   B. Using expatriates for overseas positions

   C. Employing temporary workers or contractors in foreign locations

   D. Only hiring local employees from the foreign market

12. Which type of interview focuses on assessing how a candidate handled past situations to predict future behavior?

    A. Behavioral interview

    B. Panel interview

    C. Technical interview

    D. Stress interview

13. How can structured interviews help reduce rater bias in the selection process?

    A. By allowing interviewers to ask different questions based on their preferences

    B. By ensuring each candidate is evaluated using the same set of questions and criteria

    C. By letting interviewers skip questions they feel are unnecessary

    D. By focusing only on informal, unplanned conversations with the candidate

14. What is the definition of an expatriate in a global business context?

    A. A foreign national working in their home country

    B. A freelancer working remotely for a global company

    C. A local hire in a foreign country

    D. An employee sent by their company to work in a foreign country for a temporary assignment

15. Which of the following is an example of rater bias during the selection process?

    A. A hiring manager selecting candidates based on their educational credentials

    B. A recruiter favoring candidates who attended the same college as them

    C. Only interviewing candidates who applied from a certain campus job fair

    D. Conducting multiple interviews with diverse panelists

16. What is one key difference between expatriate and local hires in global staffing?

    A. Expatriates are typically hired for temporary assignments, while local hires are usually permanent employees

    B. Local hires often receive higher compensation than expatriates

    C. Expatriates are more familiar than local hires with the local culture

    D. Local hires generally require more relocation assistance than expatriates

17. Which of the following is a typical pre-hire activity for an employer? (Choose all that apply.)

    A. Interviews

    B. Form I-9 completion

    C. Performing a background check

    D. Orientation

18. Which of the following is a common mistake interviewers should avoid during the selection process?

    A. Asking open-ended questions

    B. Using structured interview questions

    C. Incorporating personal preferences in decision-making

    D. Evaluating candidates based on job-related criteria

19. What is the purpose of Form I-9 in the post-hire process?

    A. To determine the employee's job readiness

    B. To track the employee's tax withholding preferences

    C. To verify an employee's background

    D. To verify the employee's identity and eligibility to work in the United States

20. What is a key advantage of using a global staffing method like outsourcing?

    A. It increases local employee loyalty.

    B. It reduces costs and increases flexibility.

    C. It eliminates the need for local regulations.

    D. It increases control over all aspects of operations.

aPHRi Compensation and Benefits

aPHRi EXAM OBJECTIVES COVERED IN THIS CHAPTER REQUIRE KNOWLEDGE RELATED TO FUNCTIONAL AREA 03, COMPENSATION AND BENEFITS:

✓ 03-01 Applicable laws and regulations related to compensation and benefits, such as monetary and non-monetary entitlement, wage and hour, and privacy (for example: tax treatment)

✓ 03-02 Pay structures and programs (for example: variable, merit, bonus, incentives, non-cash compensation, pay scales/grades)

✓ 03-03 Total rewards

✓ 03-04 Benefits programs (for example: healthcare plans, flexible benefits, pension scheme, health and fitness programs)

✓ 03-05 Payroll terminology (for example: pay schedule, vacation, leave, paid time off [PTO])

✓ 03-06 Data collection for salary and benefits surveys

✓ 03-07 Insurance claims, filing, or processing requirements (for example: workers' compensation, disability benefits)

✓ 03-08 Work-life balance practices (for example: flexibility of hours, telecommuting, sabbatical)

Functional area 03, Compensation and Benefits, accounts for 15% of the aPHRi exam. HRCI summarizes this exam content as "understanding concepts related to total rewards such as pay and benefits programs and responding to employee questions and handling claims and compliance with applicable laws, regulations, and company policies."

HR Done Wrong

Compass Group is a global outsourcing company that provides service workers to organizations such as caterers and cleaners in the healthcare, education, and defense industries, as examples. As global companies outsource noncore competencies, business models like Compass expand to meet demands. However, in February 2022, cleaners at London Bridge Hospital (LBH) protested the working conditions, among which were low pay and lack of basic health and safety personal protective equipment (PPE). This was not the first time that Compass had a scandal involving employees as there have been issues dating back to 2006 when the company settled a £40 million action involving bribery of a UN official for a catering contract.

In this case, the LBH cleaners are part of a subsidiary that generates almost 33% of the group's annual revenue. The number of employees is around 7,500. According to workers, they were forced to work with human waste and blood without proper supplies or PPE. They also lacked sufficient staff, requiring employees to work outside their established working hours. While the company continued to profit, their employees did not benefit from the revenues generated. When employees complained about the conditions, they faced reprisals from management.

Companies that unethically increase profit margins by shortcutting their responsibility to treat workers fairly and provide the proper health and safety equipment create an enormous risk in liabilities that eventually surface and can harm the overall corporate reputation. HR professionals have a responsibility to help management understand these risks and offer solutions to ensure workers are not exploited and that their welfare is not in danger. The referenced case and more information about these events can be found at https://corporatewatch.org/broken-compass-the-scandals-of-compass-group/.

Total Rewards

Total rewards in organizations refer to the complete package of benefits, compensation, and opportunities that employees receive in exchange for their work. This includes not just their salary, but also bonuses, health benefits, retirement plans, career development, and a positive work environment. By offering a mix of financial rewards and nonfinancial perks, companies can attract, motivate, and keep talented employees. Total rewards is a comprehensive approach used by HR professionals to attract, retain, and engage employees by offering a combination of monetary and nonmonetary rewards.

Total rewards play a big role in how satisfied employees feel and how well a company performs. Work-life balance is a key component of total rewards and includes programs and policies that help employees achieve balance in the time they dedicate to their professional and personal life. When employees feel valued and supported, they are more likely to be productive and stay with the company longer. Key terms you should be familiar with on exam day include the following:

- *Total rewards*: A combination of financial and nonfinancial benefits, like salary, bonuses, health benefits, and work environment, that an employee receives from a company
- *Wages*: The monetary compensation employees receive for their work, typically calculated by the hour, day, or as a regular salary
- *Tax treatment*: The way an employee's income and benefits are taxed according to government laws and regulations
- *Pay structures*: Systems that organize how employees are compensated, such as through bonuses, merit raises, or noncash rewards like gift cards
- *Benchmarking*: The process of comparing an organization's compensation and benefits against market rates through salary surveys and data collection to ensure competitive pay structures
- *Benefits programs*: Plans provided by employers to support employee well-being, such as healthcare, retirement savings, or fitness programs
- *Pay schedules*: The regular timing or frequency at which employees receive their pay, such as weekly, biweekly, or monthly
- *Vacation time*: Paid time off granted to employees for personal leisure or rest, separate from holidays and sick leave
- *PTO/ETO (paid time off/earned time off)*: A policy that combines vacation, sick days, and personal days into a single pool of time that employees can use at their discretion
- *Salary surveys*: Gathering information about employee pay and benefits to compare with other organizations and stay competitive
- *Insurance claims*: Procedures for filing insurance claims for things like workers' compensation or disability benefits
- *Work-life balance practices*: Company policies that help employees balance work and personal life, like flexible hours, working from home, or taking extended breaks
- *Merit pay*: A pay increase based on an employee's performance and contribution to the organization, used as part of a pay-for-performance structure

In addition to these concepts, total rewards also include recognition and rewards, training, education, and career opportunities designed to increase retention and engagement and improve employee satisfaction. By strategically integrating these elements, HR professionals can create a supportive and motivating workplace that aligns employees with the mission, vision, values, corporate goals, and organizational culture.

Compensation

Compensation is the money and benefits employees receive for doing their job. It includes wages or salaries, bonuses, and other rewards such as health insurance or retirement plans. Companies offer different types of compensation to attract and keep talented workers. These include *monetary rewards* and *nonmonetary rewards*. Extrinsic and intrinsic rewards are essential components of total compensation, each contributing to employee motivation and satisfaction in different ways. *Extrinsic rewards* are tangible and externally driven, such as salary, bonuses, benefits, and other forms of financial compensation. These rewards help meet employees' basic financial needs and provide incentives for achieving performance goals. *Intrinsic rewards*, on the other hand, are internally driven and include nonmonetary factors such as personal growth, job satisfaction, recognition, and the sense of accomplishment. Intrinsic rewards tap into employees' internal motivations and emotional well-being, which can enhance engagement and long-term commitment. Together, extrinsic and intrinsic rewards form a balanced total compensation package that attracts, motivates, and retains talent by addressing both financial needs and psychological fulfillment.

Compensation and benefits are an important function of a well-organized HR department. This means that there should be systems from which employees can clearly understand their pay, benefits, and any rewards they are entitled to. There should also be standard operating procedures for HR and payroll teams to follow to ensure pay practices are consistently delivered properly and in compliance with wage and hour regulations.

Compensation is the financial incentive and motivator for employees, and while not always the most important factor in deciding to take an offer of employment, or remain in an organization, it is almost always in the top few factors. In many cases, salary negotiations themselves can be a significant hurdle that must be navigated by HR and management to ensure that wages are fair and reasonable. Outside factors have increasingly influenced this process, such as legislation restricting employers requiring prospective employees to disclose previous salaries, the increased availability to compare job wages through websites such as Glassdoor or LinkedIn, and employees being more educated about their skills' relative value in the marketplace.

Pay Structures and Programs

Pay structures and programs organize how employees are paid based on their job level, experience, or performance. This can include fixed pay like a regular salary, bonuses for meeting goals, or noncash rewards such as gift cards or extra time off.

The HR function of pay also must consider different types of compensation. This includes *variable pay*, which changes based on performance; *merit pay*, which rewards employees for good work; and *bonuses*, which are extra payments for achieving specific goals. Incentives are rewards that motivate employees to reach certain targets, while noncash compensation includes perks like a company car or extra time off. Something to consider about increases in salary or bonuses is the impact that they have psychologically on an employee. For example, if a company gives a one dollar per hour increase in pay, that is slightly more than $2,000 gross in a given year, assuming an employee works a 40-hour work week for a year. After taxes and dividing out the pay over the various pay periods, the amount that an employee will realize is very small and may be even negligible. If the intent with the increase was to show value to the employee, they may not get that feeling. However, if a company decided to give a $1,500 one-time cash award, the employee gets the entire amount in a lump sum (excluding any taxes). While the total amount is actually less, the employee likely will have a much different attitude about the recognition. Additionally, when a company increases salary, that salary increase remains in perpetuity generally speaking, whereas a bonus can be determined year over year based on true performance. HR practitioners must understand the various pay incentives and how they affect employees in helping managers improve morale and engagement.

Wage bands, also called *pay ranges*, are set salary ranges that define the minimum and maximum pay for a specific job or job level. They help ensure that employees in similar roles are paid fairly based on their experience, skills, and performance, while also giving companies flexibility to adjust pay within the range. Wage bands are commonly used to maintain consistency in pay practices and to makes sure that employee compensation maintains internal and external equity. Similarly, a *pay grade* is a specific level within a company's salary structure. A pay grade is a category, whereas a pay range is the spread between the minimum and maximum salary boundary.

Internal Equity

Internally, the *job evaluation* process is a way for companies to figure out how much different jobs are worth within the organization. It involves reviewing the duties, responsibilities, and required skills for each job and then ranking or grading them based on their importance. This helps companies decide how much to pay employees in each position. The process also helps ensure that pay reflects the level of difficulty, responsibility, and value each job brings to the company.

Many companies use *job classification* to maintain internal equity. Jobs are grouped into categories or grades based on their duties and responsibilities. Employees in the same classification receive similar pay, which promotes internal fairness. The size of a company or number of employees is not necessarily a factor when making these comparisons but rather the scope and responsibilities of the positions are. Titles are also something to be wary of as a measure of importance. Some organizations can overinflate the overall name of a position without adding commensurate responsibilities. Job classification therefore is a critical function of the HR team to ensure that what tasks, roles, and responsibilities are being performed are consistent with the pay grade and salary structure. Giving someone a "title bump" where they gain a fancy position but no real duties actually does a disservice to the employee. In the same way, companies are trending to have unique titles for positions like "Chief of Culture" or "Lead People Person," which can make it harder to compare equivalent positions.

External Equity

External equity in compensation programs refers to the practice of ensuring that an organization's pay rates and benefits are competitive with those offered by other companies in the same industry or geographic region. To achieve external equity, businesses often conduct market *salary surveys* or *benchmark* their compensation packages against industry standards. When a company offers pay and benefits that are in line with or better than the market, it can attract and retain top talent. Ensuring external equity is important because if employees feel they are being paid less than what they could earn elsewhere, they may leave for better-paying jobs, leading to higher turnover and reduced employee satisfaction. Maintaining external equity helps a company stay competitive in attracting skilled workers while supporting long-term business success.

Data collection for salary and benefits surveys involves gathering information about how much companies pay their employees and what benefits they offer. These data are used to compare companies and make sure their compensation is competitive, helping them attract and keep workers.

Companies can conduct salary surveys in several ways to gather accurate data on market pay rates:

- **Third-party salary surveys:** Many organizations purchase salary surveys from professional associations, consulting firms, or specialized salary survey providers. These surveys offer industry-wide or region-specific data, making it easy for companies to compare their pay to the market.

- **Government data sources:** Companies can use publicly available salary data from government agencies, such as the US Bureau of Labor Statistics (BLS), which provides detailed information on wages by occupation and region.

- **Custom surveys:** Some organizations create their own salary surveys by directly reaching out to other companies in their industry or region. They collect data on specific job roles to ensure the information is highly relevant to their needs.

- **Online salary tools:** Websites like PayScale, Glassdoor, and Salary.com offer real-time salary data that companies can use to gauge market rates for different roles. These platforms aggregate user-reported salary information across various industries.

By using one or more of these methods, companies can gather reliable compensation data to maintain external equity and remain competitive in their industry.

Payroll Processing

Processing payroll involves calculating and distributing employee wages according to the company's pay schedule, which may be weekly, biweekly, or monthly:

- *Weekly payroll* means employees are paid once a week, typically on the same day, like every Friday. This schedule results in 52 paychecks per year.

- *Biweekly payroll* pays employees every two weeks, usually on the same day, like every other Friday, which totals 26 paychecks per year.

- *Bimonthly payroll* is when employees are paid twice a month, usually on set dates like the 1st and 15th, resulting in 24 paychecks a year.

- *Monthly payroll* means employees receive their pay once a month, usually on the last day or a set day of each month, resulting in 12 paychecks per year.

- *Same-day pay* is when employees get paid for the work they did that day instead of waiting until the end of the week or month. It gives employees flexibility and often increases employee retention.

During payroll processing, it's important to account for any paid time off (PTO), which includes vacation, sick leave, or personal leave that employees have used. Payroll also ensures that taxes, benefits, and other deductions are accurately applied. By keeping track of pay schedules and PTO balances, payroll professionals make sure employees are paid correctly and on time.

Coordinating payroll-related information is an important part of making sure employees are paid correctly and on time. This process includes keeping track of details like new hires and making sure their pay information is set up properly from the start. It also involves handling adjustments, such as changes in salary or work hours, and making sure PTO is counted accurately when employees take vacation or sick days. When an employee leaves the company, payroll needs to process terminations to stop the employee's pay and provide any final checks. Keeping all this information up to date helps ensure smooth payroll operations and accurate employee payments.

When hiring a new employee, consider if your company brings a new employee on at the start of a new pay period or in the middle of a pay period and its impact on the individual. Starting a new employee in the middle of a pay period may add some additional work to payroll processing, especially with deductions for benefits. Also, many companies pay individuals in arrears, meaning several days after the end of a pay period (to allow for sufficient time to process and deposit payments to employees). Consider that some employees who work paycheck to paycheck may have difficulty in making ends meet in that first week if they left a previous job and do not have a steady income due to the gap from the time worked until the time paid. This could create an unanticipated hardship, and it's important to communicate these details with new employees.

Laws and Regulations

Pay is considered an absolute right of employees, which means that as a general rule, employers are legally required to compensate employees for the work they perform according to agreed-upon terms, such as hourly wages or salaries, and must follow all applicable labor laws regarding minimum wage, overtime, and timely payment.

Privacy laws ensure that employee information, such as salary and benefits, is kept confidential. These laws vary by country and govern how personal employee data, such as salary, benefits, and health information, are collected, stored, and shared. Businesses must comply with local privacy regulations, such as General Data Protection Regulations (GDPR) in Europe, to ensure sensitive employee information is protected. Failure to adhere to these laws can lead to legal penalties and damage to a company's reputation. Maintaining privacy in total rewards programs helps build trust with employees and ensures that global companies operate within legal guidelines across different regions.

Tax treatment regulations outline how employee compensation and benefits are taxed, affecting both the company and the employee. Tax laws vary significantly among countries. Companies must carefully navigate these rules to ensure they comply with local tax regulations while offering competitive compensation packages. Failure to properly handle tax treatment can result in legal issues or financial penalties. Understanding the tax implications in different regions helps businesses create effective total rewards programs that meet both employee needs and legal requirements.

Benefits Programs

Benefits programs are a form of nonmonetary compensation designed to attract and retain a qualified workforce. Companies offer employee benefits to attract and keep good workers, improve job satisfaction, and support employee well-being. Benefits like healthcare, retirement plans, and paid time off help employees feel valued and reduce financial stress. Offering these perks also helps companies stay competitive in the job market, as workers are more likely to choose jobs that provide strong benefits in addition to a good salary.

Historically, employee benefits became more common during World War II, when companies couldn't offer higher wages due to government limits, so they started offering benefits like health insurance to attract workers. Over time, benefits have expanded to include things like retirement plans, wellness programs, and flexible work options.

There are two types of benefits: those that are mandatory, and those that are voluntary.

Mandatory benefits are those required by law, such as workers' compensation insurance in the United States or parental leave in Australia.

Voluntary benefits are those that companies choose to offer in addition to the mandatory benefits. These can include health insurance, retirement plans, paid time off, wellness programs, and gym memberships. Note that in some cases, benefits such as health insurance and paid time off are mandatory; it is important to understand the requirements based on the jurisdictions where the company operates.

Unions and works councils can significantly influence employee benefits by negotiating for better terms on behalf of workers. Through collective bargaining, unions work with employers to secure higher wages, improved healthcare plans, additional paid time off, pension plans, and other benefits.

Works councils, particularly in European countries, also play a role by representing employees in discussions with management about benefits and working conditions. They collaborate with employers to ensure that benefits packages comply with labor laws and address employee concerns. Both unions and works councils help employees have a stronger voice in shaping their benefits, often resulting in more favorable outcomes for workers.

Healthcare Plans

Healthcare plans are a large part of employee benefits that HR departments manage. HR professionals are responsible for selecting and administering healthcare options that provide employees with medical coverage for doctor visits, hospital stays, prescriptions, and preventive care. This involves negotiating with insurance providers to offer plans that balance affordability for both the company and its employees while ensuring adequate coverage.

HR also plays a key role in educating employees about their healthcare options, helping them understand the details of their plans, including costs, coverage limits, and how to use the benefits. HR also ensures compliance with relevant healthcare laws, such as the Affordable Care Act in the United States, and manages enrollment periods, making sure employees have access to the right health care at the right time.

As companies grow, the benefit plans will mature as well, but not always at the same pace. Companies can rapidly outgrow a benefits program and need to constantly evaluate the needs of a growing workforce. Age, marital status, and family status of employees all have a bearing on the types of health plans needed and the financial burden placed on the company. If a company has a relatively young, healthy, and single workforce, its health care needs will be drastically different than a company with older employees who are married with children. Health plans and all the various options are often a key factor that attracts and retains talent in a company. HR must seek to understand the differences and pros and cons associated with these variations.

Pension Schemes (Plans)

HR professionals are also responsible for setting up and maintaining *pension plans*, which help employees save for their retirement. This can include company-sponsored plans like 401(k)s in the United States or defined benefit pensions, where the company and sometimes the employee contribute funds that are invested for the future. As with all facets of total rewards, pension schemes vary from country to country:

- **Netherlands:** The Dutch occupational pension scheme is typically a defined benefit plan where both employers and employees contribute, providing guaranteed retirement income based on salary and years of service. It is known for being well-regulated and sustainable.

- **Canada:** The Canada Pension Plan (CPP) is a mandatory government-run plan, supplemented by employer-sponsored Registered Pension Plans (RPPs), which can be either defined benefit or defined contribution. Both employers and employees contribute to these plans.

- **Brazil:** The General Social Security System (RGPS) is a mandatory government-run pension plan based on years of contributions, with additional voluntary employer-sponsored complementary pension plans, which can be either defined benefit or defined contribution.

- **Iceland:** This system includes a basic state universal pension with a supplement. The country mandates compulsory contributions from both employees and employers. It also permits private pensions through voluntary personal savings plans.

- **Australia:** A system known as superannuation guarantees mandatory employer contributions to individual retirement accounts. Additionally, voluntary contributions by employees to boost their retirement savings are permitted.

- **Denmark:** The system is composed of a state pension called a Folkepension, which is a basic state pension funded by taxes. ATP (Labour Market Supplementary Pension) is a mandatory, funded pension scheme, while occupational pensions are typically defined-contribution plans agreed upon through collective bargaining

These examples illustrate the diversity in pension schemes globally, each tailored to the economic and social context of the country.

The most important thing for entry-level HR professionals to understand about managing pension schemes is that they must stay informed about the specific legal requirements and options available in each region where the company operates. HR needs to ensure that the company complies with local laws, such as mandatory contributions, tax regulations, and reporting requirements, while also communicating effectively with employees about their retirement options. Understanding how to balance government pension programs with any employer-sponsored plans and ensuring that employees are enrolled and informed about their benefits is key to successful pension management.

Flexible Benefits

Flexible benefits are employee benefit programs that give workers the ability to choose from a range of options, allowing them to customize their benefits to fit their personal needs. Instead of offering the same benefits to everyone, a flexible benefits plan lets employees pick and choose what works best for them, whether it's more vacation time, health coverage, or retirement savings. This approach makes it easier for employees to get the benefits that are most valuable to them and their families.

A *cafeteria plan* is a type of employee benefits program that allows workers to choose from a variety of benefits, such as health insurance, retirement plans, and flexible spending accounts. Employees can select the options that best meet their personal needs, much like choosing items from a cafeteria menu. This flexibility helps employees tailor their benefits package to their specific situation.

Health and Fitness Programs

Companies can offer a variety of health and fitness programs to support employee well-being. Some common types include gym memberships, where the company either provides free or discounted access to local gyms, and on-site fitness classes, such as yoga, aerobics, or strength training, which employees can join during or after work hours. Many companies also offer wellness challenges, encouraging employees to track their steps, workouts, or other healthy habits for prizes or incentives. Other programs include mental health support, like access to counseling or meditation apps, and nutritional programs, offering healthy food options in the workplace or educational workshops on diet and nutrition.

The benefits of offering these programs are significant. They can improve employee health, reducing the number of sick days and lowering healthcare costs for the company. Health and fitness programs also boost morale, as employees feel supported and valued. These programs can increase productivity, as healthier employees tend to have more energy and focus.

Case Study

According to the Centers for Disease Control and Prevention (CDC), smoking costs US employers an estimated $170 billion annually in lost productivity and healthcare expenses, including workers' compensation claims related to smoking-related illnesses. Smoking cessation programs benefit both the employer and the employee in several ways. For the employee, these programs provide support to quit smoking, leading to better health, a reduced risk of serious illnesses, and an improved quality of life. Quitting smoking can also save employees money that would otherwise be spent on cigarettes. Other ways employers can help employees quit smoking include offering counseling, nicotine replacement therapies, and incentives to quit.

Included in today's offerings of health and fitness wellness is also many mental wellness programs. These may be part of an employee assistance program (EAP) or some other benefit of visiting chaplains to have the opportunity to get a sense of the well-being of the workforce and provide insights to management without singling out specific circumstances or employees to maintain confidentiality. Another growing area of benefits is financial-readiness education and managing budgets. Employers see a positive gain in the productivity of employees who are better equipped to handle their finances and reduce the demand for ever increasing wages when there are economic downturns.

Work-life Balance Practices

Work-life balance practices are policies that help employees manage their work and personal lives more easily. These practices aim to reduce stress and improve well-being, making employees more productive and satisfied. There are specific types of work-life balance programs to be familiar with on the exam:

- *Flex hours*: Flex hours allow employees to choose when they start and finish their workday within a certain range, giving them more control over their schedule.
- *Telecommuting*: Telecommuting, or working from home, allows employees to complete their job tasks remotely, using technology to stay connected with their workplace.
- *Sabbatical*: A sabbatical is an extended period of leave, usually unpaid, that allows employees to take a break from work for personal development, travel, or rest, with the option to return to their job afterward.

Insurance Benefits

Insurance as an employment benefit is a type of protection that employers offer to help cover costs for things like medical care, dental work, or life expenses. It helps employees manage unexpected costs, providing financial security and support for them and their families.

Insurance claims are requests made by employees to receive money or benefits from their insurance, usually for medical expenses or lost wages. In HR, it's important to understand how to help employees with filing and processing requirements. This means making sure the employee completes the correct forms and submits them on time and that the company follows the rules set by the insurance provider or government.

Workers' compensation is a type of insurance that provides benefits to employees who get injured or sick because of their jobs. It covers medical bills and lost wages while the employee recovers. *Disability benefits* are for employees who are unable to work due to a short-term or long-term injury or illness. Usually, these benefits have some period of restriction, depending on when they are triggered after an accident or illness. These insurance benefits do not require the accident to have been work–related. These benefits help replace some of the employees' income when they are unable to work. HR professionals play a key role in making sure that employees understand their rights and the process for getting these benefits.

Communicating Total Rewards

Communicating total rewards to employees is important because it helps them understand the full value of what the company offers, beyond just their salary. Total rewards include things like health benefits, retirement plans, bonuses, PTO, and other perks, which can significantly boost employee satisfaction and retention.

Studies show that many employees do not fully utilize their benefits packages, often due to a lack of understanding or awareness. For example, nearly 45% of employees report that they don't fully understand all the elements of their benefits package. Additionally, employers may offer a variety of benefits that employees don't always engage with, which limits the potential value these programs could offer to both the company and the workers.[1] When employees are fully aware of these benefits, they understand their compensation and are better equipped to utilize the benefits being offered by their employer.

A *utilization review* helps HR communicate total rewards and employee benefits more effectively by analyzing how employees are actually using their benefits, such as health care, wellness programs, or PTO. Through this review, HR can identify which benefits are being used the most, which are underutilized, and whether employees fully understand the offerings.

With this information, HR can tailor its communication strategies to focus on the most valuable or underused benefits, helping employees understand how to access and maximize

---

[1] Ghosh, A. (2024). *Do employee benefits even matter if no one's using them?* Harmony blog. Available at: `https://qharmony.io/blog/do-employee-benefits-really-matter-if-no-ones-using-them`

them. For example, if the review shows that few employees are using mental health resources, HR can emphasize these programs through targeted communications, like workshops, newsletters, or one-on-one sessions. This allows HR to highlight the full scope of total rewards, making sure employees see the value in their benefits package and feel more engaged with what the company offers.

To communicate total rewards effectively, it's important to consider the diverse needs of the workforce. Different employees may prefer different methods of communication, such as emails, in-person meetings, or an online portal where they can access personalized information. Visual tools like brochures or infographics can help break down complex benefits in a way that's easy to understand.

By understanding how different groups utilize benefits, HR can adjust their messaging to highlight the most relevant offerings for each life stage. For younger employees, communication might focus on perks that support personal growth and financial wellness, while for older employees, HR can emphasize retirement planning resources and health benefits. This ensures that all employees, regardless of their age or life stage, see the value in the total rewards package and feel that the benefits cater to their individual needs.

By using a variety of communication methods, companies can ensure that all employees, regardless of their background or preferred learning style, are fully informed and able to take advantage of their total rewards package.

Case Study

How Google Communicates Total Rewards

Google, one of the largest tech companies in the world, is known for offering excellent benefits and rewards to its employees. These rewards go beyond just salary; they include health benefits, wellness programs, retirement plans, and other perks like free meals and access to fitness centers. To make sure employees understand and appreciate these benefits, Google has developed a clear and engaging way to communicate total rewards.

▪ Online Portal

   Google uses an online platform where employees can easily access information about their total rewards. This portal includes details on salary, bonuses, stock options, health care, retirement plans, and more. Employees can see how much they are earning and the value of the benefits they receive in one easy-to-read dashboard.[2]

---

[2] Culture Partners. (2024). Google's company culture: Unveiling organizational values (online). Available at: https://culturepartners.com/insights/googles-company-culture-unveiling-organizational-values/#:~:text=Flexible%20working%20hours%2C%20on%2Dsite,thrive%20both%20personally%20and%20professionally.

- Total Rewards Statements

  Each employee at Google gets a personalized total rewards statement. This document shows all the financial and nonfinancial rewards they receive, including their salary, bonuses, healthcare benefits, and perks like gym memberships. By putting everything together in one place, Google helps employees see the full value of working there.[3]

- Workshops and Presentations

  Google also holds regular workshops and presentations to explain the details of its benefits programs. This helps employees understand how to use their health benefits, retirement savings plans, and other perks. These sessions give employees the chance to ask questions and learn how to make the most of their benefits.[4]

By using these communication tools Google ensures that its employees understand the full value of their compensation package. This approach helps increase employee satisfaction and loyalty, as workers feel valued and well-supported.

Summary

Compensation and benefits are an essential element of an HR professional's responsibility to an organization. These programs more than any other drive the retention and motivation of good employees. HR professionals must understand the concept of total rewards as it goes beyond just monetary compensation. Nonmonetary compensation such as time off, work-life balance, education, and development opportunities are all factored into a comprehensive pay strategy.

HR professionals will take into consideration internal and external equity to ensure that a pay structure is fair and reasonable toward the employee. They must ensure that established pay structures are compliant with laws and regulations that govern compensation. These rules vary by country, and multinational companies must be sensitive to the various nuances created by different locations. Processing payroll involves calculating and distributing employee wages according to the company's pay schedule, which may be weekly, biweekly, or monthly. This key function of HR has many facets and requires a great deal of attention

---

[3] Glassdoor. (2020). Google employee reviews: Benefits and perks. Available at: `https://www.glassdoor.com/Overview/Working-at-Google-EI_IE9079.11,17.htm`
[4] Alex. (2024). Wellness programs available at Google: Employee perks explained. Go Tech Career. Available at: `https://gotechcareer.com/wellness-programs-available-at-google/`

to detail. Each employee is different, with pay, time off, deductions, and other withholdings so payroll processors must be diligent in their duties to ensure that proper wages are paid out in a timely manner.

Benefits vary by company but should be tailored to the needs of the employees in the organization. The most well-known benefits of employment are healthcare plans. This insurance product has a premium and deductible that factors in several elements about the covered population, which often also includes employees' family members. The utilization rates of health care have a direct impact on the general cost to the group. Health plans and all the various options are often a key factor that attracts and retains talent in a company. HR must seek to understand the differences and pros and cons associated with these variations.

In addition to medical coverage, other health plans and supplemental insurance may be offered, or a fitness/wellness plan that encourages employees to live a healthier lifestyle. HR often helps employees better understand the benefits available to them so employees can make informed decisions about their coverage options and needs. Beyond insurance plans and coverage, companies also strive to achieve a work-life balance that reduces stress and makes employees feel more satisfied with work. As a result, employees' productivity will increase and improve the overall business position of the organization.

Exam Essentials

Understand the facets of total rewards.   Total rewards includes monetary and nonmonetary compensation and benefits that are designed to attract, retain, and engage quality employees. HR professionals must know the elements, including salary, tax benefits, healthcare plans, work-life balance, pensions, and other factors that comprise all the ways a company compensates its employees.

Understand the types of benefit programs that may be offered by an employer.   Benefits are tailored to the organization to meet the needs of the employees. HR professionals must learn to customize benefit options and work with executives to deliver an effective benefits package that is well-received by the employees. In a competitive business environment where companies need to control costs, HR will seek benefits that have a good return on investment by meeting the demands of workers.

Be able to communicate total rewards.   HR professionals must be able to communicate with employees to coach them on available benefits as part of their total rewards. Often this requires having a solid understanding of what each benefit provides, the costs, and other pros and cons with enrolling in a particular plan. Additionally, they must be able to communicate with management to deliver a business case as to why it is important to offer certain benefits as part of a comprehensive compensation package.

Review Questions

You can find the answers in Appendix A.

1. Which of the following best describes the difference between monetary and nonmonetary entitlements in international HR practices?

    A. Monetary entitlements refer to vacation time, while nonmonetary entitlements include bonuses and commissions.

    B. Monetary entitlements are financial rewards such as salaries and bonuses, while nonmonetary entitlements include benefits like housing, healthcare, and flexible work arrangements.

    C. Monetary entitlements include company stock options, while nonmonetary entitlements refer only to paid vacation.

    D. Monetary entitlements are guaranteed by local laws, while nonmonetary entitlements are discretionary benefits provided by the employer.

2. What is the primary purpose of the job evaluation process within a company?

    A. To determine if jobs are paid based on market rates

    B. To review employee performance for promotions

    C. To assess the duties, responsibilities, and required skills of jobs to determine their value and pay

    D. To determine if pay levels are equitable

3. A company is building its pay structure and plans to conduct a salary survey to ensure competitive wages. What is the most important factor the company should consider when selecting the appropriate survey method?

    A. Choosing a survey that includes data from companies with similar revenue levels

    B. Selecting a survey that provides the lowest salary ranges to reduce payroll costs

    C. Using a survey that only focuses on high-demand industries

    D. Ensuring the survey includes data from companies with similar job roles and geographic locations

4. Which of the following is an example of a flex hours policy?

    A. Allowing employees to take unpaid leave for personal reasons

    B. Letting employees choose their start and end times within a given range

    C. Offering unlimited time off

    D. Allowing employees to volunteer for overtime during busy seasons

5. A multinational employer wants to offer a wellness program as a nonmonetary benefit to employees. Which of the following legal considerations should the employer prioritize to ensure compliance?

   A. Ensuring the wellness program complies with local privacy and data protection laws in each country

   B. Offering the same wellness program across all countries to maintain consistency

   C. Ensuring that participation in the wellness program is mandatory for all employees

   D. Providing financial incentives to encourage participation, regardless of legal restrictions in different countries

6. Which of the following should be the first priority when designing a fringe benefit program for employees?

   A. Understanding the tax implications of fringe benefits in different regions and their impact on employee compensation

   B. Ensuring that the benefits align with the company's global brand and image

   C. Offering benefits that include lifestyle perks, such as gym memberships and wellness programs

   D. Implementing a one-size-fits-all approach to simplify administration across all regions

7. What is a variable pay program in compensation structures?

   A. An executive compensation technique

   B. Compensation tied to performance or results

   C. A nonmonetary reward system

   D. A type of retirement plan benefit

8. A company is considering implementing a bonus program to boost employee motivation. Which of the following factors should be prioritized to ensure fairness in the distribution of bonuses?

   A. Clearly outlining the expectations when the program is announced

   B. Creating a minimum and a maximum scale to ensure flexibility

   C. Avoiding paying employees who are underperforming or who have had disciplinary action in the last 12 months

   D. Tying bonuses to clear, measurable performance goals

9. A company is reviewing its compensation structure and notices that some employees are unhappy with their pay grades. Which of the following should the company focus on to address these concerns while maintaining fairness?

   A. Conducting market research to ensure pay grades are competitive

   B. Offering merit-based pay raises to the top 5% of employees

   C. Removing pay grades and offering flat rates for all roles

   D. Increasing noncash compensation such as stock options without changing pay grades

10. A company wants to reward top performers without increasing fixed salary costs. Which pay structure would be most appropriate for this goal?

   A. Offering across-the-board raises

   B. Implementing a performance-based bonus program

   C. Using a pay grade system with yearly automatic increases

   D. Increasing the frequency of pay increases

11. Which of the following is a type of flexible benefit program?

   A. A defined pension plan

   B. A wellness program

   C. A cafeteria plan

   D. A company-wide health insurance plan

12. What is the primary purpose of pension schemes in a multinational enterprise (MNE)?

   A. To provide employees with healthcare coverage

   B. To offer retirement benefits to employees

   C. To give employees access to paid government-sponsored benefits

   D. To offer short-term disability coverage

13. Which of the following is typically included in a health, fitness, and wellness program offered by employers? (Choose all that apply.)

   A. Gym memberships

   B. Physical therapy

   C. Smoking cessation

   D. Well days

14. A company is designing a new healthcare plan for employees. What should be the first consideration to ensure the plan meets the needs of its diverse workforce?

   A. Selecting options that are desired by older and younger workers, as well as employees with and without children

   B. Surveying employees to determine what they want

   C. Minimize out-of-pocket costs as much as possible

   D. Including flexible options and locations to increase access

15. An employer wants to encourage employee participation in a wellness program. Which approach is most likely to increase participation without making it mandatory?

   A. Offering financial incentives for employees who participate

   B. Requiring employees to complete fitness assessments

   C. Making participation a condition for promotions

   D. Automatically enrolling all employees in the program

16. What is PTO?

   A. Time an employee earns as part of their base wages

   B. Vacation time that can be used throughout the year

   C. A system that combines vacation, sick leave, and personal days into one bank of hours

   D. A system that combines paid and unpaid time off throughout a specific period

17. A company is receiving complaints from employees who are unclear about how their vacation and PTO days are calculated. What is the best way for HR to resolve these concerns?

   A. Provide a detailed breakdown in the employee handbook of how vacation and PTO days are accrued

   B. Educate supervisors so they are well versed in company policies and can answer employee questions

   C. Require employees to attend a training session on vacation policies

   D. Provide weekly notifications in the company newsletter or intranet

18. What is a key requirement for filing a disability benefits claim?

   A. Proof that the employee is a US citizen

   B. Evidence of a disability that prevents the employee from working

   C. The employee's pay stub from the previous year

   D. A doctor's note confirming that the injury was work related

19. An HR manager is handling multiple workers' compensation claims and wants to streamline the filing process. What is the best first step the company should take to ensure claims are filed correctly and efficiently?

   A. Provide all employees with a detailed handbook explaining workers' compensation filing procedures

   B. Increase the number of staff members handling claims

   C. Require employees to submit claims directly to the insurance company

   D. Automate the claims process using software that tracks injuries and filing deadlines

20. A company is considering implementing telecommuting to improve work-life balance for its employees. What should the company prioritize to ensure the success of this program?

   A. Provide employees with a fixed amount of PTO

   B. Allow all employees to set their own schedule

   C. Invest in the necessary technology and set clear expectations for remote work

   D. Install productivity monitoring software on remote worker's devices

aPHRi Human Resource Development and Retention

aPHRi EXAM OBJECTIVES COVERED IN THIS CHAPTER REQUIRE KNOWLEDGE RELATED TO THE FUNCTIONAL AREA 04, HUMAN RESOURCE DEVELOPMENT AND RETENTION:

- ✔ **04-01 Applicable laws and regulations related to training and development activities (for example: acquiring and maintaining relevant credentials, qualified providers)**

- ✔ **04-02 Training delivery format (for example: virtual, classroom, on-the-job)**

- ✔ **04-03 Techniques to evaluate training programs (for example: participant surveys, pre- and post-testing, after action plan)**

- ✔ **04-04 Career development practices (for example: succession planning, dual career ladders)**

- ✔ **04-05 Performance appraisal methods (for example: timelines, ranking, rating scales)**

- ✔ **04-06 Performance management practices (for example: setting goals, feedback, mentoring)**

Functional area 04, Human Resource Development and Retention accounts for 10% of the aPHRi exam. HRCI summarizes this exam content as "understanding the techniques and methods for delivering training programs and developing individual employees."

HR Done Wrong

In 2015, Volkswagen admitted that their popular diesel vehicles had a "defeat device" that enabled the car manufacturer to give false results to emissions tests because the vehicle could recognize when it was configured in a testing mode (stationary while taking readings) and would alter the power output of the car. The resulting scandal cost the company around $35 billion internationally. At the heart of the scandal was the underlying corporate culture that impacted decision-making throughout the organization. As with other large technical companies, many policies and decisions are pushed from the top down and leave little room for collaboration or worker input.

To stay competitive in the market, these businesses will often set lofty goals that may be aspirational but are often communicated through the leadership as must-do. As a result, this breeds a sense of fear amongst the workers that success must be achieved at all costs and leads to poor ethical choices, where profit becomes the overarching focus. Of course, management often tries to shirk responsibility by claiming that the actions of subordinates, without express instructions from executives, are to blame and that the company should not be held responsible. However, as in the case with Volkswagen, these claims are almost always rejected because it is the organizational climate that has been established by the leaders that creates the conditions where this unethical behavior flourishes.

HR professionals must always be aware of the corporate culture that is being promoted not just in company literature, but in its practices. Human resource development seeks to train and build individuals and teams in a company that has high ethical standards and integrity. This training can be a safeguard to help the company truly achieve its goals without cutting corners and exposing the organization to large financial liabilities, legal, or retention problems. Workers subjected to an unethical business environment are far more likely to leave that organization, which can negatively impact the team. You can find more information about the Volkswagen scandal at https://www.newyorker.com/business/currency/the-volkswagen-settlement-how-bad-management-leads-to-big-punishment and https://www.bbc.com/news/business-34324772.

Human Resource Development and Retention Defined

Human resource development (HRD) refers to the process of enhancing employees' skills, knowledge, and abilities through training, education, and development programs. HRD aims to improve individual performance, productivity, and overall organizational effectiveness by fostering continuous learning and professional growth. This can include on-the-job training, mentoring, leadership development, and more. The goal of HRD is to better align employees with the organizational mission by developing the right skills needed to best improve the overall company by means of output or customer satisfaction. As a result of being part of a high performance team, employees feel a better sense of community and job satisfaction and are more likely to remain as part of the organization.

Retention refers to the strategies and practices used to keep talented employees within an organization over the long term. Retention efforts focus on improving employee satisfaction, engagement, and loyalty by offering competitive benefits, career development opportunities, and fostering a positive work culture. Effective retention reduces turnover costs and helps maintain a skilled, experienced workforce. Key terms to be familiar with include the following:

- *Employee development*: The process of improving employees' skills, knowledge, and abilities to enhance job performance and prepare them for future roles.

- *Training*: Structured programs designed to teach employees specific skills or knowledge to improve their job performance or adapt to new responsibilities.

- *Career path*: The progression of jobs and roles that an employee follows throughout their career, often aligned with their long-term career goals.

- *Qualified providers*: Organizations or individuals that meet specific criteria and standards to deliver training or development services to employees.

- *Training evaluation*: The process of assessing the effectiveness of a training program by measuring its impact on participants' skills, knowledge, and job performance.

- *Succession plans*: A strategy for identifying and developing employees who are capable of filling key roles in an organization when current leaders or employees leave.

- *Dual career ladder*: A system that allows employees to advance in their careers by moving either into management positions or by becoming experts in their field without switching to management.

- *Performance appraisal*: A formal evaluation of an employee's job performance, often used to provide feedback, set goals, and determine promotions or raises.

- *Feedback*: Information given to an employee about their performance, aimed at helping them improve or reinforcing positive behaviors.

- *Coaching*: A method of guiding employees through one-on-one support and feedback to help them develop skills and improve job performance.

- *Mentoring*: A professional relationship where a more experienced employee (mentor) provides guidance, advice, and support to help a less experienced employee (mentee) grow in their career.

- *Accreditation*: The process through which educational institutions or programs are officially recognized as meeting specific standards. This is important in HR for selecting qualified training providers and ensuring the validity of employee credentials.

- *Individual Development Plan (IDP)*: A personalized career development tool that outlines an employee's career goals and the steps needed to achieve them, often including skills development, training, and educational opportunities. IDPs help employees take ownership of their career growth, which can improve motivation and retention.

Career Development

As an early-career professional in HR, understanding key concepts like career development, succession planning, dual career ladders, and career development models is important for supporting employee growth and organizational success—including your own.

Career development refers to the process of helping employees grow their skills and abilities over time, so they can advance in their careers. This involves setting clear goals, providing opportunities for training, and offering feedback to help individuals reach their potential. HR plays an important role in facilitating career development by offering resources like mentoring programs, training courses, and career counseling.

Career development models are often constructed by HR to help build a cohesive strategy to guiding each new employee through their career lifecycle in the company. This process looks at what knowledge, skills, and abilities are combined with job experiences and continuing education and the paths that are created from entry-level employment to executive management. This does not mean that every new employee will grow to be a CEO but creates the maximum opportunities for any employee to grow to their maximum potential in the future.

Career Path

A career path is a planned progression of jobs or roles that an individual follows throughout their working life. It outlines the steps an employee takes to move from one position to another, often with increasing responsibility, skills, and experience. A career path can be linear, where an individual moves up within a specific department or industry, or it can be more flexible, allowing for lateral moves across different fields or roles. Career paths help

FIGURE 10.1 A typical HR career path

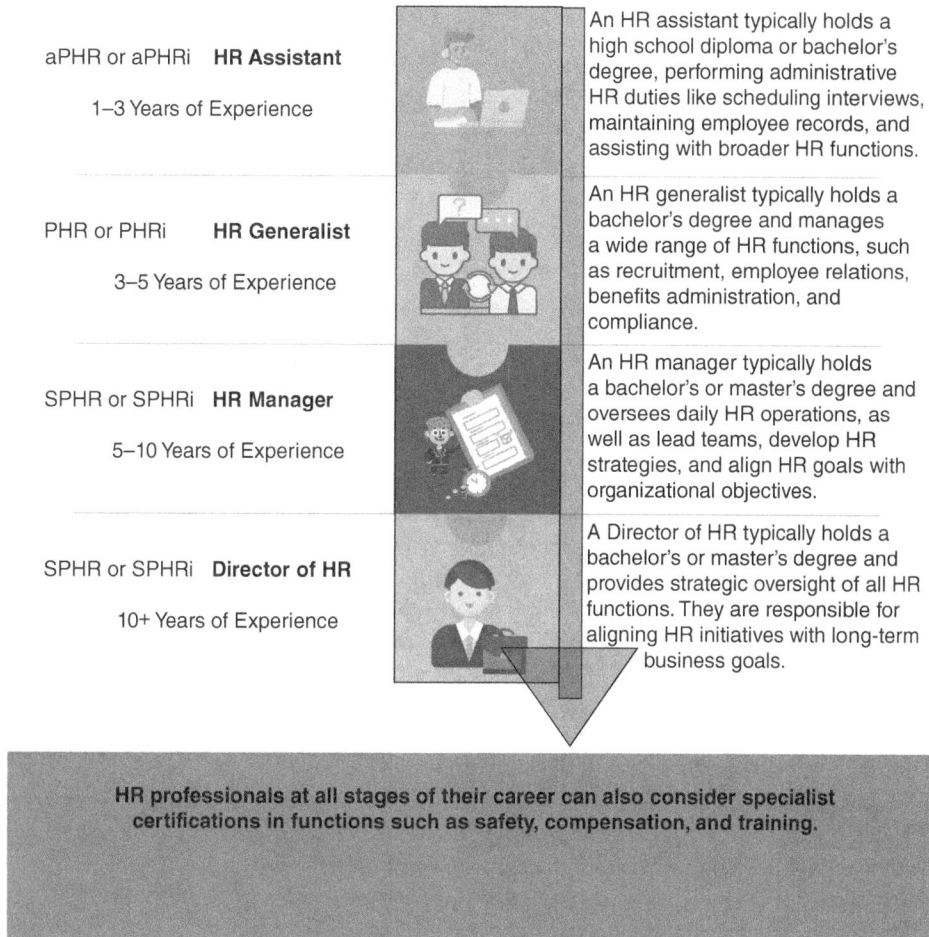

aPHR or aPHRi	**HR Assistant** 1–3 Years of Experience	An HR assistant typically holds a high school diploma or bachelor's degree, performing administrative HR duties like scheduling interviews, maintaining employee records, and assisting with broader HR functions.
PHR or PHRi	**HR Generalist** 3–5 Years of Experience	An HR generalist typically holds a bachelor's degree and manages a wide range of HR functions, such as recruitment, employee relations, benefits administration, and compliance.
SPHR or SPHRi	**HR Manager** 5–10 Years of Experience	An HR manager typically holds a bachelor's or master's degree and oversees daily HR operations, as well as lead teams, develop HR strategies, and align HR goals with organizational objectives.
SPHR or SPHRi	**Director of HR** 10+ Years of Experience	A Director of HR typically holds a bachelor's or master's degree and provides strategic oversight of all HR functions. They are responsible for aligning HR initiatives with long-term business goals.

HR professionals at all stages of their career can also consider specialist certifications in functions such as safety, compensation, and training.

individuals set long-term career goals and understand the education or experience needed to achieve them, while also providing organizations a framework for talent development and retention. Take a look at Figure 10.1 for a sample HR career path.

Coaching and Mentoring

Coaching and *mentoring* are key elements of career development that help employees grow professionally and personally. Even professional, world-class athletes have a coach to help them refine their natural talent to produce the very best possible results. In business, the goal of coaching helps employees reach their optimal performance through guidance and reflection.

Coaching typically involves a manager or HR professional providing focused guidance on specific job-related skills and performance improvements, often in the short term. Here are a few common coaching methods:

- **Directive coaching:** The coach gives clear instructions and feedback on specific tasks or skills, helping the employee improve their performance. This method is useful for immediate problem-solving or skill-building.

- **Nondirective coaching:** The coach asks open-ended questions to encourage the employee to reflect and find their own solutions. This method helps employees develop critical thinking and problem-solving skills.

- **Developmental coaching:** Focused on long-term growth, this method helps employees identify their career goals and create action plans to achieve them. It's aimed at improving leadership, communication, or other broad skills.

- **Performance coaching:** This method targets specific job performance issues. The coach works with the employee to identify weaknesses, set goals, and track progress, ensuring improvement in key areas.

Mentoring is a longer-term relationship where a more experienced professional offers advice, support, and career insights to a less experienced employee, supporting their overall career growth and development. Mentors usually fall outside of a supervisory relationship and act as a neutral evaluator to help an individual better understand their capabilities. The process involves a great deal of self-reflection and analysis of behavioral tendencies that are both positive and negative and the building of emotional intelligence. This is especially important for senior executives to still have mentors that can help refine their leadership philosophy and how they interact with subordinates. Mentors facilitate development of the whole, which includes personal and professional elements where coaches tend to focus on a short-term, specific issue or aspect of an individual.

Diversity plays an important role in coaching and mentoring by promoting inclusive growth and ensuring that all employees, regardless of their background, have access to development opportunities. In a diverse workplace, coaching and mentoring can help bridge cultural, gender, or generational gaps, allowing all employees to feel more connected and valued.

When coaches and mentors consider diverse perspectives, they can tailor their approaches to meet individual needs, which enhances learning and engagement. A diverse coaching environment also promotes innovation and broadens problem-solving abilities by encouraging the exchange of unique ideas and experiences. Additionally, diversity in mentoring can help underrepresented employees build confidence, access leadership opportunities, and overcome systemic barriers in their career paths.

Succession Planning

Succession planning is the process of identifying and preparing employees to fill key roles in the organization when current leaders or essential employees leave. This helps the company develop a pipeline of talent ready to step into important positions. For early-career

HR professionals, it's important to understand how to assess the skills and potential of employees to help them grow into future leadership roles. Succession planning is not a pre-determined outcome to pre-select individuals for future leadership but rather creates strong pathways that enable talented individuals to be identified early in their career and create multiple opportunities that are based on demonstrated potential.

Replacement charts are short-term tools that identify specific individuals who can immediately step into a role if it becomes vacant due to sudden events like resignation or illness. This method is more reactive than succession planning, focusing on finding temporary or immediate replacements for key positions without necessarily preparing those individuals for long-term leadership.

Here are a few methods to assess skill levels as part of succession or replacement planning:

- **360-degree feedback:** This method gathers feedback from an employee's supervisors, peers, subordinates, and even clients to provide a well-rounded view of their skills, strengths, and areas for improvement.

- **Skill assessments:** These are formal tests or simulations that evaluate an employee's proficiency in specific job-related tasks, helping to determine their readiness for future roles.

- **Leadership assessments:** These tools evaluate an employee's potential for leadership by testing their decision-making, problem-solving, and communication abilities, helping identify those ready for higher-level positions.

- **On-the-job observation:** Managers or HR professionals can observe employees in real work situations to assess how they handle responsibilities, solve problems, and interact with others, providing a practical assessment of their skills.

Dual Career Ladders

Dual career ladders offer employees two paths for advancement: one in management and another as a technical expert. This system allows employees who may not want to pursue leadership roles to still advance in their careers by deepening their expertise in a specific area. As an HR professional, promoting dual career ladders can help retain top talent by providing multiple pathways for growth. Some people can flourish at higher levels of responsibility and lead teams and groups. Slowly their technical expertise is needed less, and their leadership is needed more in an organization. The dual career ladder recognizes that some people do not make good managers but could be placed as the technical head of a project based on their subject matter expertise. This allows talented individuals to rise without needing to have the responsibility associated with management.

Case Study

Dual Career Paths at KPMG and Superworks

A dual career path allows professionals to advance in their careers without moving into traditional managerial roles. Instead of following a typical leadership trajectory, employees have the opportunity to focus on honing their technical skills and specialized expertise. This alternative route supports professional growth in both managerial and nonmanagerial tracks, making it a flexible solution for a wide range of career goals.

An example of a dual career path can be found in technical roles at companies like KPMG and Superworks. These companies allow professionals to choose between a management track or a technical expertise track as they advance in their careers. For instance, engineers can either move into managerial roles or continue to advance as technical experts, such as senior engineers or technical leaders, without taking on management responsibilities. This flexibility supports both employee growth and job satisfaction. There are several benefits to creating a dual career path system, and these are covered next.

Specialized Expertise

One of the major benefits described by Superworks of a dual career path is the ability to focus on specialized expertise within a particular field. Employees who choose this route can deepen their knowledge in their chosen area, whether it's engineering, finance, IT, or another technical domain. This focused expertise not only increases their value within the organization but also makes them more competitive in the broader job market.

Work-life Balance

A dual career path can also offer better work-life balance. Since these roles don't require the same managerial responsibilities—like supervising teams or managing office politics—employees can focus on their core work. This often results in more control over their workload and the flexibility to pursue personal and professional goals that matter most to them.

Employee Retention

From an employer's perspective, providing dual career paths helps retain top talent. Many employees feel forced to move into management for career advancement, even if it doesn't align with their skills or interests. A dual path ensures that they can grow and evolve professionally without transitioning to leadership roles, reducing turnover and increasing long-term loyalty to the company.

Enhanced Job Satisfaction

Employees often report higher job satisfaction when they can pursue a path that aligns with their skills and interests. Whether an employee prefers management or technical roles, offering choices increases their sense of ownership and engagement within the organization. When employees are engaged and motivated, they tend to perform better and stay committed to the company's goals.

For employees wishing to pursue a dual career path, they should first identify a specialized area of interest. Becoming a subject matter expert (SME) will guide the direction their career takes. Open communication with employers about career goals is also important. Many companies, like KPMG and Superworks, actively support dual career paths, but employees must advocate for their own growth by discussing these options with supervisors and HR.

Finally, finding mentors and seeking out development opportunities—whether through certifications, advanced training, or hands-on project involvement—help employees grow in their chosen path. Mentors can provide valuable guidance, helping professionals navigate the challenges of a dual career path and offering insights into how to become an expert in their field.

Dual career paths offer both employees and employers the flexibility needed to develop employees and retain top talent. By allowing professionals to advance without taking on managerial roles, companies can enhance job satisfaction, improve work-life balance, and create a more motivated, highly skilled workforce. For employees, it provides a rewarding way to build expertise while aligning their careers with personal goals.[1]

Career Development Models

Career development models are frameworks used to guide employees through different stages of their careers. Popular models outline the typical phases employees go through; these are covered next.

VARK Learning Styles   The VARK model is a framework used to understand individual learning preferences. It classifies people into four primary learning styles:

- **Visual learners** prefer to learn through images, diagrams, and visual aids.
- **Auditory learners** retain information better through listening, such as lectures and discussions.
- **Reading/Writing learners** excel by reading text and writing down notes.
- **Kinesthetic learners** learn best through hands-on experiences and real-world examples.

---

[1] Superworks. (2024). *Dual career path* [online]. Available at: https://superworks.com/glossary/dual-career-path/

VARK helps individuals understand their dominant learning style, which can influence career choices and workplace training methods, making learning more effective and personalized.

RIASEC   The RIASEC model, developed by psychologist John Holland, categorizes careers into six personality and work environment types:

- **Realistic:** Hands-on, practical jobs like mechanics or construction
- **Investigative:** Analytical, science-based roles such as researchers or engineers
- **Artistic:** Creative, expressive careers like designers or writers
- **Social:** Jobs focused on helping others, like teachers or counselors
- **Enterprising:** Leadership and persuasion roles, such as entrepreneurs or managers
- **Conventional:** Organized, detail-oriented jobs like accountants or administrators

This model helps individuals match their interests and strengths with compatible careers, leading to more satisfying work experiences.

Career Phases Model   The career phases model outlines the different stages people go through in their careers, helping to understand personal and professional growth. It has four main phases:

1. **Exploration:** Early stage is where individuals are figuring out their interests and gaining experience.
2. **Establishment:** Employees settle into a role, focusing on building skills and advancing.
3. **Maintenance:** Individuals refine their expertise and may focus on leadership or mentoring roles.
4. **Disengagement:** Preparing for retirement, with a focus on transferring knowledge and easing out of work.

Understanding this model helps HR professionals provide the right support and resources at each stage.

Career aptitude tests can also be beneficial to help early career professionals. Assessments such as the Truity aptitude test can identify strengths, interests, and potential career paths that align with an individual's unique skills. These tests offer insights into which roles might be the best fit, helping professionals make informed career choices. By evaluating abilities in areas like problem-solving, communication, and leadership, career aptitude tests provide guidance on job suitability and highlight areas for development, making them valuable tools for long-term career planning.

Special Assignments

Special assignments such as projects, committees, and cross-functional roles play a key role in career development by giving employees new challenges and opportunities to grow.

Project assignments allow individuals to take on leadership roles, manage resources, and solve complex problems, building skills in teamwork, communication, and time management. *Committees* expose employees to decision-making processes and collaboration with different departments, which broadens their understanding of the business. *Cross-functional assignments* support career development by exposing employees to different departments and functions, helping them build a broader skill set, improve collaboration, and understand the organization from multiple perspectives, all of which prepare them for leadership roles.

Expatriate assignments support career development by offering employees the opportunity to work in different countries, which helps them gain global experience and cross-cultural understanding. These assignments allow employees to develop new skills, adapt to diverse business environments, and expand their professional networks. Working abroad also builds leadership and problem-solving abilities, as employees often face unique challenges. Expatriate assignments can fast-track career progression by providing visibility within the company and preparing employees for future leadership roles in a globalized business environment.

In the United States Army, the concept of broadening assignments allows soldiers in a particular military occupational specialty the opportunity to work at a job outside their basic role but still necessary for the overall organization. These positions often require specialized training or skills but have broad impact to the Army. Drill sergeants, recruiters, instructors, or other similar roles give a different experience and skills to a soldier and help the institutional part of the Army develop future capabilities. Soldiers will often work 1 to 3 years outside of their regular duties to get this broadening experience that makes for a more well-rounded soldier.

Performance Management

Performance management is the process of helping employees meet their job goals and improve their work by setting clear expectations, regularly reviewing performance, and providing feedback and support. It includes a series of practices designed to help employees be successful in their roles. This is done by first setting expectations through tools such as job descriptions, standard operating procedures, and training. Once an employee knows what is expected of them, managers can set goals and provide feedback so the job is done correctly and employees can grow. Performance management is about making the organization better as a whole, and any system that is used must be consistent and measure well the areas of performance of an employee that is needed for a true assessment.

Establishing Performance Expectations

Employers establish performance expectations by using job descriptions to outline key duties, skills, and responsibilities for each role. Standard operating procedures (SOPs) provide clear, step-by-step guidelines on how tasks should be performed. On-the-job training (OJT) helps reinforce these expectations by allowing employees to learn in a real work environment, where they can apply the job's requirements and procedures directly. OJT offers hands-on learning and helps employees understand exactly how to meet the set performance standards while receiving real-time feedback from supervisors.

Employees want to know that they are being successful in a role and, if not, what they can do to be successful. Communicating often and early about the desired performance outcomes has a strong correlation to retaining an employee. Some employees quit and leave an organization. However, some quit and *stay*. That means that the employee may be present in the organization, but their level of effort or engagement declines significantly. They may do only the minimum effort to avoid being dismissed for poor performance, but their performance is certainly not exceptional. Communicating with an employee when they have reached this point can be exceptionally challenging, which is why it is imperative that supervisors and managers communicate up front with employees and always have a baseline and gauge the employee's attitude toward work and the organization, including coworkers, managers, and clients. Getting an understanding of why attitudes may change can help keep employees more engaged over time.

Setting Goals

Performance goals are specific targets that employees aim to achieve in their jobs to improve performance and contribute to the company's success. These goals can be related to productivity, skill development, or project completion. They are typically set through collaboration between the employee and their manager, ensuring the goals align with both the company's objectives and the employee's growth. Performance goals should be SMART: specific, measurable, achievable, relevant, and time-bound, which helps employees focus on clear, realistic targets and track their progress over time.

Delivering Performance Feedback

Delivering performance feedback is the process of providing employees with constructive insights about their work, helping them improve and grow. A few best practices include the following:

- **Be specific:** Provide clear examples of strengths and areas for improvement, rather than vague comments.
- **Be timely:** Give feedback soon after an event or task to make sure it's relevant and fresh.
- **Focus on behavior, not the person:** Address specific actions, rather than personal traits.
- **Balance positives and areas for growth:** Encourage by acknowledging successes while suggesting improvements.

Effective feedback supports employee development and performance improvement. Performance feedback can be informal or formal with a process and documentation. Ultimately, the manager or supervisor must be able to effectively communicate with the rated employee in a manner that helps them to adjust and align work performance to meet their stated objectives. The setting where feedback is provided is also an important element of the process. Some employees may feel intimidated in certain situations and therefore not respond as well to the feedback being provided. To combat the anxiety often associated with receiving feedback, the manager should build a level of trust and rapport with the employee.

Managing Performance Appraisals

Performance appraisals are formal reviews where managers assess an employee's work performance over a specific time, called the *rating period*. The rating period is the set time frame (usually quarterly or annually) during which an employee's work is evaluated based on previously set goals and expectations. During this time, employees are observed and measured on how well they perform their tasks, meet goals, and contribute to the company. At the end of the rating period, managers provide feedback, discuss strengths and areas for improvement, and set new goals for the next cycle. There are several methods for conducting performance appraisals:

- *360-degree feedback*: This method gathers input from multiple sources, including supervisors, peers, and sometimes clients, to provide a well-rounded view of an employee's performance.

- *Management by objectives (MBO)*: Employees and managers set specific, measurable goals together, and performance is evaluated based on how well those goals are achieved.

- *Self-assessment*: Employees evaluate their own performance, reflecting on their achievements and areas for improvement.

- *Behaviorally Anchored Rating Scales (BARS)*: Performance is rated based on specific behaviors that are linked to different levels of job performance.

- *Rating scales*: Employees are evaluated on a scale (e.g., 1 to 5) based on different job-related criteria, such as quality of work or teamwork.

- *Ranking*: Employees are ranked relative to one another, often to identify top performers or those needing improvement.

While performance appraisals are important, there are several challenges to their effectiveness:

- **Inconsistent standards:** Different managers may evaluate employees with varying criteria, leading to inconsistent results.

- **Lack of clarity:** Unclear goals or expectations can make it hard for employees to know how they're being assessed.

- **Anxiety and stress:** Employees may feel nervous or stressed about receiving feedback, which can impact their performance during appraisals.

- **Time-consuming:** Properly conducting thorough performance appraisals can take a lot of time for both managers and employees.

In addition to the previous challenges, several forms of bias can negatively influence employee ratings:

- *Halo effect*: When a positive trait in one area influences the entire evaluation, making other aspects seem better than they are

- *Horn effect*: The opposite of the halo effect, where one negative aspect overshadows the employee's overall performance

- *Recency bias*: When recent events, either positive or negative, disproportionately affect the appraisal

- *Leniency or strictness bias*: When the evaluator is consistently too lenient or too harsh across all employees

- *Similarity bias*: Favoring employees who share similar traits, backgrounds, or interests with the evaluator

To overcome challenges in performance appraisals, employers can start by training managers to recognize and reduce personal biases, to minimize the impact of or to eliminate personal bias. Some of these biases can also occur during hiring. Bias awareness training should be part of performance management training for supervisors. Establishing standardized criteria for appraisals helps create consistency in how employees are assessed. Employers should also set clear, measurable goals so employees understand expectations and how their performance is measured. Increasing the frequency of feedback can provide more meaningful, real-time suggestions on performance improvement. HR also helps track the timely completion of the delivery of performance reviews, and progress made on employee development plans. Additionally, shifting the focus from purely pay increases to personal development offers a more well-rounded approach.

Training Development and Delivery

The purpose of training and development programs is to enhance employees' skills, knowledge, and abilities to improve job performance and support career growth. Career development helps employees get prepared for future roles within the organization or to create depth in their current roles. Training, however, is more geared toward helping employees gain the knowledge and skills necessary for performance in their current role. Training programs help employees stay up to date with industry trends, comply with safety and regulatory standards, and develop new competencies where necessary. By investing in training, organizations can help align employee behaviors with business results and creating a workforce that is prepared to meet current and future challenges.

Training programs should align with organizational goals to ensure that employees gain relevant skills for their roles and can adapt to evolving business needs. For the exam, you'll need to understand how training serves both immediate and long-term objectives by fostering employee competencies, motivation, and retention. For example, onboarding programs are critical to help new hires acclimate, while ongoing training helps maintain competitiveness.

For an early-career HR professional, conducting employee training programs involves organizing and delivering sessions on important topics like safety regulations, emergency preparedness, and skills development. For example, you may conduct safety training to ensure compliance with local regulations or teach basic presentation skills to improve communication within the team. Other sessions, such as time management skills, help employees work more efficiently. These topics are identified early in the training development process.

Training content is only one element of a successful training event. In addition to presentation, the training facility itself is a key aspect for training to be absorbed by the learner. Proper lighting, equipment, audio/visual enablers, and even seating can positively or negatively impact training. Imagine sitting in an uncomfortable chair for several hours of mandatory training while a monotone instructor reads bullet points from bare colorless slides with no other visual elements. This training likely would not reach the intended audience in a way where the information was retained.

Identifying Training Needs

A *training needs assessment* is a process used to determine the gap between current employee skills and the skills needed for them to perform their jobs effectively. It helps identify which employees or departments require specific training to improve performance. This assessment involves collecting data through methods such as surveys, performance evaluations, interviews, and job analysis. By identifying these gaps, HR can develop targeted training programs that improve performance, address skill shortages, and support employee growth and organizational success. In large organizations with multiple divisions or in customer-service-based industries, training needs assessments may also be done by soliciting feedback from the clients or customers to determine what skills may be lacking.

A critical task list might be developed that lists all the essential skills that are needed for a particular position or job. Once the critical task list is created, the instructional design team can customize training that will help an employee develop the skills required to accomplish the critical tasks. This specialized training could be in the manufacturing industry or similar work.

Instructional Design

Instructional design is the process of creating effective training and learning experiences. It involves planning, developing, and delivering educational materials that meet specific learning objectives. Instructional designers consider the learners' needs and the best ways to deliver content.

An important part of training design is defined objectives. *Learning objectives* are clear, specific statements that define what learners should know or be able to do after completing a training or educational program. They help guide the design of the training and provide a focus for both instructors and learners. For example, a learning objective might be: "By the end of the session, participants will be able to explain the steps of the sales process." Well-defined objectives are measurable, making it easier to assess whether the training was effective.

You are likely to be tested on a few common methods used in instructional design:

ADDIE Model The ADDIE model is a widely used framework for instructional design that helps guide the development of effective learning programs. It consists of five phases:

1. **Analyze:** Identify training needs and learning objectives.

2. **Design:** Plan the structure, content, and delivery methods.

3. **Develop:** Create the training materials and content.

4. **Implement:** Deliver the training to learners.

5. **Evaluate:** Assess the effectiveness of the training and make improvements if needed.

Bloom's Taxonomy Bloom's Taxonomy is an instructional design model that classifies learning objectives into six levels, each representing a different level of understanding. These levels, from basic to advanced, are as follows:

Remembering: Recalling facts or information
Understanding: Explaining ideas or concepts
Applying: Using knowledge in real-life situations
Analyzing: Breaking down information into parts
Evaluating: Judging or assessing information
Creating: Building something new from knowledge

This model helps instructors design lessons that encourage deeper learning and critical thinking.

Agile and Scrum In instructional design, Agile emphasizes flexibility and collaboration to create learning experiences that can quickly adapt to changing needs. By using iterative cycles, designers can gather feedback from learners and stakeholders to make continuous improvements throughout the development process. This helps align the training materials with the evolving goals of the organization.

Scrum, as an Agile framework, applies a structured approach to instructional design. It breaks down the design process into short "sprints," allowing teams to focus on creating specific learning components, reviewing progress regularly, and adjusting as needed to enhance the learning experience.

Kirkpatrick Model The Kirkpatrick model is a widely used method for evaluating the effectiveness of training programs. It has four levels:

1. **Reaction:** Measures how participants feel about the training (e.g., satisfaction). For example, "How satisfied were you with the overall training experience? Please rate on a scale of 1 to 5, with 1 being very dissatisfied and 5 being very satisfied." This question helps assess the participant's immediate response to the training.

2. **Learning:** Assesses what knowledge or skills were gained during the training. For example, "What are the three key steps in the sales process that were covered in

the training? Please list and explain briefly." This question evaluates whether the learner has retained and understood the key concepts from the training.

3. **Behavior:** Evaluates how well participants apply what they learned on the job. For example, "Since completing the training, how often have you applied the skills or knowledge gained in your daily work? Please provide specific examples." This question evaluates whether the participant is using what they learned in the training and how it has impacted their behavior on the job.

4. **Results:** Looks at the overall impact of the training on organizational goals, like improved performance or increased efficiency. For example, "What measurable improvements have you seen in your work performance or team outcomes since completing the training? Please provide specific data or examples." This question helps evaluate the tangible impact of the training on job performance and organizational goals.

Training Delivery

Training delivery refers to the method used to present learning content and facilitate training for employees or learners. The choice of delivery depends on factors like the audience, content, and organizational goals. Effective training delivery increases learner engagement with the material for optimal results. It is important to understand the pros and cons of each format. It will help you answer questions on selecting appropriate methods for different learning objectives.

Training delivery methods vary based on the needs of learners and organizations. *In-person training* involves face-to-face interactions between instructors and participants, allowing for direct engagement and immediate feedback in a classroom or workshop setting. *Blended learning* combines both in-person and online components, offering flexibility while still maintaining personal interaction. Learners may complete some modules online while attending live sessions for deeper discussion. *Online training* is fully remote, where learners access materials through digital platforms like e-learning courses, webinars, or virtual classrooms, providing convenience and accessibility. Table 10.1 shows the pros and cons of these various delivery methods.

TABLE 10.1   Pros and Cons

Training Method	Pros	Cons
In-person	Direct interaction, immediate feedback, better engagement	Requires travel, can be costly and time-consuming
Blended Learning	Combines flexibility with personal interaction	Requires coordination of both online and in-person sessions
Online	Flexible, convenient, cost effective	Limited personal interaction, may lack engagement

In a multinational enterprise (MNE), HR professionals must be mindful of employees for whom English is a second language (ESL). When providing training, it's important to offer language support or simplified materials to ensure clear communication and understanding. This may include translation services, bilingual resources, or additional time for ESL employees to complete training. In addition to language barriers, HR professionals in international organizations must consider several factors when designing training programs:

- **Time zone differences:** Scheduling training sessions across global teams requires flexibility.

- **Cultural norms:** Training content should respect cultural differences in learning styles, communication, and feedback.

- **Technology access:** Ensure that all participants have equal access to the technology required for online or remote training.

- **Legal and regulatory compliance:** Training must align with local labor laws and industry standards in each country.

Training Laws and Regulations

In an MNE training setting, compliance with training laws and regulations is critical for avoiding legal penalties and ensuring fairness. These laws vary by country, but typically require adherence to standards around equal opportunity, preventing discrimination in training access.

Companies are responsible for confirming that employees acquire and maintain relevant credentials through certified programs, particularly in regulated industries like healthcare or finance. An example of credentialing in healthcare for an MNE is the Certified Professional in Healthcare Quality (CPHQ). This internationally recognized certification shows that employees working in healthcare management meet global standards in quality and safety. Employees in different countries may need this certification to align with international best practices and local regulations in patient care.

In finance, MNEs often require certifications like the Chartered Financial Analyst (CFA), which is globally recognized and validates that professionals meet the high standards of financial analysis and ethics required for cross-border operations.

Using qualified providers is important, as they offer accredited training that aligns with both legal standards and industry requirements, ensuring that programs meet local and international compliance. Qualified providers are often required to be certified by regulatory bodies to guarantee the quality and legal adherence to the training they deliver.

HR professionals can use *ISO standards* to build consistency and quality in training programs across multiple countries. ISO 10015, for example, focuses on quality management for training, helping HR design effective training processes that meet international benchmarks. ISO standards also provide a framework for measuring training outcomes and ensuring continual improvement across global operations. This framework, as part of the

ISO 30437 standard, provides organizations with a structured approach to evaluate the impact of learning and development programs. It categorizes metrics into three areas: efficiency (e.g., how cost-effective and utilized the training is), effectiveness (e.g., how well learning outcomes are met), and outcomes (e.g., how training supports broader business goals). This framework helps organizations track, report, and optimize their training efforts, aligning with international standards for consistent quality.[2]

Training Logistics

For an early-career HR professional, managing training logistics involves several key tasks. This includes coordinating training sessions, which includes booking venues or setting up virtual meetings, ensuring all materials (like handouts or presentations) are prepared, and managing tracking and registration of participants. Keeping accurate records of who attended and completed the training is important. Additionally, HR assistants often will handle the evaluation process, where feedback is gathered on the session's effectiveness through surveys or other tools to assess learning outcomes and areas for improvement.

Evaluation of Training

In addition to the Kirkpatrick model of training evaluation, HR can use several other methods to measure the effectiveness of training programs:

- **Surveys:** These gather feedback from participants about their satisfaction and understanding of the training. Surveys help identify areas for improvement.
- **Pre- and post-learning testing:** By comparing test results before and after training, HR can assess how much knowledge or skill participants gained.
- **After-action plan and training follow-up:** This involves creating a plan for applying what was learned and checking in later to evaluate how well the training has been implemented in practice.

Summary

HR Development and Retention are two critical functions of HR within an organization. HR professionals help managers with the career development of their employees by helping to create successful career paths using career development models that include regular and special assignments in the company over a career. Succession planning allows managers to

[2] Inglehart, D. (2023). *New ISO Standard for L&D metrics: What you need to know* [online]. ExecOnline. Available at: https://www.execonline.com/new-iso-standard-for-ld-metrics-what-you-need-to-know/

identify high potential employees early in their career and to facilitate their growth and development with opportunities that can improve their skills for increased responsibility. While there is no guarantee that an employee will be management material, the use of dual-career ladders can help give an employee who is technically advanced have an increasing role of responsibility from a technical sense without the demands of management roles. Employees may have a coach to help with specific development or seek mentors who can provide a broader, more long-term assessment and advice for an employee.

Managers and supervisors can use performance management to help develop and grow employees by aligning their skills with the needs of the organization and the overall goals of the company. Managers must become adept at delivering performance feedback to ensure that employees are giving their best performance and effort to the organization. By assessing an individual's performance against agreed-upon goals and objectives, supervisors will manage performance appraisals by delivering them in a timely manner to the rated employee. HR works with managers to help craft the right language that will best empower an employee to reach their highest performance potential and often will assist managers with creating the right conditions to deliver performance feedback to employees.

To best align performance, HR develops and delivers quality training by first identifying training needs of the organization through various methods and then designing the needed training that will help improve the skillset of the employees performing the roles and tasks that need improvement. Training delivery must comply with laws and regulations to ensure that no employee is placed at a disadvantage to receiving training or having disparate impact based on a disability or limitation to training. HR must also keep and maintain training records and continuously evaluate training that it's meeting the needs of the employees and the organization.

Exam Essentials

Understand the elements of career development models and how they apply to an organization.   Effective organizations use career development processes to identify, train, employ, and retain qualified employees to meet the goals and objectives of an organization. HR professionals must understand career paths, succession planning, and special assignments to help empower employees from initial hire to higher levels of executive leadership over a career timeline. Using coaches and mentors to develop talent is the sign of a strong organization and culture by ensuring the best employees have multiple resources to improve their skills and abilities to support the needs of the company.

Know how a performance management system operates.   HR professionals must know how to develop and employ a performance management system including appraisals, feedback, and retention of documentation on employees' performance. They should be able to work with managers who are setting goals in coordination with their employees and teach the best methods of delivering performance feedback.

Understand the essentials of instructional design and training delivery. HR professionals must be able to design training that meets the needs of the organization building the skills of the employees that enhance performance. Training must be designed and delivered in a consistent manner that complies with laws and regulations to ensure that all employees have fair access to training with or without accommodations. Delivery of training includes all the training logistics to include space and required training aids to enhance delivery. Finally, HR professionals should be able to assess and evaluate the effectiveness of training delivered using a variety of techniques that look immediately before and after training and then weeks to months later to see if the training has had an impact on altering the work habits and behaviors of employees resulting in increased performance.

Review Questions

You can find the answers in Appendix A.

1. A company wants to offer an internal certification program for its employees. What is the most important legal consideration the company should focus on when developing this program?

   A. Ensuring the certification aligns with industry standards and legal requirements

   B. Offering the certification to employees free of charge

   C. Making the certification available to all employees, regardless of job role

   D. Setting a deadline for employees to complete the certification

2. When setting performance goals, what should managers prioritize to ensure they are effective?

   A. Setting general, broad goals to encourage creativity

   B. Creating specific, measurable, achievable, relevant, and time-bound goals

   C. Allowing employees to set goals independent from management

   D. Setting the same goals for all employees to ensure fairness

3. What is one of the main principles of adult learning styles?

   A. Adults prefer to learn through memorization and repetition.

   B. Adults learn best when they are told what processes they are supposed to follow.

   C. Adults prefer to learn through graded tests and formal assessments.

   D. Adults learn best when they are actively involved and can apply new knowledge to real-life situations.

4. Which of the following is not one of the four learning styles in VARK?

   A. Visual

   B. Abstract

   C. Reading

   D. Kinesthetic

5. What does the RIASEC model assess in relation to career development?

   A. It evaluates an employee's technical skills.

   B. It assesses an individual's interests and matches them to career environments.

   C. It measures job performance based on communication styles.

   D. It predicts an employee's career success based solely on their personality traits.

6. A company is considering offering virtual training to employees. Which of the following factors should be prioritized to ensure the training is effective?

   A. Virtual training requires no planning or management.

   B. Virtual training is cost-effective and accessible, allowing employees to learn at their own pace.

C. Virtual training is primarily for technical skills and does not support soft skill development.

D. Virtual training eliminates the need for any employee interaction.

7. When choosing between classroom and virtual training formats, what is the most important consideration for the company?

   A. The cost of renting classroom space

   B. Employee preferences on how they like to learn

   C. The complexity of the material and which format will deliver it most effectively

   D. How long the training will take to complete

8. Which of the following best explains how cross-functional assignments contribute to career development?

   A. They allow employees to take extended time off for personal development, such as sabbaticals.

   B. They allow employees to work in a different country.

   C. They expose employees to different departments, broadening their skill set and understanding of the organization.

   D. They limit the number of responsibilities an employee has in a role.

9. How can expatriate assignments fast-track an employee's career progression?

   A. By limiting the employee's administrative tasks, allowing them to focus on more strategic or operational needs

   B. By allowing the employee to experience different countries and develop leadership skills through cross-cultural understanding

   C. By improving an employee's cultural competence

   D. By increasing the level of difficulty of the tasks they perform, which, in turn, increases their skills

10. A company wants to assess the effectiveness of a recent training program. Which of the following techniques would be most effective in measuring how much employees have learned?

    A. Conducting a pre- and post-test to measure knowledge gained

    B. Sending out an anonymous survey about the training experience

    C. Asking employees for feedback after the training

    D. Offering incentives for employees who completed the training

11. What is the primary purpose of succession planning in career development?

    A. To replace employees in positions that become available in less than 12 months

    B. To create success plans for individual team members

    C. To evaluate employees' current job performance

    D. To prepare employees for future leadership roles

12. What is a dual career ladder in career development?

   A. A system that allows employees to switch between different departments

   B. A ladder system designed for employees who work multiple jobs

   C. A structure that allows employees to advance either in a management track or a technical/specialist track

   D. A program designed for employees who want to pursue two separate careers simultaneously

13. One challenge of implementing a dual career ladder in a company is which of the following?

   A. Difficulty in maintaining equal pay between managerial and technical roles

   B. Finding enough candidates for the technical track

   C. Ensuring that employees on the management track don't leave the company

   D. The need for frequent job rotations to keep employees engaged

14. In a dual career ladder system, how can employees advance in their careers without moving into management?

   A. By transitioning into administrative roles within their department

   B. By working exclusively as independent consultants outside the company

   C. By rotating across various managerial roles in different departments

   D. By focusing on developing technical expertise and taking on project leadership roles

15. What is the main purpose of using rating scales in performance appraisals?

   A. To provide feedback on employee performance with objective numerical ratings

   B. To create a list of employees ranked from best to worst

   C. To set deadlines for future performance goals

   D. To identify areas where employees need additional training

16. One advantage of using the ranking method in performance appraisals is which of the following?

   A. It allows for clear differentiation between top and low performers.

   B. It gives specific feedback on how to improve performance.

   C. It reduces the amount of documentation required.

   D. It allows for more flexible timelines when assessing performance.

17. What is the main difference between 360-degree feedback and the BARS method of performance appraisal?

   A. 360-degree feedback uses only peer evaluations, while BARS uses manager evaluations.

   B. 360-degree feedback is focused on setting future goals, while BARS evaluates past performance.

C. 360-degree feedback gathers input from multiple sources, while BARS uses specific behavioral examples to rate performance.

D. 360-degree feedback measures only technical skills, while BARS measures leadership ability.

18. After completing a leadership training program, a company wants to measure its long-term effectiveness. What technique would best help assess the impact of the training over time?

A. Offering participants a survey after the training

B. Asking supervisors to send monthly feedback about the employees' behavior

C. Developing an after-action plan that tracks participant progress and application of skills

D. Conducting informal discussions with participants about the training experience

19. What is one of the key benefits of taking on special project assignments for career development?

A. They provide employees with the opportunity to build leadership skills.

B. They limit employees' involvement in decision-making processes.

C. They require minimal communication and teamwork.

D. They offer short-term roles with no long-term career impact.

20. A training provider has been hired to conduct employee development sessions. Which of the following should the company verify to comply with legal regulations?

A. The training provider's schedule availability

B. Whether the training provider is certified and qualified under applicable laws

C. The training provider's past client reviews

D. Whether the training provider offers a money-back guarantee

Chapter 11

aPHRi Employee Relations, Health, and Safety

---

aPHRi EXAM OBJECTIVES COVERED IN THIS CHAPTER REQUIRE KNOWLEDGE RELATED TO THE FUNCTIONAL AREA 05, EMPLOYEE RELATIONS, HEALTH, AND SAFETY:

✔ **05-01** Applicable laws affecting employment environments, Labor Relations, and privacy

✔ **05-02** Employee and employer rights and responsibilities (for example: privacy, substance abuse)

✔ **05-03** Methods and processes for collecting employee feedback (for example: employee attitude surveys, focus groups, exit interviews)

✔ **05-04** Workplace behavior issues (for example: absenteeism, aggressive behavior, employee conflict, workplace harassment)

✔ **05-05** Methods for investigating complaints or grievances (for example: employee and employee, employee and manager, employee and company)

✔ **05-06** Progressive discipline (for example: verbal or written warnings, escalating corrective actions, termination)

✔ **05-07** Off-boarding or termination activities (for example: exit interviews, handover process, and to service benefits, non-compete or non-solicitation)

✔ **05-08** Employee relations programs (for example: recognition, special events, diversity programs)

✔ **05-09 Workforce reduction and restructuring terminology (for example: downsizing, mergers, relocation, assignments, transfer)**

✔ **05-10 Applicable laws and regulations related to workplace health, safety, security, and privacy (for example: health and safety training, security compliance)**

✔ **05-11 Risk management in the workplace (for example emergency evacuation procedures, health and safety, employee violence, emergencies)**

✔ **05-12 Security risks in the workplace (for example data, materials, or equipment theft; equipment damage or destruction; cybercrime; password usage)**

Functional area 05, Employee Relations, Health, and Safety accounts for 20% of the aPHRi exam. HRCI summarizes this exam content as "understanding the methods organizations use to monitor and address morale, performance, and retention. Balancing the operational needs of the organization with the well-being of the individual employee. Understanding the laws, regulations, and policies that promote a safe work environment. Use risk mitigation procedures to protect against workplace hazards."

HR Done Wrong

Apple's popular iPhones have many components that are primarily manufactured in factories overseas and outsourced to suppliers. One such international company, Foxconn, continues to operate factories in multiple provinces on both mainland China and Taiwan as well as other countries in Asia. It is among the largest private employers in China. Although the company has been around since the 1970s, it's been mired in controversy regarding the working conditions of its employees for more than a decade.

Apple first discovered issues as early as 2007, but inspections showed the organization to be compliant. However, after a string of 14 suicides around 2010, undercover reporting showed the harsh working conditions, especially involving children, and illegal overtime. While a series of investigations put the company in a bad light, Apple continues to have this company as part of its supply chain.

Beginning around 2015, the company replaced half of its workforce with automation and is steadily continuing to move toward totally automated production facilities. In 2022, during the resurgence of COVID-19 in mainland China, the zero-COVID policy had an exacerbating effect on the employees once again, leading to violent worker protests and the financial lost sales of $1 billion per week in new iPhone sales. Global companies have a responsibility to treat workers fairly and be conscious and attentive to the health and safety of their employees regardless of location. While the increasing demand for cheaper goods and services often drives manufacturing overseas to lower wage workforces, this does not alleviate a company of an obligation to treat their workers humanely.

Source: Carbonaro, G. (2022). Apple criticized over worker conditions at China iPhone plant. Newsweek [online]. Available at: `https://www.newsweek.com/apple-criticized-worker-condition-china-iphone-plants-1762248`

Employee Relations, Health, and Safety Defined

Employee relations refer to the management of relationships between employers and employees, focusing on creating a positive work environment and resolving conflicts. It includes handling issues like disputes, communication, and employee and employer rights and responsibilities. Employee relations is not to be confused with labor relations, which involves union processes and collective bargaining of employees. Although, companies that often have problems with employee relations may find themselves with workers who seek to unionize to get better working conditions and concessions from management. Employee relations handles interpersonal connections and can be strongly influenced by leaders with high emotional intelligence.

Health and safety in the workplace protects employees from risks and hazards. HR is responsible for enforcing safety regulations, conducting training, and ensuring compliance with laws to prevent accidents and maintain a safe working environment. These areas help improve employee well-being and manage risk.

Key terms to remember for this functional area include the following:

- *Employee relations*: Managing the relationship between employers and employees to create a positive work environment and address issues like disputes and communication
- *Privacy*: Protecting employee personal information and ensuring it is handled according to legal and ethical standards
- *Substance abuse*: The misuse of drugs or alcohol that can negatively impact an employee's health and job performance
- *Employee feedback*: Input given by employees or employers about job performance, often to encourage improvement or acknowledge achievements
- *Absenteeism*: Frequent absence from work without valid reasons, which can affect productivity
- *Counterproductive work behaviors*: Actions by employees that harm the organization, such as theft, sabotage, or poor performance
- *Complaints and grievances*: Formal or informal expressions of dissatisfaction by employees regarding workplace conditions or treatment

- *Progressive discipline*: A step-by-step approach to address employee misconduct, starting with a warning and escalating to more serious consequences if behavior doesn't improve
- *Offboarding*: The process of managing an employee's exit from the company, including final paperwork and exit interviews
- *Workforce reduction*: The intentional decrease in the number of employees, often due to financial constraints or restructuring
- *Risk management*: Identifying and addressing potential risks to the organization, such as safety hazards, to prevent losses

Employee Relations

Employee relations has evolved significantly over time. In the early twentieth century in the United States, workplaces often had poor conditions, with little protection for workers. Today as we focus on a global workforce, we see that there are still many places where worker health and safety conditions are a primary focus. The rise of labor unions and work councils have led to greater focus on employee rights, resulting in improvements in wages, working conditions, and the establishment of labor laws. Especially in Europe, we see conditions that have led to higher wages, improved working environments, and strong safety consciousness by companies. However, in the developing world and countries with large populations such as India and China, the balance between output and productivity and working conditions is still trying to achieve a balance.

Employee relations are about setting the conditions by which HR can help corporate leadership to manage relationship dynamics in the workplace. Through policies, practices, and the development of emotional intelligence to be aware of the needs and feelings of employees, employers can more effectively relate to their workforce. Several types of relationships exist in the workplace:

- **Union–Management:** The relationship between labor unions and management, focused on collective bargaining, resolving disputes, and negotiating wages and working conditions
- **Coworker relationships:** The interactions between employees working together, which are important for teamwork, collaboration, and navigating conflict
- **Leader–Employee:** The relationship between managers or leaders and their team members, centered on guidance, support, feedback, and accountability
- **Employer–Employee:** The overall relationship between the company and its employees, which includes rights, responsibilities, and work agreements

Rights and Responsibilities

Employee and employer rights and responsibilities in the workplace refer to the legal and ethical obligations that ensure fair treatment, safety, and mutual respect between both parties. These rights and responsibilities seek to balance the relationship between the employer and the employee. Some countries have clearly defined laws and regulations that outline and specify the rights and responsibilities of both the employer and the employee. HR must be aware of the variance between countries when dealing with a multinational organization.

Employee Rights and Responsibilities

Rights: Employees have the right to fair wages, safe working conditions, and protection from discrimination or harassment. They also have the right to privacy regarding personal data and freedom from unfair dismissal. In many countries, employees can join labor unions and engage in collective bargaining.

Responsibilities: Employees are responsible for performing their duties to the best of their ability, following company policies, maintaining safety standards, and respecting coworkers and company property.

Employer Rights and Responsibilities

Rights: Employers have the right to expect employees to perform their jobs competently, follow workplace rules, and maintain productivity. They can enforce policies regarding conduct, safety, and performance.

Responsibilities: Employers must provide a safe and healthy work environment, comply with labor laws, pay employees fairly, protect their personal data, and prevent discrimination or harassment in the workplace.

Global Employment Practices

To regulate global employment practices, international labor standards are set by the United Nations (UN) through the International Labour Organization (ILO). The ILO collaborates with 187 member countries, aligning efforts between workers, employers, and governments to promote social justice and fair labor practices globally. Member countries commit to ILO standards and incorporate these regulations into their local legal frameworks. Under these guidelines, the ILO addresses key areas to improve working conditions worldwide. Some high-level policy objectives include the following:

- Prohibiting child labor
- Banning forced or compulsory labor
- Preventing workplace discrimination
- Ensuring the right to collective bargaining, including union membership
- Common issues in international employment law

In addition to the ILO's global standards, regional labor laws set further guidelines. For instance, EU labor law covers rights across EU member states, such as the following:

- Prohibition of workplace discrimination
- A minimum of four weeks' annual leave for employees
- Requirement of a written employment contract
- Freedom of movement for workers across EU states

Similarly, North American labor standards, defined under the North American Agreement on Labor Cooperation, apply to the United States, Canada, and Mexico. The following key areas are covered:

- Workers' compensation and health and safety standards
- Protection for migrant workers and equal pay for equal work
- The right to collective bargaining and the prohibition of child labor
- Universal Employment Standards

Regardless of an organization's headquarters, compliance with each country's local labor laws is essential. Beyond UN and regional regulations, several common employment standards apply globally:

- **Benefits:** Many countries mandate employer contributions to health insurance, retirement funds, workers' compensation, and unemployment insurance.
- **Minimum wage:** Nations like the United States, Canada, France, Ireland, and Australia have minimum wage laws that require employers, including those hiring independent contractors, to meet specific pay standards.
- **Employee contracts:** In numerous countries, written employment agreements are mandatory, specifying job responsibilities, hours, pay, and leave.
- **Termination:** Policies vary widely; for instance, the United States allows "at-will" termination of employment, whereas France requires justified cause and adherence to fair procedures.
- **Payroll compliance:** In most jurisdictions, employers must withhold payroll taxes for employees, typically excluding freelancers and independent contractors.

Navigating international employment law is a complex but critical aspect of global workforce management. Noncompliance can lead to penalties, fines, and damage to a company's reputation. Organizations expanding internationally must rigorously adhere to both international standards and local regulations.

Psychological Contract

In addition to legal and ethical obligations to each other is the modern *psychological contract*. This refers to the unwritten expectations between employers and employees regarding what each side will offer in the workplace. Unlike traditional contracts that focus on job security in exchange for loyalty, the modern psychological contract emphasizes flexibility, personal growth, and work-life balance. Abraham Maslow introduced his hierarchy of needs in his 1943 paper, "A Theory of Human Motivation." His psychological theory suggests that people are motivated to fulfill their needs in a specific order: physiological, safety, love and belonging, esteem, and self-actualization. As this pertains to workers, employees who don't feel physically safe in their working conditions will not be able to be concerned about a rewards and recognition program (esteem). Once basic needs are met, only then can an organization seek to further advance and develop their people. For employees, this might mean expecting opportunities for career development, meaningful work, and a positive work environment. Employers, in return, may expect high performance, adaptability, and engagement. This shift reflects changes in the workplace, where lifelong employment is less common, and both parties seek mutual benefits beyond just pay and job security.

Laws and Regulations

In an international business environment, companies must navigate a range of laws affecting employment environments. Labor laws vary across countries, covering areas like minimum wage, working hours, and employee rights. Labor relations laws also differ, with some nations supporting strong unions while others restrict union influence. Privacy regulations, such as the General Data Protection Regulations (GDPR) in Europe, require companies to protect employee data and ensure confidentiality. Health and safety regulations mandate safe working conditions, with laws requiring proper safety measures and training to prevent workplace accidents and protect employee well-being.

The general purpose of labor laws is to protect the rights and well-being of workers. These laws regulate working conditions, such as wages and working hours, provide guidelines for resolving disputes between employers and employees, and protect against discrimination. Modernized countries with a highly educated or skilled workforce will drive the demand for better working conditions, including pay.

Labor Relations Regulations

On a global scale, labor relations laws regulate the interactions between employers, employees, and unions, varying significantly by country. These laws govern collective bargaining, workers' rights to organize, and the resolution of labor disputes. In some countries, unions have strong protections and can negotiate contracts, while in others, union activity is more restricted. International organizations, like the International Labour Organization (ILO), set global labor standards to promote fair labor practices and improve working conditions worldwide. The following key standards are included:

- **Right to form and join unions:** Workers can organize and collectively bargain for better conditions.

- **Fair wages and reasonable working hours:** Ensures workers are paid fairly and have limits on working hours.

- **Elimination of forced labor and child labor:** Prohibits any form of forced or child labor.

- **Equal pay for equal work:** Guarantees that men and women receive equal pay for the same work.

- **Nondiscrimination in the workplace:** Protects workers from discrimination based on gender, race, or religion.

Part of an HR professional's job is to stay informed of trends in labor issues. One key trend to watch from the ILO is the increasing focus on responsible work and social justice, especially in the face of economic slowdowns and global crises. As labor markets recover unevenly from the pandemic, the demand for high-quality jobs with secure wages is growing. Another major trend is the impact of inflation on wages, with many workers, especially in lower-income groups, facing declining real wages due to rising costs of living. The ILO highlights the ongoing challenges faced by women and young people, who continue to experience disproportionately high levels of unemployment and lower workforce participation. The ILO is also advocating for a Global Coalition for Social Justice to help foster better labor standards and protect vulnerable workers across the globe.

Privacy

Global privacy laws focus on protecting employee data and ensuring confidentiality, with common elements across countries. These include the need for informed consent before collecting personal information, the right to access and correct personal data, and the obligation for companies to protect this data from unauthorized access or misuse. Laws like the GDPR in Europe and similar regulations in other countries require companies to be transparent about how employee data are collected, used, and stored, ensuring privacy and security across borders. The GDPR includes several key mandates for employers to follow:

- **Data minimization:** Employers must collect only the personal data necessary for a specific purpose and avoid unnecessary data collection.

- **Informed consent:** Employers must obtain explicit consent from employees before collecting or processing their personal data. Employees should be clearly informed about what data are collected and how that data will be used.

- **Right to access and correction:** Employees have the right to access their personal data held by the employer and can request corrections or deletions if the data are inaccurate or no longer needed.

- **Data protection** by design and default: Employers must implement data protection measures from the beginning of any process and ensure that privacy is a core aspect of all systems handling employee data.

- **Data breach notification:** If a data breach occurs that risks employee privacy, employers must report it to the relevant authorities within 72 hours and notify the affected employees.

- **Right to be forgotten:** Employees can request the deletion of their personal data when it is no longer needed or if they withdraw consent for its use.

These mandates help protect employee privacy and ensure that personal data are handled responsibly and transparently. The GDPR applies to any organization, regardless of location, that processes the personal data of individuals who are in the European Union, whether the organization is based inside or outside the EU. As companies use more technology and artificial intelligence (AI), the collection of big data will inevitably compete with individual privacy, and HR will need to be involved with the management and tracking of data that contains information about employees.

VB vs. Bulgarian National Revenue Agency and the GDPR

In a landmark case under the GDPR, the Bulgarian National Revenue Agency (NAP) faced a major lawsuit after a cyberattack in 2019 exposed the personal data of more than six million individuals. One of the individuals affected, referred to as "VB," filed a lawsuit claiming compensation for nonmaterial damages, specifically fear of future misuse of her personal data, even though there was no evidence that her data had been accessed or used maliciously.

Legal Context and Issues Raised

Under the GDPR, companies and organizations are required to implement appropriate security measures to protect personal data from unauthorized access, disclosure, or loss. In this case, VB argued that the breach alone was sufficient grounds for compensation. She claimed that the mere exposure of her data caused significant emotional distress, even though no actual misuse had occurred.

However, the Bulgarian NAP argued that they had taken adequate security measures and the attack was the result of a third-party breach, for which they should not be held fully accountable. They also argued that fear of potential misuse does not qualify as nonmaterial damage that should be compensated under the GDPR.

Court Ruling and Key Takeaways

The Court of Justice of the European Union (CJEU) ruled that while individuals have the right to seek compensation for nonmaterial damages, simply being involved in a data breach does not automatically entitle someone to compensation. The court established that for damages to be awarded, the claimant must demonstrate that the company failed to implement "appropriate" security measures as required under GDPR Articles 24 and 32. Additionally, the claimant must prove actual harm, not just fear of harm.

This case set a significant precedent in GDPR litigation:

- **Breach alone is insufficient:** The occurrence of a data breach alone does not automatically prove fault or entitle the claimant to compensation. Companies can be held liable only if they are proven to have failed in implementing appropriate security measures.

- **Subjectivity in harm claims:** Fear or anxiety about potential data misuse must be grounded in well-founded, objective evidence of harm. Mere speculation is not enough to qualify for damages.

- **Security measures must be proportionate:** The GDPR requires that security measures be appropriate to the nature and scope of data processing. The court highlighted that not all breaches imply a failure of security, and organizations must show that their systems were designed in proportion to the risks involved.

Implications for Companies

This case emphasizes the importance of continuously evaluating and updating data security practices to comply with the GDPR. It also highlights the need for comprehensive documentation of security measures to defend against potential claims. Organizations must be transparent with data subjects about how their personal information is handled and must be prepared to show that reasonable security measures were in place to protect it.

Maldoff, G., Loose, A., and Dragosz, K. (2023). EU Court of Justice confirms GDPR security measures can be "appropriate" even if not foolproof. Insights & Resources[online]. Goodwin. Available at: `https://www.goodwinlaw.com/en/insights/blogs/2023/12/eu-court-of-justice-confirms-gdpr-security-measures-can-be-appropriate-even-if-not-foolproof`

Workplace Harassment

Workplace harassment is any unwelcome behavior that creates a hostile, intimidating, or offensive work environment. It can take many forms, including verbal, physical, or written actions, and can be based on factors like race, gender, age, religion, sexual orientation, or disability. Harassment can severely impact an employee's mental health, job satisfaction, and overall well-being, making it crucial for organizations to address it quickly and effectively. There are four main types of harassment that can take place at work:

- **Verbal harassment:** Insults, slurs, or offensive comments about someone's race, gender, or other personal characteristics

- **Physical harassment:** Unwanted physical contact, intimidation, or physical threats

- **Sexual harassment:** Unwanted sexual advances, requests for sexual favors, or inappropriate touching

- **Cyber harassment:** Harassment through email, social media, or other online platforms, often involving offensive messages or threats

HR teams are responsible for preventing harassment in the workplace. They do this by the following:

- **Establishing clear policies:** HR establishes strict anti-harassment policies, outlining what constitutes harassment and the consequences for engaging in it.

- **Conducting or sourcing training:** Regular training sessions for employees and management on recognizing and preventing harassment ensure that everyone understands the rules and their responsibilities.

- **Creating safe reporting channels:** HR provides confidential ways for employees to report harassment, ensuring victims feel safe coming forward.

- **Taking prompt action:** When harassment is reported, HR must investigate quickly and take appropriate action, which could include mediation, counseling, or disciplinary measures like dismissal.

Workplace Investigations

Workplace investigations sometimes are necessary when an employee brings a complaint to HR's attention. An *employee grievance* is a formal complaint made by an employee about unfair treatment, workplace conditions, or violations of company policies that affect their job or well-being. Investigative best practices help ensure that these processes protect both the organization and its employees.

One of the first steps in conducting a workplace investigation is acting promptly. Once a complaint is filed, delays in starting the investigation can allow the issue to escalate, potentially worsening the work environment or damaging employee morale.

Confidentiality is another important aspect of workplace investigations. HR works to guard the details of the investigation, making sure that information is shared only with those directly involved or with a need to know. This approach helps protect both the complainant and the accused from unnecessary gossip or retaliation. It is important to recognize that HR is still part of the company and is not able to be a neutral, dis-interested party. When handling privileged information, it is best that organizations retain legal counsel that can properly advise and advocate for the best interests of the company so as not to put HR in a difficult position. While HR can advise leaders on how to handle sensitive employee issues, and often have a great deal of empathy for employees, they are always part of the organization. This can create an ethical dilemma when evaluating the needs of the employees, individual managers, corporate leadership, stakeholders, clients, legal requirements, and the organization. HR must be adept at navigating these challenges on a case-by-case basis.

It's also important that HR or the appointed investigator remains neutral throughout the process. Remaining unbiased ensures that the investigation is based solely on facts and evidence, not the personal feelings or opinions of the investigator.

Gathering evidence is another essential part of the process. Investigators need to collect all relevant information, including emails, messages, or witness statements. Part of this process includes interviewing those involved, including the complainant, the accused, and any witnesses, using open-ended, nonleading questions to gather as much detail as possible. This helps uncover the full scope of the issue.

Documentation is a foundational practice throughout the investigation. Every step, from interviews to the final findings, should be carefully documented. This not only ensures transparency but also provides a record in case the issue escalates to legal action.

Once the investigation is complete, HR must take appropriate action based on the findings. This may range from requiring additional training to dismissing an employee, depending on the severity of the issue. The complainant and the accused should be informed of the outcome, but only the necessary information should be shared to maintain confidentiality.

Finally, after the resolution, HR must monitor the situation to ensure there is no retaliation and that the work environment returns to a positive, healthy state.

Workplace investigations become even more complex in multinational enterprises (MNEs) or across different countries, where local laws and cultural norms can impact how investigations are conducted. For example, privacy laws in the European Union, such as the GDPR, place strict limits on how employee data are handled during an investigation. In some cultures, direct confrontation or reporting a superior may be seen as disrespectful, making employees less likely to file complaints. In these cases, HR must adapt the investigation process to respect local customs while ensuring fairness and compliance with both corporate policies and local laws.

Employee Relations Programs

Employee relations programs are the activities that help improve the relationship between employers and employees. These programs aim to make the workplace more positive and supportive for everyone and opportunities to improve relations exist all throughout the employee lifecycle, from recruiting to separation.

Recognition Programs

Employee recognition taps into basic behavioral psychology principles like positive reinforcement. When employees are recognized for their efforts, it strengthens desired behaviors, such as productivity and collaboration, by rewarding them with praise, rewards, or incentives. This reinforcement boosts motivation and morale, making employees feel valued and appreciated. Over time, consistent recognition helps build stronger emotional connections to the workplace. Following are several monetary and nonmonetary recognition examples:

- **Personalized thank-you notes:** A handwritten note from a manager or colleague can be meaningful. Personalize it by mentioning specific achievements or contributions.

- **Recognition wall:** Create a space in the office where employees' accomplishments are posted for everyone to see. It can be a physical wall or a digital platform where peers can celebrate each other.

- **Spotlight moments:** Feature employees in the company newsletter, social media, or during meetings. Share their stories and contributions with the entire team.

- **Experience-based rewards:** Instead of a traditional gift, offer experiences like a cooking class, concert tickets, or a weekend getaway as a reward for great work.

- **Peer-to-peer recognition:** Encourage team members to recognize each other through a system where they can nominate coworkers for a job well done. This fosters camaraderie and helps everyone feel appreciated.

- **Employee of the month:** Rotate recognition where an employee gets to enjoy special privileges like choosing music in the office, selecting lunch, or having a dedicated parking spot.

- **Cash incentives:** Provide direct cash bonuses for hitting key goals or achieving significant milestones. These can be one-time rewards or part of a structured performance incentive plan.

- **Gift cards:** Offer gift cards to popular stores, restaurants, or online platforms as a way to reward employees. Gift cards allow employees to choose what they want, adding a personal touch.

As noted earlier, recognition programs may be formal or informal. Regardless of the structure, recognition should follow basic guidelines such as being timely, specific, and relevant in order for the recognition to be credible and effective.

Special Events

In addition to employee recognition programs, companies might hold special events like holiday parties, team-building activities, or company picnics. These events help employees connect with each other outside of work. Special events during onboarding are a great opportunity to kick-start employee relations programs right from the start of the employee life cycle. By hosting team-building activities, casual meet-and-greets, or icebreakers, companies help new hires connect with their coworkers and feel welcome. These events introduce new employees to the company culture and create a sense of belonging and help new hires feel supported and included from their very first day. It is important that these special events be used to enhance a positive culture that already exists. One-off events cannot replace or replicate the authentic caring that must be demonstrated by a company toward its employees or special events will not have the intended effect.

Here are some key points related to special events that are valuable for HR professionals to understand:

- **Purpose and objectives:** Special events are more than just celebrations; they are strategic tools to enhance morale, boost engagement, and foster a sense of community. Each event should have a clear purpose, such as celebrating achievements, recognizing milestones, or building team cohesion, which aligns with broader organizational goals.

- **Budgeting and planning:** Proper budgeting is essential, as it determines the scale and scope of the event. Planning should cover all aspects, from venue selection to catering, activities, and decor, ensuring that resources are allocated in a way that matches the event's importance and aligns with organizational policies.

- **Inclusivity and representation:** Inclusivity should be a priority, making sure the event considers the diversity of employees' backgrounds and needs. This can include providing accessible venues, catering to various dietary restrictions, and ensuring everyone feels welcomed and valued.

- **Customization and personalization:** Customizing elements, such as awards, themes, and recognition speeches, to resonate with employees' specific achievements or contributions can make the event more meaningful. This personalization helps employees feel genuinely appreciated and reinforces company values.

- **Engagement and interaction:** Interactive elements like team-building activities or live polls keep employees engaged and creates a positive atmosphere. These can be tailored to match the tone of the event, whether formal or casual, and encourage participation, which strengthens connections between employees.

- **Evaluation and feedback:** Post-event feedback helps to assess the event's success and gathering insights for future improvements. Collecting responses on what employees enjoyed or felt could improve helps HR refine future events and continually enhance engagement strategies.

Diversity, Equity, and Inclusion (DEI) Programs

Diversity refers to the presence of differences within a workforce, such as varied races, genders, ages, sexual orientations, abilities, and experiences. Diversity initiatives aim to build a workforce that reflects a broad spectrum of backgrounds and perspectives. Equity focuses on creating fair opportunities for all employees by addressing structural inequalities. Equity in the workplace often involves removing barriers that may hinder certain groups and ensuring that policies support fair access to resources, promotions, and professional development. Inclusion ensures that all employees feel respected, valued, and actively engaged. Inclusive environments encourage contributions from everyone, fostering a sense of belonging across all backgrounds.

Effective DEI programs are treated with the same attention to detail as any other business strategy. This means the programs have leadership commitment, are properly resourced, and have measurable goals and accountability for outcomes.

DEI should also be considered when designing employee relations programs such as recognition and special events. Tailoring these programs to reflect the diverse backgrounds, cultures, and values of employees ensures inclusivity and helps everyone feel appreciated. This might involve recognizing different cultural holidays, offering a variety of rewards that cater to individual preferences, and ensuring that events are accessible and inclusive. This is especially important for multinational corporations or organizations that have ex-pats embedded in a foreign workforce. A genuine respect for the host nation culture and customs should be a critical part of a diversity program.

Collecting Employee Feedback

Collecting employee feedback is an important part of building positive employee relations. It helps companies understand what's working, what needs improvement, and what employees really want.

A *focus group* is a small group of employees brought together to discuss specific topics or issues. These discussions are used to gather feedback, opinions, and ideas from employees about things like company policies, products, or workplace improvements. Focus groups help companies better understand employee perspectives and make more informed decisions. For example, if a company is thinking about changing its health benefits, they might hold a focus group with employees to hear their thoughts and concerns before making any changes. This allows the company to make decisions that better meet the needs of their staff.

Employee sentiment and *attitude surveys* ask employees how they feel about their job, their team, and the company. Questions about job satisfaction, work environment, and leadership give valuable insights. The feedback helps identify areas to improve and shows that the company cares about employee opinions. HR can use AI to conduct employee surveys in several effective ways:

- **Personalized surveys:** AI can analyze employee data to tailor survey questions based on an employee's role, department, or experience, making the questions more relevant and increasing response rates.

- **Sentiment analysis:** AI can automatically analyze open-ended responses in surveys to identify employee emotions and attitudes. This helps HR quickly understand key themes, such as job satisfaction, engagement, or concerns.

- **Automated surveys:** AI can send out surveys at optimal times, like after major projects, team changes, or periodically throughout the year, ensuring timely feedback without manual effort.

- **Real-time insights:** AI-powered tools can process survey results instantly and provide real-time insights, helping HR quickly spot trends, such as declining morale or rising engagement.

- **Actionable suggestions:** By analyzing feedback patterns, AI can suggest specific actions HR can take to address common concerns or enhance employee satisfaction.

Using AI in employee surveys helps HR save time, gain deeper insights, and act on feedback faster, leading to a more engaged workforce.

Another important opportunity to gather feedback is during the separation stage of the employee lifecycle. When an employee leaves, *exit interviews* give them a chance to share honest feedback about their experience. Asking about why they're leaving and what could have been better helps companies learn and improve for future employees.

Workplace Behavior

HR plays an important role in managing employee behavior at work. One of the main ways they do this is by creating clear policies, such as codes of conduct, anti-harassment rules, and attendance guidelines. These policies help set expectations, so everyone knows what is acceptable behavior on the job. Behaviors must align with the corporate culture and mission, vision, and values of the company. Companies recognize more and more that "off-duty" behavior, which are actions employees take outside of working hours, can have an impact and reflect on the company. Some companies stipulate that actions employees take that have a negative impact on the company can result in discipline, even when those actions take place outside of work.

HR also helps by providing training to employees on topics like communication, teamwork, and conflict resolution. These training sessions teach important skills that help employees interact better with each other and handle tough situations professionally.

When conflicts arise, HR acts as a neutral party, stepping in to *mediate* and resolve disputes. To mediate means to help two or more people or groups find a solution to their disagreement by guiding a calm discussion and encouraging compromise.

Another way HR manages behavior is through performance management. HR partners with managers to address problems like poor performance or inappropriate behavior. Together, they provide feedback, coaching, and create action plans to help employees improve.

Additionally, HR supports employees through programs that promote well-being, such as *employee assistance programs (EAPs)*, wellness initiatives, and mental health resources. EAPs are work-based programs designed to help employees deal with personal or work-related problems that may affect their job performance, health, or well-being, offering services like counseling, legal advice, and stress management support.

HR also advises leadership on organizational behavior, helping guide decisions that shape the overall work environment. They provide insights on how leadership actions and company policies impact employee morale, engagement, and performance. HR also needs to model appropriate behavior, such as acting with integrity and professionalism. By analyzing employee feedback, performance data, and workplace trends, HR can recommend strategies to improve team dynamics and reduce turnover.

For example, HR might suggest leadership implement more flexible work arrangements to boost work-life balance or introduce new recognition programs to motivate staff. They also help leaders address any organizational behavior issues, such as poor communication or low engagement, by offering solutions like leadership training or revising management approaches. In this way, HR ensures that leadership decisions align with the company's values.

Counterproductive Work Behaviors

Counterproductive workplace behaviors (CWBs) are actions by employees that harm the company or create a negative environment. These can include things like wasting time, being dishonest, or acting aggressively toward others. Aggressive behaviors, such as bullying, harassment, or verbal abuse, can make the workplace uncomfortable and unproductive.

HR plays a key role in reducing CWBs and aggressive behaviors. HR can help by providing the following:

- **Clear policies:** HR creates rules on acceptable behavior and zero tolerance for aggression, such as anti-harassment and anti-bullying policies. These guidelines set expectations for how employees should act.

- **Training:** HR provides training on conflict resolution, communication, and respect in the workplace. This helps employees handle disagreements without resorting to aggression.

- **Open communication:** HR encourages employees to report aggressive behaviors and ensures there's a safe, confidential process for doing so.

By setting clear expectations, providing support, and addressing problems early, HR can help prevent and manage aggressive behaviors.

Substance Abuse

Substance abuse in the workplace refers to the misuse of drugs or alcohol by employees, which can negatively affect their job performance, safety, and overall health. Workers who abuse substances are more likely to make mistakes, cause accidents, or have conflicts with coworkers, putting themselves and others at risk. Substance abuse can lead to lower productivity, higher absenteeism, and increased workplace accidents.

The number one substance abused in the workplace is alcohol. Many employees may drink excessively outside of work or come to work under the influence, which can impair their ability to perform their tasks safely and effectively. Addressing substance abuse through employee assistance programs, health policies, and education is important for maintaining a safe and productive workplace. In the United States, alcoholism is considered a disability and is protected under the Americans with Disabilities Act (ADA). However, while individuals with alcoholism may be entitled to reasonable accommodations, the ADA does not protect individuals who are currently using alcohol in a way that impairs job performance or violates workplace conduct policies. Employers can still enforce rules regarding alcohol use and related misconduct. In many countries, like Canada and the UK, alcoholism can be considered a disability, offering some legal protection. However, rules vary, and employers are usually allowed to set policies about alcohol use at work. The focus is often on supporting recovery while maintaining job performance standards.

Substance abuse can also be the misuse of prescription medication either by someone that the medication was not intended for or by not using the medication in accordance with the doctor's instruction. Companies such as manufacturers can be at risk if someone under the influence is operating heavy equipment. Companies must ensure that there are policies and procedures in place to prevent this type of substance abuse from interfering with operations.

Conflict Management

Conflict in the workplace is common and can happen for many reasons, such as differences in opinions, personalities, misunderstandings, or competition. While conflict isn't always bad, if left unresolved, it can hurt teamwork, morale, and productivity. This is why conflict management is important for maintaining a healthy work environment.

One recognized expert in conflict management in the workplace is Kenneth Cloke,[1] a well-known mediator, arbitrator, and author. His approach focuses on the following:

- **Open communication:** Cloke encourages honest and transparent dialogue between conflicting parties, believing that open communication helps to uncover the root causes of disputes and develops mutual respect.

- **Mediation:** He uses mediation as a tool to guide employees through conflicts by acting as a neutral party, facilitating discussions that lead to mutually beneficial solutions without the need for formal disciplinary actions.

- **Creating understanding between conflicting parties:** Cloke emphasizes the importance of empathy and understanding, helping each side see the other's perspective. By building this understanding, conflicts can be resolved in ways that promote collaboration and long-term harmony in the workplace.

Progressive Discipline

Progressive discipline is a step-by-step method that employers use to deal with employee performance or behavior issues. The goal is to correct problems and help employees improve rather than just punishing them.

The process usually starts with a verbal warning, where a manager talks to the employee about the issue and what needs to change. If the problem continues, it moves to a written warning, which is more formal and usually includes specific details about what the employee did wrong and what needs to be done to fix it. If the issue isn't resolved, there may be suspension or final warnings. The last step, if there's no improvement, is often dismissal.

Progressive discipline can be effective, but there are several challenges organizations face in implementing it successfully:

- **Inconsistent application:** One of the biggest challenges is ensuring the process is applied consistently across all employees. If some employees are disciplined more harshly or leniently for similar behaviors, it can lead to claims of unfair treatment or discrimination.

---

[1] Cloke, K. (2001). *Mediating dangerously: The frontiers of conflict resolution.* San Francisco, CA: Jossey-Bass; Cloke, K. and Goldsmith, J. (2005). *Resolving conflicts at work: Ten strategies for everyone on the job.* San Francisco, CA: Jossey-Bass.

- **Subjectivity:** Supervisors may interpret rules or behaviors differently, leading to subjective enforcement of discipline. This can undermine the fairness of the process and damage employee morale.

- **Lack of documentation:** Progressive discipline requires detailed documentation at every step. If supervisors fail to properly document warnings and actions taken, it may become difficult to justify stronger disciplinary actions later on.

- **Employee pushback:** Employees may view progressive discipline as overly punitive or unfair, especially if they don't agree with the warnings or consequences. This can lead to resistance, lower morale, or even legal challenges.

- **Time-consuming:** The step-by-step nature of progressive discipline can take time to carry out, especially in cases where multiple warnings or interventions are needed. This may delay resolving ongoing issues and drain management resources.

- **Legal risks:** Improperly handling progressive discipline, such as skipping steps or failing to communicate expectations clearly, can open the door to legal risks like wrongful termination claims.

While progressive discipline is designed to give employees chances to improve their behavior, there are situations where it might be necessary to move directly to dismissal. This usually happens when the employee's behavior is so severe that it creates serious risks or damages the workplace.

For example, if an employee engages in violent behavior, like physical assault, or harassment, especially if it involves threats, it can create an unsafe environment for others. In these cases, immediate dismissal may be needed to protect coworkers and the company from further harm.

Another reason for skipping progressive discipline is theft or fraud. If an employee is caught stealing from the company, committing fraud, or deliberately breaking important rules like falsifying records, it can lead to immediate dismissal because it shows a breach of trust.

Gross misconduct—which includes things like using illegal substances at work or violating major safety protocols—can also lead to direct employment termination. Such actions can endanger the employee, their coworkers, and the company's reputation.

In situations like these, the severity of the behavior means that giving multiple warnings may not be appropriate or safe.

Health, Safety, and Security

Health, safety, and security refer to the practices and policies that protect employees from harm in the workplace. *Health* includes promoting well-being and preventing illness through policies like sick leave and wellness programs. *Safety* involves creating a hazard-free environment, following rules like wearing protective gear or regular equipment checks to prevent accidents. *Security* means protecting employees from external threats, like workplace violence or unauthorized access to sensitive areas.

Globally, different countries have regulations to ensure health and safety, such as the Occupational Safety and Health Administration (OSHA) in the United States, while Europe has strong laws under the EU's Health and Safety Directive. In regions like Asia, compliance varies, but international companies often follow global standards for consistency. Many laws and regulations share similar components, including written plans and policies, training, security best practices, and active risk management.

Health and Safety Prevention Plans and Policies

Health and safety prevention plans and policies are rules and guidelines designed to keep employees safe and healthy at work. These plans aim to prevent accidents, injuries, and illness by identifying potential hazards and taking steps to avoid them through education and other prevention efforts.

An *injury* is physical harm, like a cut, burn, or broken bone, that happens because of an incident at work. An *illness* is when a worker gets sick due to conditions at their job, such as breathing in harmful chemicals or getting sick from a contagious flu. An *accident* is an unexpected event, like slipping on a wet floor, that causes either an injury or damage to property. An *incident* is an unexpected event or situation in the workplace that can cause harm, damage, or disruption. It may not always result in injury or damage, but it still poses a risk, such as a near-miss accident, equipment malfunction, or unsafe behavior that could lead to a future problem. An injury, illness, accident, or incident may require some degree of investigation not to find fault, but rather, take steps to prevent the situation from occurring again.

Workers' compensation insurance in the United States is considered *no-fault*, which means that employees are entitled to benefits for work-related injuries or illnesses regardless of who was responsible for causing the accident or injury, and employees typically cannot sue their employer for negligence in exchange for these benefits. It is important to document incidents as a matter of practice. If, for example, an employee has an accident while working, such as a heavy piece of equipment falling, and the employee states they are fine, but three days later are complaining about a muscle pain or sore back as the result of the accident, the timeliness and reporting mechanisms become challenging. Even for seemingly minor incidents, a good practice is to report. In the United States, certain accidents must be reported and posted to comply with OSHA regulations.

A *safety and health management plan* is a formal document that outlines how a company will manage workplace safety and health risks. It provides a structured approach to identifying potential hazards and is designed to protect workers. These plans often include emergency evacuation procedures, health and safety training, and programs and procedures to address workplace security concerns, including workplace violence.

Emergency Evacuation Procedures

The US Department of Labor offers a great example of what should be included in an emergency evacuation plan, regardless of which country the business operates in. These procedures include the following:

- **Evacuation routes and exits:** Establish clear and accessible routes for safe exit from the building. These should be marked and known by all employees.

- **Reporting procedures:** Employees should know how to report emergencies like fires or chemical spills immediately, either through alarms or direct communication with emergency responders.

- **Headcounts:** After evacuating, employees should gather at a designated meeting place, where a headcount can be done to ensure everyone is accounted for.

- **Roles and responsibilities:** Assign specific roles, such as evacuation leaders, to guide the process and ensure smooth evacuation.

- **Emergency contact information:** Keep emergency phone numbers and contact information readily available and ensure employees know how to access them.

- **Drills and training:** Regularly conduct drills to ensure all employees are familiar with the procedures and can respond quickly in real emergencies.

> **NOTE** You can discover more on evacuation plans at the Department of Labor's website: `https://www.dol.gov/agencies/oasam/centers-offices/security-center/emergency-response`.

Evacuation procedures are not just for a building or facility. Significant weather conditions sometime dictate the need to evacuate a region or area such as in times of flooding or hurricanes. Procedures should be established by the company to determine how and when operations should be terminated or suspended so that employees can leave the impacted area with sufficient time to safely evacuate. The decision point of "too soon," which then impacts revenue and operational costs, or "too late," which puts employees in harm's way, is one management must navigate.

Health and Safety Training

Health and safety training teaches people how to work in a way that keeps them and others safe. Safety and health training is not universal—different industries have different training needs. For example, construction workers need to learn how to wear safety gear, like hard hats and harnesses. They also learn about fall protection and safe operation of tools. Nurses and doctors learn how to handle medical equipment safely, deal with hazardous substances, and prevent infections. Manufacturing teams need to understand how to operate machinery safely, avoid electrical hazards, and manage chemical spills.

A hazard assessment helps employers identify safety and health risks to employees. These can include the following types of risks:

- **Environmental:** Hazards caused by factors in the physical environment, such as extreme temperatures, poor lighting, or noise

- **Biological:** Risks from exposure to living organisms, like bacteria, viruses, fungi, and mold, which can cause illness or infection

- **Chemical:** Hazards due to exposure to harmful chemicals, such as acids, solvents, or fumes, which can cause burns, poisoning, or respiratory problems
- **Physical:** Risks from physical factors like machinery, tools, or falls that can cause injuries such as cuts, broken bones, or concussions
- **Ergonomic:** Hazards related to improper body positioning or repetitive movements that can cause strain or injury, especially to muscles and joints
- **Psychosocial:** Hazards affecting mental well-being, such as stress, workplace violence, or harassment, which can lead to anxiety or burnout
- **Radiological:** Risks from exposure to harmful radiation, such as X-rays or radioactive materials, which can damage cells and cause long-term health issues

Once these hazards have been identified, it is necessary to take steps to mitigate or eliminate them. *Mitigation* means decreasing the likelihood of an injury by taking steps to train, or requiring personal protective equipment (PPE) such as goggles, gloves, or hearing protection. Training should be done regularly to keep employees up to date on safety procedures, new equipment, or when procedures have been updated.

The main goal of risk management is to prevent accidents before they happen. This could mean teaching workers how to spot risks, report unsafe conditions, and follow safety rules at all times.

Workplace Security

Security risks are potential threats that can harm a company's employees, property, or data. These risks come in different forms, including theft, damage, or destruction of valuable assets.

Theft refers to the act of stealing, which can happen in several ways. Data theft occurs when someone steals sensitive information, such as customer data, trade secrets, or financial records. Data theft can lead to identity theft, fraud, or damage to a company's reputation. Companies can lose valuable resources when materials like office supplies or machinery are stolen. Equipment theft can slow down work and lead to financial losses.

Damage or destruction occurs when property is intentionally or accidentally harmed. This could include vandalism, where someone damages equipment, buildings, or other property on purpose. In some cases, damage can also result from natural disasters, but in the context of security, we focus on intentional actions like sabotage, which disrupts operations and leads to costly repairs or replacements. To protect against these risks, businesses should do the following:

- **Implement security measures:** Installing cameras, alarms, and using secure locks can help prevent theft and property damage.
- **Conduct regular audits:** Regular inspections help detect weaknesses in security systems and ensure that assets are accounted for. Audits can also help detect fraud.
- **Train employees:** Educating employees about the risks and how to report suspicious activities can significantly improve security.

In addition to the just listed risk management efforts, employers should pay special attention to cybersecurity protocols to guard against cyberattacks. A *cyberattack* is an attempt by hackers or other malicious individuals to damage, disrupt, or gain unauthorized access to computers, networks, or digital systems. The following are some of the common types of cyberattacks:

- *Phishing*: This involves sending fake emails or messages that trick people into revealing personal information, such as passwords or credit card numbers.

- *Malware*: Malware is malicious software, like viruses, worms, or ransomware, designed to damage or disable computers, steal data, or spy on users.

- *Denial of service (DoS) attacks*: In these attacks, hackers flood a network or website with so much traffic that it is unable to handle the requests, becoming unresponsive and preventing users from accessing it.

- *Ransomware*: This is a type of malware that locks users out of their systems or data until a ransom is paid to the attacker.

- *Man-in-the-middle (MitM) attacks*: In this attack, hackers intercept communications between two parties (like a user and a website) to steal data or spy on the conversation.

- *SQL injection*: This type of attack targets databases by inserting malicious code to access or manipulate sensitive information.

- *Spoofing*: Spoofing is a cyberattack where someone pretends to be a trusted source, like a website, email, or phone number, to trick people into sharing personal information or accessing secure systems.

Cyberattacks are dangerous because they can lead to the loss of sensitive data, financial damages, and even disruption of critical services like healthcare or power systems. To prevent them, individuals and organizations need to use strong passwords, update software regularly, and be cautious about clicking on suspicious links. *Authentication* is a security process that verifies a user's identity, often through passwords, fingerprints, or multifactor authentication, to prevent unauthorized access and protect against cyberattacks.

Access controls are security measures used to regulate who can view or use resources in a computing environment. They help ensure that only authorized individuals have access to sensitive data, systems, or physical areas. Access controls can involve passwords, key cards, or biometric scans (like fingerprints). These measures help prevent unauthorized users from gaining access and protect against cyberattacks or data breaches.

Workplace Violence

Workplace violence is any act or threat of physical violence, harassment, intimidation, or other disruptive behavior that happens at work. It can range from verbal threats and bullying to physical assaults. Workplace violence can happen between employees, but it can also involve customers or strangers.

Workplace violence can occur for many reasons, such as stress, personal conflicts, or mental health issues. In some cases, jobs that involve handling money, working with the public, or dealing with unstable individuals can be at a higher risk of violent incidents.

Employers have a general duty to keep employees safe, and this includes preventing and preparing for a workplace violence event. Employers should make sure that the workplace is safe, secure, and well-lit. Installing security cameras and having security personnel can help prevent violence. HR begins the prevention efforts by having clear policies outlining expected standards of behavior. Employees should be encouraged to report any violent or threatening actions immediately.

Regular training can help employees recognize the warning signs of potential violence, such as sudden anger or aggressive behavior, and teach them how to respond safely. While a goal should be to de-escalate a potentially violent situation, in some cases, the most prudent action is to shelter in place and contact law enforcement. Active shooter events are a subcategory of workplace violence and must be dealt with a rapid response. According to the FBI, 69% of these incidents end in five minutes or less, and 23% end in two minutes or less.[2] However, the devastation can be significant if measures are not put in place to respond. The most often used approach consists of avoiding or running from the threat, evading or hiding in a secure location that a perpetrator cannot access, and as a last resort, defending yourself and protecting others by fighting and standing your ground. These incidents are becoming more prevalent in the workplace, and more companies are putting mitigation measures in place, including access control, security, and safe rooms.

Workplace violence is not perpetrated by other employees alone. In some cases, such as with intimate partner violence (IPV), the threat is brought to the workplace by an outside individual. Employee support in these circumstances is paramount to protect not only the employee, but the other team members as well. If an employee is dealing with personal issues like stress or mental health problems, offering counseling services or employee assistance programs can help address these issues before they lead to violence.

Case Study

Retail workers continue to face a high rate of workplace violence. In fact, recent data shows that retail workers are among the most at-risk, with incidents of violence, including abuse and assaults, rising significantly. For example, in the UK, violence against retail workers surged by 50% in 2023, with shoplifting being a major trigger for these confrontations. The British Retail Consortium reported up to 1,300 violent incidents per day in 2023.[3] Similarly, in the United States, the retail industry remains one of the highest risk

---

[2] Federal Bureau of Investigation. (2014). *Active shooter study: Quick reference guide.* Washington, DC: Author. Available at: www.fbi.gov/file-repository/as-study-quick-reference-guide-updated1.pdf

[3] Reals, K. (2024). *Violence and abuse against shop workers up 50 per cent last year, says British Retail Consortium* [online]. British Safety Council. Available at: https://www.britsafe.org/safety-management/2024/violence-and-abuse-against-shop-workers-up-50-per-cent-last-year-says-british-retail-consortium

sectors for nonfatal workplace violence, particularly in roles involving direct customer interactions, handling money, or working in isolated settings like convenience stores.[4]

Retail environments often involve scenarios where employees may deal with irate customers, theft, or robbery attempts, contributing to the high incidence of violence. As a result, both governments and retailers are increasingly investing in preventive measures such as security cameras, de-escalation training, and anonymous reporting systems.

Workforce Reduction and Restructure

Workforce reduction and restructure are strategies that companies use when they need to change the size or shape of their workforce.

Workforce reductions happen when a company needs to reduce the number of employees. It can occur for several reasons, such as financial struggles, a decrease in demand for the company's products, or the adoption of new technologies that make some jobs unnecessary. Sometimes, this is called a "layoff" or "downsizing." The company may let go of some employees permanently, either by firing them or offering them voluntary packages to leave.

Workforce restructuring means that a company is changing how it is organized. This could involve changing people's roles, merging departments, or even creating new job positions while eliminating old ones. The goal of restructuring is usually to make the company more efficient or better suited to new challenges in the business world. Sometimes, restructuring happens alongside workforce reduction, but it doesn't always mean cutting jobs. Instead, it can mean shifting responsibilities or moving people to different areas within the company.

In both cases, companies make these changes to improve their operations or stay competitive, but they can have a big impact on employees, leading to job loss or changes in their roles. There are several types of reductions and restructures, and these are covered next.

- **Downsizing:** Downsizing is when a company reduces the number of employees to save money or become more efficient. It often happens when the business is struggling financially or when new technology makes some jobs unnecessary. Employees may lose their jobs, and the company becomes smaller.

- **Mergers:** A merger happens when two companies combine to form one larger company. This is often done to increase profits or share resources. After a merger, the companies might work more efficiently together, but there can be changes in leadership, job roles, or even layoffs as they combine their operations.

---

[4] National Institute for Occupational Safety and Health. (2024). *About workplace violence* [online]. Centers for Disease Control and Prevention. Available at: `https://www.cdc.gov/niosh/violence/about/index.html`

- **Relocation:** Relocation occurs when a company moves its offices or facilities to a new place. This might be to reduce costs or access better resources, like a larger market or cheaper labor. Employees may be asked to move to the new location, or they might be offered jobs at a different site.

- **Assignments and Transfers:** In assignments and transfers, employees are moved to new roles or different locations within the same company. This could be to help with a new project, fill a role in another department, or help the employee gain more experience. Transfers can happen within the same country or even internationally.

Offboarding and Termination Activities

Offboarding and termination activities are the steps a company takes when an employee leaves the organization, either voluntarily (resigning) or involuntarily (fired or laid off). It is the point in the lifecycle when the relationship between the employer and the employee terminates.

Offboarding refers to the entire process of managing an employee's departure from the company, which can include the following:

- **Notification of termination:** The employee is formally told they are being let go, with reasons for the decision.

- **Returning company property:** The employee must return items like laptops, keys, or ID cards.

- **Transitioning work:** The employee's tasks and responsibilities are handed over to someone else.

- **End of services:** HR explains to employees the details of their benefits, such as options to continue or when they will expire.

- **Final paycheck:** HR makes sure the employee is paid for any remaining work, vacation days, or other benefits.

NOTE

Many employers seek to enforce signed agreements once an employee has left. A nonsolicitation agreement is a legal contract that prevents an employee from encouraging coworkers or clients to leave the company or do business elsewhere after the employee departs. A noncompete agreement is a contract that restricts an employee from working for competitors or starting a similar business for a specific period after leaving the company.

Challenges to nonsolicitation and noncompete agreements include difficulty enforcing them due to varying country laws, especially in regions where courts view them as limiting job mobility. Additionally, proving violations can be complex, and overly restrictive terms may be seen as unfair or invalid.

Severance Packages

A *severance* package is a set of benefits and payments offered to employees when their employment is involuntarily terminated. Companies often provide these packages during layoffs, company restructuring, or downsizing to help employees financially as they transition out of the organization.

The most noticeable part of a severance package is usually the financial payment. This payment might come as a lump sum or in installments and is often calculated based on how long the employee worked at the company. For example, some companies might offer two weeks of pay for every year the employee was with them. This money helps the person cover their bills and living expenses while they look for a new job.

Another key part of a severance package can be health benefits. Many companies continue offering health insurance for a certain period after the employee leaves, which is important for those who are between jobs and still need medical coverage.

To help employees move on to new opportunities, some companies also provide outplacement services. These services can include things like career counseling, resume building, and job-search support. The idea is to help employees find a new job as quickly as possible.

While severance packages aren't always legally required, many companies choose to offer them. Often, in exchange for accepting the severance package, the employee might be asked to sign an agreement stating that they won't take legal action against the company or share any confidential information they learned while working there.

Severance practices vary from country to country in several key ways, which are covered next.

Legal Requirements

- **Mandatory severance:** In many countries, severance is required by law. For example, countries in the European Union (e.g., France, Germany, Spain) and Latin America (e.g., Brazil, Argentina) have strict legal requirements for severance pay, which is based on the employee's length of service.

- **Discretionary severance:** In countries like the United States and Japan, severance is not legally mandated but is often offered as a company policy or cultural practice.

Amount of Severance

- **Length-based calculation:** In many regions, severance is calculated based on the employee's years of service. For instance, Brazil and Spain require a set number of days' or months' pay per year of employment.

- **No set formula:** In countries like the United States, the amount of severance offered can vary widely and is often negotiated between the employer and the employee.

Additional Benefits

- **Comprehensive packages:** In regions like Europe and Latin America, severance packages may include not only financial payments but also additional benefits like continued health insurance, outplacement services, or retirement benefits.

- **Basic financial compensation:** In other countries like the United States and Japan, severance often consists of just financial compensation, with fewer additional benefits.

Cultural Practices

- **Generous cultural norms:** In countries like Japan and India, companies may offer severance as a cultural expectation, even if not required by law.
- **Strict legal and social expectations:** In many European Union and Latin American countries, severance is not only a legal requirement but also a strongly expected social norm.

Additionally, outplacement services can be offered to exiting employees that can be of mutual benefit by protecting brand reputation, reducing legal risks, boosting morale and retention, enhancing productivity during transition, and strengthening alumni networks.

Exit Interviews

An exit interview is a conversation that takes place between an employer and an employee who is leaving the company. The purpose of the exit interview is to gather honest feedback from departing employees about their experience working at the company. This feedback can help the organization identify areas for improvement, such as workplace culture, management practices, or specific job roles.

The benefit of exit interviews is that they offer a unique opportunity for companies to gain insight into why employees are leaving. Since the employees are no longer concerned about job security, they may feel more comfortable sharing truthful information about their experiences. It is also an important opportunity to hear about departing employees' negative experiences, allowing them to feel heard. This approach may make the former team members less likely to speak negatively about the company to others. Feedback can be incredibly valuable for improving employee retention, refining management practices, or addressing unresolved issues in the workplace.

However, there are also downsides to exit interviews. One of the main challenges is that departing employees may be reluctant to provide negative feedback, either because they don't want to burn bridges, or they feel it won't lead to change. Additionally, if the interview is not conducted in a supportive and neutral manner, it may not lead to useful insights. The effectiveness of the process largely depends on how open the company is to receiving and acting on the feedback.

Expatriation and Repatriation

An *expatriate* is a person who lives and works in a country other than their own, often for a temporary job assignment. Employees choose expatriate assignments for various reasons, including the opportunity for career growth, gaining international experience, and developing new skills. Many are motivated by the chance to take on leadership roles, work in diverse cultural environments, and enhance their resumes. Financial incentives, such as higher pay or allowances, along with personal adventure or a desire to travel, can also be strong motivators for accepting an overseas assignment.

HR supports expatriation assignments by helping to select the right candidates, offering competitive compensation packages, providing pre-departure training, and ensuring proper relocation support. HR also manages visa and work permits, oversees health and safety requirements, and facilitates cultural adjustment for employees and their families. Throughout the assignment, HR monitors performance, manages ongoing communication, and prepares for the eventual repatriation process, ensuring smooth reintegration into the home country. Additionally, HR considers long-term career development to retain expatriates after their assignment ends.

Repatriating employees after a global assignment involves returning them to their home country once their overseas job is completed. The process includes logistical arrangements like travel, housing, and reintroduction to their original or a new role within the company. It often includes support for adjusting back to local life, addressing challenges such as reverse culture shock, and reintegrating into the workplace.

Summary

Employee relations and the health and safety of the workforce are critical functions of an organization to maintain a strong and vibrant workplace. To affect employees in a positive manner, HR professionals must understand the laws and regulations that govern activities such as labor relations and the rights and responsibilities of both employees and employers. They must create a working environment that respects the privacy of employees and does its utmost to protect personal information, while ensuring that the workplace remains free from counterproductive workplace behavior such as harassment. HR can develop and implement employee recognition programs, diversity programs, and special events that celebrates the employees and builds the organizational culture. Key to these activities is collecting employee feedback to understand the needs of the workers.

Within the workplace, HR must understand the negative impact of certain behaviors and be able to manage conflict between individuals in the organization, whether they be management or employee. Progressive discipline is a method to align employees' actions with the goals, mission, and values of a company by eliminating negative behaviors that poorly impact the operations. HR must be able to conduct workplace investigations in a timely manner respecting the rights and privacy of all involved and quickly resolve any situations that have arisen.

Paramount to operations is ensuring the health, safety, and security of the entire organization. Prevention plans and policies are managed by HR professionals to be activated during a potential hazard situation. Workplace security refers to securing both persons and property in the company, which includes intellectual property such as company trade secrets. Corporate espionage, insider threats, and negligence can often put the organization at risk of losing valuable resources such as equipment or product ideas. Workplace violence is a reality in the workplace today and companies must have actionable plans that can mitigate a threat. One specific area to consider is an active shooter and how to handle such an occurrence.

Finally, workforces change over time due to market changes or other forces on the company. These changes may require reducing or restructuring the workforce to meet the changing needs of the company. Sometimes, this means reducing the force by offboarding individuals who are no longer needed for operations. They may be offered severance packages as compensation for leaving the organization. Another aspect, especially for global companies, is expatriation or repatriation of employees where key individuals with specific skills, familiar with the corporate objectives, are remotely located with the company in countries foreign to the company's country of origin. These workers understand the organizational culture and can infuse their knowledge to these distant locations.

Exam Essentials

Be able to establish an effective employee relations program.   An effective employee relations program includes policies for preventing and resolving disputes with clear guidelines on how to handle conflicts and seeks to improve working conditions with reasonable hours, pay and benefits, and work-life balance. It uses employee feedback to know if the programs are beneficial and acknowledges the contributions of employees through strong rewards and recognition programs. These components help create a positive workplace culture, improve job satisfaction, and enhance worker productivity.

Be familiar with the laws and regulations related to employee relations.   While the United States has laws such as the Fair Labor Standards Act (FLSA), the National Labor Relations Act (NLRA), and the Occupational Safety and Health Act (OSHA), international laws include the International Labour Organization (ILO) Conventions, which sets international labor standards on a wide range of topics including working conditions and employment policy. There are also EU directives that address working time, health and safety, and nondiscrimination in the workplace. The UN Global Compact encourages businesses worldwide to adopt sustainable and socially responsible policies, including labor standards. These laws and regulations aim to protect workers' rights, ensure fair treatment, and promote safe and healthy work environments.

Understand the risks associated with workplace security.   Workplace security involves managing various risks to ensure the safety of employees, infrastructure, and information. These risks include physical threats like theft or vandalism, cyber threats such as data breaches or hacking, workplace violence, natural disasters, supply chain disruptions, and health and safety hazards that could cause illness or injury. HR must implement comprehensive security measures, such as risk assessments, employee training, and security procedures that can mitigate these risks.

Know what activities constitute workplace reductions and restructuring.   Workplace reductions and restructuring involve a variety of activities to improve efficiency, competitiveness, and profitability. These may include layoffs, mergers and acquisitions, divestitures, changes in the organizational structure, outsourcing, or hiring freezes. These actions can be challenging for both the employee and employer but are necessary to adapt to changing market conditions and ensure the long-term sustainability of the business.

Review Questions

You can find the answers in Appendix A.

1. What is one of the key responsibilities of employers under global labor laws?
   - **A.** Providing workers' compensation insurance
   - **B.** Protecting employees from unsafe working conditions
   - **C.** Working with unions and councils to bargain for safety and health protections
   - **D.** Maintaining job security for employees

2. How does sentiment analysis improve the effectiveness of employee surveys?
   - **A.** By replacing quantitative data with storytelling
   - **B.** By sending automated responses to all employees to streamline processes
   - **C.** By analyzing open-ended survey responses to identify employee emotions and attitudes
   - **D.** By collecting data from managers and supervisors to measure performance scores

3. Which of the following best defines the modern psychological contract between employers and employees?
   - **A.** A mutual understanding of expectations that focuses on flexibility, personal growth, and work-life balance
   - **B.** A legal document that outlines the specific job duties of an employee
   - **C.** An employment contract with duties, responsibilities, and compensation outlined
   - **D.** A shared agreement of employee–employer rights and responsibilities

4. How does Maslow's hierarchy of needs apply to the workplace?
   - **A.** It suggests that employees must have their basic needs, such as safety, met before they can be concerned with higher-level goals like recognition.
   - **B.** It explains why both monetary and nonmonetary rewards are effective as motivators.
   - **C.** It encourages employers to focus on each need equally in order to achieve their greatest potential.
   - **D.** It notes that employees cannot be motivated toward the lower needs until the higher needs are met.

5. Which of the following is an employee responsibility in the workplace?
   - **A.** Giving two weeks' notice when they resign
   - **B.** Disclosing personal data to the employer when asked
   - **C.** Not sharing their pay rates with other employees
   - **D.** Performing job duties competently and following workplace rules

6. Which of the following are key responsibilities of employee relations in a company? (Choose all that apply.)

    A. Negotiating collective bargaining agreements with unions

    B. Managing the relationship between employers and employees to create a positive work environment

    C. Drafting health and safety regulations for the company

    D. Conducting employee performance reviews

7. How can poor employee relations lead to potential unionization efforts within a company?

    A. Employees may form unions to negotiate better working conditions if their interpersonal issues are not addressed.

    B. Employers often encourage unionization to avoid managing employee complaints.

    C. Excessive grievances automatically trigger the legal requirement for union formation.

    D. Employee relations is not related to unionization.

8. Which of the following best describes counterproductive work behaviors?

    A. Rudeness or profanity

    B. Low productivity or quality

    C. Employee sabotage or theft

    D. Frequent unexcused absences

9. Why is employee privacy an important aspect of employee relations?

    A. It helps companies monitor employee performance more effectively.

    B. It protects employee personal information and ensures it is handled according to legal standards.

    C. It allows employees to anonymously share their opinions.

    D. It helps employers comply with international privacy laws.

10. Which of the following are critical to an effective emergency response plan? (Choose all that apply.)

    A. Ensuring all employees are trained on emergency evacuation procedures

    B. Providing employees with emergency procedures, such as first aid protocols

    C. Ensuring that emergency exits are clear and accessible

    D. Having a written plan that remains consistent over time

11. Why is it important to document accidents and incidents, even if they do not result in an injury or damage to company property?

    A. Documentation may be required by unions and/or works councils.

    B. Minor incidents are reportable to workers' compensation carriers.

C. The goal of documentation is to prevent similar incidents that may result in injury or property damage.

D. It is unnecessary to document near-miss incidents.

12. Which of the following actions must an employer take in the event of a data breach under GDPR?

A. Notify the relevant authorities and affected employees within 72 hours.

B. Notify the board of directors and wait for instructions on how to proceed.

C. Notify employees immediately so they can take steps to mitigate the data exposure.

D. Inform employees once the breach has been resolved.

13. How can HR ensure that workplace harassment policies are effectively implemented?

A. By establishing clear anti-harassment policies

B. By relying on anonymous hotlines for confidential reporting

C. By training supervisors to handle complaints

D. By disciplining those accused of inappropriate behavior

14. What challenge might HR face when conducting workplace investigations in MNEs?

A. The need to address local corrupt practices

B. Local laws and cultural norms that may influence the investigation process

C. A lack of cooperation from corporate leadership

D. The need to hire external investigators for international cases

15. Why should diversity be considered when designing employee recognition and special events?

A. To tailor programs to reflect diverse backgrounds and cultures

B. To increase the number of employees recognized

C. To identify creative ways to reward employees

D. To avoid any personal or cultural preferences when designing programs

16. How can focus groups benefit a company considering changes to its health benefits?

A. By providing HR with actionable data to increase utilization

B. By gathering employee feedback and concerns to reduce the cost of employee benefit offerings

C. By consolidating employee feedback into manageable amounts

D. By shortening the time it takes to make informed decisions about employee benefits

17. What is an advantage of using AI-powered employee attitude surveys? (Choose all that apply.)

A. AI can provide employee feedback from the survey responses.

B. AI can analyze employee data and tailor survey questions to each employee's role.

    C. AI can model expected standards of behavior for employees.

    D. AI can predict patterns in employee behaviors and make recommendations.

18. In which of the following situations should you recommend that an employer bypass the company's progressive discipline policy and proceed directly to dismissal?

    A. If the employee yells at a coworker

    B. If the employee "no calls, no-shows" to work for more than two days

    C. If the employee engages in gross misconduct such as physical assault or theft

    D. It is never a good idea to bypass company policy, as it increases the risk of a wrongful discipline or discharge claim.

19. How does subjectivity impact the effectiveness of progressive discipline?

    A. It helps tailor discipline uniquely to each employee's situation.

    B. It reduces the effectiveness of feedback as it slows down the process.

    C. It improves the clarity of feedback for the employee.

    D. It leads to inconsistency in how discipline is applied.

20. Which of the following is a key mandate of the GDPR regarding employee privacy?

    A. Employers are not required to obtain informed consent prior to collecting data.

    B. Employers must allow employees to access and correct their personal data.

    C. It applies only to businesses that operate in the European Union.

    D. Employers must store all employee data for seven years.

Appendix A

Answers to Review Questions

Chapter 2: aPHR Talent Acquisition

1. B. Conducting a skills inventory involves assessing the current skills of employees to determine where there are gaps that need to be filled. The other options are less relevant: analyzing customer feedback (option A) focuses on improving products and services rather than staffing; organizing team-building activities (option C) aims to enhance teamwork and employee morale, not to identify staffing needs; and monitoring social media trends (option D) provides insights into public perception and market trends but does not address the company's internal staffing requirements.

2. C. Job analysis helps in identifying what a job entails and the skills required for it. The other options are incorrect: determining employee satisfaction (option A) is related to measuring how content employees are with their roles and work environment; redesigning jobs to improve productivity (option B) is a potential outcome of job analysis but not its primary purpose; and increasing employee engagement (option D) focuses on how involved and enthusiastic employees are about their work, which is not the main goal of a job analysis.

3. A. Forecasting allows companies to plan ahead and ensure they have the right number of employees with the necessary skills. The other options are not the main reasons for forecasting: informing the annual HR budget (option B) is a part of financial planning but not the primary focus of forecasting; identifying employee training needs (option C) is used for employee development; and analyzing past seasonal staffing needs (option D) looks at historical data rather than predicting future requirements.

4. B. Creating a company blog to share employee success stories helps build the company's reputation as a great place to work to attract potential employees. The other options, although beneficial to employees, are not focused on employer branding: offsetting commute costs for employees (option A) is a perk that can improve employee satisfaction; reducing the number of meetings per week (option C) aims to increase productivity; and increasing the company's team-building budget (option D) enhances team cohesion but doesn't specifically build the company's external image as an employer of choice.

5. A, B. Resume mining helps recruiters efficiently identify potential hires from a large pool of applicants. The other options are not part of resume mining: hosting job fairs to meet potential candidates in person (option C) is a method of talent sourcing but not related to the detailed examination of resumes, and conducting interviews to assess candidate suitability for a job (option D) is a separate stage in the hiring process after resume screening has been completed.

6. A, B, C, D. All options describe different aspects of a candidate pipeline, which is a resource that helps companies maintain a ready pool of potential candidates for current and future job openings. A candidate pipeline refers to a group of previous applicants for an open position (option A), candidates who have been selected for an interview (option B), a list of current employees who have placed a job bid (option C), and employees identified to take on a future leadership role (option D).

7. C. Using a mix of behavioral and situational questions helps interviewers gain a well-rounded understanding of a candidate's skills, experiences, and problem-solving abilities. The other options are less effective: asking mostly yes or no questions to ensure consistency (option A) limits the depth of information gathered; letting the candidate lead the conversation to assess their communication skills (option B) may not cover all necessary topics; and focusing primarily on the candidate's resume without exploring other experiences (option D) misses the opportunity to understand the candidate's full range of abilities and potential.

8. D. In the scenario described, the candidate is using the STAR method which stands for Situation, Task, Action, and Result. The candidate explained the context (Situation), what they needed to achieve (Task), the steps they took (Action), and the outcome (Result). The other options are incorrect: the structured interview method (option A) involves asking all candidates the same set of questions in a specific order, but it doesn't necessarily focus on past behavior using the STAR format. The case study interview method (option B) involves giving candidates a real or hypothetical problem to solve, which is different from describing past experiences. The unstructured interview method (option C) is more casual and doesn't follow a specific format.

9. A, C. A close-ended interview question can be answered with a simple "yes" or "no" or "closed for additional comment." The other options examples of open-ended questions as they ask for a narrative versus a simple "yes" or "no."

10. D. A job description provides detailed information about what is expected in a particular role. The other options are incorrect: job analysis (option A) is a process used to study and gather information about a job, but it does not create the specific document that describes the job. Job posting (option B) refers to the advertisement of a job opening, not the detailed document describing the job itself. Job bid (option C) is a process where employees can apply for internal job openings, and it does not refer to the document detailing job responsibilities.

11. B. In a Boolean search, "AND" ensures that the results include both terms, making it the correct choice. The other options are incorrect as they are not recognized by a Boolean search and will not yield the desired results.

12. B, C, D. The goals of the talent acquisition process include attracting and hiring skilled employees (option B), overseeing the candidate experience (option C), and communicating the employer brand (option D). These activities help the company find and retain the best talent. Option A is incorrect as improving employee engagement is typically part of employee retention and development strategies rather than the initial talent acquisition process.

13. C. The first stage of the employee lifecycle involves attracting and hiring new employees to join the organization. The other options are incorrect: performance management (option A) occurs later in the employee lifecycle and involves evaluating and improving employee performance. Onboarding (option B) is the process of integrating new hires into the company, but it happens after recruitment. Retirement (option D) is the final stage of the employee lifecycle, when employees leave the workforce, making it the last step, not the first.

14. B. The primary goal of the onboarding process is to help new hires understand how the company operates and what is expected of them to support a smooth transition into their new roles. The other options are incorrect: evaluating employee performance (option A) is part of performance management, which comes later in the employee lifecycle. Planning future training sessions (option C) is related to employee development but is not the main focus of onboarding. Conducting exit interviews (option D) occurs when an employee is leaving the company, making it part of the offboarding process rather than onboarding.

15. C. The stage of the employee lifecycle that focuses on skill improvement is dedicated to helping employees enhance their skills and advance in their careers through training, mentoring, and other growth opportunities. The other options are incorrect: recruitment (option A) involves attracting and hiring new employees, not focusing on skill improvement. Onboarding (option B) is about integrating new hires into the company and familiarizing them with company culture and procedures. Retirement (option D) is the final stage of the employee lifecycle when employees leave the workforce, not upskill or reskill.

16. B. A counteroffer in the context of job offers is when the candidate is suggesting different terms, such as salary or benefits, than those originally offered. The other options are incorrect: an offer made by an employer to a candidate after an interview (option A) is just a regular job offer, not a counteroffer. A job offer extended to multiple candidates simultaneously (option C) is simply a job offer to several people, not a counteroffer. An offer made by an employer to fill a temporary position (option D) is a temporary job offer, which is not related to counteroffers.

17. A. The primary purpose of an employment contract is to specify details like job responsibilities, salary, and benefits. The other options are incorrect: creating a commitment between the employer and a union (option B) is the purpose of a collective bargaining agreement, not an individual employment contract. Clarifying the terms and conditions of employee dismissal (option C) is just one part of an employment contract, not its main purpose. Providing details on the company's policies, procedures, and rules (option D) is the role of an employee handbook, not an employment contract.

18. D. The employee handbook is a mandatory document for new employees because it contains important policies, procedures, and expectations for employees (option D). This helps new employees understand the rules and guidelines they need to follow. The other options are incorrect: while providing detailed employment information about the company (option A) and outlining the company's mission, vision, and values (option B) are useful, they are not the primary reasons the handbook is mandatory. Protecting against employment at-will (option C) is not accurate, as employment at-will is a legal doctrine that allows employers or employees to terminate employment at any time, for any reason, or for no reason at all, without prior notice, and a handbook can help protect the right to employment at-will.

19. B. A commonly used metric to measure ROI in the talent acquisition process is cost per hire (option B). This metric calculates the total cost involved in hiring and helps companies understand their hiring efficiency. The other options are incorrect: employee satisfaction scores (option A) measure how happy employees are with their jobs, but they don't directly relate to the costs of hiring. The number of job applications received (option C) shows interest in the job openings but doesn't reflect the costs or efficiency of the hiring process. The length of employee training programs (option D) pertains to how long training lasts, not ROI in hiring.

20. C. A key indicator of a successful ROI in the talent acquisition process is a short time-to-fill for job openings (option C). This means that the company is able to quickly hire qualified candidates, showing that its hiring process is effective. The other options are incorrect: high turnover rates (option A) suggest that employees are leaving the company frequently, which is a negative sign. Low candidate response rates (option B) indicate that few people are interested in the job openings, which is not good for the company's recruitment efforts. Increased number of training sessions (option D) is important for employee development but does not directly measure the success of the talent acquisition process.

Chapter 3: aPHR Learning and Development

1. A. An example of knowledge in the workplace is understanding how to operate specific software because it involves having the information and understanding needed to use the software effectively. The incorrect options are typing at a speed of 60 words per minute (option B), which is a skill; leading a team meeting (option C), which involves skills and abilities; and handling customer complaints (option D), which also requires a combination of skills and abilities.

2. B. Resolving conflict between team members is the best example of skills because it involves using learned behaviors and techniques to handle and mediate disputes effectively. The incorrect options are knowledge (option A), which refers to information and understanding of specific subjects; abilities (option C), which are natural or innate talents; and other competencies (option D), which refer to other behavioral or personal traits that do not fall with the knowledge, skill, or abilities category.

3. B, C. Examples of abilities in the workplace include having 20/20 vision and lifting heavy objects because these are innate or natural talents that a person possesses. The incorrect options are memorizing company procedures (option A), which is more about knowledge, and writing detailed reports (option D), which is considered a skill that can be developed and improved over time.

4. A. Promoting from within can save time and resources since the employee is already familiar with the company. The incorrect options are when the position requires cutting-edge expertise not available in the current workforce (option B), which would require hiring externally; when the company is undergoing significant changes and needs new approaches (option C), which might benefit from external perspectives; and when the company is

looking to diversify its talent pool (option D), which often involves bringing in new talent from outside.

5. D. A realistic job preview allows candidates to experience the job firsthand, providing a clear picture of the role, making job shadowing the best choice. The incorrect options are: structured interview (option A), which involves a set list of questions during an interview; job bidding (option B), which is when current employees apply for a new position within the company; and paid internship (option C), which is a temporary position for gaining work experience that is tied to educational goals and lasts longer than a day.

6. A, B, C. Examples of employee orientation activities include introducing the new employee to their team (option A), providing an overview of the company's mission, values, and culture (option B), and explaining company policies and procedures (option C). These activities help new employees become familiar with the company and their role. The incorrect option is assigning the new employee their first project (option D), which is part of the onboarding process that follows orientation.

7. C. When a new employee was not given proper training materials and their workstation was not set up the best action for the HR professional is to elevate the situation to the HR Manager. This ensures that the issue is addressed at a higher level to prevent it from happening again. The incorrect options are: buying the new hire the proper equipment (option A), which may solve part of the problem but not the underlying issue; apologizing to the new hire and offering support (option B), which is necessary but not sufficient to resolve the problem; and scheduling additional training sessions (option D), which might help but doesn't address the immediate setup and material issues.

8. C. Acclimation programs may require employees to fit into a rigid company culture, which can hinder their ability to adapt and feel valued. The incorrect options are certainly challenges to employee onboarding but can be the result of other issues, such as poor organization, low employee morale, and inadequate resource management, not the acclimation program itself.

9. A, B. Managers can help set expectations for new hires by providing a detailed job description and performance standards and offering regular feedback and check-ins. These methods help the new hires understand their roles and receive guidance to re-orient their performance as needed while they settle in. The incorrect options are allowing peers to mentor them within their first 30 days (option C), as peers may not establish the proper expectations or offer the consistent feedback necessary in the early days of a job; and setting open goals to encourage creativity (option D), which may lead to confusion if expectations are not clearly defined.

10. B. Coaching focuses on improving performance in specific tasks, often with direct oversight from a manager. Mentoring, on the other hand, involves guidance and advice from someone with more experience, often focusing on broader career development. The incorrect options are coaching focuses on long-term career guidance, while mentoring focuses on short-term skill development (option A), which reverses their typical roles; coaching is informal and unstructured, while mentoring follows a specific plan (option C), which is not accurate; and coaching involves group sessions, while mentoring is always one on one (option D), which misrepresents both practices.

11. D. Career pathing involves outlining the steps and skills needed for an employee to advance to higher positions within the company. The incorrect options are performance feedback (option A), which focuses on evaluating and improving current job performance; coaching (option B), which is more about improving specific skills or tasks with a supervisor's guidance; and mentoring (option C), which involves advice and support from a more experienced colleague, rather than a structured plan for career advancement.

12. B. Training courses and workshops are ways that HR can support employee development. The incorrect options are conducting annual performance reviews (option A), which offers developmental feedback but should be done by an employee's manager; facilitating team meetings (option C), which aren't necessarily focused on skill development; and offering flexible work hours (option D), which can support employee retention but don't contribute to learning new skills.

13. B. The six personality types in the RIASEC model are Realistic, Investigative, Artistic, Social, Enterprising, and Conventional. The Realistic type is characterized by a preference for practical, hands-on activities and often involves working with tools, machines, or nature.

14. A. For a person with SEC (Social, Enterprising, Conventional) as their RIASEC code, the most suitable career path would be a human resource professional as this role involves interacting with people, organizing activities, and managing tasks. The incorrect options are accountant (option B), which is more suited for someone with Conventional and Investigative traits; electrician (option C), which may include conventional traits but aligns better with Realistic over Social and Enterprising; and retail associate (option D), which typically suits those with Realistic and Enterprising traits rather than Social and Conventional.

15. B, C, D. HR can utilize a career framework to design employee development plans (option B), help individuals identify career paths (option C), and identify reskilling or upskilling needs (option D). These correct options leverage the career frameworks (such as the RIASEC model) to align employees' personality types with suitable career development strategies. The incorrect option is to help determine employee pay increases based on performance (option A), which would not be a proper use for a career model.

16. A. A job is characterized by short-term tasks, whereas a career is characterized by long-term growth and development. This means a job focuses on immediate responsibilities and tasks, while a career involves a series of jobs and experiences that contribute to professional advancement and personal growth over time. The other answers are not true.

17. C. It is important for HR professionals to continually update their knowledge and skills to keep up with changing laws and best practices so they stay compliant with current regulations and can implement effective HR strategies. The incorrect options are maintaining their current job position (option A), which does not fully encompass the value of continuous career development; reducing the workload of other employees (option B), which is not a direct result of updating HR knowledge; and ensuring employee satisfaction (option D), which is important but not the primary reason for ongoing HR education.

18. C. Knowles' adult learning principles, also known as andragogy, emphasize that adults learn best when they understand why they need to learn something, when learning is self-directed,

when it builds on their experiences, and when it is focused on practical, real-life tasks and problem-solving. These principles highlight the importance of making learning relevant and applicable to the learner's personal and professional life.

19. D. According to Knowles' model of adult learning, learning activities should focus on real-life experiences and problem-solving (option D). This approach helps adults apply what they learn to practical situations, making the learning process more relevant and effective.

20. C. The primary difference between synchronous and asynchronous learning is that synchronous learning happens in real time with live interaction between instructors and students, such as in a live online class or a classroom setting. In contrast, asynchronous learning allows students to learn at their own pace using prerecorded materials and assignments that can be accessed anytime. The other responses are not true.

Chapter 4: aPHR Compensation and Benefits

1. A, B, C, D. Total compensation includes all forms of payment and benefits that an employee receives. This means it covers health insurance premiums (option A), bonuses (option B), housing allowance (option C), and nonmonetary perks (option D). All these options are correct because they contribute to the overall value of what an employee earns from their job, beyond just their base salary.

2. D. An employee benefit is an extra component of an employee's total rewards package. Alternative work schedules are considered a benefit because they offer flexibility in how employees manage their work hours. The other options are incorrect: a monthly salary (option A) is part of regular compensation; bonuses (option B) are additional pay based on performance; and job satisfaction (option C) is an emotional response to the job, not a tangible benefit.

3. A. The main difference between job analysis and job evaluation is that job analysis focuses on describing a job, while job evaluation assesses the job's value. The other options are incorrect: job analysis does not define wage scales, and job evaluation does not price jobs (option B). Job analysis is not solely used to define training needs, and job evaluation does not rank jobs in order of importance (option C). Finally, while job analysis data are indeed used to create job descriptions, job evaluation does not define the characteristics of jobs (option D); it evaluates their relative worth.

4. B. The primary reason for a pay increase is to maintain competitiveness with similar roles in the industry. The other options are partially correct in that they can be reasons for a pay increase, but not the primary reason for doing so: rewarding employees for daily above-average performance better describes a reason for a piece-rate pay system (option A) and pay increases only for retention purposes (option C) may not achieve desired results.

Similarly, keeping employees happy (option D) is a goal of many HR practices but is not the primary reason for adjusting pay.

5. B, C, D. Determining the appropriate salary for a job based on its duties and market data is called benchmarking compensation points (option B), pricing jobs (option C), and evaluating the internal competitiveness of wages (option D). Creating job descriptions (option A) involves outlining job responsibilities but does not set salaries.

6. B. "We strive to maintain transparency within our compensation systems and commit to paying our employees fairly and competitively to attract and retain top talent" highlights the principles of a compensation philosophy, which often include transparency, fairness, and market position as core elements. The other options are incorrect as none of them include the key elements of a compensation philosophy.

7. A, B, D. The Fair Labor Standards Act (FLSA) has several purposes: to regulate child labor (option A), to establish a threshold for minimum wage (option B), and to require all private employers to pay a minimum wage to nonexempt workers (option D). The incorrect option is C, which states that the FLSA requires employers with 50 or more employees to offer healthcare benefits; this requirement is actually part of the Affordable Care Act, not the FLSA.

8. D. Conducting a job analysis to determine the responsibilities and requirements of each position is a necessary first step for setting accurate pay rates. The other options are incorrect: understanding the company's compensation philosophy (option A) is important for guiding the pay scale, but is irrelevant without knowing the details of each job. Classifying workers as exempt or nonexempt (option B) and pricing jobs relative to market conditions (option C) rely on the information gathered during the job analysis.

9. A, C. The criteria for exemption includes being paid a salary, such as with the manager and performing certain types of job duties, such as a computer programmer. The other options are incorrect: an hourly worker in a retail store (option B) and a part-time cashier at a grocery store (option D) are usually classified as nonexempt, as they do not meet the criteria for exemption.

10. A. Based on the FLSA, overtime is calculated for hours worked over 40 in a workweek at a rate of 1.5 times the regular pay. The total hours worked are $8.25 + 8.5 + 8 + 9 + 6.5 = 40.25$ hours. The 2 hours of paid time off do not count toward overtime. The overtime hours are 0.25 hours. The correct answer is $5.53 (option A). This is calculated by taking 0.25 hours of overtime and multiplying it by 1.5 times the regular rate: 0.25 hours × ($14.75 × 1.5) = $22.13 × 0.25 hours = 5.53.

11. B. HMO members must see their primary care physician first and get a referral before seeing a specialist. The incorrect options are providing the flexibility to see any healthcare provider without a referral (option A), which is a feature of PPOs, not HMOs; offering high-deductible health plans with health savings accounts (option C), which is typical of certain insurance plans but not specific to HMOs; and allowing members to receive care from out-of-network providers at a higher cost (option D), which is another feature of PPOs, not HMOs.

12. D. Offering a comprehensive benefits package makes the company more attractive to potential employees. Most are required by regulations (option A) is not true as many benefits are voluntary; it supports an employer brand (option B) is beneficial but not the main reason; it increases employee job satisfaction (option C) is important but secondary to attracting talent in the first place.

13. A, C, D. The options that are not likely to qualify for health insurance benefits with an employer are gig workers (option A), grandparents as dependents (option C), and part-time employees (option D). Gig workers typically work as independent contractors and are not eligible for employer-provided benefits. Grandparents as dependents are usually not covered under standard employer health insurance plans. Part-time employees often do not qualify for the same benefits as full-time employees. The incorrect option is full-time employees (option B), who are generally eligible for health insurance benefits with an employer.

14. B. Complying with state and federal labor laws and avoiding penalties ensures that the employer is following legal requirements and helps prevent legal issues and fines. The incorrect options are ensuring the employees' pay is accurate (option A), which should be done with mechanisms in place prior to the paycheck being issued; providing employees with written proof of payment (option C), which is beneficial but not the main focus; and reducing the company's tax liability (option D), which is unrelated to the information required on pay stubs.

15. B, D. The correct options about an employee's final paycheck are that it must include payment for any unused vacation time, if state law requires it (option B) and must comply with state requirements (option D). The incorrect options are it can be withheld until the employee returns all company property (option A), which is not allowed as the final paycheck is owed regardless of property return, and it can include a lump-sum deduction for outstanding employee loans (option C), which is generally not permitted without the employee's consent and often governed by state law.

16. A. Outsourcing payroll allows the small business to handle payroll efficiently without needing in-house expertise. The other options are less ideal: while a company with temporary or contract workers (option B) might benefit, agencies typically have a centralized structure for payroll processing. A company with more than 1,000 employees (option C) usually has the resources for an internal payroll team. Similarly, a company with 200 employees and 1 HR person (option D) might find outsourcing helpful, but it's not as pressing as in option A.

17. B. Pay compression is defined as the situation where there is a small difference in pay between employees regardless of their skills, experience, or seniority. This can occur when new employees are hired at salaries close to or higher than those of existing employees, causing inequity. The other options are incorrect: adjusting employee salaries based on performance reviews (option A) is a practice known as merit pay; increasing salaries to match market rates (option C) refers to market adjustments; and providing bonuses to employees during peak seasons (option D) is typically known as seasonal bonuses or incentive pay.

18. B, C, D. Wage and hour laws do not require severance pay (option B), two weeks' notice of separation (option C), or paid meal periods (option D). These aspects are typically determined by individual states, company policy, or employment contracts, not mandated by law. Overtime pay must be provided to eligible employees who work more than 40 hours in a workweek.

19. D. The job evaluation method involves comparing different jobs by assigning points to various factors like skill and responsibility. The other options are incorrect: the ranking method (option A) involves ordering jobs from highest to lowest based on overall value, without detailed scoring. The point method (option B) and point factor method (option C) are similar and involve assigning points to jobs based on specific criteria, but they do not focus specifically on the detailed comparison of factors like skill and responsibility.

20. A. Job evaluation involves assessing the value of each job within the company to ensure fair and consistent pay. The other options are incorrect: benchmarking (option B) and salary surveys (option C) involve comparing pay rates and benefits with those of other companies, which are external methods. Market evaluations (option D) also focus on analyzing external market conditions to set competitive pay rates.

Chapter 5: aPHR Employee Relations

1. A, B, C. To effectively manage relationships in the workplace, the necessary HR competencies are communication (option A), conflict resolution skills (option B), and negotiation (option C). These skills help HR professionals handle interactions, resolve disputes, and reach agreements. The incorrect option is data analysis (option D), which is important for other HR functions like tracking performance metrics, but it does not directly relate to managing workplace relationships.

2. B. The primary difference between employee rights and employee responsibilities is that rights are entitlements employees have, while responsibilities are duties they must perform (option B). This means that rights are what employees are allowed to have or do, such as those granted by law. Responsibilities are tasks or actions they are required to complete, such as to perform their work in accordance with company guidelines, or to work safely. The other options are not true.

3. C. Facilitating open conversation to address the issue(s) encourages communication and helps resolve misunderstandings or disputes (option C). The incorrect options are asking the employees to try and work it out themselves first (option A), which might not always lead to a resolution; training supervisors to be effective conflict managers (option B), which is helpful but not a direct strategy for managing a specific conflict; and avoiding discussions about the conflict to prevent escalation (option D), which usually worsens the problem rather than resolving it.

4. A. An example of a company mission statement is "To provide the best customer service and improve lives through innovation" (option A). This statement clearly defines the company's purpose and goals. The incorrect options are "To become the global leader in our industry" (option B), which is more of a vision statement outlining a future goal; "Integrity, excellence, and teamwork" (option C), which describes company values; and "Our approach is centered

on continuous learning and improvement" (option D), which reflects more of a company philosophy than mission.

5. B. An example of company values is "Honesty, accountability, and respect for all individuals" (option B). This statement highlights the principles that guide the company's behavior and decisions. The incorrect options are "Our goal is to expand to new markets and increase our customer base" (option A), which is more of a business objective; "To be the most trusted brand in our field" (option C), which describes a vision for the future; and "We believe in a work-life balance and employee well-being" (option D), which reflects a company philosophy.

6. D. The primary purpose of labor laws in the workplace is to protect the rights of workers (option D). These laws ensure that employees are treated fairly and have safe working conditions. Employment laws do not exist to collect taxes (option A), supplement collective bargaining agreements (option B), or focus on retention (option C).

7. A. An example of a political factor in a PESTLE audit is a new president being elected (option A), representing a change in government that can impact business regulations and policies. The incorrect options are advances in artificial intelligence (option B), which is a technological factor; an increase in the aging population (option C), which is a demographic or social factor; and a shift in consumer fashion trends (option D), which is a social factor.

8. A, B, C. In a PESTLE audit, the impact of climate change on a business would include social (option A), economic (option B), and environmental (option C) factors. Social factors involve changes in public awareness and behavior regarding the environment. Economic factors cover the financial costs and benefits related to climate change, such as shifts in markets or the cost of sustainable practices. Environmental factors directly relate to how climate change affects natural resources and regulations. The incorrect option is legal (option D), which deals with laws and regulations but is not directly impacted by climate change itself.

9. C. An example of an opportunity in a SWOT audit is a competitor being bought out (option C) because it can open up new market opportunities and reduce competition. The incorrect options are employees gaining new skills (option A), which is an internal strength; implementation of new customer service management software (option B), which is also an internal strength; and an economic recession (option D), which is an external threat.

10. D. Forecasting (option D) involves predicting future needs based on data and trends. The incorrect options are benchmarking (option A), which involves comparing your company's performance to industry standards; sensing (option B), which involves observing current market trends without making future predictions; and analyzing (option C), which involves studying past and present data but does not necessarily include making predictions for the future.

11. C. The Delphi method (option C) uses multiple rounds of questioning to gather insights and reach agreement among experts. The incorrect options are scenario planning (option A), which involves creating and analyzing possible future scenarios; trend analysis (option B), which looks at historical data to predict future trends; and consensus building (option D),

which is a general term for group agreement but does not specifically describe the Delphi method.

12. C. In a hierarchical structure (option C), each employee has a single, direct supervisor, whereas in a matrix structure, employees may report to both a functional manager and a project manager. The incorrect options are hierarchical structures having multiple leaders and matrix structures having a single leader (option A), which is not accurate; hierarchical structures focusing on team collaboration and matrix structures emphasizing individual performance (option B), which does not correctly describe how these structures operate; and hierarchical structures being more flexible while matrix structures are more rigid (option D), which is incorrect as matrix structures are more flexible to accommodate cross-functional projects.

13. A. The primary difference among a policy, procedure, and rule is that a policy provides general guidelines, a procedure outlines specific steps, and a rule mandates strict requirements (option A). This means that a policy sets the overall direction or principles for actions, a procedure gives detailed instructions on how to carry out specific tasks, and a rule establishes clear, mandatory expectations that must be followed. The other options are not true.

14. A, D. The appropriate human resource activities for employee self-service systems are updating personal contact information (option A) and viewing pay stubs and tax documents (option D). These activities allow employees to manage their own information and access important documents easily. The incorrect options are submitting a grievance (option B), which requires direct communication and sensitive handling by HR, and conducting a self-appraisal (option C), which is usually part of a more formal performance review process involving supervisors and HR.

15. B. Positive discipline aims to improve behavior through encouragement and personal growth, while progressive discipline involves increasing consequences, starting with warnings and escalating if the issue continues (option B). Positive discipline does not focus on punishment, and progressive discipline doesn't always result in immediate dismissal (option A). Both approaches address minor and major violations (option C) and both positive and progressive discipline can be legally defensible when applied properly (option D).

16. A, B, C. To improve the effectiveness of its performance review process, a company should increase the frequency of feedback (option A), as regular feedback helps employees stay on track and improve continuously. Avoiding rater biases (option B) ensures that evaluations are fair and objective. Training supervisors and managers on how to deliver meaningful feedback (option C) helps them provide constructive and helpful insights to employees. The incorrect option is replacing the annual review with monthly feedback (option D), which may be too frequent to provide meaningful feedback and would not allow the employee adequate time to correct behaviors.

17. A, C, D. Challenges to the performance appraisal process include a lack of meaningful feedback (option A), which means employees do not get useful information on how to improve; frequency (option C), which refers to appraisals being too infrequent to effectively support development; and supervisor favoritism (option D), which means some employees may receive biased evaluations based on personal relationships. The incorrect option is unsatisfying pay increases (option B), which relates more to compensation issues rather than the appraisal process itself.

18. B. Rater bias is a tendency to rate employees based on personal feelings rather than objective criteria (option B), meaning that evaluations can be unfair and not accurately reflect an employee's performance. The incorrect options are a method to improve employee skills (option A), which is not related to rater bias; a tool for measuring employee satisfaction (option C), which has nothing to do with performance appraisals; and a method for giving employee feedback (option D), which describes part of the appraisal process but not rater bias.

19. C. Reducing toxic workplace behaviors (option C) involves creating a positive work environment by addressing and eliminating harmful behaviors. The incorrect options are managing the performance review process (option A), which focuses on employee evaluations rather than culture; conducting wage surveys (option B), which relates to compensation rather than directly improving culture; and integrating HR technology such as employee self-service (option D), which enhances HR efficiency but does not specifically address company culture.

20. D. The primary difference between diversity and equity in the workplace is that diversity refers to having a variety of backgrounds and perspectives, while equity ensures fair treatment and opportunities for all employees (option D). This means diversity is about the presence of differences, and equity is about fairness in access and treatment. The other options are untrue.

Chapter 6: aPHR Compliance and Risk Management

1. C. The Fair Labor Standards Act (FLSA) sets the minimum wage and overtime pay requirements in the United States. The other options are incorrect because they focus on different areas: (A) The National Labor Relations Act (NLRA) protects union rights, (B) the Employee Retirement Income Security Act (ERISA) deals with employee benefits, and (D) the Consolidated Omnibus Reconciliation Act (COBRA) allows employees to continue health insurance after leaving a job, but none of these regulate wages or overtime.

2. B. The Consolidated Omnibus Budget Reconciliation Act (COBRA) allows employees to continue their health insurance coverage after leaving a job. The other options are incorrect: (A) The Americans with Disabilities Act (ADA) focuses on disability rights, (C) the Fair Labor Standards Act (FLSA) regulates wages and overtime, and (D) the Occupational Safety and Health Act (OSHA) deals with workplace safety, but none of these relate to continuing health insurance coverage.

3. A, B. Employers cannot retaliate against employees for union activity, and unions cannot coerce or threaten employees into joining. The incorrect options are (C) An employer offering higher wages to employees who oppose unionization, which is also an unfair labor practice, and (D) An employer holding regular staff meetings, which is a normal business activity and not an unfair labor practice.

4.   A. The FMLA allows eligible employees to take unpaid, job-protected leave for reasons such as the birth of a child or caring for a seriously ill family member. The incorrect options are (B) Provides up to 12 weeks of paid leave, which is false because FMLA leave is unpaid; (C) Is administered on a state level, which is incorrect because FMLA is a federal law, although some states do have equivalent laws; and (D) Requires employees to first use any PTO or other available leave, which is not a requirement, although employers may allow or require it in some cases.

5.   C. ERISA stands for the Employee Retirement Income Security Act. This law ensures that employees receive protections for their retirement and health benefits. The other options are incorrect: (A) FLSA sets wage and overtime rules, (B) WARN Act requires advance notice for layoffs, and (D) NLRA protects the rights of employees to form unions, but none of these focus on retirement and health benefits.

6.   A. OSHA stands for the Occupational Safety and Health Act. This law requires employers to ensure a safe and healthy work environment by following safety regulations. The other options are incorrect: (B) ADA focuses on disability rights, (C) FMLA provides unpaid leave for family and medical reasons, and (D) COBRA allows employees to continue health insurance after leaving a job, but none of these deal with workplace safety.

7.   C. US anti-discrimination laws, such as Title VII of the Civil Rights Act, protect all employees regardless of immigration status. This means that Maria, as a DACA worker, has the right to report harassment and should feel confident in seeking help from HR or her supervisor to stop the inappropriate behavior.

8.   C. Reporting the behavior ensures that the issue is addressed properly and helps maintain a respectful workplace. The other options are incorrect: (A) Tell the employee being talked about what was said could cause more harm and discomfort, (B) Tell the group to stop might not effectively resolve the issue and could lead to confrontation, and (D) Stay out of it because it doesn't involve him directly is not appropriate, as all employees should help create a respectful work environment, even if they are not directly involved.

9.   A, C, D. Mergers and acquisitions and downsizing or layoffs are all clear examples of organizational restructuring, which involves significant changes to a company's structure or workforce. (D) Outsourcing can also be considered restructuring since it involves shifting tasks or jobs to outside organizations. However, (B) hiring is not an example of organizational restructuring, as it involves bringing in new employees but does not change the overall structure of the organization.

10.   D. HR must investigate ongoing harassment complaints and take appropriate action, which may include disciplinary measures and ensuring the victim is safe from further harm. While escalating to leadership (A) or dismissal (B) may be options in severe cases, HR should always take action and never tell the employee there's nothing more they can do (C).

11.   A, B, C, D. All of these documents are acceptable for verifying identity and employment eligibility for Form I-9. A US Passport verifies both identity and work authorization, while a

driver's license and Social Security card, or a birth certificate, together confirm identity and work eligibility. An arrival/departure record is also valid as a receipt in specific cases, such as for lawful permanent residents.

12. A, C. Fines can be imposed for improper handling of I-9 forms, and criminal charges can occur if an employer knowingly hires unauthorized workers. The incorrect answers are (B) Employee dismissal, which is not a penalty for I-9 violations, and (D) Reassignment of employees to different roles, which is unrelated to I-9 compliance penalties.

13. A, C. Moving an employee to a different department after they file a complaint and firing or demoting an employee for reporting harassment both can be forms of retaliation if done in response to the employee exercising their rights. The other options are incorrect: (B) Offering training opportunities to an employee who raised a safety concern and (D) Providing feedback to an employee who participated in an investigation are positive actions, not examples of retaliation.

14. A. The Equal Employment Opportunity Commission (EEOC), which enforces anti-discrimination laws in the workplace, ensuring employees are treated fairly regardless of race, gender, religion, or other protected characteristics. The other options are incorrect: (B) Department of Labor (DOL) focuses on wage, hour, and employment standards, (C) Occupational Safety and Health Administration (OSHA) enforces workplace safety regulations, and (D) Internal Revenue Service (IRS) handles tax collection and enforcement, none of which deal with anti-discrimination laws.

15. B. Under the Patient Protection and Affordability Care Act PPACA, large employers (typically with 50 or more full-time employees) are required to provide affordable health insurance to full-time workers and their dependents or face penalties. The other answers are not true.

16. A, B, C, D. All the options are correct under the Portal-to-portal Act. (A) Time spent traveling between work sites during the workday is compensable because it's part of the job. (B) Time spent working through a lunch break is compensable if the employee is not fully relieved from duties. (C) Time spent on mandatory training required by the employer must be paid as it's part of the job. (D) Time spent performing essential job duties before or after the official workday is compensable if it's necessary for the job, such as setting up or closing down.

17. B. The Employee Retirement Income Security Act (ERISA) requires companies to provide financial reports and audits to demonstrate compliance. The other options are incorrect: (A) Securing employment practices liability insurance is related to protecting against legal claims, not ERISA compliance. (C) Allowing employees to manage their own retirement funds without interference goes against ERISA's requirement for fiduciary oversight. (D) Matching employee contributions equally is not a requirement under ERISA, as companies are not mandated to match contributions.

18. C. The Davis-Bacon Act requires prevailing wages on federal construction projects, while the Walsh-Healy Act sets standards for wages, hours, and safety for manufacturing and supply contracts.

19. A, C. OSHA enforces workplace safety by creating safety standards and conducting inspections to ensure that employers are meeting the required regulations to keep workplaces safe for employees. OSHA also enforces safety by issuing citations and fines for violations of safety standards. This holds companies accountable and encourages them to comply with safety regulations. (B) OSHA does not offer tax incentives to companies for maintaining safe workplaces. (D) OSHA conducts its own inspections and does not hire private companies to inspect workplaces for compliance with standards.

20. B, C. (B) Providing regular harassment prevention training is an effective way for companies to educate employees on recognizing and preventing harassment. (C) Establishing clear anti-harassment policies and reporting systems ensures that employees know how to report incidents and that the company takes harassment issues seriously. (A) Ignoring minor complaints is not effective and can lead to bigger issues. (D) Delaying investigations until multiple complaints are made can allow harassment to continue and worsen.

Chapter 7: aPHRi HR Operations

1. B. PESTLE helps businesses analyze external factors that can affect them, like political, economic, social, technological, legal, and environmental changes. Internal finances (A), customer complaints, (C) and employee productivity (D) are incorrect because they focus on internal or specific company issues, not the broader outside influences PESTLE covers.

2. A, B, C. Social factors are elements in society that can influence how businesses operate. These factors include things like changes in cultural trends, where shifts in popular beliefs or behaviors can impact what products or services people want. Population growth is another social factor because changes in the number of people in a certain area can affect demand for goods and services. Shifts in consumer preferences are also a social factor because as people's tastes change, businesses need to adapt to meet their needs. New government regulations (D), falls under legal or political factors, not social factors.

3. B. The International Labour Organization (ILO) is responsible for creating and enforcing international labor standards, promoting decent work conditions, and ensuring workers' rights are respected across the world. World Trade Organization (WTO) focuses on international trade, not labor rights (A). United Nations Security Council (UNSC) deals with peace and security issues, not labor laws (C). World Health Organization (WHO) focuses on public health, not workers' rights or labor laws (D).

4. C. The main purpose of the GDPR is to protect individuals' personal data and ensure their privacy rights are respected. It gives people more control over how their data are used and stored. To protect companies from data breaches is wrong because the GDPR focuses on protecting individuals, not businesses (A). To control how individuals use the internet is incorrect because GDPR regulates how companies collect and use personal data, not how individuals browse the internet (B). To promote free trade within the European Union is also wrong because the regulation is about data protection, not trade (D).

5. A, B, C, D. Privacy laws protect various types of documents that contain personal or sensitive information. Employee personal data such as addresses and Social Security numbers are protected to ensure privacy. Employee records, like job history or contracts, also fall under privacy laws because they contain sensitive details. Business records that include personal data, such as payroll information, are safeguarded. Performance reviews, which provide personal feedback about employees, are protected to maintain privacy and fairness.

6. D. The priority in employee records management is to protect personal information by ensuring data privacy and security, which helps prevent unauthorized access and ensures compliance with privacy laws. Maximizing the amount of data collected (A) is incorrect because the focus should be on protecting relevant data, not collecting excessive amounts. Minimizing the amount of data collected (B) is partially right, but securing the data is more important than just minimizing it. Keeping records for as long as possible (C) is wrong because records should only be kept for as long as necessary, based on legal and business needs.

7. C. The main purpose of an organizational strategy is to guide the company toward achieving its long-term goals. While vision and values (A) help shape a company's identity, they are not the core focus of strategy. Similarly, strategy is not about making short-term decisions (B) but focuses on long-term objectives. Finally, strategy aims at overall growth and success, not just profit increases (D).

8. D. Goals represent the overall purpose a company wants to achieve, while objectives are the specific actions taken to reach those goals. The other options are incorrect: goals are not short term and objectives long term (B), as both can have short- or long-term focuses. Goals are not directly tied to values and objectives to mission (C), instead, both relate to achieving the company's broader strategy. Goals are not strictly about employee performance and objectives about customer satisfaction (A); both can apply to various areas within a business.

9. B. Organizational culture impacts the way employees think, act, and make decisions, which in turn influences how business strategies are developed and executed. Financial goals are not directly set by culture (A), and culture does not inherently limit access to markets (C). Culture affects more than just employee performance; it shapes broader decision-making and strategic thinking (D).

10. D. Companies can effectively communicate their strategy by using clear messages through meetings, emails, and presentations. Implementing a strategy without explanation leads to confusion and disengagement (B). Strategy should be communicated to all employees, not just top management (A). Unwritten practices are important but are not the primary means of communicating strategy (C).

11. D. Business operations refer to the daily activities and processes that help a company produce goods or provide services. The specific departments within a company (A) are part of the organizational structure, but they do not define business operations as a whole. The hiring and training of employees (B) is a function of human resources, not a description of business operations. Financial management (C) relates to accounting and managing the company's finances, but business operations cover a broader range of daily tasks.

12. C. In a matrix structure, employees typically report to more than one manager, usually a functional manager and a project manager, allowing for flexibility across departments. A flat structure (A) has few or no levels of management, so employees don't report to multiple managers. In a product structure (B), the company is organized around specific products, with teams responsible for their assigned product, but employees still report to a single manager. The divisional structure (D) organizes the company into divisions based on products, markets, or geography, with each division operating semi-independently, but employees do not report to more than one manager.

13. A. A flat structure has few or no levels of management, giving employees direct access to top leaders and allowing for quick decision-making. A product structure (B) organizes teams around specific products, but this doesn't eliminate management levels, so decisions may still need approval from multiple levels. A matrix structure (C) involves employees reporting to multiple managers, which can slow decision-making due to the need for coordination. The divisional structure (D) divides the company into semi-independent divisions, which still have layers of management.

14. A. A matrix reporting structure is characterized by employees reporting to multiple project or product managers. In a product structure (B), employee reporting is organized around specific products. Dividing the company by geographic regions (C) is a feature of a divisional structure, not a product structure. Having few or no management levels (D) describes a flat structure, not a product-based one.

15. C. One of the key challenges HR professionals must overcome to improve HR operations is developing a stronger understanding of business operations. This allows HR to be more involved in strategic and operational decisions, enhancing their impact on the organization. Being distracted by underperforming employees (A) is incorrect because managing employee performance is a necessary part of HR, not a distraction. Overcoming documentation requirements (B) is a challenge, but it is also a necessary part of HRs role. Being limited to administrative tasks (D) is incorrect because the bigger challenge is developing a stronger understanding of business operations. This understanding allows HR to contribute more effectively to the company's overall strategy and operations, making the department's role more impactful beyond basic administrative duties.

16. A, B, C, D. The purpose of having policies, procedures, and rules in human resources management includes ensuring employees are treated fairly (A), providing supervisors and leaders with guidelines for managing employees (B), making sure employees understand what is required of them (C), and ensuring compliance with labor laws (D). These elements work together to create a fair and structured work environment.

17. B. A policy provides general guidelines on how things should be done in an organization, setting broad expectations for employee behavior and operations. A rule, on the other hand, outlines the specific do's and don'ts for acceptable behavior, giving clear boundaries for what is allowed. Rules are specific, not general suggestions (A). While rules support policies, they are not strict interpretations but rather clear directives. Rules are often company-specific and not necessarily based on legal requirements (D); that would be more the role of a written policy.

18. D. High employee engagement indicates that employees are satisfied and invested in their work, which can reduce turnover. Low engagement often signals dissatisfaction and can lead to higher turnover rates. Retention rate (A) measures how many employees stay at the company, but it doesn't predict future turnover as directly as employee engagement. Turnover in the first six months (B) reflects a specific period of turnover but doesn't give a broader view of engagement or future retention. Time to hire (C) is related to the efficiency of the recruitment process and is not directly linked to predicting turnover.

19. B. The key difference between HR performance measures and measures of effectiveness is that HR performance measures assess the efficiency of HR activities, such as how well processes like recruitment or training are carried out. These metrics focus on how smoothly and efficiently HR tasks are completed.

20. D. Accurate payroll processing depends on maintaining well-organized employee records, including salary information and work hours. Developing more training programs (A) wouldn't directly address payroll issues, as it's focused on employee skills. Improving recruitment strategies (C) deals with hiring and wouldn't help with payroll accuracy. Conducting employee satisfaction surveys (B) might provide insight into morale but wouldn't solve the technical problem of payroll management.

Chapter 8: aPHRi Recruitment and Selection

1. C. The GDPR's main purpose is protecting personal data and privacy. The incorrect options: (A) focuses on companies, not individuals, (B) is related to labor laws, and (D) is about trade, not data protection, which all miss the main focus of GDPR.

2. A. Companies must report a data breach to the authorities within 72 hours because a core requirement of the GDPR is to ensure prompt action. The incorrect answers miss the point of this requirement: (B) suggests notifying employees immediately regardless of severity, but the law prioritizes notifying authorities first; (C) is wrong because waiting to act goes against GDPR's urgency; and (D) is incorrect because no breach should be ignored, regardless of the number of people involved.

3. C. The GDPR applies to any company, regardless of its location, as long as it handles the personal data of individuals in the European Union. The incorrect answers are misleading: (A) mistakenly limits GDPR's scope to companies within the EU, (B) wrongly claims that non-EU companies are exempt, and (D) incorrectly focuses only on companies doing business with EU governments, ignoring the broader application of the law to any entity processing EU citizens' data.

4. D. Social media recruiting can reach candidates with a wide range of experience levels, while university recruitment focuses on entry-level talent. This distinction is key because social media platforms connect with a broad audience, including both experienced professionals and entry-level candidates, while university recruitment generally targets students or recent graduates for entry-level positions. (A) Social media recruiting is not typically limited to entry-level roles, and (B) social media recruiting can attract both active and passive job seekers, while university recruitment generally focuses on students or recent graduates who are actively pursuing entry-level opportunities. (C) University recruitment can be effective for building long-term talent pipelines, particularly for future entry-level roles.

5. B. Automating resume screening and candidate matching, as AI is often used to quickly sort through large volumes of resumes and match candidates based on job requirements. The incorrect options are less relevant to AI's typical use in recruitment: (A) conducting interviews is generally a human task; (C) job training is not a primary function of AI in recruiting; and (D) negotiating salaries is generally handled by HR professionals or managers, not AI systems.

6. B. ATS can unintentionally filter out qualified candidates if they use different words or phrasing that don't match preset keywords. The incorrect options, (A), (C), and (D), do not reflect the main bias issue associated with an ATS.

7. A, B, C. An employment visa (A) permits work in specific roles, while (B) a Green Card or EAD authorizes broader employment. (C) A Social Security card is necessary for tax reporting and employment verification purposes but does not alone grant work authorization. The incorrect option, (D), is a US passport, which is only required for US citizens and cannot be used by foreign nationals to obtain work authorization.

8. A, B. A work permit or visa from the home country is often necessary, as some countries require additional documentation from the worker's country of citizenship to support the foreign work authorization process. A work permit or visa from the host country is typically essential, as most countries require foreign workers to obtain legal authorization to work within their borders. (C) A US driver's license is not usually required for work authorization abroad; it primarily serves as identification for driving within the United States. (D) A letter of recommendation from a US employer may support an application but is not generally required for legal work authorization in another country.

9. B. An employment contract is legally binding, while an offer letter is generally not. An offer letter may become legally binding if it includes terms that contradict at-will employment, such as specifying guaranteed employment for a set period, as this can imply that the employee cannot be dismissed without cause during that time. The other answers are false.

10. A, C, D. The correct answers, (A), (C), and (D), are common mistakes. Omitting benefits, failing to include compensation details, and using unclear language can lead to confusion or miscommunication. The incorrect option, (B), is not a mistake, as clearly stating the job title and start date is an essential part of a well-written offer letter.

11. C. The correct answer, (C), is using temporary workers or contractors, which is a flexible staffing method that allows companies to adapt quickly to global needs. The incorrect answers include (A), hiring exclusively from the home country is not an alternative method); (B), as expatriates are a traditional method, not alternative; and (D), hiring only local employees doesn't leverage alternative global methods like contractors or freelancers.

12. A. The correct answer, (A), is a behavioral interview, which focuses on past experiences to gauge how candidates might behave in future situations. The incorrect options include (B), as panel interviews involve multiple interviewers but don't focus specifically on past behavior; (C), as technical interviews assess job-specific skills; and (D), because stress interviews test how candidates handle high-pressure situations.

13. B. Structured interviews reduce bias by using the same set of questions and evaluation criteria for all candidates, promoting fairness. Asking different questions can introduce bias (A), skipping questions undermines consistency (C), and unplanned conversations increase the chance of bias (D).

14. D. An expatriate is an employee sent by their company to work in a foreign country on a temporary assignment. The other answers are not true.

15. B. Bias can exist when interviewers favor candidates with a personal connection, in this case, going to the same college. The incorrect options, educational credentials are a valid criterion (A), selecting from campus fairs may be part of targeted recruiting (C), and using diverse panelists reduces bias (D).

16. A. Expatriates are often hired for temporary international assignments, while local hires are usually permanent employees in their home country. The other options are not true.

17. A, C. Interviews are typically conducted to assess a candidate's fit for the job, and background checks are performed to verify qualifications and ensure the candidate meets company requirements. The incorrect options include (B), as Form I-9 completion is a post-hire activity to verify work eligibility, and (D), since orientation typically occurs after hiring to introduce new employees to company policies and culture.

18. C. Interviewers should avoid allowing personal biases to affect their decisions. The incorrect options include (A) as open-ended questions help gather more information, (B) because structured interviews ensure fairness, and (D) as evaluating based on job-related criteria is an effective selection method.

19. B. Form I-9 is used to verify an employee's identity and eligibility to work in the United States, a legal requirement for all US employers.

20. B. Outsourcing reduces costs and increases flexibility by hiring external talent, often at a lower cost. The incorrect options include (A) as loyalty can be lower in outsourced roles, (C) because local regulations must still be followed, and (D) as outsourcing often reduces direct control over day-to-day operations.

Chapter 9: aPHRi Compensation and Benefits

1. B. Monetary entitlements in international HR practices include financial rewards such as salaries, bonuses, and commissions. Nonmonetary entitlements refer to benefits provided by the company, such as housing, healthcare, or flexible work arrangements, which enhance employee well-being but are not directly tied to financial compensation. (A) Incorrectly categorizes vacation as a monetary entitlement, (C) focuses too narrowly on stock options, and (D) does not accurately describe the distinction between guaranteed and discretionary benefits.

2. C. The job evaluation process within a company helps ensure that employees are compensated fairly based on the complexity, responsibility, and contribution of each job to the organization. (A) Determining if jobs are paid based on market rates is part of market analysis, not job evaluation. (B) Reviewing employee performance for promotions is separate from the job evaluation process, which focuses on the role itself. (D) While job evaluation supports pay equity, the primary focus is on understanding the job's value within the company.

3. D. When conducting a salary survey to build a pay structure, it is most important to select a survey that includes data from companies with similar job roles and geographic locations to make sure that the pay structure is competitive and relevant to the specific labor market. (A) Similar revenue levels are helpful but less important than job roles and location. (B) Using a survey with the lowest salary ranges would not help attract or retain talent. (C) Focusing only on high-demand industries may skew the data and not reflect the company's actual needs.

4. B. An example of a flex hours policy is allowing employees to manage their work schedules while maintaining coverage during core business hours, supporting work-life balance. (A) Allowing employees to take unpaid leave for personal reasons is related to time off, not flex hours. (C) Offering unlimited time off refers to a leave policy, not a flex hours policy. (D) Allowing employees to volunteer for overtime is related to extra hours, not flexibility in daily scheduling.

5. A. When offering a wellness program across multiple countries, it is essential to prioritize compliance with local privacy and data protection laws, as regulations vary by region and failure to comply can result in legal issues. (B) Offering the same wellness program across all countries may not take into account the differing legal requirements in each region. (C) Making participation mandatory could violate employment laws in some countries where wellness programs must be voluntary. (D) Providing financial incentives may not always be compliant with local laws.

6. A. The first priority when designing a fringe benefit program should be understanding the tax implications, as this can affect both the company's costs and employees' net compensation. Without addressing tax compliance, the company risks financial and legal challenges. (B) Aligning benefits with the company's brand is important but secondary to legal and tax considerations. (C) Lifestyle perks are attractive but not as crucial as ensuring tax compliance. (D) A one-size-fits-all approach may not work due to varying legal and tax requirements in different regions.

7. B. A variable pay program provides employees with financial incentives based on their individual or team performance, encouraging higher productivity and achievement of specific goals. (A) Variable pay can apply to all levels of employees, not just executives. (C) Nonmonetary reward systems are different from variable pay, which directly involves financial compensation. (D) Retirement plan benefits are typically long-term and not tied to immediate performance or results.

8. D. The company should prioritize tying bonuses to clear, measurable performance goals to ensure that bonuses are distributed fairly based on the specific contributions and achievements of employee. (A) While clear communication helps, the most effective way to maximize the company's return on investment on bonus payouts is by tying them to measurable performance goals. Option (B) is incorrect because simply creating a minimum and maximum scale does not directly ensure fairness; it only provides flexibility but doesn't guarantee that bonuses are tied to objective performance criteria. (C) Avoiding payment to underperforming employees or those with disciplinary action might be a consideration, but the main priority should be on overall performance-based criteria, which offer a more comprehensive evaluation of an employee's contribution to the company's success.

9. A. Conducting market research ensures that pay grades are competitive and aligned with industry standards, addressing concerns about fairness. (B) Offering merit raises to only a small percentage could cause discontent. (C) Removing pay grades might eliminate structure and fairness. (D) Increasing noncash compensation without addressing pay concerns might not fully resolve employee dissatisfaction.

10. B. The most appropriate pay structure for rewarding top performers without increasing fixed salary costs is implementing a performance-based bonus program. This structure allows the company to provide financial rewards based on performance, without increasing the base or hourly labor cost. (A) Offering across-the-board raises would increase fixed costs for all employees, regardless of performance. (C) A pay grade system with automatic increases would also raise fixed costs and may not directly reward high performance. (D) Increasing the frequency of pay increases would similarly lead to higher long-term salary costs rather than focusing on rewarding performance.

11. C. A cafeteria plan is a flexible benefit program that allows employees to choose from various benefits based on their needs. (A) A defined pension plan is not flexible, as it provides fixed retirement benefits. (B) A wellness program and (D) a company-wide health insurance plan with no customization are also not considered flexible benefits programs.

12. B. A pension scheme is designed to provide employees with financial support after they retire. (A) Healthcare coverage and (D) short-term disability coverage are unrelated to the purpose of a pension scheme. (C) Government benefits vary country by country.

13. A, C. A health, fitness, and wellness program help promote a healthier lifestyle and well-being for employees, encouraging physical activity and supporting efforts to quit smoking. (B) Physical therapy is usually covered under medical insurance or workers' compensation insurance, rather than being a standard part of a wellness program. (D) Well days are not as commonly included as gym memberships and smoking cessation programs in wellness initiatives and often vary from employer to employer.

14. B. Surveying employees allows the company to gather direct feedback, which will highlight the range of healthcare needs across different demographics, such as age, family status, and health conditions. Without this input, designing a plan may risk overlooking key aspects that are important to various employee groups. (A) can be achieved after employees share their preferences. (C) is incorrect because minimizing out-of-pocket costs alone does not ensure that the healthcare plan aligns with the actual needs of the employees. Option (D) is incorrect because programs should be based on employee feedback to ensure that any included options and locations are relevant to the workforce.

15. A. Offering financial incentives encourages employees to voluntarily participate in wellness programs without making it mandatory. (B) Requiring fitness assessments and (C) making participation a condition for promotions could discourage involvement and be discriminatory. (D) Automatic enrollment may be effective, but it does not encourage active participation in the same way that incentives do and may come with some transparency issues.

16. C. PTO, or paid time off, is a system that combines vacation, sick leave, and personal days into one bank of hours. This allows employees to use their allotted time off as they see fit, whether for personal needs, illness, or vacation, giving them more flexibility in managing their time off. (A) PTO is not part of base wages but a separate benefit. (B) While vacation time can be used throughout the year, PTO is broader and includes sick leave and personal days. (D) PTO generally includes paid time off, while unpaid time off is managed separately in most systems.

17. A. Providing a detailed breakdown in the employee handbook of how vacation and PTO days are accrued gives employees clear, written guidelines they can refer to at any time, reducing confusion and promoting transparency. (B) Educating supervisors is helpful but does not provide employees with direct access to the information they need. (C) Requiring employees to attend a training session could be burdensome and unnecessary for resolving this issue. (D) Providing weekly notifications in the company newsletter or intranet may not be sufficient for detailed, comprehensive explanations.

18. B. A key requirement for filing a disability benefits claim is providing evidence of a disability that prevents the employee from working to demonstrate that the employee qualifies for benefits under disability policies. (A) Proof of US citizenship is not required for disability claims. (C) Pay stubs from the previous year may be needed for other purposes but are not typically the key requirement for filing a disability claim. (D) To qualify for disability benefits, an injury or illness does not have to be work-related. Disability benefits can cover both work-related and non-work-related conditions, as long as the disability prevents the employee from working.

19. D. Software solutions specifically designed to handle claims management can reduce human error, track deadlines, and provide real-time updates on the status of claims. Option (A) does not address the efficiency of the process or eliminate potential errors. (B) Increasing the number of staff can help manage claims volume, but it does not inherently improve the accuracy or efficiency of the filing process. (C) Requiring employees to submit claims directly could add unnecessary complexity and may lead to incomplete or improperly filed claims if employees are not trained.

20. C. Having the right tools and a clear framework helps employees stay productive and aligned with company goals while working remotely. (A) Providing a fixed amount of PTO does not directly impact the effectiveness of telecommuting. (B) Allowing all employees to set their own schedule without structure could lead to miscommunication and reduced productivity.

(D) Installing productivity monitoring software may be part of a larger technology strategy, and care must be taken to ensure trust and transparent practices.

Chapter 10: aPHRi Human Resource Development and Retention

1. A. Ensuring the certification aligns with industry standards and legal requirements makes sure that the certification is recognized, credible, and compliant with regulations that may govern the field or industry, making the program valuable to employees and the organization. (B) Offering the certification free of charge is a positive incentive, but it is not a legal requirement. (C) While inclusivity is important, certain certifications may only apply to specific job roles, making availability to all employees less relevant. (D) Setting deadlines helps with program management but is secondary to legal compliance and industry standards.

2. B. Specific, measurable, achievable, relevant, and time-bound (SMART) goals ensures that goals are clear, actionable, and aligned with both individual and organizational objectives, making them more effective in driving performance. (A) Broad goals may encourage creativity but lack the clarity needed for employees to understand expectations. (C) Allowing employees to set goals independently from management can lead to misalignment with company priorities. (D) Setting the same goals for all employees may not account for individual roles or strengths, reducing the effectiveness of performance management.

3. D. One of the main principles of adult learning styles is that adults learn best when they are actively involved and can apply new knowledge to real-life situations, which helps adults connect learning to their experiences, making it more relevant and meaningful. (A) Memorization and repetition are less effective for adult learners who prefer practical application. (B) Being told what processes to follow may not engage adult learners fully. (C) While formal assessments can be helpful, adults generally benefit more from hands-on, experiential learning.

4. B. The VARK model categorizes learning preferences into Visual, Auditory, Reading/Writing, and Kinesthetic. These styles help individuals understand how they best absorb and process information. "Abstract" is not a recognized learning style within this model.

5. B. The RIASEC model assesses an individual's interests and matches them to career environments. It categorizes people into six personality types—Realistic, Investigative, Artistic, Social, Enterprising, and Conventional—to help align their interests with suitable career paths. (A) The RIASEC model does not focus on technical skills. (C) It does not measure job performance based on communication styles. (D) While personality is a factor, the model assesses broader interests, not just personality traits, to predict suitable career environments rather than career success.

6. B. Virtual training provides flexibility, reduces travel and material costs, and allows employees to engage in training at times that best suit their schedules, making it both a cost-effective and accessible option for companies.

7. C. The most important consideration when choosing between classroom and virtual training formats is the complexity of the material and which format will deliver it most effectively as some content may require hands-on learning, while other material might be better suited for virtual platforms, depending on the depth of engagement required. (A) The cost of renting classroom space is important but secondary to how effectively the training is delivered. (B) While employee preferences matter, the format that best supports learning outcomes should take priority. (D) The length of the training is a factor, but not the most important one when it comes to choosing an effective format.

8. C. Cross-functional assignments contribute to career development by helping employees build a well-rounded knowledge base, improve collaboration skills, and prepare for leadership roles by giving them a broader view of how the company operates. (A) Extended time off for personal development, like sabbaticals, is unrelated to cross-functional assignments. (B) Working in a different country refers to expatriate assignments, not cross-functional roles. (D) Cross-functional assignments typically increase, rather than limit, responsibilities by involving employees in various aspects of the business.

9. B. Working in a different country provides employees with exposure to diverse business environments, helping them adapt to new challenges, improve problem-solving abilities, and gain global leadership skills. (A) Limiting administrative tasks alone does not fast-track career progression. (C) While improving cultural competence is important, the key benefit is the broader leadership development gained through cross-cultural experiences. (D) Increasing the difficulty of tasks may contribute to growth, but it is the exposure to global environments and leadership challenges that truly accelerates career progression.

10. A. Conducting a pre- and post-test to measure knowledge gained allows the company to compare employees' knowledge before and after the training, providing concrete evidence of what has been learned. (B) Sending out an anonymous survey may give insight into how employees felt about the training but doesn't directly measure learning. (C) Asking for feedback can help gauge opinions but doesn't assess knowledge gained. (D) Offering incentives encourages completion but does not evaluate the effectiveness of the training in terms of learning.

11. D. Succession planning ensures that a company has a pipeline of talented employees ready to step into key positions when they become available, helping to maintain stability and continuity in leadership. (A) Succession planning is typically focused on long-term leadership development, not just short-term replacements. (B) While individual success plans may be part of development, the focus of succession planning is broader, addressing leadership transitions. (C) Evaluating current job performance is part of ongoing management but not the primary goal of succession planning.

12. C. A dual career ladder enables employees who may not want to pursue management roles to still advance and gain recognition in their area of expertise. (A) Switching between departments is unrelated to the dual career ladder. (B) The dual career ladder is not about

working multiple jobs but about providing two paths for career progression. (D) Pursuing two separate careers is different from advancing within the company in either a managerial or technical role.

13. A. Ensuring that employees in technical or specialist tracks are compensated fairly compared to those in management can be challenging, as companies often associate higher pay with managerial roles. (B) Finding enough candidates for the technical track may be a concern, but it's not a central challenge of the dual career ladder structure. (C) Employee retention is important, but it's not specifically tied to the dual career ladder system. (D) Frequent job rotations are not a requirement of dual career ladders and don't directly relate to its challenges.

14. D. A dual career ladder system allows employees to progress by building specialized skills and leading projects, providing advancement without moving into management. (A) Administrative roles focus on support tasks, not the specialized growth emphasized in a dual career ladder. (B) Consulting outside the company doesn't fit a dual career ladder's internal advancement path. (C) Rotating through management contradicts the dual career ladder's focus on nonmanagerial, technical expertise.

15. A. Rating scales help quantify performance in a standardized way, making it easier to evaluate and compare employees based on specific criteria. (B) Creating a list of employees ranked from best to worst is more aligned with ranking methods, not rating scales. (C) Setting deadlines for future goals is part of performance management but not the primary purpose of rating scales. (D) While rating scales can highlight areas for improvement, their primary focus is on providing objective feedback through ratings.

16. A. By ranking employees, companies can easily identify their strongest and weakest performers, which can be useful for decision-making in promotions, compensation, and development. (B) The ranking method does not provide detailed feedback on how to improve performance. (C) The ranking method does not necessarily reduce the amount of documentation required. (D) Ranking does not typically offer flexibility in timelines for performance assessment.

17. C. The main difference between 360-degree feedback and the behaviorally anchored rating scales (BARS) method is that 360-degree feedback collects performance evaluations from a range of sources—such as peers, supervisors, subordinates, and sometimes customers—offering a comprehensive view of the employee's performance. In contrast, BARS focuses on rating performance based on specific, predefined behaviors that are directly tied to job expectations.

18. C. Developing an after-action plan that tracks participant progress and application of skills allows the company to monitor how employees are applying what they learned over time, providing a clear measure of the program's lasting impact on their performance. (A) Offering a survey immediately after training does not track long-term application. (B) Monthly supervisor feedback is helpful, but an after-action plan offers a more structured and comprehensive evaluation. (D) Informal discussions lack the consistency and depth of an after-action plan.

19. A. Special projects often involve managing resources, solving complex problems, and collaborating with others, which helps employees develop critical leadership and problem-solving abilities. (B) Special projects typically involve significant decision-making. (C) Communication and teamwork are essential in project assignments, making option

(C) incorrect. (D) Special project assignments can have a lasting impact on an employee's career by showcasing their ability to lead and manage complex tasks, so they are not just short-term roles with no long-term effect.

20. B. Ensuring that the provider meets industry standards and legal requirements is important to offering legitimate and effective employee development sessions. (A) Schedule availability is important for logistics but is not a legal requirement. (C) Past client reviews can be helpful in assessing the quality of the provider, but they do not address compliance with regulations. (D) A money-back guarantee may be a bonus but does not ensure that the training provider is legally qualified.

Chapter 11: aPHRi Employee Relations, Health, and Safety

1. B. Employers must ensure that workplace hazards are minimized and that proper safety measures are in place to protect employees' health and well-being. This is a core requirement in many countries' labor regulations. (A) Providing workers' compensation is important but not the primary focus of global labor laws, nor is it universally required. (C) Working with unions and councils is relevant in certain cases but also not a universal responsibility for all employers. (D) Maintaining job security for employees is typically based on contractual agreements and not a global labor law requirement.

2. C. Sentiment analysis helps companies better understand employee feelings by examining open-ended responses, allowing HR to spot trends and identify concerns more effectively. (A) Replacing quantitative data with storytelling doesn't provide measurable insights from employee surveys. (B) Sending automated responses doesn't address employee emotions or attitudes. (D) Collecting data from managers and supervisors primarily measures performance, not employee sentiment or attitudes.

3. A. The modern psychological contract refers to the unwritten expectations between employers and employees, emphasizing aspects like personal growth, adaptability, and work-life balance rather than just job security or pay. (B) A legal document outlining specific job duties refers to a formal employment contract, not the psychological contract. (C) An employment contract with duties and compensation outlined is not part of the psychological contract, as it is more formal and structured. (D) A shared agreement of employee–employer rights and responsibilities focuses more on legal aspects, while the psychological contract deals with expectations beyond the written agreements.

4. A. Maslow's hierarchy of needs explains that employees are motivated to fulfill their basic needs (like safety and security) first. Only when these are met can they focus on higher-level needs, such as esteem and self-actualization, which include recognition and personal growth. (B) While monetary and nonmonetary rewards can be effective motivators, Maslow's theory focuses on the order of needs rather than types of rewards. (C) Maslow's hierarchy prioritizes needs, starting with basic ones, and does not suggest focusing on all needs equally.

(D) Maslow suggests that lower needs must be met before higher needs can be addressed, not the other way around.

5. D. Employees are responsible for fulfilling their job duties to the best of their ability while adhering to the company's policies and guidelines. (A) Giving two weeks' notice when resigning is a common courtesy but not a legal responsibility in many places. (B) Disclosing personal data is typically subject to privacy laws and is not always mandatory. (C) Employees have the right to discuss their pay with others under labor laws in many countries, so withholding pay information is not a responsibility.

6. A, B, C. Employee relations involve handling negotiations with unions, ensuring a healthy work environment through positive relationships, and establishing health and safety standards to protect employees. (D) Conducting employee performance reviews is typically part of performance management, not a direct responsibility of employee relations.

7. A. Poor employee relations, such as unresolved conflicts, dissatisfaction, or lack of communication, can push employees toward unionization as a means of improving their work environment and negotiating for better conditions. (B) Employers do not typically encourage unionization; they aim to resolve issues internally. (C) Union formation is not automatically triggered by grievances, though unresolved issues may lead to it. (D) Employee relations are closely related to unionization, as poor management of employee relations can increase the likelihood of union efforts.

8. C. Counterproductive work behaviors refer to actions that harm the organization, such as sabotage, theft, or intentional rule violations that undermine the company. (A) Rudeness or profanity may be negative behaviors but are not necessarily counterproductive unless the behavior reaches a point of harassment or violence. (B) Low productivity or quality could be related to poor performance but is not as extreme as counterproductive behaviors like theft. (D) Frequent unexcused absences are problematic but are typically classified under absenteeism, not counterproductive work behaviors.

9. B. Employee privacy is a critical aspect of employee relations because it ensures that personal data are protected and managed in compliance with legal standards. (A) Monitoring employee performance is not directly related to privacy protection. (C) Privacy does support confidentiality, but the primary focus is on protecting personal information, not just anonymity. (D) Although compliance with international privacy laws is part of the correct answer, the broader importance of employee privacy is ensuring personal information is managed properly and ethically.

10. A, B, C. Ensuring all employees are trained on emergency evacuation procedures, providing employees with emergency procedures, and ensuring that emergency exits are clear and accessible are essential to ensure that employees know what to do during an emergency, can access safe exits, and are equipped to handle medical situations if needed. (D) A written plan should be reviewed and updated regularly, not kept consistent over time, to address new risks and changes in the workplace.

11. C. Even if an accident or incident doesn't cause immediate harm, documenting it helps identify potential risks and take steps to prevent future accidents that could result in injuries

or damage. (A) Documentation is typically required by safety regulations or company policies, not unions or works councils. (B) Only incidents involving injury or illness are reportable to workers' compensation carriers. (D) It is necessary to document near-miss incidents to ensure workplace safety and prevent future issues.

12. A. Under GDPR, employers must report data breaches to the appropriate supervisory authority within 72 hours and notify affected employees if the breach poses a risk to their personal data. (B) Waiting for instructions from the board of directors could delay the response and violate the 72-hour requirement. (C) Immediate notification to employees is important, but it is not required by the GDPR and may not give the employer adequate time to create a response plan. (D) Informing employees after resolving the breach would not comply with the GDPR's 72-hour rule.

13. A. Having clear, well-communicated policies is critical for setting expectations and guidelines for behavior in the workplace, helping employees understand what constitutes harassment and the consequences for engaging in it. (B) Anonymous hotlines can be a helpful tool for reporting, but relying on them for reporting lacks comprehensiveness. (C) Training supervisors is important but will be ineffective as an exclusive remedy if the supervisor is part of the problem. (D) Disciplining those accused of inappropriate behavior is premature, as an accusation without an investigation is insufficient to prove harassment or other inappropriate behavior.

14. B. In MNEs, HR must navigate different legal systems and cultural expectations, which can complicate how investigations are conducted and resolved. (A) While local corruption could be an issue, it is not a common challenge specific to HR investigations. (C) A lack of cooperation from corporate leadership is not a typical challenge in conducting investigations. (D) Hiring external investigators may be necessary at times but is not the main challenge HR faces in multinational enterprises.

15. A. Considering diversity in employee recognition and special events ensures that programs are inclusive and appreciate the unique contributions of employees from various backgrounds. (B) Increasing the number of recognized employees is important, but diversity is about inclusivity, not quantity. (C) While creativity in rewards is beneficial, the main reason for considering diversity is to reflect cultural inclusivity. (D) Avoiding personal or cultural preferences could lead to exclusion, which is why diversity should be a key consideration.

16. A. Focus groups allow HR to gather detailed feedback and insights directly from employees, helping the company understand how to improve and increase the use of its health benefits offerings. (B) While cost reduction may be a consideration, the primary goal of focus groups is gathering employee input, not necessarily cutting costs. The findings could actually increase the costs, depending on what employees need and want. (C) Consolidating feedback is helpful but not necessarily the result of a focus group. (D) Focus groups aim to provide valuable insights and may require that more time is taken to understand the employee feedback.

17. B, D. AI-powered surveys provide more personalized and relevant feedback by tailoring questions to individual roles, and they can analyze large sets of data to identify trends and offer actionable insights. (A) While AI can help analyze responses, the actual feedback comes from employees, not the AI itself. (C) AI doesn't model behavior standards; its role is primarily in data analysis and pattern recognition.

18. C. Gross misconduct, including severe violations like physical violence or theft, poses significant risks to the company and other employees, often justifying immediate dismissal rather than following progressive discipline steps. (A) Yelling at a coworker, while inappropriate, may not rise to the level necessary to justify bypassing a progressive discipline policy. (B) No-call, no-show situations might require progressive steps depending on company policy, and understanding the reasons behind the issue. (D) While generally following policy is important, gross misconduct often warrants immediate action to protect the company and its employees.

19. D. Subjectivity is when opinions, feelings, or personal preferences influence decisions rather than facts or objective standards. In progressive discipline, this can cause supervisors to apply rules or consequences differently for similar behaviors, which can undermine fairness and consistency in the process. (A) Subjectivity often creates more harm by introducing bias rather than improving fairness. (B) Subjectivity doesn't necessarily slow down the process but rather reduces the fairness of feedback. (C) Subjectivity typically decreases the clarity of feedback, as different supervisors may interpret behaviors in various ways.

20. B. Under GDPR, employees have the right to access the personal data held by their employers and request corrections if the data are inaccurate or no longer necessary. (A) Under certain circumstances, such as contractual necessity or other legal obligation, the GDPR requires employers to obtain informed consent before collecting personal data. (C) The GDPR applies to any organization that processes the personal data of individuals in the European Union, regardless of where the business is located. (D) The GDPR does not mandate a specific seven-year data retention period; data should only be kept as long as necessary for the purpose it was collected.

Appendix B

Case Studies

Case Study 1: Impact of Changes to US Military Service Policy

By Colonel Seana Jardin and Lieutenant Colonel Angie Chipman, United States Army

The "Don't Ask, Don't Tell" (DADT) policy, enacted in 1993 under President Bill Clinton, barred military personnel from discriminating against closeted LGBTQ (lesbian, gay, bisexual, transgender, queer) members while simultaneously prohibiting these service members from disclosing their sexual orientation. This compromise policy faced significant opposition and led to the discharge of more than 13,000 service members. The policy was officially repealed on September 20, 2011, under President Barack Obama's administration, allowing LGBTQ individuals to serve openly in the military (Raghavan, 2021). The lifting of this ban was only the beginning of addressing the diverse needs of this group, such as ensuring equal access to military benefits for same-sex partners, preventing discrimination based on sexual orientation or gender identity, and addressing the unique mental health challenges faced by LGBTQ service members.[1]

The Case

Decentralized lifting of these restrictions did not address ongoing harassment that would continue to occur at the tactical level. Additionally, it did not address individual state and country laws and policies that denied support to LGBTQ Service Members, especially access to benefits like housing, financial benefits, etc.

Once the Defense Department rescinded the DADT policy, there were no established measures of performance or effectiveness at the tactical or operational level to determine the impacts on units or service members. Lifting the ban eliminated required administrative actions to remove admitted or exposed LGBTQ service members. However, there was no consideration of the benefits that the Defense Department should extend to them like their heterosexual counterparts who were, at the time, enrolled in state-sanctioned domestic partnerships before the legalization of same-sex marriage (Chappell, 2015).

The Defense Department considered several strategies. First, senior leaders require engagement with their Equal Opportunity (EO) advisors to provide recommendations and educational services to them and their junior leaders. EO advisors were untrained on the specific impacts lifting the ban would cause or the follow-on benefits that would need to be implemented for LGBTQ service members to ensure they were receiving the same treatment as their heterosexual counterparts. This gap was a failure at the strategic level to fully understand the extent of changes required as they allowed openly LGBTQ service members to remain in service. As subject matter experts on perceptions of discrimination and its impacts on the overall force, these valuable advisors can help leaders shape their internal policies and monitor their organizations. They are poised to provide data at the tactical, operational, and strategic levels to help leaders at every echelon understand the effectiveness of implemented changes and potential issues resulting from an ill-formed plan

---

[1] Pruitt, S. (2018). *Was "don't ask, don't tell" a step forward for LGBT in the military?* [online] HISTORY. Available at: https://www.history.com/news/dont-ask-dont-tell-repeal-compromise

that did not fully grasp the extent to which support would need to change to ensure complete and practical integration.

Second, from an HR perspective, it is necessary to provide leadership data analytics enabling them to see themselves and how their behaviors toward LGBTQ service members were different from their behaviors toward heterosexual service members. HR professionals must provide information on service members' issues (marriage benefits, housing benefits, pay issues for same-sex couples, promotions, professional military education, selection for nominative assignments, etc.). HR professionals and leaders must discuss the impacts of internalized bias on talent management at varying echelons. Whether you're a chief executive officer (CEO), chief human resources officer (CHRO), or someone who works within the HR structure, every organization working on their diversity, equity, and inclusion (DEI) efforts should consider that equitable treatment of personnel translates to improved performance, retention, and overall job satisfaction. It costs more to find and train new personnel rather than create an environment where the ones you have feel valued and welcomed. Additionally, collaboration and innovative problem-solving increase with diversity of thought and experiences as long as you have a diverse team that is fully empowered.

The integration of LGBTQ service members after the end of the ban was adequate if the only desired end state was to stop unnecessary service member discharges. The results varied by location because the Defense Department did not clearly articulate a desired end-state. Federal recognition of same-sex marriage was necessary to get the services to grant full benefits to LGBTQ service members. Little was done to hold individual persons accountable for any potential discriminatory behaviors while there was an undefined statute across the federal government. Human Resources Command (HRC) likely took individual circumstances into consideration when determining follow-on assignments, but often, the needs of the service will always trump the desires of the service members if the need is a high enough priority.

Review Questions

1. From an HR perspective, what are some of the negative or positive impacts of lifting the ban without examining how service members were treated differently based on sexual orientation (both good and bad)?

2. What are some of the HR data analytics you could provide to help the leadership team see themselves more effectively?

3. What are some of the strategies you would have incorporated to help the full integration of openly serving LGBTQ service members more smoothly?

Answer Explanations

1. A few areas were directly impacted by the DoD's failure to recognize the various impacts:

    ■ Retention of personnel (Positive: they didn't discharge them anymore; negative: they failed to treat persons equally.)

    ■ Use of personnel to enhance recruiting efforts (Negative)

    ■ Overall feelings of acceptance (Mixed)

- Perception of individual value brought to the organization (Mixed)
- Promotion rates of openly serving LGBTQ service members (undetermined)
- Selection for leadership roles/nominative positions (Undetermined)

2. Data analytics related to this issue are the following:

   - Promotion rates
   - Retention rates
   - Recruitment rates
   - Defense Organizational Climate Survey (DEOCS) Assessment
   - Re-enlistment for same unit vs. different unit/location

3. Strategies to incorporate would have included the development of manner of effectiveness measurements vs. manner of performance. Just because you stopped discharging personnel does not mean they've been effectively integrated or that you've now created an environment where they feel treated with equality. Have you developed an educational strategy to address misinformation and internalized biases? Is there a support team on hand to provide additional guidance, oversight, and emphasis on the importance of the initiative (EO, Inspector General, Chaplain, well-respected members of the unit who are supportive, etc.) ?

Case Study 2: Integration of Women into Combat Arms

The US Army opened Combat Arms (branches previously closed to women, which were Infantry, Armor, Special Forces, certain echelon of Field Artillery, etc.) in 2016 after a phased approach started in 2013. Integration of women done at the aggregate level does not constitute successful integration at the tactical level.

The Case

Although the United States Army Forces Command (FORSCOM) was monitoring the integration of women into combat arms units and branches, it was only monitoring the integration of women at a basic level. This means they were ensuring women were assigned to the unit, but they were monitoring it from the strategic level, and not providing corrective guidance, direction, or oversight involving the tactical level where the integration was occurring. The term integration for the strategic level did not mean that they ensured women were integrated into the jobs for which they had enlisted, trained, and would ultimately be professionally managed. In 2020, in the wake of the Vanessa Gullen murder at Fort Hood, Texas, members of Congress and numerous senior leaders descended upon Killeen, Texas, to determine the depth and scope of sexual harassment, sexual assault, and sexual discrimination alleged to exist in the units. General Paul M. Funk, Jr. (then TRADOC Commander) met with multiple women from Brigade Combat Teams within the 1st Cavalry Division who represented newly opened branches of Infantry and Armor to speak with them about their experiences as newly integrated Tankers and Bradley Crew members. While others reported successful integration and excellent collaboration with their leadership from the tactical level up, the 2nd Brigade Combat Team reported that all women who had been transferred to support integration efforts in its organization had been relegated to administrative, medical, or support roles for months. These women were not currently operating in their designated professional specialties on tanks or Bradley Fighting Vehicles. Upon further review and engagement with the Brigade Commander, he acknowledged that they were not integrating women into the tanks and Bradley Fighting Vehicles for months to "assess" their abilities and determine their best-fit for crew assignments. When asked if he did the same for his newly assigned males, the answer was no.

Senior leaders took several steps to respond to the issues. First, senior leaders require engagement with their Equal Opportunity Advisors to provide recommendations and educational services to them and their junior leaders. As subject matter experts on issues pertaining to perceptions of discrimination and the impacts it has on the overall force, these valuable advisors can help leaders shape their internal policies and monitor their organizations. Second, from an HR perspective, obtain data analytics to provide leadership information that enables them to see themselves and how their behaviors toward one gender versus another were different. Provide information on impacts for HR issues affecting the service members in question (promotions, professional military education, selection for nominative assignments, etc.) when their talent management is done differently than that of their counterparts. Finally, while examining the levels at which various requirements are best tracked, helps both the lower and higher echelons to develop both measures of performance and measures of effectiveness that can be implemented and owned fully by the leadership within that organization. In order to fully own a process, one must be directly involved in that process.

Because the strategic level oversight provided by FORSCOM did not delve into unit level management of integration for women into the combat arms, results varied by unit. Overall efficacy was higher in units that took on a highly proactive stance on the integration of women into teams at the lowest echelons. Results were less promising in units that slowed the integration of women resulting in a lower retention rate.

Review Questions

1. From an HR perspective, what are some of the negative or positive impacts of the 2nd Brigade Commander when he decided to "assess" newly integrated women for their first few months to determine what crew they should belong to?

2. What are some of the HR data analytics you could provide to help the leadership team see themselves more effectively?

3. What are some of the strategies you would have incorporated to help the full integration of women into newly opened positions more smoothly?

Answer Explanations

1. A few areas were directly impacted by the 2nd Brigade Commander:

   ■ Retention of personnel (Negative)

   ■ Use of personnel to enhance recruiting efforts (Negative)

   ■ Overall feelings of acceptance (Negative)

   ■ Perception of individual value brought to the organization (Negative)

   ■ Promotion rates of women within those units/MOSs (Varied)

   ■ Selection for leadership roles/nominative positions (Varied)

   ■ Perception of thoughtful placement on crews (Positive)

2. Data analytics related to this issue are the following:

   ■ Promotion rates

   ■ Retention rates

   ■ Recruitment rates

   ■ Placement rates

   ■ Crew qualification rates

   ■ DEOCS assessment

   ■ Re-enlistment for same unit vs. different unit/location

3. Strategies to incorporate would have included the development of manner of effectiveness measurements vs. manner of performance. Just because you have women in the unit does not mean they've been effectively integrated. How many are there? What is the number of incidents of SHARP-related offenses when compared to other like-type units? Have you developed an educational strategy to address misinformation and internalized biases? Is there a support team on hand to provide additional guidance, oversight, and emphasis on the importance of the initiative (EO, IG, Chaplain, well-respected members of the unit who are supportive, etc.)?

Appendix C

Federal Employment Legislation and Case Law

The body of federal employment legislation and case law is extensive. This appendix provides a good introduction to this area of knowledge.

Affirmative Action Plans (AAPs)

All federal contractors and subcontractors who have at least 50 employees and designated monetary levels of government contracts or subcontracts must prepare and update annually two or three affirmative action plans (AAPs). Each AAP has specific requirements dictated by regulations. The three potential AAPs are as follows:

Vietnam Era Veterans' Readjustment Assistance Action (VEVRAA) of 1974, as amended, 38 U.S.C. 4212 AAP: Covers protected veterans and is required for each establishment, if a government contractor (or subcontractor) has 50 or more employees and has a government contract (or subcontract) of at least $150,000. Federally assisted construction contractors must also prepare the same type of AAP. The categories of protected veterans are disabled veteran, recently separated veteran (three-year period), active duty wartime or campaign badge veteran, or an armed forces service medal veteran.

Section 503 of the Rehabilitation Act of 1973, as amended, 29 U.S.C. 793 AAP: Covers individuals with disabilities and is required for each establishment, if a government contractor (or subcontractor) has 50 or more employees and a government contract (or subcontract) of at least $50,000. Federally assisted construction contractors must also prepare the same type of AAP. The government allows the VEVRAA AAP and the Section 503 AAP to be combined into one if both are required.

The Office of Federal Contract Compliance Programs (OFCCP) in the U.S. Department of Labor constructs and enforces the affirmative action regulations. The OFCCP periodically will audit federal contractors and subcontractors on the contents of their AAPs and other regulatory requirements. Contractors and subcontractors are prohibited from discharging or otherwise discriminating against applicants or employees who inquire about, discuss, or disclose their compensation or that of others, subject to certain limitations.

Note that employers may not override an applicant's gender self-identification based on an employer's visual observation. Should an employee or applicant self-identify as nonbinary, the contractor must still include the individual in their AAP submission but may exclude that individual's data from the gender-based analyses that is part of the reporting requirements.

VEVRAA AAP

The required components of the VEVRAA AAP include the following. Note that when the term *contractor* is used, it also applies to subcontractors.

Policy Statement   The contractor's equal opportunity policy statement should be included in the AAP and be posted on the organization's bulletin board.

Review of Personnel Processes   The contractor shall periodically review such processes and make any necessary modifications to ensure that its obligations are carried out. A description of the review and any modifications should be documented.

Physical and Mental Qualifications   Provides for a schedule for the periodic review of all physical and mental job qualification standards to ensure that to the extent that qualification standards tend to screen out qualified disabled veterans, they are job-related for the position in question, and are consistent with business necessity.

Reasonable Accommodation to Physical and Mental Limitations   Includes a statement that the contractor will make reasonable accommodation to the known physical or mental limitations of an otherwise qualified disabled veteran unless it can demonstrate that the accommodation would impose an undue hardship on the operation of the business.

Harassment   Includes a statement about what the contractor has done to develop and implement procedures to ensure that its employees are not harassed because of their status as protected veterans.

External Dissemination of Policy, Outreach, and Positive Recruitment   Includes listing the organization's outreach efforts, including sending written notification of the organization's EEO/AA policy to all subcontractors, vendors, and suppliers. Also requires the contractor to review, on an annual basis, the outreach and recruitment efforts it has taken over the previous 12 months to evaluate their effectiveness in identifying and recruiting qualified protected veterans. If not effective, the contractor shall identify and implement alternative efforts. These assessments are to be retained for a three–year period.

Internal Dissemination of Policy   The contractor outlines its efforts to implement and disseminate its EEO/AA policy internally.

Audit and Reporting System   The contractor describes and documents the audit and reporting system that it designed and implemented to measure the effectiveness of its affirmative action program, among other things.

Responsibility for Implementation   The contractor documents which official of the organization has been assigned responsibility for implementation of the contractor's affirmative action program. Their identity should appear on all internal and external communications regarding the contractor's affirmative action program.

Training   Describes the efforts made to train all personnel involved in the recruitment, screening, selection, promotion, disciplinary actions, and related processes on the contractor's commitments in the affirmative action program.

Other VEVRAA requirements not included in the AAP, but required by the regulations, include:

Data Collection Analysis   Annual documentation, maintained for a three-year period, of the number of applicants who self-identified as protected veterans, the total number of job openings and the total number of jobs filled, the total number of applicants for all jobs, the number of applicants hired, and the number of protected veterans hired.

Hiring Benchmark   The contractor shall either establish and document a hiring benchmark for protected veterans, based on specific criteria, or use the OFCCP-dictated hiring benchmark, which is 5.2 percent as of the time of publication (2024). The annual veteran hiring benchmark is updated every year. Stay up-to-date by scheduling an annual review at www.dol.gov/agencies/ofccp/vevraa/hiring-benchmark in March of each year to stay in compliance.

Section 503, Individuals with Disabilities AAP

Under Section 503 of the Rehabilitation Act of 1973, federal contractors are required to develop and maintain an Affirmative Action Program for individuals with disabilities. The required components of a Section 503 affirmative action program include:

- **Equal Opportunity Policy Statement:** A policy statement affirming the contractor's commitment to equal employment opportunity for individuals with disabilities and outlining the procedures for handling complaints of discrimination.

- **Review of Personnel Processes:** The contractor must periodically review its personnel processes to ensure that they provide for careful, thorough, and systematic consideration of the job qualifications of applicants and employees with disabilities.

- **Physical and Mental Qualifications:** The contractor must review all physical and mental job qualification standards to ensure that they are job-related and consistent with business necessity and safe performance of the job.

- **Reasonable Accommodation:** The contractor must ensure that reasonable accommodations are provided to qualified individuals with disabilities, unless providing such accommodation would cause undue hardship.

- **Harassment Prevention Statement:** The AAP must include a commitment to ensuring that employees are not harassed based on disability.

- **External Dissemination of Policy, Outreach, and Positive Recruitment:** The contractor must undertake appropriate outreach and positive recruitment activities to recruit individuals with disabilities.

- **Internal Dissemination of Policy:** The contractor must internally disseminate its equal opportunity policy to employees and applicants.

- **Audit and Reporting System:** The contractor must design and implement an audit and reporting system that measures the effectiveness of the AAP and indicates any need for remedial action.

- **Responsibility for Implementation:** The AAP must specify the responsibilities of individuals assigned to implement the program.

- **Training:** The contractor must provide training to all personnel involved in recruitment, hiring, and management to ensure they understand the AAP and their responsibilities.

- **Data Collection Analysis:** The contractor must collect and analyze data on applicants and hires to assess the effectiveness of its outreach and recruitment efforts.

- **Utilization Goals:** Contractors must establish a utilization goal of 7 percent for the employment of qualified individuals with disabilities within each job group of their workforce.

- **Invitation to Self-Identify:** The contractor must invite applicants and employees to voluntarily self-identify as individuals with disabilities at the pre-offer and post-offer stages of employment, and periodically thereafter.

Age Discrimination in Employment Act of 1967 (ADEA)

The purpose of the Age Discrimination in Employment Act (ADEA) is to "promote employment of older persons based on their ability rather than age; to prohibit arbitrary age discrimination in employment; to help employers and workers find ways of meeting problems arising from the impact of age on employment."

The ADEA prohibits discrimination against persons 40 years of age or older in employment activities, including hiring, job assignments, training, promotion, compensation, benefits, terminating, or any other privileges, terms, or conditions of employment. The ADEA applies to private businesses, unions, employment agencies, and state and local governments with more than 20 employees. As with Title VII, the ADEA provides for the following exceptions:

- Bona fide occupational qualifications (BFOQs) that are reasonably necessary to business operations

- The hiring of firefighters or police officers by state or local governments

- Retirement of employees age 65 or older who have been in executive positions for at least two years and are eligible for retirement benefits of at least $44,000 per year

- Retirement of tenured employees of institutions of higher education at age 70

- Discharge or discipline for just cause

Individuals who think they have been subjected to an unlawful employment practice must file charges with the Equal Employment Opportunity Commission (EEOC), which has federal enforcement responsibility for the ADEA, or with the state equal employment agency (if one exists for the location in which the incident occurred). Timely filing of charges is essential for complainants, since the EEOC will not investigate charges that are not made according to the guidelines.

Older Worker Benefit Protection Act Amendment to the ADEA

The Older Worker Benefit Protection Act (OWBPA) amended the ADEA in 1990 to include a prohibition on discrimination against older workers in all employee benefit plans unless any age-based reductions are justified by significant cost considerations. This amendment allows seniority systems as long as they do not require involuntary terminations of employees based on their age and extends ADEA protections to all employee benefits, as well as guidelines for legal severance agreements.

The OWBPA defines the conditions under which employees may waive their rights to make claims under the act. To be acceptable, waivers must include the following components:

- Waiver agreements must be written in a way that can be understood by the average employee.

- Waivers must refer specifically to the rights or claims available under the ADEA.

- Employees may not waive rights or claims for actions that occur subsequent to signing the waiver.

- Employees must receive consideration in exchange for the waiver in addition to anything to which they are already entitled.

- The waiver must advise employees of their right to consult an attorney prior to signing the document.

- In individual cases, employees must be given 21 days to consider the agreement before they are required to sign; when a group of employees is involved, employees age 40 and older must be given 45 days to consider their decision.

- Once the waiver is signed, employees may revoke the agreement within seven days.

- In cases of group terminations (such as a reduction in force or early retirement program), employees must be advised of the eligibility requirements for any exit incentive programs, any time limits for the programs, and a list of the job titles and ages of employees who have been selected or who are eligible for the program.

The federal agency responsible for enforcement of the OWBPA is the EEOC.

Americans with Disabilities Act of 1990 (ADA) and Amendments

The Americans with Disabilities Act (ADA) of 1990 was based in large part on the Rehabilitation Act of 1973 (discussed later in this appendix), and it extended protected class status to qualified persons with disabilities. Employment discrimination is covered by Title I of the act and identifies covered entities as employment agencies, labor unions, joint labor-management committees, and employers with 15 or more employees (including those who work on a part-time or temporary basis) for each working day in each of 20 weeks in the current or previous calendar year. Excluded from coverage are the federal government and 501(c) private membership clubs. The ADA prohibits discrimination in job application procedures; the hiring, advancement, or discharge of employees; employee compensation; job training; and other terms, conditions, and privileges of employment.

The ADA requires covered entities to make *reasonable accommodation* to develop employment opportunities for qualified persons with disabilities in two areas:

- Facilities should be accessible to persons with disabilities.

- Position requirements may be adjusted to accommodate qualified persons with disabilities.

The ADA allows that accommodations constituting an *undue hardship* to the business are not required and defines undue hardship as an accommodation that places an excessive burden on the employer. The act identifies the factors to be considered in determining whether an accommodation is an undue hardship by looking at the cost, the financial resources of the organization, the size of the organization, and other similar factors.

In 2008, Congress enacted the ADA Amendments Act of 2008, which took effect on January 1, 2009. According to language in the amendment, Congress took the action to clarify the intention of the original legislation, which was to make the definition of "disability" consistent with the way the courts had defined the term under the Rehabilitation Act of 1973. In fact, court interpretations under the ADA had "narrowed the broad scope of protection" originally intended. The amendment more clearly defined the intent of Congress in the following ways:

Broadly Defines "Disability" A disability is a physical or mental impairment that causes *substantial limitation* to one or more *major life activities* for an individual, a record of impairment for an individual, or an individual who is regarded as being impaired.

Defines "Major Life Activity" The amendment defines major life activities in two areas: general activities and major bodily functions. Table C.1 lists activities Congress cites in the law as examples but is not meant to be a complete list.

Ignores Mitigating Measures Congress directs that, except for "ordinary glasses or contact lenses," mitigating measures such as medication, prosthetics, hearing aids, mobility devices, and others may not be used to limit the definition of disability for an individual.

Clarifies the Definition of "Regarded As" This amendment requires that individuals who are able to demonstrate that they have been the subject of prohibited activities under the ADA, whether or not they actually have some type of impairment, are protected by its requirements.

Explicitly Authorizes the EEOC to Regulate Compliance The amendment mandates the EEOC to develop and implement regulations and guidance for employers to follow, specifying the inclusion of a definition for "substantially limits" that is consistent with the intent of Congress in the legislation.

Prohibits "Reverse Discrimination" Claims The amendment clearly states that individuals without disability may not use the ADA to file claims of discrimination when disabled individuals receive favorable employment actions.

TABLE C.1 Major Life Activities

General activities	Major bodily functions
Caring for oneself, performing manual tasks, seeing, hearing, eating, sleeping, breathing, learning, reading, concentrating, thinking, communicating, working	Functions of the immune system; normal cell growth; and functions of the digestive, bowel, bladder, neurological, brain, respiratory, circulatory, endocrine, and reproductive systems

A key element of ADA compliance is the requirement to engage in an interactive process with disabled individuals requesting a reasonable accommodation that will enable them to perform essential job functions.

Civil Rights Act of 1964 (Title VII)

Title VII of the Civil Rights Act of 1964 introduced the concepts of *protected classes* and *unlawful employment practices* to American businesses. Unlawful employment practices are those that have an adverse impact on members of a protected class, which is a group of people who share common characteristics and are protected from discriminatory practices. Title VII established the basis for two types of unlawful practices: disparate treatment and disparate impact. *Disparate treatment* happens when employers treat some candidates or employees differently, such as requiring women to take a driving test when they apply for a job but not requiring men to take the test when they apply for the same job. Practices that have a *disparate impact* on members of protected classes seem fair on their face but result in adverse impact on members of protected classes, such as requiring all candidates for firefighter positions to be a certain height. Although the requirement applies to all candidates equally, some Asian and female candidates who might otherwise qualify for the position might be eliminated because they are generally shorter than male candidates of other races.

The act identified five protected classes: race, color, religion, national origin, and sex. It also defined the following unlawful employment practices:

- Discriminatory recruiting, selection, or hiring actions
- Discriminatory compensation or benefit practices
- Discriminatory access to training or apprenticeship programs
- Discriminatory practices in any other terms or conditions of employment

Legitimate seniority, merit, and piece-rate payment systems are allowable under Title VII as long as they do not intentionally discriminate against protected classes.

Title VII allowed for limited exceptions to its requirements, some of which are listed here:

- Bona fide occupational qualifications (BFOQs) occur when religion, sex, or national origin is "reasonably necessary to the normal operation" of the business.
- Educational institutions were not originally subject to Title VII.
- Religious organizations may give preference to members of that religion.
- A potential employee who is unable to obtain, or loses, a national security clearance required for the position is not protected.
- Indian reservations may give preference to Indian applicants and employees living on or near the reservation.

Title VII created the Equal Employment Opportunity Commission (EEOC) with a mandate to promote equal employment opportunity, educate employers, provide technical assistance, and study and report on its activities to Congress and the American people. The EEOC is the enforcement agency for Title VII and other discrimination legislation.

Amendments to Title VII

Title VII was amended in 1972, 1978, and 1991 to clarify and expand its coverage.

Equal Employment Opportunity Act of 1972

Created in 1972, the Equal Employment Opportunity Act (EEOA) provides litigation authority to the EEOC in the event that an acceptable conciliation agreement cannot be reached. In those cases, the EEOC is empowered to sue nongovernmental entities, including employers, unions, and employment agencies.

The EEOA extended coverage of Title VII to entities that had been excluded in 1964:

- Educational institutions
- State and local governments
- The federal government

In addition, the EEOA reduced the number of employees needed to subject an employer to coverage by Title VII from 25 to 15 and required employers to keep records of the discovery of any unlawful employment practices and provide those records to the EEOC upon request.

The EEOA also provided administrative guidance for the processing of complaints by providing that employers be notified within 10 days of receipt of a charge by the EEOC and that findings be issued within 120 days of the charge being filed. The EEOC was empowered to sue employers, unions, and employment agencies in the event that an acceptable conciliation agreement could not be reached within 30 days of notice to the employer. The EEOA also provided protection from retaliatory employment actions against whistleblowers.

Pregnancy Discrimination Act of 1978

Congress amended Title VII with the Pregnancy Discrimination Act of 1978 to clarify that discrimination against women on the basis of pregnancy, childbirth, or any related medical condition is an unlawful employment practice. The act specified that pregnant employees should receive the same treatment and benefits as employees with any other short-term disability.

Pregnant Worker Fairness Act (PWFA)

The Pregnant Workers Fairness Act (PWFA) went into effect on June 27, 2023. It requires employers to provide reasonable accommodations to workers affected by pregnancy, childbirth, or related medical conditions, unless doing so would cause undue hardship to the employer. This includes modifications to work duties, schedules, and other job functions as needed to accommodate their health and well-being.

The key difference between the PDA and the PWFA is that the PDA prohibits discrimination based on pregnancy but doesn't require specific accommodations. In contrast, the PWFA mandates reasonable accommodations for pregnant workers, similar to those for disabilities under the ADA.

Civil Rights Act of 1991

The Civil Rights Act (CRA) of 1991 contained amendments that affected Title VII, the Age Discrimination in Employment Act (ADEA), and the Americans with Disabilities Act (ADA) in response to issues raised by the courts in several cases that were brought by employees based on Title VII.

The purpose of the Civil Rights Act (CRA) of 1991, as described in the act itself, is fourfold:

1. To provide appropriate remedies for intentional discrimination and unlawful harassment in the workplace

2. To codify the concepts of "business necessity" and "job relatedness" articulated by the Supreme Court in *Griggs v. Duke Power Co.* and in other Supreme Court decisions

3. To confirm statutory authority and provide statutory guidelines for the adjudication of disparate impact suits under Title VII of the Civil Rights Act of 1964

4. To respond to recent decisions of the Supreme Court by expanding the scope of relevant civil rights statutes in order to provide adequate protection to victims of discrimination

Amendments contained in the CRA affected Title VII, the ADEA, and the ADA. One of the issues addressed is that of disparate impact, first introduced by the *Griggs v. Duke Power Co.* case in 1971. Disparate impact occurs when an employment practice, which appears on its face to be fair, unintentionally discriminates against members of a protected class. The CRA places the burden of proof for discrimination complaints on the complainant when there is a job-related business necessity for employment actions. When an individual alleges multiple discriminatory acts, each practice in itself must be discriminatory unless the employer's decision-making process cannot be separated, in which case the individual may challenge the decision-making process itself. The CRA also provides additional relief for victims of intentional discrimination and harassment, codifies the concept of disparate impact, and addresses Supreme Court rulings over the previous few years that had weakened equal employment opportunity laws.

The CRA made the following changes to Title VII:

- Provided punitive damages when employers engage in discriminatory practices "with malice or with reckless indifference"

- Excluded back pay awards from compensatory damages

- Established a sliding scale for compensatory and punitive damages based on company size

- Provided that any party to a civil suit in which punitive or compensatory damages are sought may demand a jury trial

- Expanded Title VII to include congressional employees and some senior political appointees

- Required that the individual alleging that an unlawful employment practice is in use prove that it results in disparate impact to members of a protected class

- Provided that job relatedness and reasonable business necessity are defenses to disparate impact and that if a business can show that the practice does not result in disparate impact, it need not show the practice to be a business necessity

- Provided that business necessity is not a defense against an intentional discriminatory employment practice

- Established that if discrimination was a motivating factor in an employment practice it was unlawful even if other factors contributed to the practice

- Allowed that if the same employment decision would have been made whether or not an impermissible motivating factor was present, no damages would be awarded

- Expanded coverage to include foreign operations of American businesses unless compliance would constitute violation of the laws of the host country

Common Law Doctrines

Common law doctrines are the result of legal decisions made by judges in cases adjudicated over a period of centuries. A number of doctrines have implications for employment relationships, the most common of which is the concept of *employment at will*. Other common law issues that affect employment relationships are *respondeat superior*, constructive discharge, and defamation.

Employment at Will

In *Payne v. The Western & Atlantic Railroad Company* in 1884, Justice Ingersoll of the Tennessee Supreme Court defined employment at will in this way: ". . .either party may terminate the service, for any cause, good or bad, or without cause, and the other cannot complain in law." This definition allowed employers to change employment conditions, whether it was to hire, transfer, promote, or terminate an employee, at their sole discretion. It also allowed employees to leave a job at any time, with or without notice. In the absence of a legally enforceable employment contract, this definition was unaltered for more than 70 years.

Although there have always been exceptions to at-will employment based on employment contracts, beginning in 1959 the doctrine began to be eroded by both court decisions and statutes. This erosion resulted in several exceptions to the at-will concept, including public policy exceptions, the application of the doctrine of good faith and fair dealing to employment relationships, and the concepts of promissory estoppel and fraudulent misrepresentation.

Contract Exceptions

Employment-at-will intentions may be abrogated by contracts, either express or implied. An *express contract* can be a verbal or written agreement in which the parties state exactly what they agree to do. Employers have been known to express their gratitude for a job well done with promises of continued employment, such as "Keep doing that kind of work and you have a job for life" or "You'll have a job as long as we're in business." Statements such as these can invalidate the at-will doctrine.

An *implied contract* can be created by an employer's conduct and need not be specifically stated. For example, an employer's consistent application of a progressive discipline policy can create an implied contract that an employee will not be terminated without first going through the steps set forth by the policy. A disclaimer can offset the effects of an implied contract; however, there is little agreement in the courts as to what and how the disclaimer must be presented in order to maintain at-will status.

Statutory Exceptions

The at-will doctrine has been further eroded by legislation. At-will employment may not be used as a pretext for terminating employees for discriminatory reasons as set forth in equal opportunity legislation or other legislation designed to protect employee rights.

Public Policy Exceptions

Erosion of the doctrine of at-will employment began in 1959 when the California Court of Appeals heard *Petermann v. International Brotherhood of Teamsters*, in which Mr. Petermann, a business agent for the union, alleged that he was terminated for refusing to commit perjury on behalf of the union at a legislative hearing. The court held that it is "... obnoxious to the interest of state and contrary to public policy and sound morality to allow an employer to discharge any employee, whether the employment be for a designated or unspecified duration, on the ground that the employee declined to commit perjury, an act specifically enjoined by statute."

The public policy exception to employment at will was initially applied conservatively by the courts, but over time, its application has been expanded. In general, the public policy exception has been applied in four areas. The first is exemplified by the *Petermann* case—an employee who refuses to break the law on behalf of the employer can claim a public policy exception. The second application covers employees who report illegal acts of their employers (whistleblowers); the third covers employees who participate in activities supported by public policy, such as cooperating in a government investigation of wrongdoing by the employer. Finally, the public policy exception covers employees who are acting in accordance with legal statute, such as attending jury duty or filing a workers' compensation claim.

While the public policy exception to at-will employment originated in California, it has been adopted by many, although not all, states.

Duty of Good Faith and Fair Dealing

This tenet of common law provides that parties to a contract have an obligation to act in a fair and honest manner with each other to ensure that benefits of the contract may be realized. The application of this doctrine to at-will employment issues varies widely from state to state. The Texas Supreme Court, for example, has determined that there is no duty for good faith and fair dealing in employment contracts. On the other hand, the Alaska Supreme Court has determined that the duty is implied in at-will employment situations.

Promissory Estoppel

Promissory estoppel occurs when an employer entices an employee (or prospective employee) to take an action by promising a reward. The employee takes the action, but the employer does not follow through on the reward. For example, an employer promises a job to a candidate who resigns another position to accept the new one and then finds the offered position has been withdrawn. If a promise is clear, specific, and reasonable, and an employee acts on the promise, the employer may be required to follow through on the promised reward or pay equivalent damages.

Fraudulent Misrepresentation

Similar to promissory estoppel, fraudulent misrepresentation relates to promises or claims made by employers to entice candidates to join the company. An example of this might be a company that decides to close one of its locations in six months but, in the meantime, needs to hire a general manager to run the operation. If, when asked about the future of the company during the recruiting process, the company tells candidates that the plant will be expanded in the future and withholds its intention to close the plant, the company would be fraudulently misrepresenting the facts about the position.

Respondeat Superior

The Latin meaning of *respondeat superior* is "let the master answer." What this means is that an employer can be held liable for actions of its employees that occur within the scope and course of assigned duties or responsibilities in the course of their employment, regardless of whether the act is negligent or reckless. This concept has implications for many employment situations; one is sexual harassment, which will be discussed later in this appendix. Another could be an auto accident where a third party is injured when an employee hits another vehicle while driving an employer's delivery truck. *Respondeat superior* could also come into play if a manager promised additional vacation time to a candidate and the candidate accepted the position based on the promise. Even if the promise was not in writing and was outside the employer's normal vacation policy, and the manager made the promise without prior approval, the employer could be required to provide the benefit based on this doctrine.

Constructive Discharge

Constructive discharge occurs when an employer makes the workplace so hostile and inhospitable that an employee resigns. In many states, this gives the employee a cause of action against the employer. The legal standard that must be met varies widely between the states, with some requiring the employee to show that the employer intended to force the resignation, and others requiring the employee to show only that the conditions were sufficiently intolerable that a reasonable person would feel compelled to resign.

Defamation

Accusations of defamation in employment relationships most often occur during or after termination. Defamation is a communication that damages an individual's reputation in the community, preventing the person from obtaining employment or other benefits. When an employer, out of spite or with a vengeful intent, sets out to deliberately damage a former employee, the result is malicious defamation.

Concerns about defamation have caused many employers to stop giving meaningful references for former employees, in many cases responding to reference requests only with dates of employment and the individual's last title. Employers are generally protected by the concept of "qualified privilege" if the information provided is job-related, truthful, clear, and unequivocal. Obtaining written authorization prior to providing references and limiting responses to the information being requested without volunteering additional information can reduce the risks of being accused of defamation.

Copyright Act of 1976

The use of musical, literary, and other original works without permission of the owner of the copyright is prohibited under most circumstances. The copyright owner is the author of the work with two exceptions. The first is that an employer who hires employees to create original works as part of their normal job duties is the owner of the copyright because the employer paid for the work to be done. The second exception is that the copyright for work created by a freelance author, artist, or musician who has been commissioned to create the work by someone else is owned by the person who commissioned the work. These exceptions are known as *work-for-hire* exceptions.

For trainers who want to use the work of others during training sessions, two circumstances do not require permission. The first is related to works that are in the *public domain*. Copyrights protect original works for the life of the author plus 70 years; after that, the works may be used without permission. Works-for-hire are protected for the shorter of 95 years from the first year of publication or 120 years from the year of creation.

Other works in the public domain include those produced as part of the job duties of federal officials and those for which copyright protection has expired. Some works published without notice of copyright before January 1, 1978, or those published between then and March 1, 1989, are also considered to be in the public domain.

The second circumstance for use of published works without permission is known as the *fair use doctrine*. The act specifies that use of a work for the purposes of criticism, commentary, news reporting, or teaching (including multiple copies for classroom use, scholarship, or research) is not an infringement, depending on four factors:

- **The purpose and character of the use:** Is it to be used for a profit or for a nonprofit educational purpose?
- **The nature of the work itself:** Is it a work of fiction? Or is it based on facts? How much creativity did it require?
- **The amount of work:** How much of the work (one copy or 50?) or what portion (a paragraph or an entire chapter?) will be used?
- **The effect:** What effect will the use of the material have on the potential market value of the copyrighted work?

Permission for the use of copyright-protected material that is outside the fair use exceptions can generally be obtained by contacting the author or publisher of the work.

Davis–Bacon Act of 1931

The Davis–Bacon Act was the first federal legislation to regulate minimum wages. It requires that construction contractors and their subcontractors pay at least the prevailing wage for the local area in which they are operating if they receive federal funds. Employers with federal construction contracts of $2,000 or more must adhere to the Davis–Bacon Act.

Drug-Free Workplace Act of 1988

The Drug-Free Workplace Act of 1988 applies to businesses with federal contracts of $100,000 or more each year. Contractors subject to the act must take the following steps to be in compliance:

Develop and publish a written policy.   Contractors must develop a written policy clearly stating that they provide a drug-free workplace and that illegal substance abuse isn't an acceptable practice in the workplace. The policy must clearly state what substances are covered and the consequences for violating the policy.

Establish an awareness program.   The employer must develop a program to educate employees about the policy, communicate the dangers of drug abuse in the workplace, discuss the employer's policy, inform employees of the availability of counseling or other programs to reduce drug use, and notify employees of the penalties for violating the policy. The program can be delivered through a variety of media—seminars, brochures, videos, web-based training—whatever methods will most effectively communicate the information in the specific environment.

Notify employees about contract conditions.   Employees must be made aware that a condition of their employment on a federal contract project is that they abide by the policy and inform the employer within five days if they're convicted of a criminal drug offense in the workplace.

Notify the contracting agency of violations.   If an employee is convicted of a criminal drug offense in the workplace, the employer must notify the contracting agency within 10 days of being informed of the conviction by the employee.

Establish penalties for illegal drug convictions.   The employer must have an established penalty for any employees convicted of relevant drug offenses. Within 30 days of notice by an employee of a conviction, the employer must take appropriate disciplinary action against the employee or require participation in an appropriate drug-rehabilitation program. Any penalties must be in accordance with requirements of the Rehabilitation Act of 1973.

Maintain a drug-free workplace.   Contractors must make a good-faith effort to maintain a drug-free workplace in accordance with the act, or they're subject to penalties, including suspension of payments under the contract, suspension or termination of the contract, or exclusion from consideration from future contracts for a period of up to five years.

This act supersedes individual state laws.

EEO Survey

The EEO survey promotes equal employment opportunity by requiring employers to collect and report detailed workforce data on the representation of various demographic groups, such as race and gender. This data helps identify potential discrimination or disparities in hiring, promotions, wages and other employment practices. The EEOC and OFFCP worked together to develop the reporting form, known as the EEO-1 survey or report. It must be filed on or before September 30 of each year using employment data from one pay period in July, August, or September of the current survey year. All employers who meet the following criteria must complete the report:

- All federal contractors who are private employers and (a) are not exempt as provided by 41 CFR Section 60-1.5; (b) have 50 or more employees; *and* (i) are prime contractors or first-tier subcontractors, and have a contract, subcontract, or purchase order amounting to $50,000 or more, or (ii) serve as a depository of government funds in any amount, or (iii) are a financial institution that is an issuing and paying agent for U.S. Savings Bonds. Only those establishments located in the District of Columbia and the 50 states are required to submit. No reports should be filed for establishments in Puerto Rico, the Virgin Islands, or other American protectorates.

- All private employers who are subject to Title VII of the Civil Rights Act of 1964, as amended, with 100 or more employees.

Exceptions to the EEO-1 reporting requirements include:

- State and local governments

- Primary and secondary school systems

- Institutions of higher education

- Indian tribes

- Tax-exempt private membership clubs (other than labor organizations)

The preferred method for filing the EEO-1 survey is through the online filing application. Refer to the EEOC website at www.eeoc.gov for information on how to file the EEO-1 survey.

The "workforce snapshot period" is October 1 to December 31 (the fourth quarter of each year). In other words, each employer may choose any pay period during this three-month "workforce snapshot period" to count its full-time and part-time employees for the EEO-1 report. The deadline to file is generally early June, although the exact date may vary from year to year. Verify the deadline and file online at www.eeocdata.org/eeo1.

Report Types

Employers with operations at a single location or establishment complete a single form, whereas those who operate at more than one location or establishment must file employment data on multiple forms.

Headquarters Report   All multiple-establishment employers must file a Headquarters Report, which is a report covering the principal or headquarters office.

Establishment Report   Locations with 50 or more employees file a separate Establishment Report for each location employing 50 or more persons.

Locations with fewer than 50 employees may be reported on an Establishment Report or on an Establishment List. The Establishment List provides the name, address, and total number of employees for each location with fewer than 50 employees along with an employment data grid combining this data by race, sex, and job category.

Employees who work remotely and/or telework must be included in an employer's EEO-1 report(s) by the specific establishment to which the employees report. Under no circumstances should an employee's home address be reported on any EEO-1 Component 1 submission or report. According to the EEOC, "if a remote employee is not assigned to and does not report to any physical location on a permanent basis, the employee should be counted at the establishment to which the employee's manager reports or is assigned. If an employee does not report to an establishment and the employee's manager also does not report to an establishment, the employee (and their manager) should be included on the employer's 'Headquarters Report.'"

Consolidated Report   Data from all the individual location reports and the headquarters report are combined on the Consolidated Report. The total number of employees on this report must be equal to data submitted on all the individual reports.

Parent corporations that own a majority interest in another corporation report data for employees at all locations, including those of the subsidiary establishments.

Race and Ethnicity Categories

Employers are required to report on seven categories of employees:

- Hispanic or Latino
- White
- Black or African American
- Native Hawaiian or Other Pacific Islander
- Asian
- American Indian or Alaska Native
- Two or More Races (not Hispanic or Latino)

Job Categories

The EEO-1 report requires employers to group jobs into job categories based on the average skill level, knowledge, and responsibility of positions within their organizations:

- Executive/senior-level officials and managers
- Midlevel officials and managers
- Professionals
- Technicians
- Sales workers
- Administrative support workers
- Craft workers
- Operatives
- Laborers and helpers
- Service workers

Data Reporting

Private employers and federal contractors with 100 or more employees, the EEO-1 report requires additional reporting components of employment data. These reports include:

Employee Report   Total employees in the workforce snapshot for each job category and pay band

Pay Report   W-2 Box 1 earnings for all employees identified in the workforce snapshot

Hours Worked Report   Hours worked for all employees in the snapshot in their job category and pay band

The 12 pay bands are:

- $19,239 and under
- $19,240–$24,439
- $24,440–$30,679
- $30,680–$38,999
- $39,000–$49,919
- $49,920–$62,919
- $62,920–$80,079
- $80,080–$101,919
- $101,920–$128,959
- $128,960–$163,799
- $163,800–$207,999
- $208,000 and over

Employment Retirement Income Security Act of 1974 (ERISA)

The Employment Retirement Income Security Act (ERISA) was created by Congress to set standards for private pensions and some group welfare programs such as medical and life insurance.

ERISA requires organizations to file three types of reports: a summary plan description, an annual report, and reports to individual participants of their benefit rights.

Summary Plan Description (SPD)

A *summary plan description (SPD)* provides plan participants with information about the provisions, policies, and rules established by the plan and advises them on actions they can take in utilizing the plan. ERISA requires that the SPD include the name and other identifying information about plan sponsors, administrators, and trustees, along with any information related to collective bargaining agreements for the plan participants. The SPD must describe what eligibility requirements must be met for participating in the plan and for receiving benefits, as well as the circumstances under which participants would be disqualified or ineligible for participation or be denied benefits.

The SPD must also describe the financing source for the plan and the name of the organization providing benefits. Information on the end of the plan year and whether records are maintained on a calendar, plan, or fiscal year basis must be included in the description.

For health and welfare plans, the SPD must describe claim procedures, along with the name of the U.S. Department of Labor (DOL) office that will assist participants and beneficiaries with Health Insurance Portability and Accountability Act (HIPAA) claims. The SPD must also describe what remedies are available when claims are denied.

A new SPD reflecting all changes made must be prepared and distributed every five years unless no changes have occurred. Every 10 years, a new SPD must be distributed to participants whether or not changes have occurred.

Annual Reports

ERISA requires annual reports (Form 5500) to be filed for all employee benefit plans. The reports must include financial statements, the number of employees in the plan, and the names and addresses of the plan fiduciaries. ERISA mandates that any persons compensated by the plan (such as an accountant) during the preceding year be disclosed, along with the amount of compensation paid to each, the nature of the services rendered, and any relationship that exists between these parties and any party in interest to the plan. Information that is provided with regard to plan assets must be certified by the organization that holds the assets, whether it is the plan sponsor, an insurance company, or a bank.

The annual report must be summarized and distributed to plan participants. The summary annual report (SAR) provides participants with an overview of the plan's financial status and operations.

The annual reports must be audited by a CPA or other qualified public accountant, and any actuarial reports must be prepared by an enrolled actuary who has been licensed jointly by the Department of the Treasury and the Department of Labor to provide actuarial services for U.S. pension plans.

Once submitted, annual reports and other documents become public record and are made available in the DOL public document room. The DOL may also use this information to conduct research and analyze data.

Participant Benefit Rights Reports

Participants may request a report of the total benefits accrued on their behalf along with the amount of the benefit that is nonforfeitable. If there are no nonforfeitable amounts accrued at the time the report is requested, the earliest date that benefits will become nonforfeitable must be provided. Participants are entitled to receive the report no more than once per year.

ERISA records must be maintained for six years from the date they were due to be filed with the DOL. In addition to requiring the preparation of these reports, ERISA regulations stipulate that annual reports are to be filed with the DOL within 210 days of the end of the plan year. The

DOL may reject reports that are incomplete or that contain qualified opinions from the CPA or actuary. Rejected plans must be resubmitted within 45 days, or the DOL can retain a CPA to audit the report on behalf of the participants. ERISA authorizes the DOL to bring civil actions on behalf of plan participants if necessary to resolve any issues.

In addition to the reporting requirements, ERISA sets minimum standards for employee participation or eligibility requirements, as well as vesting requirements for qualified pension plans.

Employee Participation

A participant is an employee who has met the eligibility requirements for the plan. The law sets minimum participation requirements as follows:

- When one year of service has been completed or the employee has reached the age of 21, whichever is later, unless the plan provides for 100 percent vesting after two years of service. In that case, the requirement changes to completion of two years of service or reaching age 21, whichever is later.

- Employees may not be excluded from the plan on the basis of age; that is, they may not be excluded because they have reached a specified age.

- When employees have met the minimum service and age requirements, they must become participants no later than the first day of the plan year after they meet the requirement, or six months after the requirements are met, whichever is earlier.

Vesting

Qualified plans must also meet minimum vesting standards. Vesting refers to the point at which employees own the contributions their employer has made to the pension plan whether or not they remain employed with the company. The vesting requirements established by ERISA refer only to funds that are contributed by the employer; any funds contributed by plan participants are owned by the employee. Employees are always 100 percent vested in their own money but must earn the right to be vested in the employer's contribution.

Vesting may be immediate or delayed. Immediate vesting occurs when employees are 100 percent, or fully, vested as soon as they meet the eligibility requirements of the plan. Delayed vesting occurs when participants must wait for a defined period of time prior to becoming fully vested. There are two types of delayed vesting:

- With *cliff vesting*, participants become 100 percent vested after a specified period of time. ERISA sets the maximum period at five years for qualified plans, which means that participants are zero percent vested until they have completed the five years of service, after which they are fully vested.

- *Graded vesting*, which is also referred to as graduated or gradual vesting, establishes a vesting schedule that provides for partial vesting each year for a specified number of years. A graded vesting schedule in a qualified plan must allow for at least 20 percent vesting after three years and 20 percent per year after that, with participants achieving full vesting after seven years of service. See Table C.2 for a graded vesting schedule that complies with ERISA requirements.

TABLE C.2   ERISA Graded Vesting Schedule

Years of service	Percent vested
3	20 percent
4	40 percent
5	60 percent
6	80 percent
7	100 percent

Benefit Accrual Requirements

ERISA sets specific requirements for determining how much of an accrued benefit participants are entitled to receive if they leave the company prior to retirement. Plans must account for employee contributions to the plan separately from the funds contributed by the employer since the employees are entitled to all the funds contributed by them to the plan when they leave the company.

Form and Payment of Benefits

ERISA sets forth specific requirements for the payment of funds when participants either reach retirement age or leave the company. The act also provides guidance for employers to deal with qualified domestic relations orders (QDROs), which are legal orders issued by state courts or other state agencies to require pension payments to alternate payees. An alternate payee must be a spouse, former spouse, child, or other dependent of a plan participant.

ERISA also defines funding requirements for pension plans and sets standards for those who are responsible for safeguarding the funds until they are paid to employees. Finally, ERISA provides civil and criminal penalties for organizations that violate its provisions.

Funding

An enrolled actuary determines how much money is required to fund the accrued obligations of the plan, and ERISA requires that these funds be maintained in trust accounts separate from a business's operating funds. These amounts must be deposited on a quarterly basis; the final contribution must be made no later than eight and a half months after the end of the plan year.

Fiduciary Responsibility

For purposes of ERISA, a fiduciary is a person, corporation, or other legal entity that holds property or assets on behalf of, or in trust for, the pension fund. ERISA requires fiduciaries to operate pension funds in the best interests of the participants and their beneficiaries and at the lowest possible expense to them. All actions taken with regard to the plan assets must be in accord with the prudent person standard of care, a common law concept that requires all actions be undertaken with "the care, skill, prudence, and diligence. . .that a prudent [person] acting in like capacity" would use, as defined in ERISA itself.

Fiduciaries may be held personally liable for losses to the plan resulting from any breach of fiduciary responsibility that they commit and may be required to make restitution for the losses and be subject to legal action. They are not held liable for breaches of fiduciary responsibility that occur prior to the time they became fiduciaries.

ERISA specifically prohibits transactions between pension plans and parties in interest.

Safe Harbor Provisions

The safe harbor provisions under ERISA provide a framework that exempts certain fiduciaries from liability for investment decisions made by participants in individual account plans, such as 401(k) plans. These provisions allow plan sponsors to offer a selection of investment options and require them to provide participants with sufficient information to make informed investment choices. By following specific guidelines—such as offering a diverse range of investment options and providing clear communication—plan sponsors can limit their liability for participants' investment losses, as long as the decisions were made independently by the participants.

Administration and Enforcement

The Employee Benefits Security Administration (EBSA) conducts investigations of criminal violations of ERISA, including kickbacks, false statements, and embezzlement. Criminal penalties for willful violations of ERISA include fines beginning at $5,000 and imprisonment. The decision to seek criminal actions are based on the egregiousness and magnitude of the violation; the desirability and likelihood of incarceration as a deterrent and as a punishment; and whether the case involves a prior ERISA violator. Civil actions may be brought by plan participants or their beneficiaries, by fiduciaries, or by the DOL to recover benefits or damages or to force compliance with the law.

Amendments to ERISA

Amendments to ERISA include COBRA and HIPAA.

Consolidated Omnibus Budget Reconciliation Act of 1986 (COBRA)

Prior to 1986, employees who were laid off or resigned from their jobs lost any healthcare benefits that were provided as part of those jobs. ERISA was amended in 1986 by the Consolidated Omnibus Budget Reconciliation Act (COBRA), which requires businesses with 20 or more employees to provide health plan continuation coverage under certain circumstances. Employers who meet this requirement must continue benefits for those who leave the company or for their dependents when certain qualifying events occur.

Employers must notify employees of the availability of COBRA coverage when they enter the plan and again within 30 days of the occurrence of a qualifying event. Table C.3 shows the qualifying events that trigger COBRA, as well as the length of time coverage must be continued for each event.

TABLE C.3   COBRA Qualifying Events and Coverage Requirements

Qualifying event	Length of coverage
Employee death	36 months
Divorce or legal separation	36 months
Dependent child no longer covered	36 months
Reduction in hours	18 months
Reduction in hours when disabled[a]	29 months
Employee termination	18 months
Employee termination when disabled[a]	29 months
Eligibility for SSA benefits	18 months
Termination for gross misconduct	0 months

[a] An employee who is disabled within 60 days of a reduction in hours or a termination becomes eligible for an additional 11 months of COBRA coverage.

Employers may charge COBRA participants a maximum of 102 percent of the group premium for coverage and must include them in any open enrollment periods or other changes to the plans. Employers may discontinue COBRA coverage if payments are not received within 30 days of the time they are due.

Employees must notify the employer within 60 days of a divorce, a separation, or the loss of a child's dependent status. Employees who fail to provide this notice risk the loss of continued coverage.

Health Insurance Portability and Accountability Act of 1996 (HIPAA)

The Health Insurance Portability and Accountability Act (HIPAA) was another amendment to ERISA and prohibits discrimination on the basis of health status as evidenced by an individual's medical condition or history, claims experience, utilization of healthcare services, disability, or evidence of insurability. It also places limits on health insurance restrictions for preexisting conditions, which are defined as conditions for which treatment was given within six months of enrollment in the plan. Insurers may exclude those conditions from coverage for 12 months or, in the case of a late enrollment, for 18 months.

Insurers may discontinue an employer's group coverage only if the employer neglects to pay the premiums, obtained the policy through fraudulent or intentional misrepresentation, or does not comply with material provisions of the plan. Group coverage may also be discontinued if the insurer is no longer offering coverage in the employer's geographic area, if none of the plan participants reside in the plan's network area, or if the employer fails to renew a collective bargaining agreement or to comply with its provisions.

In April 2001, the Department of Health and Human Services (HHS) issued privacy regulations that were required by HIPAA. The regulations defined protected health information (PHI), patient information that must be kept private, including physical or mental conditions, information about healthcare given, and payments that have been made. Although these regulations were directed at covered entities that conduct business electronically, such as health plans, healthcare providers, and clearinghouses, they have had a significant impact on the way employers handle information related to employee health benefits. Many employers had to redesign forms for open enrollment periods and new hires, and update plan documents and company benefit policies to reflect the changes. The regulations have an impact on employers in other ways as well.

Although flexible spending accounts (FSAs) are exempt from other HIPAA requirements, they are considered group health plans for privacy reasons, so employers who sponsor FSAs must comply with the privacy requirements for them.

Employers who are self-insured or who have fully insured group health plans and receive protected health information are required to develop privacy policies that comply with the regulations, appoint a privacy official, and train employees to handle information appropriately.

Although the HIPAA regulations do not prevent employees from seeking assistance from HR for claim problems or other issues with the group health plan, they do require employees to provide the insurance provider or third-party administrator with an authorization to release information about the claim to the HR department. Note that in 2023, plans were announced to update HIPAA regulations for healthcare organizations to improve cybersecurity performance goals to protect patient privacy.

The regulations include stiff civil and criminal sanctions for violations; civil penalties of $137 per violation and up to $68,928 depending on the level of culpability. There are three levels of criminal penalties:

- A conviction for obtaining or disclosing PHI can result in one year in prison.

- Obtaining PHI under false pretenses can result in five years in prison.

- Obtaining or disclosing PHI with the intent of selling, transferring, or using it to obtain commercial advantage or personal gain can be punished with up to 10 years in prison.

Executive Orders

Executive orders (EOs) are presidential proclamations that, when published in the Federal Register, become law after 30 days. EOs have been used to ensure that equal employment opportunities are afforded by federal agencies and private businesses that contract or subcontract with those agencies. Certain executive orders relating to equal employment issues are enforced by the OFCCP.

Executive Order 11478, Amended by 13087, 13152, and 13672   Executive Order 11478, issued in 1969, requires the federal government to provide equal employment opportunities for all employees, regardless of race, color, religion, sex, national origin, or age. Amendments to the order expanded protections: Executive Order 13087 added sexual orientation, Executive Order 13152 included parental status, and Executive Order 13672 added gender identity. These changes ensure that federal employees are treated fairly and without discrimination, promoting a more inclusive workplace in the federal government.

Executive Order 12138   In 1979, with the implementation of EO 12138, the National Women's Business Enterprise policy was created. This EO also required federal contractors and subcontractors to take affirmative steps to promote and support women's business enterprises.

Executive Order 12989, Amended by 13286 and 13465   This order requires contractors with qualifying federal contracts to electronically verify employment authorization of: (1) all employees hired during the contract term, and (2) all employees performing work in the United States on contracts with a Federal Acquisition Regulation (FAR) E-Verify clause. A federal contractor may be exempt from these clauses if any of the following apply:

- The contract is for fewer than 120 days.

- It is valued at less than $150,000, the simplified acquisition threshold.

- All work is performed outside the United States.

- It includes only commercially available off-the-shelf (COTS) items and related services.

Fair Credit Reporting Act of 1970 (FCRA)

The Fair Credit Reporting Act of 1970 (FCRA) was first enacted in 1970 and has been amended several times since then, most recently with the Fair and Accurate Credit Transactions (FACT) Act in 2003. Enforced by the Federal Trade Commission (FTC), the FCRA requires employers to take certain actions prior to the use of a consumer report or an investigative consumer report obtained through a consumer reporting agency (CRA) for use in making employment decisions.

Familiarity with three terms is valuable for understanding why these consumer protection laws are important for HR practitioners:

- A consumer reporting agency (CRA) is an individual, business, or nonprofit association that gathers information about individuals with the intent of supplying that information to a third party.

- A consumer report is a written document produced by a CRA containing information about an individual's character, reputation, lifestyle, or credit history for use by an employer in determining that person's suitability for employment.

- An investigative consumer report is a written document produced by a CRA for the same purpose as a consumer report but is based on information gathered through personal interviews with friends, coworkers, employers, and others who are acquainted with the individual.

The FCRA established the following four-step process for employers to follow when using CRAs to perform background investigations:

1. A clear and conspicuous disclosure that a consumer report may be obtained for employment purposes must be made in writing to the candidate before the report is acquired.

2. The candidate must provide written authorization for the employer to obtain the report.

3. Before taking an adverse action based in whole or in part on the credit report, either the employer must provide the candidate with a copy of the report and a copy of the FTC notice, "A Summary of Your Rights Under the Fair Credit Reporting Act," or, if the application was made by mail, telephone, computer, or similar means, the employer must notify the candidate within three business days that adverse action is being taken based in whole or in part on the credit report. This notice must provide the name, address, and telephone number of the CRA and indicate that the CRA did not take the adverse action and cannot provide the reasons for the action to the candidate. If a candidate requests a copy of the report, the employer must provide it within three days, along with a copy of the FTC notice just described.

4. Candidates must be advised of their right to dispute the accuracy of information contained in the report.

When employers request investigative consumer reports on candidates, they must comply with the following additional steps:

- Provide written disclosure of its intent to the candidate within three days of requesting the report from a CRA.

- Include a summary of the candidate's FCRA rights with the written notice.

- Advise the candidate that they have a right to request information about the type and extent of the investigation.

- If requested, provide complete disclosure of the type and extent of the report within the later of five days of the request or receipt of the report.

The FCRA was amended in 2003 by the Fair and Accurate Credit Transactions (FACT) Act of 2003. Designed to improve the accuracy of consumer credit information, it gives consumers one free credit report per year. The act also requires disclosure to consumers who are subject to risk-based pricing (less favorable credit offers) or who are denied credit altogether because of a credit-related record.

FACT describes "reasonable measures" for destroying credit reports, depending on the medium:

- Paper documents must be shredded, pulverized, or burned in a way that prevents them from being reassembled.

- Electronic files or media must be erased in a way that prevents them from being reconstructed.

- Either type may be destroyed by an outside vendor once the employer has conducted due diligence research to ensure the vendor's methods are reliable.

Fair Labor Standards Act of 1938 (FLSA)

Enacted in 1938, the Fair Labor Standards Act (FLSA) today remains a major influence on basic compensation issues for businesses in the United States. FLSA regulations apply to workers who are not already covered by another law. For example, railroad and airline employers are subject to wage and hour requirements of the Railway Labor Act, so the FLSA does not apply to their employees.

There are two categories of employers subject to the requirements of the FLSA: enterprise and individual. Enterprise coverage applies to businesses employing at least two employees with at least $500,000 in annual sales and to hospitals, schools, and government agencies. Individual coverage applies to organizations whose daily work involves interstate commerce. The FLSA defines interstate commerce so broadly that it includes those who have regular contact by telephone with out-of-state customers, vendors, or suppliers; on that basis, it covers virtually all employers in the United States.

The FLSA established requirements in five key areas to HRM:

- It introduced a minimum wage for all covered employees.
- It identified the circumstances in which overtime payments are required and set the overtime rate at one and one half times the regular hourly wage.
- It identified the criteria for determining what jobs are exempt from FLSA requirements.
- It placed limitations on working conditions for children to protect them from exploitation.
- It identified the information employers must keep about employees and related payroll transactions.

Minimum Wage

The FLSA regulates the federal minimum wage, which is set at $7.25 per hour as of 2024. The federal minimum wage for tipped employees is $2.13 per hour, however, the tipped minimum wage and amount of tips must reach at least $7.25; if not, the employer must make up the difference. Some states, such as Alaska, California, and New York, have set the minimum wage at a higher rate than the federal government; when this is the case, the state requirement supersedes the federal minimum wage. The DOL provides a useful map showing current minimum wage requirements by state at www.dol.gov/whd/minwage/ america.htm.

Nonexempt employees must be paid at least the minimum wage for all compensable time. The FLSA defines compensable time as the time an employee works that is "suffered or permitted" by the employer. For example, a nonexempt employee who continues to work on an assignment after the end of the business day to finish a project or make corrections must be paid for that time.

Maximum Hours and Overtime

The FLSA defined the maximum workweek for nonexempt employees as 40 hours per week and required overtime to be paid for any compensable time that exceeds that maximum. The FLSA defined overtime for nonexempt workers as one and one half times the regular hourly wage rate for all compensable time worked that exceeds 40 hours in a workweek (also commonly known as time and a half).

Although double-time, or two times regular pay, is not required by the FLSA, it may be required by some states or may be part of a labor agreement.

While the FLSA does not require payment of overtime for exempt employees, it also does not prohibit overtime payments for them. Employers who choose to compensate exempt employees for hours worked exceeding the regular workweek are free to do so without risking the loss of exemption status. As long as overtime payments are in addition to the regular salary, exemption status is not affected. Exempt overtime can be paid at straight time, at time and a half, or as a bonus.

State or local government agencies may compensate employees with what is known as compensatory time off, or comp time, instead of cash payment for overtime worked. For example, a road maintenance worker employed by a city government may work 20 hours of overtime during a snowstorm. Instead of being paid time and a half for the overtime hours, the employee may receive 30 hours of additional paid time off (1.5 times 20 hours) to be used just as paid vacation or sick leave. From time to time, initiatives to expand comp time to private employers are presented in Congress, but at this time, the FLSA does not permit private employers to use comp time.

Overtime calculations are based on time actually worked during the week. For example, in a week with a paid holiday, full-time nonexempt employees will actually work 32 hours even though they are paid for 40 hours. If some employees then work 6 hours on Saturday, for a total of 38 actual hours worked during the week, those hours are paid at straight time, not time and a half (unless, of course, a state law or union contract requires otherwise). This requirement also applies when employees use paid vacation or sick leave or some other form of paid time off (PTO).

To accurately calculate overtime payments, it is necessary to understand the difference between compensable time—hours that must be paid to nonexempt employees—and noncompensable time. The FLSA defines several situations for which nonexempt employees must be paid, such as the time spent preparing for or cleaning up after a shift by dressing in or removing protective clothing. Other types of compensable time include the following.

Waiting Time

Time spent by nonexempt employees waiting for work is compensable if it meets the FLSA definition of engaged to wait, which means that employees have been asked to wait for an assignment. For example, a marketing director may ask an assistant to wait for the conclusion of a meeting in order to prepare a Microsoft PowerPoint presentation needed for a client meeting early the next morning. If the assistant reads a book while waiting for the meeting to end, that time is still compensable.

Time that is spent by an employee who is waiting to be engaged is not compensable. For example, time spent by an employee who arrives at work 15 minutes early and reads the newspaper until the beginning of a shift is not considered to be compensable.

On-Call Time

The FLSA does not require employees who are on call away from the worksite and are able to effectively use the time for their own purposes to be paid for time they spend waiting to be called. These employees may be required to provide the employer with contact information. If, however, the employer places other constraints on the employee's activities, the time could be considered compensable.

Employees who are required to remain at or close to the worksite while waiting for an assignment are entitled to on-call pay. For example, medical interns required to remain at the hospital are entitled to payment for all hours spent at the hospital waiting for patients to arrive.

Rest and Meal Periods

Although rest and meal periods are not required by the FLSA, if they are provided, that time is subject to its requirements. Commonly referred to as breaks, short periods of rest lasting less than

20 minutes are considered compensable time. Meal periods lasting 30 minutes or longer are not compensable time unless the employee is required to continue working while eating. For example, a receptionist who is required to remain at the desk during lunch to answer the telephone must be paid for that time.

Lectures, Meetings, and Training Programs

Nonexempt employees are not required to be paid to attend training events when all four of the following conditions are met:

- The event takes place outside normal work hours.
- It is voluntary.
- It is not job-related.
- No other work is performed during the event.

Travel Time

Regular commute time (the time normally spent commuting from home to the regular worksite) is not compensable. There are, however, some situations in which the FLSA requires that nonexempt employees receive payment for travel time.

Emergency Travel from Home to Work

Any time an employee is required to return to work for an emergency after working a full day, the employee must be compensated for travel time.

One-Day Off-Site Assignments

When nonexempt employees are given a one-day assignment at a different location than their regular worksite, the travel time may be considered compensable in certain circumstances. For example, if an employee drives to the off-site assignment, the travel time is compensable, but if they are a passenger in the car, the travel time is not compensable.

Travel Between Job Sites

Nonexempt employees (such as plumbers or electricians) who are required to drive to different worksites to perform their regular duties must also be paid for the driving time between worksites.

Travel Away from Home

Travel away from home is defined as travel that keeps employees away from their homes overnight. When nonexempt employees must travel overnight, the FLSA considers the travel time during regular work hours as compensable time. This includes time traveled on non-workdays (weekends, for example) when it occurs during the employee's regular work hours. The DOL excludes the time spent outside of working hours as a passenger on an airplane, train, boat, bus, or automobile from compensable time calculations. If the employee is driving or working while traveling, the time is compensable.

Exemption Status

The FLSA covers all employees except those identified in the law as exempt from the regulations. All other employees are considered nonexempt and must be paid in accordance with FLSA requirements.

Certain positions may be exempt from one or all of the FLSA requirements (minimum wage, overtime, or child labor). For example, police officers and firefighters employed by small departments of fewer than five employees are exempt from overtime requirements but not exempt from the minimum wage requirement. On the other hand, newspaper delivery jobs are exempt from the minimum wage, overtime, and child labor requirements.

The determination of exemption status is often misunderstood by both employers and employees. Employers often think that they will save money by designating jobs as exempt and paying incumbent employees a salary. Employees often see the designation of a job as exempt as a measure of status within the company. Neither of these perceptions is accurate, and jobs that do not meet the legal exemption requirements can have costly consequences for employers.

To assist employers in properly classifying positions, the DOL regulations include exemption tests to determine whether a job meets those requirements and is therefore exempt from FLSA regulations.

The U.S. Department of Labor announced a significant update to overtime and minimum wage exemptions in 2023. On July 1, 2024, the minimum salary threshold for exempt executive, administrative, and professional employees rose from $684 per week ($35,568 annually) to $844 per week ($43,888 annually). It will further increase to $1,128 per week ($58,656 annually) by January 1, 2025. The total annual compensation threshold for highly compensated employees will also rise from $107,432 to $132,964, and subsequently to $151,164.

Note that only a month after the final rule was adopted, legal challenges sought to invalidate or, at minimum, delay implementation. It is important that you are well versed in the status of the law *at the time of your testing*, so check for the most recent updates at www.dol.gov.

Executive Exemption

Employees who meet the salary basis requirement may be exempt as executives if they meet all of the following requirements:

- They have as their primary duty managing the enterprise, or managing a customarily recognized department or subdivision of the enterprise.
- They customarily and regularly direct the work of at least two other full-time employees.
- They have the authority to hire, fire, promote, and evaluate employees or to provide input regarding those actions that carry particular weight.
- Employees who own at least a 20 percent equity interest in the organization and who are actively engaged in management duties are also considered bona fide exempt executives.

Administrative Exemption

Employees who meet the salary basis requirement may qualify for the administrative exemption if they meet all of the following requirements:

- The primary duty is to perform office or nonmanual work directly related to management or general business operations.

- The primary duty requires discretion and independent judgment on significant matters.

Professional Exemption

The DOL identifies two types of professionals who may qualify for exemption:

- **Learned Professional Exemption:** Employees who meet the salary basis requirement may qualify for exemption as learned professionals if they also meet both of the following criteria:

  - The primary duty requires the use of this advanced knowledge for work that requires the consistent use of discretion and judgment.

  - They have advanced knowledge in a field of science or learning acquired through a prolonged course of intellectual instruction.

- **Creative Professional Exemption:** Employees who meet the salary basis requirement may qualify for exemption as creative professionals if the primary duty requires invention, imagination, originality, or talent in a recognized field of artistic or creative endeavor.

Highly Compensated Employee Exemption

Highly compensated employees may also be considered exempt. To meet this exemption requirement, employees must perform office or nonmanual work and, on a customary and regular basis, at least one of the duties listed earlier for the executive, administrative, or professional exemptions.

The salary threshold for highly compensated employees (HCEs) under the U.S. Department of Labor's final 2024 rule was increased. As of July 1, 2024, the threshold is $132,964. It will further increase to $151,164 per year by January 1, 2025. Additionally, automatic updates to these thresholds will occur every three years beginning in 2027.

Computer Employee Exemption

Employees who meet the weekly salary requirement ($684) or who are paid at least $27.63 per hour may qualify for the computer employee exemption if they perform one of the following jobs:

- Computer systems analyst
- Computer programmer
- Software engineer
- Other similarly skilled jobs in the computer field

and if they perform one or more of the following primary duties as part of the job:

- Apply systems analysis techniques and procedures, including consulting with users, to determine hardware, software, or system functional specifications.

- Design, develop, document, analyze, create, test, or modify computer systems or programs, including prototypes, based on and related to user or system design specifications.

- Design, document, test, create, or modify computer programs related to machine operating systems.
- Perform a combination of the previously described duties, at a level requiring the same skill.

Outside Sales Exemption

Unlike the other exemptions, there is no salary requirement for outside sales personnel. To qualify for this exemption, employees must meet both of the following requirements:

- The primary duty of the position must be making sales or obtaining orders or contracts for services or for the use of facilities for which a consideration will be paid by the client or customer.
- The employee must be customarily and regularly engaged away from the employer's place of business.

Salary Deductions

There are certain circumstances where an employer may make deductions from the pay of an exempt employee. The DOL defines permissible salary deductions as the following:

- Absence for one or more full days for personal reasons other than sickness or disability
- Absence for one or more full days because of sickness or disability if the deduction is made in accordance with a bona fide plan, policy, or practice of providing compensation for salary lost due to illness
- To offset amounts employees receive for jury or witness fees or military pay
- For good-faith penalties imposed for safety rule infractions of major significance
- Good-faith, unpaid disciplinary suspensions of one or more full days for infractions of workplace conduct rules
- During the initial or terminal weeks of employment when employees work less than a full week
- Unpaid leave under the Family and Medical Leave Act

Employers who have an "actual practice" of improper deductions risk the loss of exemption status for all employees in the same job classification, not just for the affected employee. The loss of exemption status will be effective for the time during which the improper deductions were made.

Actual Practice

The DOL looks at a variety of factors to determine whether employers have an actual practice of improper deductions from exempt pay. These factors include the following:

- The number of improper deductions compared to the number of employee infractions warranting deductions
- The time period during which the improper deductions were made

- The number of employees affected
- The geographic location of the affected employees and managers responsible for the deductions

Safe Harbor

The DOL provides a safe harbor provision for payroll errors that could affect exemption status. The safe harbor applies if all of the following are met:

- There is a clearly communicated policy prohibiting improper deductions that includes a complaint mechanism for employees to use.
- The employer reimburses employees for improper deductions.
- The employer makes a good-faith commitment to comply in the future.

Employers who meet these criteria will not lose exemption status for the affected employees unless they willfully violate the policy by continuing to make improper deductions after receiving employee complaints.

Child Labor

The FLSA regulates the employment of workers under the age of 18. Children 16 years of age and up may work for an unlimited amount of hours. Children of any age may work for businesses owned entirely by their parents, unless they would be employed in mining, manufacturing, or other hazardous occupations. There are no restrictions on a youth 18 years of age or older.

Children 14 and 15 years of age can work in nonmanufacturing, non-mining, and nonhazardous jobs outside of school hours if they work the following hours:

- No more than 3 hours on a school day or 18 hours in a workweek
- No more than 8 hours on a non-school day or 40 hours in a non-school workweek

During the school year, youths between the ages of 14 and 15 can work between 7 a.m. and 7 p.m. During the summer months, June 1 through Labor Day, the workday can be extended to 9 p.m.

Recordkeeping

There are two common methods for reporting time worked: positive time reporting, in which employees record the actual hours they are at work along with vacation, sick, or other time off, and exception reporting, in which only changes to the regular work schedule are recorded, such as vacation, sick, or personal time. Although the DOL regulations accept either method, in general the positive time method is best for nonexempt employees because it leaves no doubt as to actual hours worked by the employee and protects both the employee and the employer if there is ever a question about overtime payments due. Exception reporting is more appropriate for exempt employees because their pay is not based on hours worked.

The FLSA does not prevent employers from tracking the work time of exempt employees. These records may be used for billing customers, for reviewing performance, or for other administrative purposes, but they may not be used to reduce pay based on the quality or quantity of work produced. Reducing the salary invalidates the exemption status and subjects the employee to all requirements of the FLSA.

The FLSA requires the maintenance of accurate records by all employers. The information that must be maintained includes the following:

- Personal information, including full name, Social Security number (SSN), home address, occupation, sex, and date of birth if younger than 19 years old
- The hour and day when the workweek begins
- The total hours worked each workday and each workweek
- The basis on which employee's wages are paid (e.g., "$15 per hour" or "$640 per week")
- The total daily or weekly straight-time earnings
- The regular hourly pay rate for any week, including overtime
- Total overtime pay for the workweek
- Deductions and additions to wages
- Total wages paid each pay period
- The pay period dates and payment date

These FLSA records are usually maintained by the payroll department. Records must be preserved for at least three years. They must include payroll records, collective bargaining agreements, and sales and purchase records.

Penalties and Recovery of Back Wages

It is not uncommon for an employer to make an inadvertent error in calculating employee pay. In most cases when that happens, the employer corrects the error as soon as the employee points it out or the employer catches the error in some other way. Although distressing for employees, employers who make a good-faith effort to rectify the error in a timely manner remain within FLSA requirements.

In other cases, employers intentionally violate FLSA regulations by either paying employees less than the minimum wage, not paying overtime, or misclassifying employees as exempt to avoid overtime costs. These and other employee complaints about wage payments are investigated by state or federal agencies. If the complaints are justified, the employers are required to pay retroactive overtime pay and penalties to the affected employees. The investigation of a complaint by a single employee at an organization can trigger a government audit of the employer's general pay practices and exemption classification of its other employees and may result in additional overtime payments or penalties to other employees if they are found to be misclassified.

Employees whose complaints are verified can recover back wages using one of the following four methods the FLSA provides. The least expensive cost to the employer requires payment of the back wages.

- The Wage and Hour Division of the DOL can supervise the payment of back wages.
- The DOL can file a lawsuit for the amount of back wages and liquidated damages equal to the back wages.

- Employees can file private lawsuits to recover the wages plus an equal amount of liquidated damages, attorney fees, and court costs.
- The DOL can file an injunction preventing an employer from unlawfully withholding minimum wage and overtime payments.

There is a two-year statute of limitations for back pay recovery unless the employer willfully violated the FLSA. In those cases, the statute extends to three years. Employers may not terminate or retaliate against employees who file FLSA complaints. Willful violators of the FLSA may face criminal prosecution and be fined up to $10,000; if convicted a second time, the violator may face imprisonment. A civil penalty of up to $1,100 per violation may be assessed against willful or repeat violators.

FLSA Amendments

The FLSA has been amended numerous times since 1938, most often to raise the minimum wage to a level consistent with changes in economic conditions. Two significant federal amendments have been added to the FLSA since 1938: the Portal to Portal Act and the Equal Pay Act. Additionally, the Patient Protection and Affordable Care Act, commonly referred to as Obamacare, affected the FLSA requirements.

Portal to Portal Act (1947)

The Portal to Portal Act clarified what was considered to be compensable work time and established that employers are not required to pay for employee commute time. This act requires employers to pay nonexempt employees who perform regular work duties before or after their regular hours or for working during their lunch period.

Equal Pay Act (EPA) (1963)

The Equal Pay Act, the first antidiscrimination act to protect women, prohibits discrimination on the basis of sex. Equal pay for equal work applies to jobs with similar working conditions, skill, effort, and responsibilities. The Equal Pay Act applies to employers and employees covered by FLSA and is administered and enforced by the Equal Employment Opportunity Commission (EEOC). The EPA allows differences in pay when they are based on a bona fide seniority system, a merit system, a system that measures quantity or quality of production, or any other system that fairly measures factors other than sex. Prior to the EPA, the comparable worth standard was used by the U.S. government to make compensation decisions. When Congress passed the EPA, it deliberately rejected the comparable worth standard in favor of the equal pay standard.

The first act signed by former President Obama was the Lilly Ledbetter Fair Pay Act. The purpose of this act was to restore the protection against pay discrimination by clarifying that the 180-day statute of limitations for filing an equal-pay lawsuit resets with each new discriminatory paycheck.

Patient Protection and Affordable Care Act (PPACA) (2010)

In March 2010, President Barack Obama signed into law the Patient Protection and Affordable Care Act (PPACA). Largely intended as substantial healthcare reform, it included provisions for lactation accommodation in the workplace. The amendment requires that employers provide a reasonable break time for an employee to express breast milk for her nursing child for one year after the child's birth each time such employee has need to express the milk, and an appropriate place (other than a bathroom) that provides privacy.

There is some dispute as to whether this time must be paid, however. While the amendment states that the time need not be compensated, current FLSA language reads otherwise: "Rest periods of short duration, generally running from 5 minutes to about 20 minutes, are common in industry. They promote the efficiency of the employee and are customarily paid for as work time. It is immaterial with respect to compensability of such breaks whether the employee drinks coffee, smokes, goes to the rest room, etc." This is an excellent example of when existing employment practices must be considered when applying the law. For example, if an employer allows additional paid break time for employees who smoke (unprotected activity), it may be prudent for said employer to count lactation accommodation (protected activity) as paid time as well.

Family and Medical Leave Act of 1993 (FMLA)

In 1993, President Bill Clinton signed the Family and Medical Leave Act (FMLA), which was created to assist employees in balancing the needs of their families with the demands of their jobs. In creating the FMLA, Congress intended that employees should not have to choose between keeping their jobs and attending to seriously ill family members.

In addition to protecting employees from adverse employment actions and retaliation when they request leave under the FMLA, the act provides three benefits for eligible employees in covered organizations:

- Twelve weeks of unpaid leave within a 12-month period (26 months for military caregiver leave)
- Continuation of health benefits
- Reinstatement to the same position or an equivalent position at the end of the leave

Designation of FMLA Leave

Employers are responsible to designate leave requests as FMLA-qualified based on information received from employees or someone designated by employees to speak on their behalf. When the employee does not provide enough information for the employer to determine if the leave is for a reason protected by the FMLA, it is up to the employer to request additional information. The FMLA regulations do not require employees to specifically request FMLA leave, but they must provide enough information to allow the employer to determine if the request is protected by the FMLA. If leave is denied based on a lack of information, it is up to the employee to provide enough additional information for the employer to ascertain that the leave is protected by the FMLA.

The regulations allow employers to retroactively designate leave as FMLA-qualified, as long as sufficient notice is given to the employee and the retroactive designation does not cause harm or injury to the employee. The retroactive designation can be made by mutual agreement between the employee and employer. When an employer fails to appropriately designate that a leave is FMLA-qualified at the time of the employee's request, the employee may be entitled to any loss of compensation and benefits caused by the employer's failure. This can include monetary damages, reinstatement, promotion, or other suitable relief.

Failure to Designate in a Timely Manner

In 2008, the FMLA was amended by the National Defense Authorization Act (NDAA). One of the changes incorporated the Supreme Court ruling in *Ragsdale v. Wolverine Worldwide, Inc.*, a case that addressed what happens when an employer fails to designate a leave as FMLA-qualified in a timely manner. Prior to the *Ragsdale* case, some employees interpreted the regulations in a way that required employers to provide more than the 12 weeks of unpaid leave required by the FMLA. The regulations now state that, if an employer neglects to designate leave as FMLA, employees who are harmed may be entitled to restitution for their losses.

Waiver of Rights

Prior to the 2008 changes, the DOL required any settlement of past claims, even those mutually agreeable to both parties, to be approved by either the DOL or a court. The 2008 final rules amend this, allowing employers and employees who mutually agree on a resolution to settle past claims between them, avoiding costly and unnecessary litigation. However, the regulations do not permit employees to waive their future FMLA rights.

Substitution of Paid Leave

DOL regulations permit employees to request, or employers to require, the use of all accrued paid vacation, personal, family, medical, or sick leave concurrently with the FMLA leave. Eligible employees who do not qualify to take paid leave according to policies established by their employers are still entitled to the unpaid FMLA leave.

Perfect Attendance Awards

Employers may now deny perfect attendance awards to employees whose FMLA leave disqualifies them as long as employees who take non-FMLA leave are treated the same way.

Light-Duty Assignments

Under the Family and Medical Leave Act (FMLA), the final ruling on light-duty work assignments states that employers are not required to offer or provide light-duty assignments as an alternative to FMLA leave. Employees who cannot perform the essential functions of their original position due to a physical or mental condition are not entitled to restoration to a different, light-duty position under the FMLA. If an employee accepts a light-duty assignment, this does not count against their FMLA leave entitlement, and their right to job restoration is held in abeyance during the light-duty period. Note that the right to FMLA is absolute, meaning that an employee cannot be compelled to forfeit their leave for a light-duty assignment.

Recordkeeping Requirements

FMLA leave records must be kept in accordance with recordkeeping standards established by the Fair Labor Standards Act (FLSA) and may be maintained in employee personnel files. The FMLA does not require submission of FMLA leave records unless requested by the DOL, but they must be maintained and available for inspection, copying, or transcription by DOL representatives for no less than three years. The DOL may not require submission more than once during any 12-month period without a reasonable belief that a violation has occurred.

Employers Covered

The FMLA applies to all public agencies and schools, regardless of their size, and to private employers with 50 or more employees working within a 75-mile radius. The law provides detailed descriptions on how employers determine whether these requirements apply to them.

Fifty or More Employees

Employers must comply with the FMLA when they employ 50 or more employees for each working day during each of 20 or more calendar workweeks in the current or preceding year. The statute does not require the workweeks to be consecutive. Guidelines in the FMLA count the number of employees at a worksite as being determined by the number of employees on the payroll for that site.

Employers remain subject to FMLA rules until the number of employees on the payroll is less than 50 for 20 nonconsecutive weeks in the current and preceding calendar year. This means that if employers with 50 employees on the payroll for the first 20 weeks in 2025 reduce the number of employees for the rest of 2025 and remain at the reduced level throughout 2026, they must continue to comply with FMLA through the end of 2026.

Worksites within a 75-Mile Radius

The number of employees at each worksite is based on the employees who report to work at that site or, in the case of outside sales representatives or employees who telecommute, the location from which their work is assigned. This can be either a single place of business or a group of adjacent locations, such as a business park or campus.

A worksite may also consist of facilities that are not directly connected if they are in reasonable geographic proximity, are used for the same purpose, and share the same staff and equipment.

Employees such as construction workers or truck drivers who regularly work at sites away from the main business office are counted as employees in one of the three following ways:

- At the business site to which they report
- At the worksite that is their home base
- At the site from which their work is assigned

However, these employees may not be counted at a worksite where they may be temporarily deployed for the duration of a project.

Notice Obligations

Employers have two notice obligations for the FMLA: The first obligation is to inform employees of their FMLA rights and the second requires specific information to be provided in response to an FMLA leave request.

Informational Notice

Upon hire, employers must provide employees with a general informational notice in two formats. The DOL provides a poster (WH Publication 1420) explaining FMLA rights and responsibilities. Employers must post this information in an area frequented by employees.

Employers must also provide information about employee rights and responsibilities in the employee handbook, collective bargaining agreement (CBA), or other written documents. When an employer does not have a handbook or CBA, DOL provides Fact Sheet #28, a four-page summary of the FMLA that the employer may distribute to employees.

Notice in Response to Leave Request

Once an employee requests an FMLA leave, the final rules require employers to respond within five business days. At this time, employers must inform employees of their eligibility, rights, and responsibilities for an FMLA leave, and designate the leave as FMLA. The DOL provides two forms for this purpose: WH-381 and WH-382.

The eligibility, rights, and responsibilities notice (Form WH-381) informs employees of the following:

- The date of leave request, and beginning and ending dates of the leave
- The reason for the leave (birth or adoption of a child or serious health condition of employee or family member)
- Employee rights and responsibilities under the FMLA
- That employee contributions toward health insurance premiums continue and whether or not the employee will be required to reimburse the employer for premiums paid if the employee does not return to work after the leave
- Whether or not the employer will continue other benefits
- Whether or not the employee is eligible for an FMLA leave
- Whether or not the employee is designated as a *key employee* and therefore may not be restored to employment upon the end of the leave
- Whether or not the employer requires periodic reports on the employee's status and intention to return to work

The designation notice (Form WH-382) informs employees of the following:

- Whether or not the requested leave will be counted against their FMLA leave entitlement
- Whether or not a medical certification is required
- Whether or not the employer requires them to use their accrued paid leave for the unpaid FMLA leave; if not required, whether or not the employee chooses to substitute accrued paid leave for all or part of the FMLA leave
- Whether or not the employer requires a fitness-for-duty certificate prior to the employee's return to work

Employers are not required to use the DOL forms, but if a substitute form is used, it must include all information required by the regulations.

Employers may not revoke an employee's eligibility, once confirmed. Similarly, if an employer neglects to inform an employee that they are ineligible for FMLA leave prior to the date the leave begins, the employee is considered eligible to take the leave, and the employer may not deny it at that point.

Employees Eligible for FMLA

The FMLA also provides guidelines for determining which employees are eligible for leave. This includes employees who:

- Work for an employer that is subject to FMLA as described previously.
- Have been employed by the employer for at least 12 months, which need not be consecutive, but time worked prior to a break in service of seven or more years does not need to be counted unless the service break was to fulfill a military service obligation. Employees who received benefits or other compensation during any part of a week are counted as having been employed for that week.
- Worked at least 1,250 hours during the 12 months immediately preceding the leave, based on the FLSA standards for determining compensable hours of work. If accurate time records are not maintained, it is up to the employer to prove that the employee did not meet the requirement; if this is not possible, the law provides that the employee will be presumed to have met the requirement. The determination of whether an employee meets the requirement for 1,250 hours of work within the past 12 months is counted from the date the leave begins.

Key Employee Exception

An FMLA leave is available to all employees of covered organizations who meet the FMLA eligibility requirements. FMLA includes a provision that key employees may be denied reinstatement to the position they held or an equivalent position if the employer demonstrates that the reinstatement would cause "substantial and grievous economic injury" to its operations. A key employee is defined by FMLA as a salaried employee among the highest-paid 10 percent of employees at the worksite as defined previously. The law requires that the determination of which employees are the highest paid is calculated by taking the employee's year-to-date earnings (base salary, premium pay, incentive pay, and bonuses) and dividing the total earnings by the number of weeks worked. Whether an employee meets the definition of a key employee is to be determined at the time leave is requested. The employee must be advised of this status, either in person or by certified mail, as soon as possible. The employer must also explain why restoring the employee's job will cause substantial and grievous economic injury.

If the employee decides to take the leave after being informed of the implications of key employee status, the employee may still request reinstatement upon return to work. The employer must review the circumstances again and, if substantial and grievous economic injury would still occur under the circumstances at that time, notify the employee in writing, in person, or by certified mail that restoration is denied.

Key employees continue to be protected by the FMLA unless they notify their employer that they will not return to work, or until the employer denies reinstatement at the end of the leave.

Employee Notice Requirement

One FMLA requirement that caused difficulty for employers was an interpretation of previous rules that employees had up to two full days after an FMLA-qualifying event occurred to notify their employers of the need for FMLA leave. This made it difficult for employers to meet production schedules and ensure necessary coverage of critical work needs.

The 2008 final rules eliminated this language and clarified the timing of employee notices for two situations: foreseeable and unforeseeable leaves. In either case, employees must provide verbal notice so that the employer is aware of the need for FMLA-qualified leave, the expected timing and length of the leave, and information about the medical condition described in the upcoming section, "Reasons for FMLA Leave." Employees are not required to specifically request FMLA leave or mention FMLA for the first occurrence of a qualified event, but they are required to answer reasonable questions about the need for leave so that employers can determine whether the leave is qualified under the FMLA.

Foreseeable Leave

When the need for leave is foreseeable, FMLA rules require employees to notify their employers at least 30 days prior to the anticipated start date of leaves such as for the birth of a child, adoption, placement of a foster child, or planned medical treatment for a serious health condition. If the circumstances surrounding the planned leave change (such as a child is born earlier than expected), notice must be given as soon as practicable. This means as soon as both practical and possible, on the same day or the next business day. In these circumstances, a family member or someone else representing the employee may provide notice.

If the leave is foreseeable more than 30 days in advance and an employee fails to provide notice at least 30 days in advance without a reasonable excuse for delaying, the employer may delay FMLA coverage until 30 days after the date the employee provided notice.

If the need for FMLA leave is foreseeable less than 30 days in advance and the employee fails to notify the employer as soon as practicable, the employer may delay FMLA coverage of the leave. The amount of delay depends on the circumstances of each leave request and is evaluated on a case-by-case basis. Generally, the employer may delay the start of FMLA leave by the amount of delay in notice by the employee.

Unforeseeable Leave

At times, employees may be unable to notify their employers of the need for FMLA leave in advance. In these circumstances, the 2008 change to FMLA rules requires employees to provide notice in accordance with the usual and customary practice for calling in an absence unless unusual circumstances prevent the employee from doing so. An employee's representative, such as a spouse or another responsible person, may provide the notice if the employee is unable to do so. In emergencies when employees are unable to contact employers, they are permitted to supply the notice when they are able to use a telephone.

In order for employees to provide notice in accordance with the regulations, they must be aware of their responsibility to do so. The FMLA provides that proper posting of FMLA notice requirements by employers satisfies this requirement. Employers may waive FMLA notice requirements or their own rules on notice for employee leaves of absence at their discretion. In the absence of unusual circumstances, employers may choose not to waive their internal notice rules for employees who fail to follow those rules when requesting FMLA leaves, as long as those actions are consistent with practices regarding other leave requests. This is acceptable under the regulations as long as the actions do not discriminate against employees taking FMLA leave or violate the FMLA requirements described earlier.

Reasons for FMLA Leave

FMLA presents covered employers with a list of circumstances under which FMLA leave must be provided if requested by an eligible employee. Passage of the 2008 NDAA added care for military personnel and their families in some circumstances to existing circumstances that qualify for leave:

- **The Birth of a Child and Caring for the Infant:** FMLA leave is available to both fathers and mothers; however, if both parents work for the same employer, the combined total of the leave may not exceed the 12-week total. In addition, the leave must be completed within 12 months of the child's birth.

- **Placement of an Adopted or Foster Child with the Employee:** The same conditions that apply to the birth of a child apply here as well; in this case, the leave must be completed within 12 months of the child's placement.

- **To Provide Care for the Employee's Spouse, Son, Daughter, or Parent With a Serious Health Condition:** For purposes of FMLA leave, a spouse must be recognized as such by the state in which the employee resides.

A parent can be the biological parent of the employee or one who has legal standing *in loco parentis*, a Latin term that means "in place of the parent" and applies to those who care for a child on a daily basis. *In loco parentis* does not require either a biological or a legal relationship.

A son or daughter may be a biological child, adopted or foster child, stepchild, legal ward, or the child of someone acting *in loco parentis*. A child must also be younger than 18 years of age or, if older than 18, unable to care for themselves because of a physical or mental disability. Under the FMLA, persons who are *in loco parentis* include those with day-to-day responsibilities to care for or financially support a child. Courts have indicated some factors to be considered in determining *in loco parentis* status:

- The age of the child
- The degree to which the child is dependent on the person

- The amount of financial support, if any, provided
- The extent to which duties commonly associated with parenthood are exercised

In a 2015 amendment to the definition of spouse, eligible employees in legal same-sex marriages are able to take FMLA leave to care for their spouse or family member, regardless of where they live. The 2015 change means that eligible employees, regardless of where they live, will be able to take:

- FMLA leave to care for their lawfully married same-sex spouse with a serious health condition
- Qualifying exigency leave due to their lawfully married same-sex spouse's covered military service
- Military caregiver leave for their lawfully married same-sex spouse
- FMLA leave to care for their stepchild (child of employee's same-sex spouse) regardless of whether the *in loco parentis* requirement of providing day-to-day care or financial support for the child is met
- FMLA leave to care for a stepparent who is a same-sex spouse of the employee's parent, regardless of whether the stepparent ever stood *in loco parentis* to the employee

Employers may require those employees requesting FMLA leave to provide reasonable documentation to support the family relationship with the person for whom they will be providing care.

Employees may qualify for FMLA leave for their own serious health condition, defined as an illness, injury, impairment, or a physical or mental condition that requires the following:

- Inpatient care or subsequent treatment related to inpatient care
- Continuing treatment by a healthcare provider because of a period of incapacity of more than three consecutive calendar days. Incapacity refers to an inability to work, attend school, or perform other daily activities as a result of the condition.
- Incapacity because of pregnancy or prenatal care
- Treatment for a serious, chronic health condition

FMLA time is available to employees who need to provide care for a covered service member with a serious injury or illness sustained while on active duty. In this situation, family members are eligible to take up to 26 weeks of leave in a 12-month period.

Additionally, FMLA-protected time is available to eligible employees for qualifying exigencies for families of members of the National Guard and Reserves. Qualifying exigencies include the following:

- Short-notice deployments
- Military events and related activities
- Child care and school activities
- Financial and legal arrangements
- Counseling
- Rest and recuperation
- Post-deployment activities
- Leave for other related purposes when agreed to by the employee and employer

Medical Certification Process

FMLA regulations allow employers to require medical certifications to verify requests for any qualified leave as long as the employee is notified of the requirements. The DOL provides the following forms for this purpose:

- WH-380-E (for employee's serious health condition)
- WH-380-F (for family member's serious health condition)
- WH-384 (for exigency leave for military families)
- WH-385 (for serious injury or illness to covered service member)

Employers should request initial certification within five business days of the employee's leave request. Additional certifications may be required at a later date to verify that the leave continues to be appropriate. Employers must provide at least 15 calendar days for the employee to submit the certification but may allow more time.

FMLA regulations require employees to provide "complete and sufficient" certification for the employer. If the certification does not meet the complete and sufficient standard, employers may request, in writing, the additional information needed to comply. A certification is not considered complete and sufficient if one or more of the entries on the form are not completed or if the information is vague, ambiguous, or nonresponsive. Employees must be allowed a minimum of seven days to return the form with the additional information. When employers request the certification or additional information, they must advise employees of the consequences for failing to provide adequate certification of the serious illness or injury. If employees do not return the certification or they fail to provide a complete and sufficient certification upon notice of deficiencies in what was submitted, FMLA regulations allow employers to deny the FMLA leave.

Employers are not required to use the DOL forms but may only request information that is directly related to the serious health condition necessitating the leave, including the following:

- Contact information for the healthcare provider.
- Approximate date the serious health condition began and an estimate of how long it will last.
- A description of the medical facts about the health condition, such as symptoms, diagnosis, hospitalization, doctor visits, prescribed medication, treatment referrals, or continuing treatments.
- For employees with serious health conditions, the certification must establish the inability to perform essential job functions, describe work restrictions, and indicate the length of the inability to perform job functions.
- For family members with serious health conditions, the certification must establish that the patient requires care, how often, and how long care will be necessary.
- Information that confirms the medical necessity for reduced or intermittent leave with estimated dates and length of treatment.

FMLA leave certifications may be complicated when workers' compensation, ADA, or employer-provided paid leave programs are used concurrently. FMLA regulations address certifications under these circumstances as follows:

- When FMLA runs concurrently with a workers' compensation leave, employers are prohibited from collecting information for workers' compensation purposes that exceeds what is allowed for FMLA purposes.

- Employers may require additional information in accordance with a paid leave or disability program but must advise employees that the additional information is required in conjunction with the paid-leave plan, not with the FMLA leave. Whatever information is collected may be used to evaluate continuation of the FMLA leave. Failure to provide the additional information does not affect continuation of the FMLA leave.

- When FMLA leave runs concurrently with ADA, employers may follow ADA procedures for collecting information. This information may be used to evaluate the claim for FMLA-protected leave.

Employees are responsible for providing their own medical certifications. If they choose to do so, they may provide employers with an authorization or release to obtain information directly from their healthcare providers, but employers may not require them to do so.

Types of FMLA Leave

FMLA provides for three types of leave: continuous, reduced leave, and intermittent. A *continuous FMLA leave* is one in which the employee is absent from work for an extended period of time. A reduced *FMLA leave schedule* is one in which the employee's regular work schedule is reduced for a period of time. This can mean a reduction in the hours worked each day or in the number of days worked during the week. An *intermittent FMLA leave* is one in which the employee is absent from work for multiple periods of time because of a single illness or injury. When utilizing intermittent leave, employees must make an effort to schedule the leave to avoid disruption of regular business operations. In addition, the employer may assign an employee requesting intermittent leave to a different position with equivalent pay and benefits in order to meet the employee's needs.

Calculating the FMLA Year

FMLA provides four possible methods for employers to use in calculating the FMLA year, the 12-month period during which employees may use the 12 weeks of leave. An FMLA year can be calculated as any of the following:

- The calendar year
- Any fixed 12-month period (such as the fiscal year or anniversary date)
- The 12-month period beginning when an FMLA leave begins
- A rolling 12-month period that is measured back from the date FMLA is used by an employee

Although the most difficult to administer, for many employers the rolling 12-month period is best. Other methods are more open to abuse of FMLA by some employees, resulting in the use of 24 weeks of leave by bridging two 12-month periods, allowing an employee to be on continuous FMLA leave for 24 weeks.

If an employer does not have a stated policy, the FMLA year must be calculated in the way that provides the most benefit to employees. Whichever method is selected, it must be used to calculate FMLA for all employees. Employers that decide to change the way they calculate the FMLA year must provide written notice to employees 60 days in advance of the change and obtain written acknowledgment of the change.

Tracking Reduced and Intermittent FMLA Leave

Although keeping track of the amount of FMLA used for a continuous leave is fairly straightforward, ensuring that accurate records of reduced and intermittent FMLA records are maintained can be a bit more difficult. In either case, only the amount of leave used may be deducted from the 12 weeks available to the employee. For example, an employee whose regular work schedule of 40 hours per week is reduced to 20 hours per week would be charged one-half week FMLA leave for each week that the employee works the reduced schedule.

For intermittent leave, employers may charge for leave in increments of not less than one hour. Employees should provide at least two days' notice of the need to utilize the intermittent leave whenever possible.

Ending FMLA Leave

FMLA leave ends when the employee has used the full 12 weeks of leave, the serious illness of the employee or family member ends, or, in some cases, when the family member or the employee dies. When one of these three circumstances occurs (other than the employee's own death), the employee may return to the same or an equivalent position with no loss of benefits. If the employee wants to continue the leave at that point, the company is under no obligation to grant it, unless there is a company policy in place to provide a longer leave.

Employers may require employees returning from FMLA leaves to provide a fitness-for-duty certification from their healthcare providers, attesting to their ability to return to work. If they choose to do so, employers may require the fitness-for-duty report to specify the employee's ability to perform the essential functions of the job. Employers that choose this type of certification must provide a job description or list of the employee's essential job functions with the designation notice provided to the employee. Similarly to medical certifications, employers may contact healthcare providers to clarify and authenticate information contained in the fitness-for-duty certificate, but they may not request information unrelated to the serious health condition that is the reason for the FMLA leave. Employees may be required to provide the fitness-for-duty certification prior to returning to work. Employees who neither provide the certificate nor request an extension of the leave are no longer entitled to reinstatement.

FMLA Implications for Employers

HR professionals need to ensure that supervisors and managers throughout their organizations are aware of the requirements for FMLA leaves and the consequences for noncompliance. FMLA requirements are complex and confusing, particularly when used in conjunction with workers' compensation or the ADA, and managers of other functional areas may not be aware of their obligations for FMLA requests.

There are some things employers can do to ensure that they comply with FMLA requirements. To start, review current leave practices to ensure that they comply with FMLA requirements and any state laws with more stringent requirements. FMLA leave policies should be included in the employee handbook; new hires must be advised of their rights to take leave under the act. It is important for HR professionals to work with supervisors and managers throughout the organization to ensure that they understand the implications for situations that may be subject to FMLA regulations and encourage them to talk to HR about potential FMLA leave situations. HR needs to take an active role in educating the management team about the interaction of FMLA, ADA, and workers' compensation requirements. Before an FMLA situation occurs, a documentation procedure and policy should be developed, and HR should take an active role in ensuring that all leaves comply with established procedures to avoid possible claims of discriminatory practices. When workers' compensation and FMLA leaves occur simultaneously, make sure to advise the employee that the leaves run concurrently.

Foreign Corrupt Practices Act of 1977

The Foreign Corrupt Practices Act (FCPA) of 1977 made it unlawful for certain classes of people and entities to make payments to foreign government officials to assist in obtaining or retaining business. Made up of antibribery provisions, the FCPA prohibits people and entities from making any offer, payment, promise to pay, or authorization of the payment of money or anything of value to any person, while knowing that all or a portion of such money or thing of value will be offered, given or promised, directly or indirectly, to a foreign official to influence the foreign official in their official capacity, induce the foreign official to do or omit to do an act in violation of their lawful duty, or to secure any improper advantage in order to assist in obtaining or retaining business for or with, or directing business to, any person.

In 1988, amendments applied the antibribery provisions to foreign persons, prohibiting them from engaging in any of these activities within the United States.

The FCPA requires companies whose securities are listed in the United States to keep accurate records and maintain accounting controls to ensure that the records accurately and fairly represent corporate financial transactions.

Genetic Information Nondiscrimination Act of 2008 (GINA)

When research into the use of human genomic information made it possible to identify genetic predisposition to particular diseases, many people became uncomfortable with the idea of information so personal being made available to insurance companies or employers that could use it for discriminatory purposes. For more than 10 years, Congress worked on legislation that would prevent that from happening. President George W. Bush signed the resulting legislation, the Genetic Information Nondiscrimination Act (GINA), into law in May 2008.

GINA prohibits employers from unlawfully discriminating against employees or their family members in any of the terms or conditions of employment included in Title VII. The Act defines genetic information as the results of genetic tests for employees and their family members or as information about genetic diseases or disorders revealed through genetic testing.

The act makes it unlawful for employers to request, require, or purchase genetic information but does not penalize them for inadvertently obtaining the information. GINA allows employers to obtain the information for wellness or health programs they offer when the employee authorizes access to the information in writing. In those cases, the information obtained through genetic testing may be provided only to healthcare professionals or board-certified genetic counselors providing services to employees. This information may be provided to employers only in aggregate form that does not identify specific employees.

Employers may request the information as required by the Family and Medical Leave Act (FMLA) or similar state laws but may use it only as required by those laws. Employers can also use genetic information if federal or state laws require genetic monitoring of biological effects from toxic substances in the workplace, but only if the employee receives written notice and provides informed, written consent to the monitoring and the monitoring complies with federal and state laws. Any test results may be provided to employers only in aggregate form without identifying individual information.

The DOL issued a request for comments on the implementation of GINA prior to beginning the rule-making process. The submission period ended in December 2008, and the DOL began evaluating regulatory needs with the Department of Health and Human Services and the Treasury Department since aspects of the law impact agencies in those departments as well.

Glass Ceiling Act of 1991

In 1991, Senator Robert Dole introduced legislation known as the Glass Ceiling Act, which was eventually signed into law as an amendment to Title II of the Civil Rights Act of 1991. An article in the *Wall Street Journal* in 1986 had coined the term *glass ceiling* to describe the limitations faced by women and minorities when it came to advancing into the senior ranks of corporate management. The act established a commission whose purpose was to determine whether a glass ceiling existed and, if it did, to identify the barriers to placing more women and minorities in senior management positions. The commission found that although CEOs understood the need to include women and minorities in the ranks of senior management, this belief was not shared at all levels in the organization. The study went on to identify three barriers that prevented women and minorities from advancing to senior levels:

Societal Barriers   Societal barriers result from limited access to educational opportunities and biases related to gender, race, and ethnicity.

Internal Structural Barriers   Internal structural barriers encompass a wide range of corporate practices and shortcomings over which management has some control, including outreach and recruiting programs that do not try to find qualified women and minorities, as well as organizational cultures that exclude women and minorities from participation in activities that will lead to advancement, such as mentoring, management training, or career development assignments.

Governmental Barriers   Governmental barriers are related to inconsistent enforcement of equal opportunity legislation and poor collection and dissemination of statistics that illustrate the problem.

The commission also studied organizations that have successfully integrated glass ceiling initiatives into their operations and found some common traits that can be adopted by other organizations. Successful initiatives begin with full support of the CEO, who ensures that the initiative becomes part of strategic planning in the organization and holds management accountable for achieving goals by tracking and reporting on progress. These comprehensive programs do not exclude white men but do include a diverse workforce population. Organizations implementing programs to increase diversity benefit from improved productivity and bottom-line results for shareholders.

As a result of the study, the EEOC conducts glass ceiling audits to monitor the progress that organizations make toward including women and minorities at all levels.

Illegal Immigration Reform and Immigrant Responsibility Act of 1996 (IIRIRA)

The Illegal Immigration Reform and Immigrant Responsibility Act of 1996 reduced the number and types of documents allowable to prove identity, employment eligibility, or both in the hiring process and established pilot programs for verification of employment eligibility. It also allowed for sanctions against employers who failed to comply with the hiring requirements.

Immigration Reform and Control Act of 1986 (IRCA)

The Immigration Reform and Control Act (IRCA) was enacted in 1986 to address illegal immigration into the United States. The law applied to businesses with four or more employees and made it illegal to knowingly hire or continue to employ individuals who were not legally authorized to work in the United States. Unfair immigration-related employment practices were defined as discrimination on the basis of national origin or citizenship status.

Employers were required to complete Form I-9 for all new hires within the first three days of employment. Employers were also required to review documents provided by the employee that establish identity, employment authorization, or both from lists of acceptable documents on the Form I-9. IRCA requires employers to maintain I-9 files for three years from the date of hire or one year after the date of termination, whichever is later, and allows, but does not require, employers to copy documents presented for employment eligibility for purposes of complying with these requirements. The act also provides that employers complying in good faith with these requirements have an affirmative defense to inadvertently hiring an unauthorized alien. Substantial fines for violations of both the hiring and record-keeping requirements were provided in the law.

In addition to fines, employers that knowingly hire unauthorized workers are subject to both civil and criminal penalties for the following violations:

- Civil Violations

    - Knowingly hired, or to have knowingly recruited or referred for a fee, an unauthorized noncitizen for employment in the United States or to have knowingly continued to employ an unauthorized noncitizen in the United States

    - Failing to comply with Form I-9 employment verification requirements

    - Committing or participating in document fraud for satisfying a requirement or benefit of the employment verification process or the INA

    - Committing document abuse

    - Unlawful discrimination against an employment-authorized individual in hiring, firing, or recruitment or referral for a fee

    - Failing to notify DHS of a Final Nonconfirmation (FNC) of an employee's employment eligibility

    - Requiring an individual to post a bond or security or to pay an amount or otherwise to provide financial guarantee or indemnity against any potential liability arising under the employment verification requirements

- Criminal Violations

  - Engaging in a pattern or practice of hiring, recruiting or referring for a fee unauthorized noncitizens

According to the USCIS, employers "may retain Form I-9 using either a paper or electronic system, or a combination of both . . ." Any electronic system you use to generate Form I-9 or retain completed Forms I-9 must include:

- Reasonable controls to ensure the system's integrity, accuracy, and reliability

- Reasonable controls designed to prevent and detect the unauthorized or accidental creation of, addition to, alteration of, deletion of, or deterioration of an electronically completed or stored Form I-9, including the electronic signature, if used

- An inspection and quality assurance program that regularly evaluates the system and includes periodic checks of electronically stored Form I-9, including the electronic signature, if used

- An indexing system that allows users to identify and retrieve records maintained in the system

- The ability to reproduce legible and readable paper copies

Form I-9 are periodically updated, and employers are responsible for using the most current version. Stay up-to-date by visiting www.uscis.gov/i-9.

E-Verify

E-Verify is a free service offered through the USCIS. It is a tool that helps employers comply with IRCA's requirement that employers must verify the identity and employment eligibility of new employees. Accessed through the Internet, the employer inputs basic information gleaned from the Form I-9 and receives a nearly instant "employment authorized" or "tentative nonconfirmation" (TNC) reply from the website. The employer then prints the results. A TNC result will give the employee more information about the mismatch and a statement of their rights and responsibilities under the law. It is important to note that an employer may not terminate an employee for the initial TNC; it is only when a final nonconfirmation is received that an employer may terminate under E-Verify.

To get started in the program, an employer must first enroll the company, distribute a memorandum of understanding (MOU), and commit to using E-Verify for every new employee at the affected hiring site. Under federal law, the use of E-Verify may be designated to certain locations, although this may be restricted under some state laws.

Amendment to IRCA: Immigration Act of 1990

The Immigration Act of 1990 made several changes to IRCA, including adding the requirement that a prevailing wage be paid to H-1B immigrants to ensure that U.S. citizens did not lose jobs to lower-paid immigrant workers. The act also restricted to 65,000 annually the number of immigrants (with an additional 20,000 for applicants with an advanced degree) allowed under the H-1B category and created additional categories for employment visas, as shown in Table C.4.

In 2023, the United States increased the number of available H-2B visas in part to address the shortage of seasonal workers in industries such as hospitality and tourism.

For more information, visit the "Working in the US page" found at www.uscis.gov/working-united-states/working-us.

TABLE C.4 Employment Visas

Visa	Classification
	Visas for temporary workers
H-1B	Specialty occupations, DOD workers, fashion models
H-1C	Nurses going to work for up to three years in health professional shortage areas
H-2A	Temporary agricultural workers
H-2B	Temporary workers: skilled and unskilled, nonagricultural
H-3	Trainees
J-1	Visas for exchange visitors
	Visas for intracompany transfers
L-1A	Executive, managerial
L-1B	Specialized knowledge
L-2	Spouse or child of L-1
	Visas for workers with extraordinary abilities
O-1	Extraordinary ability in sciences, arts, education, business, or athletics
	Visas for athletes and entertainers
P-1	Individual or team athletes
P-1	Entertainment groups
P-2	Artists and entertainers in reciprocal exchange programs
P-3	Artists and entertainers in culturally unique programs
	Visas for religious workers
R-1	Religious workers
	Visas for NAFTA workers
TN	Trade visas for Canadians and Mexicans

International Labour Organization (ILO)

The *International Labour Organization (ILO)* was established in 1919 by the Treaty of Versailles to address working conditions and living standards in all countries. It has a tripartite structure consisting of member states' government, employers, and workers. The ILO currently has 185 member countries that agree to the labor standard development outcomes of *ILO conventions* and recommendations. Conventions are legally binding directives, whereas recommendations are nonbinding guidelines.

In 2000, the ILO adopted the Declaration of Fundamental Principles and Rights at Work, which includes the commitment by businesses to support, respect, and protect international human rights; the recognition of worker rights to organize and collectively bargain; to abolish child labor; and to eliminate unlawful discrimination.

International Trade Organizations

For many reasons, some countries have found it to be mutually beneficial to enter into trade agreements. These agreements clarify expectations and establish rules that impact tariffs, employment visas, and employee rights between blocs of trading countries. Though not without controversy, the most prominent of these agreements are reviewed next.

European Union (EU)

The European Union is the world's largest international trading bloc, formed of a common market around which tariffs are reduced and free trade is established. It is designed to clarify the rules of trade, people movement (immigration), and social rights between member countries. Examples include standardized taxes and the rights of most service providers to practice in all member countries. Nineteen of the member countries use the euro as their form of currency.

The EU has both social and political influence over HR practices. The Social Charter of the EU was first adopted in 1989, establishing the 12 fundamental rights of workers. Since their passage, the EU has been working to translate the rights into specific directives to be observed by member countries. Various treaties have been adopted to reinforce the fundamental rights, including employee rights to data protection, the rights of asylum, equality under the law, nondiscriminatory treatment, protection against unfair dismissal, and access to social security. These directives in some form or another apply to all organizations, both local and foreign owned.

The EU currently has 27 member states: Austria, Belgium, Bulgaria, Croatia, Cyprus, Czech Republic, Denmark, Estonia, Finland, France, Germany, Greece, Hungary, Ireland, Italy, Latvia, Lithuania, Luxembourg, Malta, Netherlands, Poland, Portugal, Romania, Slovakia, Slovenia, Spain, and Sweden.

The Schengen area is the geographic locations where legal residents may move freely between member countries without special visas. Ireland and the United Kingdom have declined to participate.

Mercosur

Mercosur is a Southern trading bloc made up of five countries: Argentina, Brazil, Paraguay, Uruguay, and Bolivia. Venezuela was suspended in 2016 for failing to incorporate trade and human rights elements into its laws; also in 2016, Bolivia was in the final stages of becoming a member. Chile, Colombia, Ecuador, Guyana, Peru, and Suriname are considered associate members. Founded in 1991, Mercosur aims to form a common market, allowing for a common external tariff and free movement of goods, services, and people across member nations. A Common Market Council makes decisions, and a Trade Commission deals with tariffs and foreign affairs. The Economic and Social Consultative Forum was established in 1994 to serve in an advisory role to the Trade Commission about labor and social issues. One major goal of Mercosur is to establish a trade agreement with the European Union.

Mine Safety and Health Act of 1977 (MSHA)

The Mine Safety and Health Act of 1977 established the Mine Safety and Health Administration (MSHA) to ensure the safety of workers in coal and other mines. The act establishes mandatory safety and health standards for mine operators and monitors operations throughout the United States. MSHA has developed a comprehensive website (www.msha.gov) that is a resource for miners and mine operators, providing access to information on prevention of accidents, information on year-to-date fatalities, and guidance on specific mine hazards. The site also contains a link to the complete text of the act.

Occupational Safety and Health Act of 1970 (OSHA)

For more than 100 years beginning in 1867, sporadic legislation was enacted by different states and the federal government to address specific safety concerns, usually in regard to mine safety or factory conditions, but there was no comprehensive legislation requiring employers to protect workers from injury or illness. That changed with the Occupational Safety and Health Act of 1970 (the OSH Act), a comprehensive piece of federal legislation that continues to have an impact on employers in virtually every company in America.

Although normally this law is referred to as OSHA, this appendix talks at length about both the act and the agency that is known by the same initials. For the sake of clarity, the law is referred to as the OSH Act throughout the discussion.

In the years prior to passage of the OSH Act, there was a growing recognition that employers were largely unwilling to take preventive steps to reduce the occurrence of injuries, illnesses, and fatalities in the workplace. On December 6, 1907, a total of 362 miners died in an explosion at the Monongah coal mine in West Virginia—the worst mining disaster in American history. In that year alone, a total of 3,242 coal miners lost their lives. As a result, in 1910 Congress established the Bureau of Mines to investigate mining accidents.

There was a long period of time in the United States when it was cheaper for employers to fight lawsuits filed on behalf of workers killed or injured on the job than it was to implement safety programs. Because the courts rarely held employers accountable for worker injuries, many chose this approach. Employer attitudes in this regard didn't change until the shortage of skilled workers during World War II gave employees plentiful options for places to work—and they opted to work for employers that provided safe environments over those that didn't.

The tragic nature of large accidents in the railroad and mining industries captured public attention and created pressure on the federal government to take action. This led Congress to enact legislation requiring safety improvements in the coal mining and railroad industries, but these measures were specifically targeted to those industries. Little attention was paid to equally dangerous workplace safety and illness issues that didn't produce the spectacular accidents prevalent in mines or on railroads. In the late 1960s, some 14,000 American workers lost their lives each year due to injuries or illnesses suffered while on the job. The federal government had been working on solutions but was mired in bureaucratic turf battles over which agency should have control of the process. The Department of Health, Education, and Welfare wanted legislation that applied only to federal contractors, and the DOL, spurred by Secretary W. Willard Wirtz's personal interest in the subject, wanted to protect *all* American workers. After several years of this infighting, the proposal by the DOL was sent to the Congress and enacted as the Occupational Safety and Health Act of 1970. A key component of this legislation was the creation of the Occupational Safety and Health Administration (OSHA), which now sets safety standards for all industries. OSHA enforces those standards with the use of fines and, in the case of criminal actions, can call on the Department of Justice to file charges against offenders.

The intent of Congress, as stated in the preamble to the OSH Act, is to ensure safe and healthful working conditions for American workers. To accomplish this purpose, the act establishes three simple duties:

- Employers must provide every employee with a place to work that is "free from recognized hazards that are causing or are likely to cause death or serious physical harm."

- Employers must comply with all safety and health standards disseminated in accordance with the OSH Act.

- Employees are required to comply with occupational safety and health standards, rules, and regulations that have an impact on their individual actions and behavior.

As mentioned previously, the OSH Act created OSHA and gave it the authority to develop and enforce mandatory standards applicable to all businesses engaged in interstate commerce. The definition of interstate commerce is sufficiently broad to cover most businesses, except only those sole proprietors without employees, family farms employing only family members, and mining operations, which are covered by the Mine Safety and Health Act (discussed earlier in this appendix). The act encouraged OSHA to work with industry associations and safety committees to build upon standards already developed by specific industries, and it authorized enforcement action to ensure that employers comply with the standards. OSHA was charged with developing reporting procedures to track trends in workplace safety and health so that the development of preventive measures would be an ongoing process that changed with the development of new processes and technologies.

The OSH Act also created the National Institute of Occupational Safety and Health (NIOSH) as part of the Department of Health and Human Services. NIOSH is charged with researching and evaluating workplace hazards and recommending ways to reduce the effect of those hazards on workers. NIOSH also supports education and training in the field of occupational safety and health by developing and providing educational materials and training aids and sponsoring conferences on workplace safety and health issues.

In 2011, OSHA celebrated 40 years in the business of protecting American workers. Its focus in the coming years includes increasing enforcement of the standards through additional hiring, and making sure vulnerable workers, such as those who speak English as a second language, are heard. How this translates into the workforce remains to be seen, but we can infer from the statements several key points, discussed next.

More Inspections

With OSHA pushing for an increased budget, it stands to reason that the hiring of additional enforcement officers means more inspections and fines.

Emphasis on Safety Communication

The 2010 National Action Summit for Latino Worker Health and Safety helped to launch OSHA's Diverse Workforce Limited Proficiency Outreach program, designed to "enhance (vulnerable) workers' knowledge of their workplace rights and improve their ability to exercise those rights." Conducting training and providing material in a language all workers can understand is a logical outcome from this focus.

Reporting of Injuries

In 2016, OSHA issued a new rule prohibiting employers from discouraging workers from reporting an injury or illness, including through safety-incentive programs rewarding employees for no injuries being reported. This rule requires employers to inform employees of their right to report work-related injuries and illnesses free from retaliation, which can be satisfied by posting the already required OSHA workplace poster. The rule also clarifies the existing implicit requirement that an employer's procedure for reporting work-related injuries and illnesses must be reasonable and not deter or discourage employees from reporting, and it incorporates the existing statutory prohibition on retaliating against employees for reporting work-related injuries or illnesses. These provisions became effective.

Finally, the OSH Act encourages the states to take the lead in developing and enforcing safety and health programs for businesses within their jurisdictions by providing grants to help states identify specific issues and develop programs for enforcement and prevention.

Employer Responsibilities

The OSH Act has three requirements, two of which pertain to employers. Not only must employers provide a workplace that is safe and healthful for employees, but they must also comply with established standards. OSHA has established other requirements for employers as required by the law:

- Employers are expected to take steps to minimize or reduce hazards, and ensure that employees have and use safe tools, equipment, and personal protective equipment (PPE) that are properly maintained.

- Employers are responsible for informing all employees about OSHA, posting the OSHA poster in a prominent location, and making employees aware of the standards that apply in the worksite. If employees request a copy of a standard, the employer must provide it to them.

- Appropriate warning signs that conform to the OSHA standards for color coding, posting, or labels must be posted where needed to make employees aware of potential hazards.

- Compliance with OSHA standards also means employers must educate employees about safe operating procedures and train them to follow the procedures.

- Businesses with 11 or more employees must maintain records of all workplace injuries and illnesses and post them on Form 300A from February 1 through April 30 each year.

- Within eight hours of a fatal accident or one resulting in hospitalization for three or more employees, a report must be filed with the nearest OSHA office.

- An accident report log must be made available to employees, former employees, or employee representatives when reasonably requested.

- When employees report unsafe conditions to OSHA, the employer may not retaliate or discriminate against them.

Under an OSHA rule effective January 1, 2017, certain employers must electronically submit injury and illness data that they are already required to record on their on-site OSHA Injury and Illness forms. Analysis of this data will be a factor used by OSHA to determine how to allocate its enforcement and compliance resources. Some of the data will also be posted to the OSHA website.

The reporting requirements were phased in over two years:

■ Establishments with 250 or more employees in industries covered by the recordkeeping regulation had to submit information from their 2016 Form 300A by July 1, 2017. These same employers were required to submit information from all 2017 forms (300, 300A, and 301) by July 1, 2018. Beginning in 2019 and every year thereafter, the information must be submitted by March 2. These employers are required to submit OSHA Form 301, where prior to this new rule, they could submit either an OSHA Form 301 or other equivalent documentation such as workers' compensation records.

■ Establishments with 20 to 249 employees in certain high-risk industries had to submit information from their 2016 Form 300A by July 1, 2017 and their 2017 Form 300A by July 1, 2018. Beginning in 2019 and every year thereafter, the information must be submitted by March 2. A list of industries covered by this provision can be found at www.osha.gov/record keeping/NAICScodesforelectronicsubmission.html.

OSHA State Plan states must adopt requirements that are substantially identical to the requirements in this final rule within six months after publication of this final rule.

Employer Rights

Employers have some rights as well, including the right to seek advice and consultation from OSHA and to be active in industry activities involved in health and safety issues. Employers may also participate in the OSHA Standard Advisory Committee process in writing or by giving testimony at hearings. Finally, employers may contact NIOSH for information about substances used in work processes to determine whether they are toxic.

At times, employers may be unable to comply with OSHA standards because of the nature of specific operations. When this happens, they may apply to OSHA for temporary or permanent waivers to the standards along with proof that the protections developed by the organization meet or exceed those of the OSHA standards.

Employee Rights and Responsibilities

When the OSH Act was passed in 1970, employees were granted the basic right to a workplace with safe and healthful working conditions. The act intended to encourage employers and employees to collaborate in reducing workplace hazards. Employees have the responsibility to comply with all OSHA standards and with the safety and health procedures implemented by their employers. The act gave employees the specific rights to do the following:

■ Seek safety and health on the job without fear of punishment.

■ Know what hazards exist on the job by reviewing the OSHA standards, rules, and regulations that the employer has available at the workplace.

■ Be provided with the hazard-communication plan containing information about hazards in the workplace and preventive measures employees should take to avoid illness or injury, and to be trained in those measures.

- Access the exposure and medical records employers are required to keep relative to safety and health issues.

- Request an OSHA inspection, speak privately with the inspector, accompany the inspector during the inspection, and respond to the inspector's questions during the inspection.

- Observe steps taken by the employer to monitor and measure hazardous materials in the workplace, and access records resulting from those steps.

- Request information from NIOSH regarding the potential toxic effects of substances used in the workplace.

- File a complaint about workplace safety or health hazards with OSHA and remain anonymous to the employer.

OSHA Enforcement

OSHA's success is the result of strong enforcement of the standards it has developed. As demonstrated in the 19th and 20th centuries, without the threat of financial penalty, some business owners would choose to ignore injury- and illness-prevention requirements. Construction and general industry continue to be the sources of the most frequently cited OSHA standards' violations through 2018. That being the case, OSHA established fines and penalties that can be assessed against businesses when violations occur. Table C.5 describes the violation levels and associated penalties for noncompliance that are in effect as of January 2024. Students should note that OSHA plans to update these penalties every January to adjust for inflation.

OSHA Recordkeeping Requirements

OSHA requires employers to record health and safety incidents that occur each year and to document steps they take to comply with regulations. Records of specific injuries and illnesses are compiled, allowing OSHA and NIOSH to identify emerging hazards for research and, if warranted, create new standards designed to reduce the possibility of similar injury or illness in the future. These records include up-to-date files for exposures to hazardous substances and related medical records, records of safety training meetings, and OSHA logs that record work-related injuries and illnesses.

TABLE C.5   Categories of Penalties for OSHA Violations

Violation	Description	Fine
Willful or repeated	Evidence exists of an intentional violation of the OSH Act or "plain indifference" to its requirements; OSHA previously issued citations for substantially similar conditions.	Up to $161,323 per violation
Serious	Hazards with substantial probability of death or serious physical harm exist.	Up to $16,131 per violation

(Continued)

TABLE C.5 Categories of Penalties for OSHA Violations (*Continued*)

Violation	Description	Fine
Other than serious and posting requirements	An existing hazard could have a direct and immediate effect on the safety and health of employees.	Up to $16,131 per violation
Failure to abate	The employer failed to abate a prior violation.	Up to $16,131 per day beyond the abatement date

Source: Adapted from https://www.osha.gov/penalties

As of January 1, 2002, OSHA revised the requirements for maintaining records of workplace injuries and illnesses in order to collect better information for use in prevention activities, simplify the information collection process, and make use of advances in technology. Three new forms were developed:

- OSHA Form 300, Log of Work-Related Injuries and Illnesses
- OSHA Form 300A, Summary of Work-Related Injuries and Illnesses
- OSHA Form 301, Injury and Illness Incident Report

Completion of the forms doesn't constitute proof of fault on the part of either the employer or the employee and doesn't indicate that any OSHA violations have occurred. Recording an injury or illness on the OSHA forms also doesn't mean that an employee is eligible for workers' compensation benefits.

The following paragraphs cover the basic requirements for OSHA recordkeeping, including who should file OSHA reports, which employers are exempt from filing, and what injuries are considered work-related.

Who Must Complete and File OSHA Forms?

All employers with 11 or more employees are required to complete and file the OSHA forms just discussed.

Are There Any Exemptions?

Employers with 10 or fewer employees aren't required to file the forms. In addition, OSHA has identified industries with low injury and illness rates and exempted them from filing reports. These include the retail, service, finance, insurance, and real estate industries. Unless OSHA has notified a business in writing that reports must be filed, the business is exempt from the requirement.

What Must Be Recorded?

OSHA regulations specify which employees are covered for reporting purposes. Injury or illness to any employee on the employer's payroll must be recorded, regardless of how the employee is classified: full-time or part-time, regular or temporary, hourly or salary, seasonal, and so on.

Injuries to employees of temp agencies, if under the employer's direct supervision on a daily basis, must also be recorded. The owners and partners in sole proprietorships and partnerships aren't considered employees for OSHA reporting purposes.

*Privacy concern case*s are new protections developed by OSHA to protect employee privacy by substituting a case number for the employee name on the OSHA Form 300 log. Cases where this is appropriate include injury or illness that involved an intimate body part or resulted from a sexual assault; HIV infection, hepatitis, or tuberculosis; needle-stick injuries involving contaminated needles; and other illnesses when employees request that their names not be included on the log.

An injury or illness is generally considered to be work-related if it occurred in the workplace or while performing work-related duties off-site. The basic OSHA requirement records any work-related injury or illness that causes death, days away from work, restricted or limited duty, medical treatment beyond first aid, or loss of consciousness. Diagnosis of an injury or illness by a physician or other healthcare professional, even if it doesn't result in one of the circumstances listed, must also be reported.

Once the employer has determined that the injury or illness is work-related, the employer must determine whether this is a new case or a continuation of a previously recorded case. To a certain extent, this decision is left to the employer's common sense and best judgment. OSHA considers a new case to have occurred when an employee hasn't had a previous injury or illness that is the same as the current occurrence or when the employee has recovered completely from a previous injury or illness of the same type.

Annual Summary

At the end of each year, employers must review the OSHA Form 300 log and summarize the entries on Form 300A, which must then be certified by a company executive as correct and complete and posted, as previously mentioned, in February of the following year.

Retention

The OSHA Form 300 log and annual summary, privacy case list, and Form 301 Incident Report forms must be retained for five years following the end of the calendar year they cover.

Employee Involvement

Employers are required to provide employees and employee representatives, former employees, or a personal representative of an employee with information on how to properly report an injury or illness, and they're also required to allow employees or their representatives limited access to the records of injury and illness.

The OSHA Form 300 log must be provided to these requestors by the end of the following business day.

The OSHA Form 301 Incident Report must be provided by the end of the next business day when the employee who is the subject of the report requests a copy. When an employee representative requests copies, they must be provided within seven calendar days, and all information except that contained in the "Tell Us About the Case" section must be removed.

OSHA Assistance

OSHA provides many sources for employers and employees to obtain information about workplace health and safety issues. Chief among these is an extensive website (www.osha.gov) that provides access to the laws, regulations, and standards enforced by OSHA as well as general information on prevention. In addition to the website, OSHA publishes a number of pamphlets, brochures, and training materials that are available to employers. While OSHA exists to protect workers' safety rights, there are services such as consultation and voluntary participation programs that exist specifically to aid employers in complying with the standards.

OSHA Consultants

Educating employers and employees about workplace health and safety issues is key to preventing injuries and illnesses in the workplace. OSHA provides training programs for consultants who work with business owners in establishing effective health and safety programs. These free consultation services give employers an opportunity to learn which of the standards apply in their worksite, involve employees in the safety process, and correct possible violations without a citation and penalty. Once the consultant becomes involved, the employer must abate any violations, or the consultant will refer the violation to an OSHA inspector.

The *Safety and Health Achievement Recognition Program (SHARP)* recognizes small, high-hazard employers that have requested a comprehensive OSHA consultation, corrected any violations, and developed an ongoing safety management program. To participate in the program, the business must agree to ask for additional consultations if work processes change.

Partnerships and Voluntary Programs

The *Strategic Partnership Program* is a means for businesses and employees to participate in solving health and safety problems with OSHA. Partnerships currently exist in 15 industries, including construction, food processing, logging, and healthcare, to develop solutions specific to their businesses.

The *OSHA Alliance Program* provides a vehicle for collaboration with employer organizations interested in promoting workplace health and safety issues. The program is open to trade and professional organizations, businesses, labor organizations, educational institutions, and government agencies, among others.

The *Voluntary Protection Program (VPP)* is open to employers with tough, well-established safety programs. VPP participants must meet OSHA criteria for the program and, having done so, are removed from routine scheduled inspection lists. The program serves to motivate employees to work more safely, reducing workers' compensation costs, and to encourage employers to make further improvements to safety programs. Acceptance into the VPP is an official recognition of exemplary occupational safety and health practices.

Health and Safety Inspections

The OSH Act authorizes both OSHA and NIOSH to investigate health or safety hazards in the workplace. The majority of OSHA inspections are focused on industries with higher hazard risks based on injury and illness rates. Some inspections occur at the request of an employer or employee in a specific organization. Less than 1 percent of OSHA inspections occur as part of the agency's Enhanced Enforcement Program that monitors employers with a history of repeat or willful violations.

NIOSH inspections, known as *health hazard evaluations*, always occur in response to the request of an employer, an employee, or a government agency.

No matter which agency conducts an investigation, employees who request or participate in them are protected by the OSH Act from retaliation or adverse employment actions.

OSHA Inspections

Most OSHA inspections are conducted without notice by a compliance safety and health officer (CSHO) who has been trained on OSHA standards and how to recognize safety and health hazards in the workplace. OSHA has established a hierarchy of situations to give priority to inspection of the most dangerous workplace environments.

During an inspection, OSHA follows a distinct procedure. In advance of the inspection, the CSHO prepares by reviewing records related to any previous incidents, inspections, or employee complaints. The inspector also determines what, if any, special testing equipment will be necessary for the inspection. Upon the inspector's arrival at the worksite, the inspection commences with an opening conference, proceeds to a workplace tour, and ends with a closing conference:

1. The CSHO arrives at the worksite and presents credentials. If the credentials aren't presented, the employer should insist on seeing them before the inspection begins. It's critical that any employee who may be the first person approached at the worksite be instructed as to who should be contacted when a CSHO arrives. Employers have the right to require the inspector to have a security clearance before entering secure areas. Any observation of trade secrets during the inspection remains confidential; CSHOs who breach this confidentiality are subject to fines and imprisonment.

2. The CSHO holds an *opening conference* during which the inspector explains why the site was selected, the purpose of the visit, and the scope of the inspection, and discusses the standards that apply to the worksite. The CSHO requests an employee representative to accompany the CSHO on the inspection along with the management representative. If no employee accompanies the inspector on the tour, the CSHO will talk to as many employees as necessary to understand the safety and health issues in the workplace.

3. The next step is a tour of the facilities. During the tour, the inspector determines what route to take, where to look, and which employees to talk to. During this part of the inspection, the CSHO may talk privately to employees, taking care to minimize disruptions to work processes. Activities that can occur during an inspection include the following:

   - Reviewing the safety and health program

   - Examining records, including OSHA logs, records of employee exposure to toxic substances, and medical records

   - Ensuring that the OSHA workplace poster is prominently displayed

   - Evaluating compliance with OSHA standards specific to the worksite

   - Pointing out unsafe working conditions to the employer and suggesting possible remedial actions

4. The inspector holds a *closing conference* where the inspector, the employer, and, if requested, the employee representative discuss the observations made and corrective actions that must be taken. At this time the employer may produce records to assist in resolving any corrective actions to be taken. The CSHO discusses any possible citations or penalties that may be issued, and the OSHA area director makes the final determination based on the inspector's report.

Should the OSHA area director determine that citations are necessary to ensure employer compliance with OSHA, the director will issue the citations and determine the penalties to be assessed according to established guidelines that consider various factors, including the size of the company. The OSHA area director also determines the seriousness of the danger(s), how many employees would be impacted, and good-faith efforts on the part of the employer to comply with the standards, among others.

During the course of an OSHA inspection, an employer may raise an affirmative defense to any violations observed by the inspector. Possible affirmative defenses include the following:

■ It is an isolated case caused by unpreventable employee misconduct. This defense may apply when the employer has established, communicated, and enforced adequate work rules that were ignored by the employee.

■ Compliance is impossible based on the nature of the employer's work, and there are no viable alternative means of protection.

■ Compliance with the standard would cause a greater hazard to employees, and there are no alternative means of protection.

The employer has the burden to prove that an affirmative defense exists. If it is successfully proven, the OSHA area director may decide that a citation and penalty aren't warranted.

Employers have specific responsibilities and rights during and after the inspection:

■ Employers are required to cooperate with the CSHO by providing records and documents requested during the inspection and by allowing employees or their representatives to accompany the inspector on the worksite tour.

■ Should a citation be issued during the inspection, the employer must post it at or near the worksite involved, where it must remain for three working days or until the violation has been abated, whichever is longer. It goes without saying, of course, that the employer is required to abate the violation within the time frame indicated by the citation.

■ Employers may file a *Notice of Contest* within 15 days of a citation and proposed penalty. If there will be an unavoidable delay in abating a violation because the materials, equipment, or personnel won't be available, the employer may request a temporary variance until the violation can be corrected.

Within 15 days of receipt of a citation by an employer, employees have the right to object in writing to the abatement period set by OSHA for correcting violations. Employees who have requested an inspection also have the right to be advised by OSHA of the results of the inspection.

NIOSH Evaluations

The NIOSH mandate contained in the OSH Act is to identify and evaluate potential workplace hazards and recommend actions to reduce or eliminate the effects of chemicals, biological agents, work stress, excessive noise, radiation, poor ergonomics, and other risks found in the workplace. NIOSH established the *Health Hazard Evaluation (HHE)* program to respond to concerns about these and other risks expressed by employers, employees, unions, and government agencies.

In response to a request, NIOSH will provide a written acknowledgement within a few weeks. They then review the request and, depending on the nature and severity of the hazard being described, responds in one of three ways:

■ NIOSH may have written materials that address the concern or may refer the request to another government agency better equipped to respond. If written materials aren't available, a project officer is assigned to assess the need for further assistance.

- The project officer telephones the requestor to discuss the request. In some cases, the request is resolved during the call.

- The project office may determine that the appropriate response is a site visit.

If a site visit is required, NIOSH will conduct an investigation, gathering information by touring the site, meeting with management and employees, and reviewing relevant records maintained by the employer. The project office may also use other investigative procedures such as sampling devices or medical tests to gather information. During a site visit, employees, employee representatives, and NIOSH project officers have seven legal rights considered nonnegotiable by NIOSH:

- NIOSH has the right to enter the workplace to conduct an HHE.

- NIOSH has the right to access relevant information and records maintained by the employer.

- NIOSH has the right to meet privately with management and employees for confidential interviews.

- An employee requestor or other employee representative has the right to accompany NIOSH during the evaluation inspection. NIOSH may also request participation from other employees if necessary to complete the evaluation.

- Employee representatives have the right to attend opening and closing conferences.

- Employees and managers have the right to participate in the investigation by wearing sampling devices and to take part in medical tests or in the use of sampling devices.

- The interim and final HHE reports must be made available to employees; the employer must either post the final report in the workplace for 30 days or provide NIOSH with employee names and addresses so that the report can be mailed to them.

Once the information-gathering phase is complete, NIOSH analyzes the data collected during the HHE and compiles a written report that is provided to the employer, employee, and union representatives.

Many activities that occur during either an OSHA consultation or NIOSH HHE seem similar and may cause confusion about which type of assistance is appropriate for any given situation. Table C.6 provides guidelines for determining which agency should be involved.

Organisation for Economic Co-operation and Development (OECD): Guidelines for Multinational Enterprises (MNEs)

The mission of the Organisation for Economic Co-operation and Development (OECD) is to promote policies that will improve the economic and social well-being of people around the world. This group works with government agencies and makes recommendations to address social, economic, and corruption/fairness issues in business dealings across boundaries (geographic, social, and political), all with a focus on the well-being of global citizens. The Guidelines for Multinational Enterprises lists responsible business conduct. They provide voluntary principles and standards in the areas of employment and industrial relations, human rights, environment, information disclosure, combating bribery, consumer interests, science and technology, competition, and taxation.

TABLE C.6 OSHA Consultation Versus NIOSH HHE

OSHA consultation	NIOSH HHE
Identify workplace hazards.	Identify the cause of employee illness.
Suggest ways to correct hazards.	Evaluate the potential for hazard from exposure to unregulated chemicals or working conditions.
Assist in creating an effective safety and health program.	Investigate adverse health effects from permissible exposures to regulated chemicals or working conditions.
Assist in reducing workers' compensation costs.	Conduct medical or epidemiologic hazard investigations.
Assist in improving employee morale.	Investigate higher-than-expected occurrences of injury or illness.
	Evaluate newly identified hazards.
	Investigate the possible hazard of exposure to a combination of agents.
	Evaluate the potential for hazard from exposure to unregulated chemicals or working conditions.

The OECD recently updated its guidelines in 2023, marking the first revision since 2011. These updates address the social, environmental, and technological issues that have emerged over the past decade. Key changes include strengthened recommendations for risk-based due diligence, especially regarding human rights and environmental impacts, and enhanced expectations for transparency in business practices, including lobbying activities. The updated guidelines also emphasize the importance of aligning business operations with international climate goals and biodiversity protection.

The governments committed to adhering to the principles are responsible for establishing a National Contact Point (NCP). The NCPs establish relationships with other participants, the business community, labor unions, and any other group needing implementation support of the Guidelines. Governments must commit to the following through their NCP: visibility, accessibility, transparency, and accountability. The NCPs facilitate grievances, called "specific instances," although they are not judicial bodies. The NCPs facilitate problem-solving through methods of conciliation and mediation.

Additionally, OECD Watch supports nongovernmental organizations (NGOs), helping them identify and hold businesses accountable for sustainable development and the eradication of poverty through policy development, education, and interactions with businesses and unions.

Patient Protection and Affordable Care Act of 2010 (PPACA, ACA, Obamacare)

On March 23, 2010, President Barack Obama signed into law a healthcare reform bill that had several employer implications. It established criteria to ensure that Americans had access to affordable healthcare.

It is important to note that the PPACA does not require that employers provide healthcare insurance. It does, however, impose penalties on large employers who fail to provide access to affordable "minimal essential coverage." A large employer is defined as those who employed an average of at least 50 full-time equivalent employees during the preceding calendar year, with an employee working 30 hours a week counted as one full-time worker, and the others prorated.

The PPACA has been significantly modified since its inception, often tied to American elections. As of this publication, here are the key provisions affecting employers:

- **Reporting Requirements:** Applicable large employers (ALEs) must file annual information returns with the IRS and provide statements to employees about the health insurance coverage offered. Forms 1094-C and 1095-C are used to report this information.

- **Preventive Services:** Employer-sponsored health plans must cover a set of preventive services without charging employees co-payments, co-insurance, or deductibles. This includes services such as vaccinations, screenings, and contraceptive methods.

- **Nondiscrimination Rules:** The ACA prohibits employer health plans from discriminating in favor of highly compensated individuals regarding eligibility and benefits. This means benefits and contributions must be fairly distributed among all employees.

- **Coverage for Adult Children:** Employers must extend coverage to employees' adult children up to age 26, regardless of whether the child is a dependent for tax purposes.

- **Essential Health Benefits:** Employer-sponsored plans, particularly those offered through the small group market, must cover essential health benefits such as emergency services, maternity care, mental health services, and prescription drugs.

- **Waiting Period Limitations:** Employers cannot impose waiting periods longer than 90 days before new employees are eligible for health coverage.

- **Summary of Benefits and Coverage (SBC):** Employers must provide a standardized Summary of Benefits and Coverage document to employees, detailing the health plan's coverage and costs. This requirement is designed to help employees understand and compare different health plans.

- **W-2 Reporting:** Employers are required to report the total cost of employer-sponsored health coverage on employees' W-2 forms. This is for informational purposes and does not affect the employees' taxable income.

Pension Protection Act of 2006 (PPA)

The main focus of the Pension Protection Act of 2006 was to require employers to fully fund their pension plans to avoid future cash shortfalls in the plans as employees retire. Beginning in 2008, companies had seven years to bring their plans into compliance; for those that didn't comply, the act provided a penalty in the form of a 10 percent excise tax. The act also specified funding notices that must be provided by defined benefit plans.

One of the biggest changes to pension rules made by the PPA was to allow employers to automatically enroll employees in 401(k) plans. Employees who do not want to participate must now opt out of the plan. Another change was that plan advisers may now provide investment advice to plan participants and their beneficiaries under certain conditions.

Largely as a result of the Enron scandal, the PPA included a requirement for defined contribution plans that include employer stock to provide at least three alternative investment options and allow employees to divest themselves of the employer's stock.

When the Economic Growth and Tax Relief Reconciliation Act of 2001 (EGTRRA) was enacted, Congress increased contribution limits for 401(k) plans and individual retirement accounts (IRAs) and allowed catch-up contributions for taxpayers older than 50 years of age. These changes were set to expire in 2010, but the PPA made them permanent. Employees older than age 50 will be able to make 401(k) catch-up contributions to retirement funds. For 2009, the maximum contribution is $5,500; this amount may be adjusted for inflation in multiples of $500 each year.

Privacy Act of 1974

The Privacy Act of 1974 was an attempt by Congress to regulate the amount and type of information collected by federal agencies and the methods by which it was stored in an effort to protect the personal privacy of individuals about whom the information had been collected. The act requires written authorization from an individual prior to releasing information to another person. The act does not currently apply to private employers.

First, the act provides individuals with the right to know what kind of information is being collected about them, how it is used and maintained, and whether it is disseminated. The act prevents this information from being used for purposes other than that for which it was collected, and it allows individuals to obtain copies of the information, review it, and request amendments to inaccurate information. The act requires the government to ensure that information collected is not misused. Except under specific circumstances covered by the Privacy Act, such as law enforcement or national security needs, the information collected by one agency must not be shared with another. Damages for violation of these requirements may be sought in federal district court and, if found by the judge to be warranted, are subject to reimbursement of attorney's fees and litigation costs, as well as a fine for actual damages incurred by the individual of up to $1,000 paid by the federal government.

Rehabilitation Act of 1973, Sections 501, 503, and 505

The Rehabilitation Act of 1973 was enacted to expand the opportunities available for persons with physical or mental disabilities. The act prohibits discrimination in hiring, promotion, training, compensation, benefits and other employment actions. The employment clauses of the act apply to agencies of the federal government and federal contractors with contracts of $10,000 or more during a 12-month period. Section 501 addresses employment discrimination, while Section 505 details the remedies available for those who have been subjected to unlawful employment practices. The EEOC has enforcement responsibility for Section 501. Under Section 503, individuals with disabilities who think a federal contractor has violated the requirements of the

Rehabilitation Act may also file complaints with the Department of Labor through the Office of Federal Contract Compliance Programs (OFCCP).

Sarbanes–Oxley Act of 2002 (SOX)

Although the main focus of *Sarbanes–Oxley Act (SOX)* compliance is the reporting of financial transactions and activities, HR professionals may be called on to participate in SOX reporting requirements. SOX requires information that materially affects an organization's financial status to be reported to the Securities and Exchange Commission (SEC), in some cases immediately, when the organization becomes aware of the information. Some instances where this would apply to HR management are the following:

- Ensuring that material liabilities from pending lawsuits or settlements of employment practices' claims are reported in the financial statements.

- Participating in the review and testing of internal controls for hiring, compensation, and termination practices.

- Reporting immediately any material changes to the organization's financial condition. Although in most cases this wouldn't be an HR responsibility, the settlement of a large class action lawsuit could potentially reach the threshold of a material change.

Failure to provide this information within the time frames required by SOX can result in criminal penalties, including incarceration, for employees who obstruct legal investigations into financial reporting issues. SOX also prohibits employers from retaliating against whistleblowers who report financial conduct that they reasonably believe violates federal laws designed to protect shareholders from fraudulent activity.

Service Contract Act of 1965 (SCA)

The McNamara–O'Hara Service Contract Act of 1965 requires any federal service contractor with a contract exceeding $2,500 to pay its employees the prevailing wage and fringe benefits for the geographic area in which it operates, provide safe and sanitary working conditions, and notify employees of the minimum allowable wage for each job classification, as well as the equivalent federal employee classification and wage rate for similar jobs.

The SCA expands the requirements of the Davis–Bacon and Walsh–Healey Acts to contractors providing services to the federal government, such as garbage removal, custodial services, food and lodging, and the maintenance and operation of electronic equipment. Federal contractors already subject to the requirements of Davis–Bacon, Walsh–Healey, or laws covering other federal contracts, such as public utility services or transportation of people or freight, are exempt from the SCA.

Uniformed Services Employment and Reemployment Rights Act of 1994 (USERRA)

Congress enacted the Uniformed Services Employment and Reemployment Rights Act (USERRA) in 1994 to protect the rights of reservists called to active duty in the armed forces. The act provides reemployment and benefits rights and is administered through the Veterans

Employment and Training Service (VETS) of the Department of Labor. USERRA applies to all public and private employers in the United States, including the federal government. The DOL issued revised rules for employers that became effective on January 18, 2006. These revisions clarified some of the requirements previously issued. Its stipulations include the following:

Coverage

- All employers, regardless of size, are required to comply with USERRA regulations.
- Members of all uniformed services are protected by USERRA.
- USERRA prohibits discrimination due to past, current, or future military obligations.
- In addition to service during times of war or national emergency, USERRA protects any voluntary or involuntary service such as active duty, training, boot camp, reserve weekend duty, National Guard mobilizations, and absence due to required fitness for duty examinations.

Notice Requirements

- In most circumstances, employees must give verbal or written notice to the employer that they have been called to active service. If an employee is unable to give notice, a military representative may provide the notice.
- If military necessity prevents advance notice, or if giving notice is impossible or unreasonable, employees are still protected by USERRA.
- To be eligible for reemployment rights, service members must report back to work within time frames that vary according to the length of service. Table C.7 shows the reporting time requirements established by USERRA for returning to work based on varying lengths of service.

TABLE C.7   USERRA Reemployment Reporting Times

Length of service	Reporting time
1 to 30 days *or* absence for "fitness for service" exam	The first regularly scheduled full workday that begins eight hours after the end of the service completion.
31 to 180 days	Submit application for reemployment no later than 14 days after the end of service or on the next business day after that.
181 or more days	Submit application for reemployment no later than 90 days after the end of service or on the next business day after that.
Disability incurred or aggravated	Reporting or application deadline is extended for up to two years.

Duration

- The employer must grant a leave of absence for up to five years, although there are several exceptions that extend coverage beyond five years.

    - Types of leave protected without limits include the following:

    - Boot camp

    - Initial service period

    - Waiting for orders

    - Annual two-week mandatory training

- Employees are permitted to moonlight during off-duty hours without losing reinstatement rights.

- Employees do not lose reinstatement rights if they leave their jobs to prepare for mobilization, but the mobilization is canceled.

Compensation

- USERRA does not require employers to pay employees during military absences, unless the employer has an established policy of doing so.

- Employers may not require employees to apply accrued vacation pay to their military leaves, but employees may choose to do so.

Benefit Protection

- Employees on military leave are entitled to the same benefits employers provide for others on a leave of absence.

- Employees continue to accrue seniority and other benefits as though they were continuously employed.

- For leave greater than 30 days but less than 240 days in duration, the employer must offer COBRA-like health coverage upon request of the employee; for service less than 31 days, and at the employee's request, the employer must continue health coverage at the regular employee cost.

- Returning service members are entitled to participate in any rights and benefits provided to employees returning from nonmilitary leaves of absence.

Pension Protection

- Employee pension rights are protected by USERRA.

- Vesting and accrual for returning service members are treated as though there was no break in employment.

- Employer pension contributions must be the same as though the military leave did not occur.

- For defined contribution plans, service members must be given three times the period of the military leave absence (not to exceed five years) to make up contributions that were missed during the leave. Plans with an employer matching component are required to match the makeup funds.

Reinstatement

- The employer must "promptly" reinstate regular employees to positions that the employees would have earned had they remained on the job, referred to as an *escalator position*. The act does not specify a definition of "promptly," since the timing will depend on the length of the leave. For example, an employee on leave for annual two-week training would be expected to be reemployed on the first workday following the end of leave. On the other hand, someone who has been serving on active duty for five years may be promptly reemployed after notice to vacate the position is given to the incumbent.

- Temporary employees do not have reinstatement rights.

- Seasonal or fixed-term contract employees are not entitled to reinstatement.

- Reemployment rights are forfeited if the employee has been discharged dishonorably or other than honorably from the service, has been expelled as a result of a court martial, or has been absent without leave (AWOL) for 90 days.

Continued Employment

- Employees returning to work from leaves of more than 30 but less than 181 days may not be discharged without cause for six months after the date of reemployment.

- Employees returning to work from leaves of 181 days or more may not be discharged without cause for one year from the date of reemployment.

Disabled Veterans

The employer must make reasonable accommodation to provide training or retraining to reemploy a returning service member disabled as a result of service; if reasonable accommodation creates an undue hardship, reemployment can be made to a position "nearest approximate" in terms of status and pay and with full seniority to which the person is entitled.

United States–Mexico–Canada Agreement (USMCA)

The United States–Mexico–Canada Agreement (USMCA) is a comprehensive trade agreement that replaced the North American Free Trade Agreement (NAFTA). Negotiated between the United States, Mexico, and Canada, the USMCA came into effect on July 1, 2020.

The USMCA affects employers through stricter rules of origin, particularly in automotive manufacturing. It imposes higher North American content requirements for tariff-free trade, influencing supply chains and sourcing decisions. Labor and environmental standards are bolstered, necessitating compliance with laws on working conditions, minimum wages, and environmental regulations. Intellectual property protections are strengthened, impacting industries reliant on intellectual property like technology and pharmaceuticals. Digital trade provisions eliminate customs duties on electronic transmissions and protect cross-border data flows, benefiting e-commerce and digital service sectors. Dispute resolution mechanisms are established to address trade disputes between member countries. Overall, employers must adapt to the USMCA's provisions by ensuring compliance with labor, environmental, intellectual property, and digital trade standards, potentially requiring adjustments to business practices, supply chains, and legal strategies.

The agreement aims to modernize and rebalance North American trade, addressing concerns such as labor rights and environmental protections, while also aiming to encourage more domestic manufacturing and job creation.

United States Patent Act of 1790

A *patent* allows inventors exclusive rights to the benefits of an invention for a defined period of time. Generally, the term of a new patent is 20 years from the date on which the application for the patent was filed in the United States or, in special cases, from the date an earlier related application was filed, subject to the payment of maintenance fees. U.S. patent grants are effective only within the United States, U.S. territories, and U.S. possessions. Patents protect an inventor's "right to exclude others from making, using, offering for sale, or selling" the invention in the United States or "importing" the invention into the United States. Patent laws in the United States define three types of patents:

- *Design patents* protect new, original, and ornamental designs of manufactured items. Design patents are limited to 14 years.

- *Utility patents* protect the invention of new and useful processes, machines, manufacture or composition of matter, and new and useful improvements to the same. Utility patents are limited to 20 years.

- *Plant patents* protect the invention or discovery of asexually reproduced varieties of plants for 20 years.

Wage Garnishment Law, Federal

The Federal Wage Garnishment Law is found in Title III of the Consumer Credit Protection Act (CCPA) of 1968 and applies to all employers and employees. Employers are required to withhold funds from an employee's paycheck and send the money to an entity designated in the court order or levy document.

Title III of the CCPA protects employees in three ways:

- Prohibits employers from terminating employees whose wages are garnished for any one debt, even if the employer receives multiple garnishment orders for the same debt.

- Sets limits on the amount that can be garnished in any single week. Currently, the weekly amount may not exceed the lesser of two figures: 25 percent of the employee's disposable earnings, or the amount by which an employee's disposable earnings are greater than 30 times the federal minimum wage (currently $7.25 an hour).

- Defines how disposable earnings are to be calculated for garnishment withholdings.

Earnings that may be garnished include wages, salaries, bonuses, and commissions. Other income from pension plans or employer-paid disability may be subject to garnishment as well. The law does not protect employees from termination if the employer receives garnishments for more than one debt.

Walsh–Healey Public Contracts Act of 1936

The Walsh–Healey Public Contracts Act requires government contractors with contracts exceeding $10,000 (for other than construction work) to pay their employees the prevailing wage for their local area as established by the Secretary of Labor.

Worker Adjustment Retraining and Notification Act of 1988 (WARN)

The WARN Act was passed by Congress in 1988 to provide some protection for workers in the event of mass layoffs or plant closings. The Act requires that 60 days' advance notice be given to either the individual workers or their union representatives. The intent of Congress was to provide time for workers to obtain new employment or training before the loss of their jobs occurred. The WARN Act is administered by the Department of Labor and enforced through the federal courts.

Employers with 100 or more full-time employees or those with 100 or more full- and part-time employees who work in the aggregate 4,000 hours or more per week are subject to the provisions of the WARN Act. The employee count includes those who are on temporary leave or layoff with a reasonable expectation of recall.

The WARN Act established that a mass layoff occurs when either 500 employees are laid off or at least 50 employees making up 33 percent of the workforce and are laid off. A plant closing occurs when 50 or more full-time employees lose their jobs because a single facility shuts down, either permanently or temporarily. In cases where the employer staggers the workforce reduction over a period of time, care must be taken that appropriate notice is given if the total reductions within a 90-day period trigger the notice requirement.

The WARN Act also established rules on notice. For instance, notice is required to be given to all affected employees or their representatives, the chief elected official of the local government, and the state dislocated worker unit. Notice requirements vary according to which group the notices are being sent to, but they must contain specific information about the reasons for the closure, whether the action is permanent or temporary, the address of the affected business unit, the name of a company official to contact for further information, the expected date of closure or layoff, and whether bumping rights exist.

The WARN Act provides for three situations in which the 60-day notice is not required, but the burden is on the employer to show that the reasons are legitimate and not an attempt to thwart the intent of the act:

■ The faltering company exception applies only to plant closures in situations where the company is actively seeking additional funding and has a reasonable expectation that it will be forthcoming in an amount sufficient to preclude the layoff or closure and that giving the notice would negatively affect the ability of the company to obtain the funding.

■ The unforeseeable business circumstance exception applies to plant closings and mass layoffs and occurs when circumstances take a sudden and unexpected negative turn that could not have reasonably been predicted, such as the cancellation of a major contract without previous warning.

■ The natural disaster exception applies to both plant closings and mass layoffs occurring as the result of a natural disaster, such as a flood, an earthquake, or a fire.

Workers' Compensation

Workers' compensation laws require employers to assume responsibility for all employee injuries, illnesses, and deaths related to employment. These laws are enacted and enforced by the individual states. The laws provide benefits for employees that cover medical and rehabilitation expenses, provide income replacement during periods of disability when employees are unable to work, and pay benefits to their survivors in the event of an employee's death.

The amount of compensation paid is based on actuarial tables that take into account the seriousness of the injury, whether the disability is permanent or temporary, whether it is a full or partial disability (such as the loss of an eye or hand), and the amount of income lost because of the injury. In most cases, employers fund workers' compensation obligations by purchasing coverage through private insurance companies or state-sponsored insurance funds. The premiums for workers' compensation coverage are based on a percentage of the employer's payroll in various job categories. The percentages are different and depend on previous claim activity in each category. The rate charged for a roofer, for example, is much higher than that for an office worker because of the inherent danger of the job and the number and severity of claims that result.

In some states, companies may self-fund workers' compensation programs, meaning that they pay the total costs of any injuries or illnesses when they occur instead of paying insurance premiums. These are known as *nonsubscriber plans* and are rare; generally, self-funded insurance plans make economic sense only for very large organizations with the financial base to support the payment of large claims when they occur.

Although increased emphasis on safety programs and training has led to a reduction in the number of nationwide workers' compensation claims filed each year, the insurance rates are increasing largely because of increased medical costs. This is most evident in California, where employers saw costs double between 2000 and 2003, but it has also led to state reform of workers' compensation programs in Florida, West Virginia, Washington, and Texas.

Implementing programs aimed at reducing the cost of workers' compensation coverage for their organizations is one way HR professionals can show a positive impact on the bottom line. Implementing safety training and injury prevention programs is one way to reduce job-related injury and illness and to prevent claims. The costs of individual claims can be reduced by ensuring the availability of jobs that meet "light-duty" medical requirements so that employees are able to return to work earlier, shortening the length of their leave.

Quick Reference Guide: Agencies, Court Cases, Terms, and Laws; General Recordkeeping Guidelines

Table C.8 presents information on agencies, court cases, terms, and laws, and Table C.9 provides general recordkeeping guidelines.

TABLE C.8 Agencies, Court Cases, Terms, and Laws

Name	Description
Adverse impact	According to the Uniform Guidelines on Employee Selection Procedures, adverse impact is a substantially different rate of selection in hiring, promotion, or other employment decision, which works to the disadvantage of members of a race, sex, or ethnic group. Occurs when the selection rate (hiring, training, promotion, etc.) for protected class groups is less than four-fifths, or 80 percent, of the selection rate for the group with the highest selection rate.
Albemarle Paper v. Moody	Required that employment tests be validated; subjective supervisor rankings aren't sufficient validation; criteria must be tied to job requirements.
Automobile Workers v. Johnson Controls, Inc.	In response to a sex-based discrimination suit filed by women "capable of bearing children," the U.S. Supreme Court found that "decisions about the welfare of the next generation must be left to the parents who conceive, bear, support and raise them, rather than to the employers who hire those parents."
Bates v. United Parcel	Established that when employers apply an unlawful standard that bars employees protected by the ADA from an application process, the employees don't need to prove they were otherwise qualified to perform essential job functions. The employer must prove the standard is necessary to business operations.
Black Lung Benefits Act (BLBA)	Provided benefits for coal miners suffering from pneumoconiosis due to mine work.
Bureau of Labor Statistics (BLS)	An agency within the DOL that was established to study and publish statistical economic and industrial accidents' data.
Burlington Northern Santa Fe Railway Co. v. White	Established that all retaliation against employees who file discrimination claims is unlawful under Title VII, even if no economic damage results.
Circuit City Stores v. Adams	Arbitration clauses in employment agreements are enforceable for employers engaged in interstate commerce except for transportation workers.
Citizen and Immigration Services, United States (USCIS)	A component of the Department of Homeland Security charged with overseeing lawful immigration to the United States. Individuals wishing to live or work in the United States must submit applications through the USCIS; employers must comply with Form I-9 and/or E-Verify for new hires.

Name	Description
Civil law	Regulations set by countries or legislative groups about the rights of people (different from common laws, which are set by judges).
Clause	A part of a document, agreement, proposal, or contract that gives more detail.
Clayton Act	Limited the use of injunctions to break strikes; exempted unions from the Sherman Antitrust Act.
Commercial diplomacy	The effort by multinational corporations to influence foreign government policy on issues such as tariffs, banking, and other financial regulations; antitrust/competition laws; workplace standards such as safety; data privacy; and corporate conduct in areas such as corruption, governance, and social responsibility.
Congressional Accountability Act (CAA)	Required all federal employment legislation passed by Congress to apply to congressional employees.
Consolidated Omnibus Budget Reconciliation Act (COBRA)	Allows employees and their families to temporarily continue their health insurance coverage after experiencing a qualifying event, such as job loss or reduction in work hours, that would otherwise result in the loss of benefits. COBRA applies to employers with 20 or more employees and requires that coverage be offered at group rates, though beneficiaries must pay the full premium plus an administrative fee.
Davis v. O'Melveny & Myers	Established that arbitration clauses in employment agreements won't be enforced if they're significantly favorable to the employer and the employee doesn't have a meaningful opportunity to reject the agreement.
Department of Labor (DOL)	Charged with the administration and enforcement of U.S. labor laws.
Disability	A physical or mental condition that limits, but does not prevent, the performance of certain tasks.
Disparate impact	Occurs when protected class groups are treated differently than other groups in employment-related decisions; includes practices that are neutral on the surface but have a negative effect on protected groups (such as requiring a high school diploma in areas where minority groups have a lower graduation rate than nonminority groups).

(Continued)

TABLE C.8   Agencies, Court Cases, Terms, and Laws (*Continued*)

Name	Description
Due process	The way a government enforces laws; in the United States, the way a government enforces its laws to protect its citizens (e.g., guaranteeing a person a fair trial).
Energy Employees Occupational Illness Compensation Program Act (EEOICPA)	Provided compensation for employees and contractors subjected to excessive radiation during production and testing of nuclear weapons.
Energy Policy Act of 1992	Allowed employers to provide a nontaxable fringe benefit to employees engaged in qualified commuter activities such as bicycling and mass transit.
Epilepsy Foundation of Northeast Ohio v. NLRB	Extended *Weingarten* rights to nonunion employees by allowing employees to request a coworker be present during an investigatory interview that could result in disciplinary action.
Equal employment opportunity (EEO)	U.S. laws that guarantee equal treatment and respect for all employees.
Equal Employment Opportunity Act (EEOA)	Established that complainants have the burden of proof for disparate impact; provided litigation authority for the EEOC; extended the time to file complaints.
Equal Employment Opportunity Commission (EEOC)	U.S. agency charged with investigating complaints of job discrimination based on race, color, religion, sex (including pregnancy, gender identity, and sexual orientation), national origin, disability, age (40 or older), or genetic information, and with taking action to stop the discriminatory behavior when found.
Extraterritorial laws	Laws from a multinational enterprise's home country that have application in other countries. U.S. laws with extraterritorial application include Sarbanes–Oxley, Foreign Corrupt Practices Act, Americans with Disabilities Act, Age Discrimination in Employment Act, and Title VII of the Civil Rights Act of 1964. These laws give American workers the right to sue in the United States for unlawful acts that occurred outside of the country.
Federal Employees Compensation Act (FECA)	Provided benefits similar to workers' compensation for federal employees injured on the job.

Name	Description
Federal Insurance Contributions Act (FICA)/Social Security Act	Required employers and employees to pay Social Security taxes.
Federal regulations	In the United States, laws that apply in every state (as opposed to laws unique to every state).
Federal Unemployment Tax Act (FUTA)	Required employers to contribute a percentage of payroll to an unemployment insurance fund.
Forum shopping	Looking for a legal venue most likely to result in a favorable outcome; the practice of trying to get a trial held in a location that is most likely to produce a favorable result.
Griggs v. Duke Power	Required employers to show that job requirements are related to the job; established that lack of intention to discriminate isn't a defense against claims of discrimination.
Immigration and Nationality Act (INA)	Eliminated national origin, race, and ancestry as bars to immigration; set immigration goals for reunifying families and preference for specialized skills.
Intellectual property	Creations or inventions protected by law; an original invention or something created by the mind, which is usually protected by patents, trademarks, or copyrights.
Internal Revenue Service (IRS)	The U.S. government agency responsible for collecting taxes and enforcing tax laws.
Jespersen v. Harrah's Operating Co.	Established that a dress code requiring women to wear makeup doesn't constitute unlawful sex discrimination under Title VII.
Jurisdiction	The right and power to interpret and apply the law, often within a certain geographical region.
Labor-Management Relations Act (LMRA; Taft–Hartley)	Prohibited closed shops; restricted union shops; allowed states to pass "right to work" laws; prohibited jurisdictional strikes and secondary boycotts; allowed employers to permanently replace economic strikers; established the Federal Mediation and Conciliation Service; allowed an 80-day cooling-off period for national emergency strikes.

(*Continued*)

TABLE C.8 Agencies, Court Cases, Terms, and Laws (*Continued*)

Name	Description
Labor-Management Reporting and Disclosure Act (LMRDA; Landrum–Griffin)	Controlled internal union operations; provided a bill of rights for union members; required a majority vote of members to increase dues; allowed members to sue the union; set term limits for union leaders.
Licensing	Giving permission to use, produce, or sell; a written contract in which the owner of a trademark or intellectual property gives rights to a licensee to use, produce, or sell a product or service.
Lobbying	The act of monitoring and seeking to influence new labor laws and regulations by contacting local, state, and national representatives of the U.S. government.
Longshore and Harbor Workers' Compensation Act	Provided workers' compensation benefits for maritime workers injured on navigable waters of the United States or on piers, docks, and terminals.
Mental Health Parity Act (MHPA)	Required insurers to provide the same limits for mental health benefits that are provided for other types of health benefits.
National Labor Relations Act (NLRA; Wagner Act)	Protected the right of workers to organize and bargain collectively; identified unfair labor practices; established the National Labor Relations Board (NLRB).
Needlestick Safety and Prevention Act	Mandated recordkeeping for all needle-stick and sharps injuries; required employee involvement in developing safer devices.
NLRB: *IBM Corp.*	NLRB reversed its 2000 decision in *Epilepsy*, withdrawing *Weingarten* rights from nonunion employees.
NLRB: *M. B. Sturgis, Inc.*	Established that temporary employees may be included in the client company's bargaining unit and that consent of the employer and temp agency aren't required to bargain jointly.
NLRB v. J. Weingarten, Inc.	U.S. Supreme Court: Established that union employees have the right to request union representation during any investigatory interview that could result in disciplinary action.
Norris–La Guardia Act	Protected the right to organize; outlawed yellow-dog contracts.
Payne v. The Western & Atlantic Railroad Company	Defined employment at will.

Name	Description
Personal Responsibility and Work Opportunity Reconciliation Act	Required employers to provide information about all new or rehired employees to state agencies to enforce child support orders.
Pharakhone v. Nissan North America, Inc.	Established that employees who violate company rules while on FMLA leave may be terminated.
Phason v. Meridian Rail Corp.	Established that when an employer is close to closing a deal to sell a company, WARN Act notice requirements are triggered by the number of employees actually employed and the number laid off on the date of the layoff, even if the purchasing company hires some of the employees shortly after the layoff.
Proprietary	Relating to an owner or ownership; rights of property ownership relating to key information, materials, or methods developed by an organization.
Public Contracts Act (PCA; Walsh–Healey Act)	Required contractors to pay prevailing wage rates.
Railway Labor Act	Protected unionization rights; allowed for a 90-day cooling-off period to prevent strikes in national emergencies. Covers railroads and unions.
Repa v. Roadway Express, Inc.	Established that when an employee on FMLA leave is receiving employer-provided disability payments, the employee may not be required to use accrued sick or vacation leave during the FMLA absence.
Retirement Equity Act	Lowered the age limits on participation and vesting in pension benefits; required written spousal consent to not provide survivor benefits; restricted conditions placed on survivor benefits.
Rule of law	A political system in which the law is supreme; all citizens are subject to the laws of their country, no individual is above the law, and everyone must obey it.
Service Contract Act	Required government contractors to pay prevailing wages and benefits.
Sherman Antitrust Act	Controlled business monopolies; allowed court injunctions to prevent restraint of trade. Used to restrict unionization efforts.

(*Continued*)

TABLE C.8 Agencies, Court Cases, Terms, and Laws (*Continued*)

Name	Description
Sista v. CDC Ixis North America, Inc.	Established that employees on FMLA may be legally terminated for legitimate, nondiscriminatory reasons, including violations of company policy if the reason is unrelated to the exercise of FMLA rights.
Small Business Job Protection Act	Redefined highly compensated individuals; detailed minimum participation requirements; simplified 401(k) tests; corrected qualified plan and disclosure requirements.
Small Business Regulatory Enforcement Fairness Act (SBREFA)	Provided that a Small Business Administration (SBA) ombudsman act as an advocate for small business owners in the regulatory process.
Smith v. City of Jackson, Mississippi	Established that ADEA permits disparate impact claims for age discrimination comparable to those permitted for discrimination based on sex and race.
Supra-national laws	Agreements, standards, and laws that transcend national boundaries or governments. Examples include directives and regulations from the EU to its member countries.
Taxman v. Board of Education of Piscataway	Found that in the absence of past discrimination or underrepresentation of protected classes, preference may not be given to protected classes in making layoff decisions.
Taylor v. Progress Energy, Inc.	Established that the waiver of FMLA rights in a severance agreement is invalid. FMLA clearly states that "employees cannot waive, nor may employers induce employees to waive, any rights under the FMLA."
Uniform Guidelines on Employee Selection Procedures (UGESP)	Established guidelines to ensure that selection procedures are both job-related and valid predictors of job success.
Velazquez-Garcia v. Horizon Lines of Puerto Rico, Inc.	Established that the burden of proof that a termination wasn't related to military service is on an employer when an employee protected by USERRA is laid off.
Visas and work permits	Documents used by various countries to control immigration and job placement of foreign workers. Most countries require a work permit whenever a foreign individual is transferred or takes a job in the country for a period of six months or more.

Name	Description
Washington v. Davis	Established that employment selection tools that adversely impact protected classes are lawful if they have been validated to show future success on the job.
World Trade Organization (WTO)	An international body in which members negotiate tariffs and trade barriers, and trade disputes are reviewed and adjudicated.
Works council	Groups that represent employees; organizations that function like trade unions and represent the rights of workers. Work councils are most common in Europe and the United Kingdom.

TABLE C.9   General Recordkeeping Guidelines

Record type	Length of retention	Requirements
Affirmative action plan/data	Two years	Applications and other personnel records that support employment decisions (e.g., hires, promotions, terminations) are considered "support data" and must be maintained for the present AAP and the prior AAP. Records required by 41CFR60-300.44(f)(4), 60-300.44(k), and 60-300.45(c) must be kept for a period of three years from the date of making the record. This also applies to records required by 41CFR60-741.44(f)(4) and (k).
Applications for employment	One year from making the record or making the hiring decision, whichever is later; two years if a federal contractor or subcontractor has 150 or more employees and a government contract of at least $150,000	If a charge or lawsuit is filed, the records must be kept until the charge is disposed.

(*Continued*)

TABLE C.9   General Recordkeeping Guidelines (*Continued*)

Record type	Length of retention	Requirements
Drug test records	One year for non-DOT employers	Department of Transportation records for commercial drivers: 1 year: Negative drug test results. Alcohol test results less than 0.02. 2 years: Records related to the alcohol and drug collection process. 3 years: Previous employer records. 5 years: Annual MIS reports. Employee evaluation and referrals to SAPs. Follow-up tests and follow-up schedules. Refusals to test. Alcohol test results 0.02 or greater. Verified positive drug test results. EBT calibration documentation.
EEO-1	Annually, unless a federal contractor or subcontractor	The current EEO-1 report must be kept on file. Federal contractors and subcontractors must produce three years' worth of EEO-1 reports, if audited by the OFCCP.
Employment benefits	Until no longer relevant to determine benefits due to employees	Except for specific exemptions, ERISA's reporting and disclosure requirements apply to all pension and welfare plans, including summary plan descriptions, annual reports, and plan termination. Pension and insurance plans for the full period the plan is in place.
Family Medical Leave records	Three years	Basic employee data, including name, address, occupation, rate of pay, terms of compensation, daily and weekly hours worked per pay period, additions to/deductions from wages, and total compensation. Dates of leave taken by eligible employees. Leave must be designated as the FMLA leave. For intermittent leave taken, the hours of leave. Copies of employee notices and documents describing employee benefits or policies and practices regarding paid and unpaid leave. Records of premium payments of employee benefits. Records of any dispute regarding the designation of leave.
Form I-9	Three years after date of hire or one year after date of termination, whichever is later	For example, if an employee works for a company for two years, the employer must retain the I-9 for one more year after the employment ends (three years from the hire date). If an employee works for five years, the employer must keep the form for one year after their employment ends.

Record type	Length of retention	Requirements
Merit and seniority pay systems	Two years	Includes wage rates, job evaluations, seniority and merit systems, and collective bargaining agreements or any other document that explains the basis for paying different wages to employees of opposite sexes in the same establishment.
Payroll records, etc.	Three years (EEOC, FLSA, ADEA): Payroll records, collective bargaining agreements, sales and purchase records. Two years: Timecards and piecework tickets, wage rate tables, work and time schedules, and records of additions to or deductions from wages	If a charge is filed, all related records must be kept until the charge is settled. Basic payroll records that must be kept according to the FLSA are: Employee's full name and Social Security number Address, including zip code Birth date, if younger than 19 Sex and occupation Time and day of week when employee's workweek begins Hours worked each day Total hours worked each workweek Basis on which employee's wages are paid (e.g., "$9 per hour," "$440 a week," "piecework") Regular hourly pay rate Total daily or weekly straight-time earnings Total overtime earnings for the workweek All additions to or deductions from the employee's wages Total wages paid each pay period Date of payment and the pay period covered by the payment
Personnel records	One year from making the record or taking the action, whichever is greater (EEOC). Three years if applicable under the Davis–Bacon Act. Two years if a federal contractor or subcontractor with 150 or more employees, or government contract of $150,000 or more	Records related to promotions, demotions, transfers, performance appraisals, terminations, requests for reasonable accommodations.

(Continued)

TABLE C.9 General Recordkeeping Guidelines (*Continued*)

Record type	Length of retention	Requirements
Polygraph test records	Three years	Polygraph test result(s) and the reason for administering.
Selection and hiring records	One year after creation of the document or the action is taken, whichever is later. Two years if a federal contractor or subcontractor with 150 or more employees, or government contract of $150,000 or more	Job ads, assessment tools, credit reports, interview records, and other documents related to hiring decisions.
Tax records	Four years from date tax is due or paid	Amounts of wages subject to withholding. Agreements with employee to withhold additional tax. Actual taxes withheld and dates withheld. Reason for any difference between total tax payments and actual tax payments. Withholding forms.
Work permits	No retention requirements	Employers must keep current work permits for minors.

Index

Note: Page numbers in **bold** refer to figures or tables.

Online Test Bank

To help you study for your aPHR and aPHRi certification exams, register to gain one year of FREE access after activation to the online interactive test bank—included with your purchase of this book!

To access our learning environment, simply visit www.wiley.com/go/sybextestprep, follow the instructions to register your book, and instantly gain one year of FREE access after activation to:

- Hundreds of practice test questions, so you can practice in a timed and graded setting.
- Flashcards
- A searchable glossary